Practical religion

J. C. Ryle

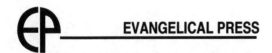

EVANGELICAL PRESS

EVANGELICAL PRESS
Faverdale North Industrial Estate, Darlington, DL3 0PH, England

Evangelical Press USA
P. O. Box 84, Auburn, MA 01501, USA

e-mail: sales@evangelical-press.org

web: http://www.evangelicalpress.org

First published 2001

British Library Cataloguing in Publication Data available

ISBN 0 85234 449 X

Printed and bound in Great Britain by Creative Print and Design Wales, Ebbw Vale.

Contents

Preface

The volume now in the reader's hands is intended to be a companion to two other volumes that I have already published, entitled *Knots Untied*, and *Old Paths*.

Knots Untied consists of a connected series of papers, systematically arranged, about the principal points that form the subject of controversy among Christians today. All who are interested in such disputed questions as the nature of the church, the ministry, baptism, regeneration, the Lord's Supper, the Real Presence, worship, confession, and the Sabbath, will find them more fully discussed in *Knots Untied*.

Old Paths consists of a similar series of papers about those leading doctrines of the gospel that are generally considered necessary to salvation. The inspiration of Scripture, sin, justification, forgiveness, repentance, conversion, faith, the work of Christ, and the work of the Holy Spirit are the principal subjects handled in *Old Paths*.

The present volume contains a series of papers about 'practical religion', and deals with the daily duties, dangers, experience and privileges of all who profess and call themselves true Christians. Read in conjunction with another work I have previously put out, called *Holiness*, I think it will throw some light on what every believer ought to be, to do, and expect.

One common feature will be found in all three volumes. I frankly declare at the outset, and will not keep it back for a moment. The standpoint I have tried to occupy, from first to last, is that of an Evangelical.

I say this deliberately and emphatically. I am fully aware that Evangelical religion is not popular and acceptable in this day. It is despised by many, and has 'no beauty or majesty' in their eyes. To declare attachment to Evangelical views, in some quarters, is to provoke a sneer, and to bring on yourself the reproach of being an 'uneducated and ignorant man'. But none of these things move me. I am not ashamed of my opinions. After forty years of Bible-reading and praying, meditation and theological study, I find myself clinging more tightly than ever to 'Evangelical' religion, and more than ever satisfied with it. It wears well: it stands the fire. I know of no system of religion that is better. In the faith of it I have lived for the third of a century, and in the faith of it I hope to die.

The plain truth is, that I see no other ground to occupy, and find no other rest for the sole of my foot. I lay no claim to infallibility, and desire to be no man's judge. But the longer I live and read, the more I am convinced and persuaded that Evangelical principles are the principles of the Bible. Holding these views, I cannot write other than I have written.

I now send forth this volume with an earnest prayer that God the Holy Spirit may bless it, and make it useful and helpful to many souls.

J. C. Ryle
Vicar of Stradbroke

November 1878

I.
Self-examination

*'Let us now go back and visit our brethren in every city where
we have preached the word of the Lord, and see how they
are doing'* (Acts 15:36).

The above text contains a proposal that the apostle Paul made
to Barnabas after their first missionary journey. He proposed to
revisit the churches they had founded, and to see how they
were getting along. Were their members continuing steadfast in
the faith? Were they growing in grace? Were they going forward,
or standing still? Were they prospering, or falling away? 'Let us
now go back and visit our brethren in every city where we have
preached the word of the Lord, and see how they are doing.'

This was a wise and useful proposal. Let us take it to heart,
and apply it to ourselves today. Let us search our ways, and
find out how matters stand between ourselves and God. Let us
'see how we are doing'. I ask every reader of this volume to
begin its perusal by joining me in self-examination. If ever self-
examination about religion was needed, it is needed today.

We live in an age of unusual *spiritual privileges*. Since the
world began there has never been such an opportunity for a
man's soul to be saved as there is in England at this time. There
have never been so many signs of religion in the land, so many
sermons preached, so many services held in churches and
chapels, so many Bibles sold, so many religious books and tracts
printed, so many societies for evangelizing mankind supported,
so much outward respect paid to Christianity. Things are done

everywhere nowadays which a hundred years ago would have been thought impossible.

Ministers support the boldest and most aggressive efforts to reach the unconverted. Clergy of the most formal and structured denominations advocate special missions, and vie with the Evangelical brethren in proclaiming that going to church on Sunday is not enough to take a man to heaven.

In short, there is a stir about religion nowadays to which there has been nothing to compare since England was a nation, and which the cleverest sceptics and agnostics cannot deny. If Romaine, and Venn, and Berridge, and Rowlands, and Grimshaw, and Hervey, had been told that such things would come to pass about a century after their deaths, they would have been tempted to say, with the Samaritan nobleman, 'Now look, if the LORD would make windows in heaven, could such a thing be?' (2 Kings 7:19). But the Lord has opened the windows of heaven. There is more taught nowadays in one week in England of the real gospel and of the way of salvation by faith in Jesus Christ than there was in a year in Romaine's time. Surely I have a right to say that we live in an age of spiritual privileges. But are we any better for it? In an age like this it is right to ask, 'How is it going with our souls?'

We live in an age of particular *spiritual danger*. Never perhaps since the world began was there such an immense amount of mere outward profession of religion as there is in the present day. A painfully large proportion of all the congregations in the land consists of unconverted people, who know nothing of heart-religion, never come to the Lord's Table, and never confess Christ in their daily lives. Myriads of those who are always running after preachers, and crowding to hear special sermons, are nothing better than empty tubs, and tinkling cymbals, without any real vital Christianity at all at home.

It is curious and instructive to observe how history repeats itself, and how much similarity there is in the human heart in every age. Even in the Early Church, as Robertson said, 'Many persons were found at church for the great Christian ceremonies, and at the theatres, or even at the temples, for the heathen spectacles. The ritual of the church was viewed as a theatrical spectacle. The sermons were listened to as the display of rhetoricians; and eloquent preachers were cheered, with clapping of hands, stamping of feet, waving of handkerchiefs, cries of "Orthodox", "Thirteenth Apostle", and such like demonstrations, which such teachers as Chrysostom and Augustine tried to restrain, that they might persuade their flocks to a more profitable manner of hearing. Some went to Church for the sermon only, alleging that they could pray at home. And when the more attractive parts of the service were over, the great mass of the people departed without remaining for the Eucharist.'[1]

The parable of the sower is continually receiving most vivid and painful illustrations. The pathway hearers, the stony-ground hearers, the thorny-ground hearers abound on every side.

In this age, the life of many religious persons, I fear, is nothing better than a continual course of spiritual tasting. They are always morbidly craving fresh excitement; and they seem to care little what it is if only they can get it. All preaching seems to be the same to them; and they appear unable to 'see differences' so long as they hear what is clever, have their ears tickled, and are part of a crowd. Worst of all, there are hundreds of young believers who are so infected with the same love of excitement, that they actually think it their duty to be always seeking after it. Insensible almost to themselves, they take up a kind of hysterical, sensational, sentimental Christianity, until they are never content with the 'old paths' and, like the Athenians, are always running after something new.

To see a calm-minded young believer, who is not stuck up, self-confident, self-conceited, and more ready to teach than learn, but who is content with a daily steady effort to grow up into Christ's likeness, and to do Christ's work quietly and inconspicuously, at home, is really becoming almost a rarity! Too many show how little deep root they have, and how little knowledge they have of their own hearts, by noise, forwardness, readiness to contradict and put down older Christians, and overweening trust in their own supposed soundness and wisdom! Many young professors of this age will do well if, after being tossed about for a while, and 'carried to and fro by every wind of doctrine', they do not end up joining some petty, narrow-minded, censorious sect, or embracing some senseless, unreasoning heresy. Surely, in times like these, there is great need for self-examination. When we look around us, we may well ask, 'How is it with our souls?'

In handling this question, I think the shortest plan will be to suggest a list of subjects for self-examination, and to go through them in order. By so doing I shall hope to cover the situation of every one into whose hands this volume may fall. I invite every one of my readers to join me in calm, searching self-examination, for a few short minutes. I desire to speak to myself as well as to you. I approach you not as an enemy, but as a friend. 'Brethren, my heart's desire and prayer to God for Israel is that they may be saved' (Romans 10:1). Bear with me if I say things that at first sight look harsh and severe. Believe me, he is your best friend who tells you the most truth.

Do we think about our souls?

Let me ask, in the first place, whether we ever think about our souls at all. Thousands of people, I fear, cannot answer that question satisfactorily. They never give the subject of religion any place in their thoughts. From the beginning of the year to the end they are absorbed in the pursuit of business, pleasure, politics, money, or self-indulgence of some kind or another. Death, and judgement, and eternity, and heaven, and hell, and a world to come, are never calmly looked at and considered. They live on as if they were never going to die, or rise again, or stand at the bar of God, or receive an eternal sentence! They do not openly oppose Christianity, for they do not reflect on it enough to do so; but they eat and drink, and sleep, and get money, and spend money, as if Christianity was a mere fiction and not a reality.

They are neither Roman Catholics, nor Socinians, nor infidels, nor High Church, nor Low Church, nor Broad Church. They are just *nothing at all*, and do not take the trouble to form opinions. A more senseless and unreasonable way of living cannot be conceived; but they do not pretend to reason it out. They simply never think about God, unless frightened for a few minutes by sickness, death in their families, or an accident. Barring such interruptions, they appear to ignore Christianity altogether, and hold on to their way, cool and undisturbed, as if there was nothing worth thinking about except this world.

It is hard to imagine a life more unworthy of an immortal creature than such a life as I have just described, for it reduces a man to the level of a beast. But it is literally and truly the life of multitudes and as they pass away, their place is taken by multitudes like them. The picture, no doubt, is horrible, distressing and revolting but, unhappily, it is only too true. In every large town, in every market, on every stock exchange, in every club, you may see specimens of this type of person by the score — men who think of everything under the sun except the one thing necessary, the salvation of their souls.

Like the Jews of old they do not 'consider their ways', they do not 'consider their latter end'; they do not 'know that they do evil' (Isaiah 1:3; Haggai 1:7; Deuteronomy 32:29; Ecclesiastes 5:1). Like Gallio they 'took no notice of these things': they are not in their way (Acts 18:17). If they prosper in the world, and get rich, and succeed in their line of life, they are praised, and admired by their contemporaries. Nothing succeeds today like success! But for all this, they cannot live for ever. They will have to die and appear before the bar of God, and be judged; and then what will the end be? When a large group of such people exists in our country, no reader need wonder why I ask whether he belongs to it. If you do, you ought to have a mark set on your door, as there used to be on a plague-stricken house two centuries ago, with the words, 'Lord have mercy on us,' written on it. Look at the type of person I have been describing, and then look at your own soul.

Do we do anything about our souls?

Let me ask, in the second place, whether we ever do anything about our souls. There are multitudes who think occasionally about Christianity, but unhappily never get beyond thinking. After a stirring sermon, or after a funeral, or under the pressure of illness, or on Sunday evening, or when things go wrong in their families, or when they meet some bright example of a Christian, or when they come across some striking, religious book or tract, they will then think a good deal, and even talk a little about religion in a vague way. But they stop short, as if thinking and talking were enough to save them. They are always meaning, and intending, and purposing, and resolving, and wishing, and telling us that they 'know' what is right, and 'hope' to be found right in the end, but they never take any action.

There is no actual separation from the world and sin, no real taking up the cross and following Christ, no positive *doing* in their Christianity. Their life is spent in playing the part of the son in our Lord's parable, to whom the father said, '"Son, go, work today in my vineyard"… And he answered and said, "I go, sir," but he did not go' (Matthew 21:28-30).

They are like those whom Ezekiel describes, who liked his preaching, but never practised what he preached: 'So they come to you as people do, they sit before you as my people, and they hear your words, but they do not do them … Indeed you are to them as a very lovely song of one who has a pleasant voice and can play well on an instrument; for they hear your words, but they do not do them' (Ezekiel 33:31-32).

In a day like this, when hearing and thinking without doing is so common, no one can rightly wonder why I press upon men the absolute need for self-examination. Once more, then, I ask my readers to consider the question of my text, 'How is it with our souls?'

Are we satisfied with formal religion?

Let me ask, in the third place, whether we are trying to satisfy our consciences with a mere formal religion. There are myriads at this moment who are being shipwrecked on this rock. Like the Pharisees of old, they make much ado about the outward part of Christianity, while the inward and spiritual part is totally neglected. They are careful to attend all the services of their place of worship, and regularly participate in all the church ordinances. They are never absent from Communion when the Lord's Supper is administered. Sometimes they are most strict in observing lent, and attach great importance to saints' days. They are often keen partisans of their own church, or sect, or congregation, and are ready to contend with anyone who does not agree with them. Yet all the time there is no heart in their religion.

Anyone who knows them intimately can see with half an eye that their affections are set on things below, and not on things above; and that they are trying to make up for the lack of inward Christianity by an excessive quantity of outward show. And this formal religion does them no real good. They are not satisfied. Beginning at the wrong end, by performing the outward things first, they know nothing of inward joy and peace, and pass their days in a constant struggle, secretly conscious that there is something wrong, and yet not knowing why. It would be well, indeed, if they do not go on from one stage of formality to another, until in despair they take a fatal plunge, and fall into Roman Catholicism! When there are so many of this kind of professing Christian, no one need wonder if I press upon him the paramount importance of close self-examination. If you love life, do not be content with the husk, and shell, and scaffolding of religion. Remember our Saviour's words about the Jewish formalists of his day: 'These people draw near to me with their mouth, and honour me with their lips, but their heart is far from me. And in vain they worship me, teaching as doctrines the commandments of men' (Matthew 15:8-9).

It needs something more than going diligently to church, and receiving the Lord's Supper, to take our souls to heaven. These things are useful in their way, and God seldom does anything for his church without them. But let us beware of being shipwrecked on the very lighthouse that helps to show the channel into the harbour. Once more I ask, 'How is it with our souls?'

Have we received forgiveness?

Let me ask, in the fourth place, whether we have received the forgiveness of our sins. Few reasonable people would think of denying that they are sinners. Many perhaps would say that they are not as bad as others, and that they have not been really wicked, and so forth. But few, I repeat, would pretend that they had always lived like angels, and never done, or said, or thought a wrong thing all their life. In short, all of us must confess that we are 'sinners', and, as sinners, are guilty before God; and, as guilty, we must be forgiven, or be lost and condemned for ever at the last day. Now it is the glory of the Christian religion that it provides for us the very forgiveness that we need — full, free, perfect, eternal and complete. It is a fundamental belief of the Christian faith that we are forgiven.

This forgiveness of sins has been purchased for us by the eternal Son of God, our Lord Jesus Christ. He has purchased it for us by coming into the world to be our Saviour, and by living, dying and rising again, as our Substitute, on our behalf. He has bought it for us at the price of his own most precious blood, by suffering in our place on the cross, and making satisfaction to God for our sins. But this forgiveness, great and full, and glorious as it is, does not become the property of every man and woman as a matter of course. It is not a privilege that every member of a church possesses, merely because they are a member of a church. It is something that each individual must receive for himself by his own personal faith, grab hold of by faith, appropriate by faith, and make his own by faith; or else, so far as he is concerned, Christ will have died in vain. 'He who believes in the Son has everlasting life; and he who does not believe the Son shall not see life, but the wrath of God abides on him' (John 3:36).

No terms can be imagined more simple, and more suitable to man. As good old Latimer said in speaking of the matter of justification, 'It is but believe and have.' It is only faith that is required; and faith is nothing more than the humble, heartfelt trust of the soul that desires to be saved. Jesus is able and willing to save; but man must come to Jesus and believe. All who believe are at once justified and forgiven: but without believing there is no forgiveness at all.

Now here is exactly the point, I am afraid, where multitudes of churchgoers fail, and are in imminent danger of being lost for ever. They know that there is no forgiveness of sin except in Christ Jesus. They can tell you that there is no Saviour for sinners, no Redeemer, no Mediator, except the one who was born of the Virgin Mary, and was crucified under Pontius Pilate, died, and was buried. But here they stop, and get no further! They never come to the point of actually laying hold of Christ by faith, and becoming one with Christ and Christ in them. They can say he is a Saviour, but not 'my Saviour' — a Redeemer, but not 'my Redeemer' — a Priest, but not 'my Priest' — an Advocate, but not 'my Advocate'; and so they live and die unforgiven! No wonder that Martin Luther said, 'Many are lost because they cannot use possessive pronouns.' When this is the state of many in this day, no one need wonder that I ask men whether they have received the forgiveness of sins.

An eminent Christian lady once said, in her old age, 'The beginning of eternal life in my soul was a conversation I had with an old gentleman who came to visit my father when I was only a little girl. He took me by the hand one day and said, "My dear child, my life is nearly over, and you will probably live many years after I am gone. But never forget two things. One is, that there is such a thing as having our sins forgiven while we live. The other is, that there is such a thing as knowing and feeling that we are forgiven." I thank God I have never forgotten his words.' How is it with us? Let us not rest till we 'know and feel' that we are forgiven. Once more let us ask, in the matter of forgiveness of sins, 'How is it with our souls?'

Do we know anything of conversion to God?

Let me ask, fifthly, whether we know anything by experience of conversion to God. Without conversion there is no salvation.

'Unless you are converted and become as little children, you will by no means enter the kingdom of heaven' (Matthew 18:3).
'Unless one is born again, he cannot see the kingdom of God' (John 3:3).
'If anyone does not have the Spirit of Christ, he is not his' (Romans 8:9).
'If anyone is in Christ, he is a new creation' (2 Corinthians 5:17).

We are all by nature so weak, so worldly, so earthly-minded, so inclined to sin, that without a thorough change we cannot serve God in life, and could not enjoy him after death. Just as ducks, as soon as they are hatched, take naturally to water, so do children, as soon as they can do anything, take to selfishness, lying and deceit; and none pray or love God, unless they are taught. Rich or poor, gentle or simple, we all need a complete change — a change that the Holy Spirit gives to us. Call it what you please — new birth, regeneration, renewal, new creation, quickening, repentance — we must possess it if we are to be saved: and if we have it, it will be *seen*.

Sense of sin and deep hatred of it, faith in Christ and love to him, delight in holiness and longing after more of it, love for God's people and distaste for the things of the world — these, these are the signs and evidences which always accompany conversion. Myriads around us, it may be feared, know nothing about it. They are, in Scripture language, dead, and asleep, and blind, and unfit for the kingdom of God. Year after year, perhaps, they go on repeating the words, 'I believe in the Holy Spirit,' but they are utterly ignorant of his changing power on the inward man. Sometimes they flatter themselves they are born again, because they have been baptized, and go to church, and receive the Lord's Supper; while they are totally destitute of the marks of the new birth, as described by John in his first Epistle. And all this time the words of Scripture are clear and plain, 'Unless you are converted and become as little children, you will by no means enter the kingdom of heaven' (Matthew 18:3).

In times like these, no reader ought to wonder why I press the subject of conversion on men's souls. No doubt there are plenty of sham conversions in such a day of religious excitement as this. But a bad coin is no proof that there is no good money: no, rather it is a sign that there is some money in circulation which is valuable, and is worth imitation. Hypocrites and sham Christians are indirect evidence that there is such a thing as real grace among men. Let us search our own hearts then, and see how it is with ourselves. Once more let us ask, in the matter of conversion, 'How is it with us?'

Do we know anything of practical Christian holiness?

Let me ask, in the sixth place, whether we know anything of practical Christian holiness. It is as certain as anything in the Bible that without holiness 'no one will see the Lord' (Hebrews 12:14). It is equally certain that it is the invariable fruit of saving faith, the real test of regeneration, the only sound evidence of indwelling grace, the certain consequence of vital union with Christ.

Holiness is not absolute perfection and freedom from all faults. Nothing of the kind! The wild words of some who talk of enjoying 'unbroken communion with God' for many months are greatly to be condemned, because they raise unscriptural expectations in the minds of young believers, and so do harm. Absolute perfection is for heaven, and not for earth, where we have a weak body, a wicked world, and a busy devil continually near our souls. Nor is real Christian holiness ever attained, or maintained, without a constant fight and struggle. The great Apostle, who said, 'I discipline my body and bring it into subjection' (1 Corinthians 9:27), would have been amazed to hear of sanctification without personal effort, and to be told that believers only need to sit still, and everything will be done for them!

Yet, weak and imperfect as the holiness of the best saints may be, it is real and true, and has a character as unmistakable as light and salt. It is not something that begins and ends with noisy profession: it will be *seen* much more than *heard*. Genuine scriptural holiness will make a man do his duty at home, and adorn his doctrine in the little trials of daily life. It will exhibit itself in passive as well as active graces. It will make a man humble, kind, gentle, unselfish, good-tempered, considerate of others, loving, meek and forgiving. It will not force him to go out of the world, and shut himself up in a cave, like a hermit. But it will make him do his duty in whatever situation God has called him to, on Christian principles, and after the pattern of Christ.

Such holiness, I know well, is not common. It is a style of practical Christianity that is painfully rare in these days. But I can find no other standard of holiness in the Word of God, no other which comes up to the pictures drawn by our Lord and his Apostles. In an age like this no reader should wonder if I press this subject also on men's attention. Once more let us ask: In the matter of holiness, how is it with our souls? 'How are we doing?'

Do we know anything of the means of grace?

Let me ask, in the seventh place, whether we know anything of enjoying the means of grace. When I speak of the means of grace, I have in mind five principal things:

The reading of the Bible
Private prayer
Public worship
The taking of the Lord's Supper
The rest of the Lord's Day

They are means that God has graciously appointed in order to convey grace to man's heart by the Holy Spirit, or keep up the spiritual life after it has begun. As long as the world stands, the state of a man's soul will always depend greatly on the manner and spirit in which he uses means of grace. The manner and spirit, I say deliberately and purposefully. Many people use the means of grace regularly and formally, but know nothing of enjoying them: they attend to them as a matter of duty, but without any feeling, interest, or affection at all. Yet even common sense might tell us that this formal, mechanical use of holy things is utterly worthless and unprofitable. Our feeling about them is just one of the many tests of the state of our souls. How can we think a man loves God, when he reads about God and his

Christ as a mere matter of duty, content and satisfied if he has just moved his bookmark onward over so many chapters? How can a man suppose he is ready to meet Christ when he never takes any trouble to pour out his heart to him in private as a Friend, and is satisfied with repeating a string of words every morning and evening, under the name of prayer, scarcely thinking what he is doing? How could a man be happy in heaven for ever, when he finds Sunday a dull, gloomy, tiresome day — when he knows nothing of hearty prayer and praise, and cares nothing whether he hears truth or error from the pulpit, or scarcely listens to the sermon? What can be the spiritual condition of the man whose heart never 'burns within him' when he receives that bread and wine, which specially remind us of Christ's death on the cross, and the atonement for sin?

These inquiries are very serious and important. If means of grace had no other use, and were not such great aids towards heaven, they would be useful in supplying a test of our real state in the sight of God. Tell me what a man does with regard to Bible-reading and praying, to Sunday, public worship, and the Lord's Supper, and I will soon tell you what he is, and on which road he is travelling. How is it with ourselves? Once more let us ask: In the matter of means of grace, 'How are we doing?'

Do we ever try to do any good in the world?

Let me ask, in the eighth place, whether we ever try to do any good in the world. Our Lord Jesus Christ continually 'went about doing good', while he was on earth (Acts 10:38). The Apostles, and all the disciples in Bible times, were always striving to walk in his steps. A Christian who was content to go to heaven himself and cared not what became of others, whether they lived happy and died in peace or not, would have been regarded in primitive times as a kind of monster, who did not have the Spirit of Christ. Why should we suppose for a moment that a lower standard will suffice in the present day? Why should fig trees that bear no fruit be spared in the present day, when in our Lord's time they were to be cut down because they 'use up the ground'? (Luke 13:7). These are serious inquiries, and demand serious answers.

There is a generation of professing Christians nowadays who seem to know nothing of caring for their neighbours, and are completely swallowed up in the concerns of 'number one' — that is, their own and their family's. They eat, and drink, and sleep, and dress, and work, and earn money, and spend money, year after year; and whether others are happy or miserable, well or ill, converted or unconverted, travelling towards heaven or towards hell, appear to be questions about which they are utterly indifferent. Can this be right? Can it be reconciled with the religion of the one who spoke the parable of the good Samaritan, and commanded us to 'Go and do likewise'? (Luke 10:37). I doubt it completely.

There is much to be done everywhere. There is not a place that does not have a field for work and an open door for being useful, if anyone is willing to enter it. There is not a Christian who cannot find some good work to do for others, if he has only a heart to do it. The poorest man or woman, without a single penny to give, can always show his deep sympathy to the sick and sorrowful, and by simple good nature and tender helpfulness can lessen the misery and increase the comfort of somebody in this troubled world. But no, the vast majority of professing Christians, whether rich or poor, faithful church attendees or not, seem possessed with a devil of detestable selfishness, and do not know the luxury of doing good. They can argue by the hour about baptism, and the Lord's Supper, and the forms of worship, and the union of Church and State, and other dry-bone questions. But all this time they seem to care nothing for their neighbours. The plain practical point, whether they love their neighbour as the Samaritan loved the traveller in the parable, and can spare any time and trouble to do him good, is a point they never touch with any of their fingers.

In too many places, both in the city and the country, true love seems almost dead, both in church and chapel, and wretched denomination spirit and controversy are the only fruits that Christianity appears able to produce. In a day like this, no reader should wonder why I press this plain old subject on his conscience. Do we know anything of genuine Samaritan love to others? Do we ever try to do any good to anyone beside our own friends and relatives, and our own denomination or cause? Are we living like disciples of the one who always 'went about doing good', and commanded his disciples to take him for their 'example'? (John 13:15). If not, how shall we meet him on Judgement Day? In this matter also, how is it with our souls? Once more I ask, 'How are we doing?'

Do we live in habitual communion with Christ?

Let me ask, in the ninth place, whether we know anything of living the life of habitual communion with Christ. By 'communion', I mean that habit of 'abiding in Christ' which our Lord speaks of, in the fifteenth chapter of John's Gospel, as essential to Christian fruitfulness (John 15:4-8). Let it be distinctly understood that union with Christ is one thing, and communion is another. There can be no communion with the Lord Jesus without union first; but unhappily there may be union with the Lord Jesus, and afterwards little or no communion at all. The difference between the two things is not the difference between two distinct steps, but the higher and lower ends of an inclined plane. Union is the common privilege of all who feel their sins, and truly repent, and come to Christ by faith, and are accepted, forgiven and justified in him. Too many believers, it may be feared, never get beyond this stage! Partly from ignorance, partly from laziness, partly from the fear of man, partly from secret love of the world, partly from some unmortified besetting sin, they are content with a little faith, and a little hope, and a little peace, and a little measure of holiness. And they live all their lives in this condition, doubting, weak, hesitant, and bearing fruit only 'thirty-fold' to the very end of their days!

Communion with Christ is the privilege of those who are continually striving to grow in grace, and faith, and knowledge, and conformity to the mind of Christ in all things: 'forgetting those things which are behind', and 'not counting [themselves] to have apprehended', but pressing 'toward the goal for the prize of the upward call of God in Christ Jesus' (Philippians 3:13-14). Union is the bud, but communion is the flower; union is the baby, but communion is the strong man. He who has union with Christ does well; but he who enjoys communion with him does far better. Both have one life, one hope, one heavenly seed in their heart — one Lord, one Saviour, one Holy Spirit, one eternal home: but union is not as good as communion! The grand secret of communion with Christ is to be continually living by faith in the Son of God, and drawing out of him every hour the supply that every hour requires. 'For to me,' said Paul, 'to live is Christ' — 'it is no longer I who live, but Christ lives in me' (Philippians 1:21; Galatians 2:20).

Communion like this is the secret of the abiding 'joy and peace in believing', which eminent saints like Bradford and Rutherford notoriously possessed. None were ever more humble, or more deeply convinced of their own infirmities and corruption. They would have told you that the seventh chapter of Romans precisely described their own experience. They would have said continually, 'The remembrance of our sins is grievous to us; the burden of them is intolerable.' But they were always looking to Jesus, and in him they were always able to rejoice. Communion like this is the secret of the splendid victories that such men as these won over sin, the world and the fear of death. They did not sit still idly, saying, 'I leave it all to Christ to do for me,' but, strong in the Lord, they used the divine nature he had implanted in them, boldly and confidently, and were 'more than conquerors through him who loved [them]' (Romans 8:37). Like Paul they would have said, 'I can do all things through Christ who strengthens me' (Philippians 4:13).

Ignorance of this life of communion is one among many reasons why so many in this age are prey to formal religions and strange doctrines. Such errors often spring from imperfect knowledge of Christ, and obscure views of the life of faith in a risen, living and interceding Saviour.

Is communion with Christ like this a common thing? No! It is very rare indeed! The majority of believers seem content with the barest elementary knowledge of justification by faith, and half-a-dozen other doctrines, and go doubting, limping, groaning along the way to heaven, experiencing little of the sense of victory or of joy.

The churches of these latter days are full of weak, powerless and uninfluential believers, saved at last, but only as one escaping through the flames; but never shaking the world, and knowing nothing of a rich welcome (1 Corinthians 3:15; 2 Peter 1:11). Despondency, Feeble-mind and Much-afraid, in *Pilgrim's Progress*, reached the celestial city as really and truly as Valiant-for-the-truth and Greatheart. But they certainly did not reach it with the same comfort, and did not do a tenth of the same good in the world! I fear there are many like them in these days! When things are like this in the churches, no reader can wonder that I inquire how it is with our souls. Once more I ask: In the matter of communion with Christ, 'How are we doing?'

Are we ready for Christ's second coming?

Let me ask, in the tenth and last place, whether we know any-thing of being ready for Christ's second coming. That he will come again the second time is as certain as anything in the Bible. The world has not yet seen the last of him. As surely as he went up visibly and in the body on the Mount of Olives before the eyes of his disciples, so surely will he come again in the clouds of heaven, with power and great glory (Acts 1:11). He will come to raise the dead, to change the living, to reward his saints, to punish the wicked, to renew the earth, and take the curse away — to purify the world, even as he purified the temple — and to establish a kingdom where sin will have no place, and holiness will be the universal rule. The doctrines that we repeat and profess to believe continually declare that Christ is coming again.

The early Christians made it a part of their religion to look for his return. They looked *backward* to the cross and the atonement for sin, and rejoiced in Christ crucified. They looked *upward* to Christ at the right hand of God, and rejoiced in Christ interceding. They looked *forward* to the promised return of their Master, and rejoiced in the thought that they would see him again. And we ought to do the same.

What have we really got from Christ? What do we know of him? What do we think of him? Are we living as if we long to see him again, and love his appearing? Readiness for that appearing is nothing more than being a real, consistent Christian. It requires no man to cease from his daily business. The farmer need not give up his farm, nor the shopkeeper his counter, nor the doctor his patients, nor the carpenter his hammer and nails, nor the bricklayer his mortar and trowel. Each and every one cannot do better than be found doing his duty, but doing it *as a Christian*, and with a heart packed up and ready to be gone. In the face of truth like this no reader can feel surprised if I ask: How is it with our souls in the matter of Christ's second coming?

The world is growing old and running to seed. The vast majority of Christians seem like the men in the time of Noah and Lot, who were eating and drinking, marrying and giving in marriage, planting and building, up to the very day when flood and fire came. The words of our Master are very solemn and heart-searching: 'Remember Lot's wife'; 'But take heed to yourselves, lest your hearts be weighed down with carousing, drunkenness, and cares of this life, and that day come on you unexpectedly' (Luke 17:32; 21:34). Once more I ask: In the matter of being ready for Christ's second coming, 'How are we doing?'

A few words of application

I end my inquiries here. I might easily add to them; but I trust I have said enough, at the beginning of this volume, to stir up self-inquiry and self-examination in many minds. God is my witness that I have said nothing that I do not feel of paramount importance to my own soul. I only want to do good to others. Let me now conclude with a few words of practical application.

1. *Are you asleep and utterly thoughtless about Christianity?*

Oh, awake and sleep no more! Look at the cemeteries. One by one the people around you are dropping into them, and you must lie there one day. Look forward to a world to come, and lay your hand on your heart, and say, if you dare, that you are ready to die and meet God. Ah! You are like one sleeping in a boat drifting down the stream towards Niagara Falls! 'What do you mean, sleeper? Arise, call on your God'; 'Awake, you who sleep, arise from the dead, and Christ will give you light' (Jonah 1:6; Ephesians 5:14).

2. *Are you feeling self-condemned, and afraid that there is no hope for your soul?*

Cast aside your fears, and accept the offer of our Lord Jesus Christ to sinners. Hear him saying, 'Come to me, all you who labour and are heavy laden, and I will give you rest' (Matthew 11:28). 'If anyone thirsts, let him come to me and drink' (John 7:37). 'The one who comes to me I will by no means cast out' (John 6:37).

Do not doubt that these words are for you as well as for anyone else. Bring all your sins, and unbelief, and sense of guilt, and unfitness, and doubts, and infirmities — bring all to Christ. This man welcomes sinners, and he will welcome you (Luke 15:2). Do not stand still, wavering between two opinions, and waiting for a convenient time. 'Be of good cheer. Rise, he is calling you.' Come to Christ this very day (Mark 10:49).

3. Are you a professing believer in Christ, but without much joy and peace and comfort?

Take advice this day. Search your own heart, and see whether the fault is not entirely your own. Very likely you are sitting at ease, content with a little faith, and a little repentance, a little grace and a little sanctification, and unconsciously shrinking back from extremes. You will never be a very happy Christian at this rate, if you live to the age of Methuselah. Change your plan, if you love life and would see good days, without delay. Come out boldly, and act decidedly. Be thorough, thorough, very thorough in your Christianity, and set your face fully towards the sun. Lay aside every weight, and the sin that so easily overtakes you. Strive to get nearer to Christ, to abide in him, to cling to him, and to sit at his feet like Mary, and drink full portions out of the fountain of life. 'And these things', says John, 'we write to you that your joy may be full' (1 John 1:4). 'But if we walk in the light as he is in the light, we have fellowship with one another' (1 John 1:7).

4. Are you oppressed with doubts and fears, on account of your weakness, infirmity and sense of sin?

Remember the text that says of Jesus, 'A bruised reed he will not break, and smoking flax he will not quench' (Matthew 12:20). Take comfort in the thought that this text is for you. What if your faith is weak? It is better than no faith at all. The least grain of life is better than death. Perhaps you are expecting too much in this world. Earth is not heaven. You are still in the body. Expect little from self, but much from Christ. Look more to Jesus, and less to self.

5. *Finally, are you sometimes downcast by the trials you meet with on the way to heaven: bodily trials, family trials, trials of circumstances, trials from neighbours, and trials from the world?*

Look up to a sympathizing Saviour at God's right hand, and pour out your heart before him. He can be touched with the feelings of your trials, for he himself suffered when he was tempted. Are you alone? So was he. Are you misrepresented and slandered? So was he. Are you forsaken by friends? So was he. Are you persecuted? So was he. Are you wearied in body and grieved in spirit? So was he. Yes! He can feel for you, and he can help as well as feel. Then learn to draw nearer to Christ. The time is short. In just a little while, all will be over: we shall soon be 'with the Lord'. 'For surely there is a hereafter, and your hope will not be cut off' (Proverbs 23:18). 'For you have need of endurance, so that after you have done the will of God, you may receive the promise: "For yet a little while, and he who is coming will come and will not tarry"' (Hebrews 10:36-37).

Note

1. Robertson, *Church history,* B. II, ch. vi, p. 356.

2.
Self-effort

'Strive to enter through the narrow gate, for many, I say to you, will seek to enter and will not be able' (Luke 13:24).

There once was a man who asked our Lord Jesus Christ a very serious question. He said to him, 'Lord, are only a few people going to be saved?'

Who this man was we do not know. What his motive was for asking this question we are not told. Perhaps he wished to gratify an idle curiosity; perhaps he wanted an excuse for not seeking salvation himself. The Holy Spirit has kept all this from us: the name and motive of the seeker are both hidden.

But one thing is very clear, and that is the vast importance of the words of our Lord to which the question gave rise. Jesus seized the opportunity to direct the minds of all around him to their own plain duty. He knew the train of thought that the man's inquiry had set moving in their hearts: he saw what was going on within them. 'Strive,' he cries, 'to enter through the narrow gate.' Whether few are saved or many, your course is clear — make every effort to enter in. Now is the accepted time. Now is the day of salvation. A day will come when many will seek to enter and will not be able. 'Strive to enter in now.'

I wish to bring the solemn lessons that the words of the Lord Jesus are meant to teach to the serious attention of all who are reading this. They are words that deserve special remembrance in the present day. They teach unmistakably that mighty truth, our own personal responsibility for the salvation of our souls. They show the immense danger of putting off the great business of Christianity, as so many unhappily do. On both these points the witness of our Lord Jesus Christ in the text is clear. He, who is the eternal God, and who spoke the words of perfect wisdom, says to the sons of men, 'Strive to enter through the narrow gate, for many, I say to you, will seek to enter and will not be able' (Luke 13:24).

1. Here is a *description* of the way of salvation. Jesus calls it 'the narrow gate'.
2. Here is a plain *command*. Jesus says, 'Strive to enter through'.
3. Here is a frightful *prophecy*. Jesus says, 'Many will seek to enter and will not be able.'

May the Holy Spirit apply the subject to the hearts of all into whose hands this publication may fall! May all who read it know the way of salvation experimentally, obey the command of the Lord practically, and be found safe in the great day of his Second Coming!

The way of salvation

Firstly, here is a description of the way of salvation. Jesus calls it 'the narrow gate'.

There is a gate that leads to forgiveness, peace with God, and heaven. Whoever goes in through that gate will be saved. Never, surely, was a gate more needed.

Sin is a vast mountain between man and God. How will a man climb over it?

Sin is a high wall between man and God. How will man get
through it?

Sin is a deep gulf between man and God. How will man
cross over it?

God is in heaven, holy, pure, spiritual, undefiled, light without
any darkness at all, a being who cannot bear that which is evil,
or look upon sin. Man is a poor fallen worm, crawling on earth
for a few years — sinful, corrupt, erring, defective — a being
whose imagination is only evil, and whose heart is deceitful
above all things, and desperately wicked. How will man and
God be brought together? How will man ever draw near to his
Maker without fear and shame? Blessed be God, there is a
way! There is a road. There is a path. There is a gate. It is the
gate spoken of in the words of Christ — 'the narrow gate'.

Made for sinners

This gate was made for sinners by the Lord Jesus Christ. From
all eternity he covenanted and promised that he would make
it. In the fulness of time he came into the world and made it, by
his own atoning death on the cross. By that death he made
satisfaction for man's sin, paid man's debt to God, and bore
man's punishment. He built a great gate at the cost of his own
body and blood. He raised a ladder on earth whose top reached
to heaven. He made a door by which the chief of sinners may
enter into the holy presence of God, and not be afraid. He
opened a road by which the vilest of men, believing in him,
may draw near to God and have peace. He cries to us, 'I am
the door. If anyone enters by me, he will be saved' (John 10:9).
'I am the way ... No one comes to the Father except through
me' (John 14:6). 'In whom,' says Paul, 'we have boldness and
access with confidence through faith in him' (Ephesians 3:12).
Thus was the gate of salvation formed.

The narrow gate

This gate is called the narrow gate, and it is not called so without reason. It is always narrow, constricted and difficult to pass
through to some people, and it will be so, as long as the world
remains. It is narrow to all who love sin, and are determined
not to part with it. It is narrow to all who set their affection on
this world, and seek first its pleasures and rewards. It is narrow
to all who dislike trouble, and are unwilling to take pains and
make sacrifices for their souls. It is narrow to all who like company, and want to keep in with the crowd. It is narrow to all
who are self-righteous, and think they are good people, and
deserve to be saved. To all these, the great gate, which Christ
made, is narrow and constricted. In vain they seek to pass
through. The gate will not admit them. God is not unwilling to
receive them; their sins are not too many to be forgiven: but
they are not willing to be saved God's way. In the last twenty
centuries, thousands have tried to make the gateway wider;
thousands have worked and toiled to get to heaven on their
terms. But the gate never alters. It is not elastic; it will not stretch
to accommodate one man more than another. It is still the
narrow gate.

The only way to heaven

Narrow as this gate is, it is the only one by which men can get
to heaven. There is no side gate; there is no side road; there is
no gap or low-place in the wall. All who are *ever* saved will be
saved only by Christ, and only by simple faith in him — not
one will be saved by simply repenting. Today's sorrow does not
wipe off yesterday's score. Not one will be saved by his own
works. The best works that any man can do are little better
than impressive sins. Not one will be saved by his formal regular

use of the outward means of grace (going to church, reading his Bible, praying, taking the Lord's Supper, and honouring the Lord's Day). When we have done it all, we are nothing but poor 'unprofitable servants'. Oh, no! It is a mere waste of time to seek any other road to eternal life. Men may look to the right and to the left, and weary themselves with their own methods, but they will never find another door. Proud men may dislike the gate if they want. Depraved men may scoff at it, and make fun of those who use it. Lazy men may complain that the way is hard. But men will discover no other salvation than that of faith in the blood and righteousness of a crucified Redeemer. There stands between us and heaven one great gate: it may be narrow, but it is the only one. We must either enter heaven by the narrow gate, or not at all.

Always ready to open

Narrow as this gate is, it is a gate always ready to open. No sinners of any kind are forbidden to draw near: whoever will, may enter in and be saved. There is but one condition of admission: that condition is that you really feel your sins and desire to be saved by Christ in his own way. Are you really aware of your guilt and vileness? Have you a truly broken and contrite heart? Look at the gate of salvation, and come in. He who made it declares, 'the one who comes to me I will by no means cast out' (John 6:37). The question to be considered is not whether you are a great sinner or a little sinner; whether you are elect or not; whether you are converted or not. The question is simply this: 'Do you feel your sins? Do you feel burdened and heavy-laden? Are you willing to put your life into Christ's hands?' Then if that is the case, the gate will open to you at once. Come in this very day. 'Why do you stand outside?' (Genesis 24:31).

Thousands have gone in and been saved

Narrow as this gate is, it is one through which thousands have gone in and been saved. No sinner who was utterly sick of his sins was ever turned back and told he was too bad to be admitted. Thousands of all sorts have been received, cleansed, washed, forgiven, clothed, and made heirs of eternal life. Some of them seemed very unlikely to be admitted: you and I might have thought they were too bad to be saved. But he who built the gate did not refuse them. As soon as they knocked, he gave orders that they should be let in.

Manasseh, King of Judah, went up to this gate. None could have been worse than he up to that time. He had despised his good father Hezekiah's example and advice. He had bowed down to idols. He had filled Jerusalem with bloodshed and cruelty. He had slain his own children. But as soon as his eyes were opened to his sins, and he fled to the gate for forgiveness, it flew wide open and he was saved.

Saul the Pharisee went up to this gate. He had been a blasphemer of Christ, and a persecutor of Christ's people. He had laboured hard to stop the progress of the gospel. But as soon as his heart was touched, and he found out his own guilt and fled to the gate for forgiveness, at once it flew wide open, and he was saved.

Many of the Jews who crucified our Lord went up to this gate. They had been grievous sinners indeed. They had refused and rejected their own Messiah. They had delivered him to Pilate, and pleaded that he might be slain. They had wanted Barabbas to be let go, and the Son of God to be crucified. But on the day when they were convicted in their heart by Peter's preaching, they fled to the gate for forgiveness, and at once it flew open, and they were saved.

The jailer at Philippi went up to this gate. He had been a cruel, hard, godless man. He had done all in his power to ill-treat Paul and his companion. He had thrust them into the inner prison, and locked their feet in the stocks. But when his conscience was aroused by the earthquake, and his mind enlightened by Paul's teaching of the Word of God, he fled to the gate for forgiveness, and at once it flew open, and he was saved.

But why need I stop at Bible examples? Why should I not say that multitudes have gone to 'the narrow gate' since the days of the Apostles, and have entered in by it and been saved? Thousands of all ranks, classes and ages — educated and uneducated, rich and poor, old and young — have tried the gate and found it ready to open; have gone through it and found peace for their souls. Yes, thousands of people still living have proved the effectiveness of the gate, and found it the way to real happiness. Noblemen and commoners, merchants and bankers, soldiers and sailors, farmers and tradesmen, labourers and workmen, are still upon earth, who have found the narrow gate to be 'a way of pleasantness and a path of peace'. They have not made any evil report of the way inside the gate. They have found Christ's yoke to be easy, and his burden to be light. Their only regret has been that so few enter in, and that they themselves did not enter in before.

This is the gate that I want every one, into whose hands this publication may fall, to enter. I don't want you merely to go to church, but to go with heart and soul to the gate of life. I don't want you merely to believe there is such a gate, and to think it a good thing, but to enter by faith and be saved.

Think *what a privilege* it is to have a gate at all. The angels who did not remain faithful to God fell, never to rise again. To them there was no door of escape opened. Millions of pagans have never heard of any way to eternal life. What would they have given, if they could only have heard one plain sermon about Christ? The Jews in Old Testament times only saw the gate dimly and far away. 'The way into the Holiest of All was not yet made manifest while the first tabernacle was still standing' (Hebrews 9:8). You have the gate set plainly before you; you have Christ and full salvation offered to you, without money and without price. You need never be at a loss which way to turn. Oh, consider what a mercy this is! Beware that you do not despise the gate and perish in unbelief. Better a thousand times not to know of the gate than to know of it and yet remain outside. How will you escape if you neglect so great a salvation?

Think *what a thankful man* you ought to be if you have really gone in at the narrow gate. To be a pardoned, forgiven, justified soul; to be ready for sickness, death, judgement and eternity; to always be provided for in both worlds — surely this is a matter for daily praise. True Christians ought to be more full of thanksgiving than they are. I fear that few sufficiently remember what they were by nature, and what debtors they are to grace. A heathen remarked that singing hymns of praise was one special mark of the early Christians. It would be good for Christians in the present day if they knew more of this frame of mind. It is no evidence of a healthy state of soul when there is much complaining and little praise. It is an amazing mercy that there is any gate of salvation at all; but it is a still greater mercy when we are taught to enter in by it and be saved.

A plain command

Secondly, here is a plain command. Jesus says to us, 'Strive to enter through the narrow gate.'

There is often much to be learned in a single word of Scripture. The words of our Lord Jesus in particular are always full of matter for thought. Here is a word that is a striking example of what I mean. Let us see what the great Teacher would have us glean from the word 'strive'.

Strive teaches that a man must use means diligently, if he would have his soul saved. There are means that God has appointed to help man in his efforts to approach him. There are ways in which a man must walk if he desires to be found by Christ. Public worship, reading the Bible, hearing the gospel preached — these are the kind of things to which I refer. They lie, as it were, in the middle, between man and God. Doubtless no one can change his own heart, or wipe away one of his sins, or make himself in the least degree acceptable to God; but I do say that if man could do nothing but sit still, Christ would never have said, 'Strive'.

Strive teaches that man is a free agent, and will be dealt with by God as a responsible being. The Lord Jesus does not tell us to wait, and wish, and feel, and hope, and desire. He says, 'Strive'. I call that which teaches people to be content with saying, 'We can do nothing ourselves,' and allows them to continue in sin, a worthless religion. It is as bad as teaching people that it is not their fault if they are not converted, and that God only is to blame if they are not saved. I find no such theology in the New Testament. I hear Jesus saying to sinners, 'Come — repent — believe — labour — ask — seek — knock.' I see plainly that our salvation, from beginning to end, is entirely *of God*; but I see no less clearly that our ruin, if we are lost, is wholly and entirely *of ourselves*. I maintain that sinners are always addressed as accountable and responsible; and I see no better proof of this than what is contained in the word 'strive'.

Strive teaches that a man must expect many adversaries and a hard battle if he would have his soul saved. And this, as a matter of experience, is utterly true. There are no 'gains without pains' in spiritual things any more than in temporal. That roaring lion, the devil, will never let a soul escape from him without a struggle. The heart that is naturally sensual and earthly will never be turned to spiritual things without a daily fight. The world, with all its opposition and temptations, will never be overcome without a conflict. But why should all this surprise us? What great and good thing was ever done without trouble? Wheat does not grow without ploughing and sowing; riches are not obtained without care and attention; success in life is not won without hardship and work; and heaven, above all, is not to be reached without the cross and the battle. The 'kingdom of heaven suffers violence, and the violent take it by force' (Matthew 11:12). A man must 'strive'.

Strive teaches that it is worthwhile for a man to seek salvation. If there is anything that deserves a struggle in this world, it is the prosperity of the soul. The objects for which the great majority of men strive are comparatively poor and trifling things. Riches, and greatness, and rank, and learning are 'a corruptible crown'. The incorruptible things are all within the narrow gate. The peace of God which passes all understanding — the bright hope of good things to come — the sense of the Spirit dwelling in us — the consciousness that we are forgiven, safe, ready, insured, provided for in time and eternity, whatever may happen — these are true gold, and lasting riches. It is right and good that the Lord Jesus calls on us to 'strive'.

Strive teaches that laziness towards Christianity is a great sin. It is not merely a misfortune, as some believe — something for which people are to be pitied, and a matter of regret. It is far more than this. It is a breach of a clear commandment. What will be said of the man who violates God's law, and does something that God says, 'You will not do'? There can be but one answer. He is a sinner. 'Whoever commits sin also commits lawlessness, and sin is lawlessness' (1 John 3:4). And what will be said of the man who neglects his soul, and makes no effort to enter the narrow door? There can be only one reply. He is omitting an explicit duty. Christ says to him, 'Strive', and behold, he sits still!

Strive teaches that all those outside the narrow gate are in great danger. They are in danger of being lost and tormented for ever. There is but a step between themselves and death. If death finds them in their present condition, they will perish without hope. The Lord Jesus saw that clearly. He knew the uncertainty of life and the shortness of time; he would gladly have sinners hurry and not delay, unless they put off the matters concerning their soul until it is too late. He speaks as one who saw the devil drawing near to them daily, and the days of their life gradually ebbing away. He wished them to take great care not to wait too long; therefore he cries, 'Strive'.

That word *strive* raises solemn thoughts in my mind. It is full of condemnation for thousands of baptized persons. It condemns the ways and practices of multitudes who profess and call themselves Christians. There are many who neither swear, nor murder, nor commit adultery, nor steal, nor lie; but one thing unhappily cannot be said of them: they cannot be said to be 'striving' to be saved. The 'spirit of slumber' possesses their hearts in everything that concerns Christianity. They are very busy over the things of the world: they rise early, and go to bed late; they work; they labour; they are busy; they are careful; but the one thing they need to accomplish they never do — they never 'strive' towards the things of God.

Irregular public worship

What shall I say of those who are irregular about public worship on Sundays? There are thousands who answer this description. Sometimes, if they feel disposed, they go to some church, and attend a religious service; at other times they stay at home and read the paper, or idle about, or look over their accounts, or seek some amusement. 'Is this striving?' I speak to men with common sense. Let them judge what I say.

Attendance out of habit

What shall I say of those who come regularly to a place of worship, but come entirely out of habit? There are many in every part of our country in this condition. Their fathers taught them to come; their custom has always been to come: it would not be respectable to stay away. But they care nothing for the worship of God when they do come. Whether they hear law or gospel, truth or error, it is all the same to them. They remember nothing afterwards. They take off their form of religion with their Sunday clothes, and return to the world. Is this 'striving'? I speak to men with common sense. Let them judge what I say.

Seldom read the Bible

What shall I say of those who seldom or never read the Bible? There are thousands of people, I fear, who answer this description. They know the Book by name; they know it is commonly regarded as the only Book that teaches us how to live and how to die; but they can never find time for reading it, Newspapers, reviews, novels, romances, they can read, but not the Bible. Is this 'striving' to enter in? I speak to men with common sense. Let them judge what I say.

Never pray

What shall I say of those who never pray? There are multitudes, I firmly believe, in this condition. Without God they rise in the morning, and without God they lie down at night. They ask for nothing; they confess nothing; they return thanks for nothing; they seek nothing. They are all dying creatures, and yet they are not even on speaking terms with their Maker and their Judge! Is this 'striving'? I speak to men with common sense. Let them judge what I say.

It is a solemn thing to be a minister of the gospel. It is a painful thing to look on, and see the ways of mankind in spiritual matters. We hold in our hands that great law book of God, which declares that without repentance, and conversion, and faith in Christ, and holiness, no man living can be saved. In discharge of our office we urge men to repent, believe and be saved; but, to our grief, how frequently we have to lament that our labour seems all in vain. Men attend our churches, and listen, and approve; but do not 'strive' to be saved. We show the sinfulness of sin; we unfold the loveliness of Christ; we expose the vanity of the world; we set forth the happiness of Christ's service; we offer the living water to the wearied and heavy-laden sons of toil; but, to our dismay, how often we seem to speak to the winds. Our words are patiently heard on Sundays; our arguments are not refuted; but we see plainly in the week that men are not 'striving' to be saved. Then on Monday morning the devil comes, and offers his countless snares. Then comes the world, and holds out its illusive prizes: our hearers follow them greedily. They work hard for this world's goods; they toil at Satan's bidding; but the one thing they need to do they won't — they will not 'strive' at all.

I am not writing from hearsay. I speak what I have seen. I write down the result of thirty-seven years' experience in the ministry. I have learned lessons about human nature during that period that I never knew before. I have seen how true are our Lord's words about the narrow road. I have discovered how few there are that 'strive' to be saved.

Seriousness about fleeting matters is common enough. Striving to be rich and prosperous in this world is not rare at all. Pains about money, and business, and politics; pains about trade, and science, and fine arts, and amusements; pains about rent, and wages, and labour, and land; pains about such matters I see in abundance both in the city and the country. But I see few who take pains about their souls. I see few anywhere who 'strive' to enter in through the narrow gate.

I am not surprised at all this. I read in the Bible that it is only what I am to expect. The parable of the great supper is an exact picture of things that I have seen with my own eyes ever since I became a minister (Luke 14:16). I find, as my Lord and Saviour tells me, that 'men make excuse'. One has his piece of land to see; another has his oxen to prove; a third has his family hindrances. But all this does not prevent my feeling deeply grieved for the souls of men. I grieve to think that they should have eternal life so close to them, and yet be lost because they will not 'strive' to enter in and be saved.

I do not know in what state of soul many of my readers may be. But I warn you to take heed that you do not perish for ever because you did not 'strive'. Do not suppose that it needs some great scarlet sin to bring you to the pit of destruction. You have only to sit still and do nothing, and you will find yourself eventually in hell. Yes! Satan does not ask you to walk in the steps of Cain, and Pharaoh, and Ahab, and Belshazzar, and Judas Iscariot. There is another road to hell that is guaranteed to get you there — the road of spiritual sluggishness, spiritual laziness, and spiritual sloth. Satan has no objection to you being known as a respectable member of the Christian Church. He will let you give your offerings; he will allow you to sit comfortably in church every Sunday that you live. He knows full well that so long as you do not 'strive', you must come in the end to the place where the destroying maggot never dies, and the fire is never quenched. Be careful that you do not come to this end. I repeat: 'You have only to do nothing, and you will be lost.'

If you have been taught to 'strive' for your soul's well-being, I beg you never to suppose you can go too far. Never give way to the idea that you are too concerned about your spiritual condition, and that there is no need for so much carefulness. Rather, be convinced in your own mind that 'in all labour there is profit', and that no labour is so profitable as that bestowed on the soul. It is a maxim among good farmers that the more they do for the land the more the land does for them. I am sure it should be a maxim among Christians that the more they do for their Christianity, the more their Christianity will do for them.

Watch out for the slightest inclination to be careless about such things as reading the Bible, going to church, praying and taking the Lord's Supper. Beware of shortening your prayers, your Bible reading, your private communion with God. Be careful that you do not give way to a thoughtless, lazy manner of using the weekly services of the church. Fight against any rising disposition to be sleepy, critical and fault-finding, while you listen to the preaching of the gospel. Whatever you do for God, do it with all your heart, mind and strength. In other things be moderate, and dread running into extremes. In matters of the soul fear moderation just as you would fear the plague. Don't care what men may think of you. Let it be enough for you that your Master says, 'Strive'.

Frightful prediction

The last thing I wish to consider is the dreadful prediction that the Lord Jesus delivers. He says, 'Many will seek to enter and will not be able.' When will this be? At what time will the gate of salvation be shut for ever? When will the 'striving' to enter in be of no use? These are serious questions. The gate is now ready to open to the chief of sinners; but a day is coming when it will open no more.

The time foretold by our Lord is the time of his own Second Coming to judge the world. The patience of God will at last be at an end. The throne of grace will at last be taken down, and the throne of judgement will be set up in its place. The fountain of living waters will finally be closed. The narrow gate will at last be barred and bolted. The day of grace will be passed and over. The day of reckoning with a sin-laden world will finally begin. And then the solemn prediction of the Lord Jesus will come about: 'Many will seek to enter and will not be able.'

All prophecies of Scripture that have been fulfilled up to this time have been fulfilled to the very letter. They have seemed to many unlikely, improbable, even impossible, up to the very time of their accomplishment; but not one word of them has ever failed.

The promises of *good things* have come to pass, in spite of difficulties that seemed impossible.

1. Sarah had a son when she was well past the age for bearing children.

2. The children of Israel were brought out of Egypt and established in the Promised Land.

3. The Jews were redeemed from the captivity of Babylon, after seventy years, and enabled once more to build the temple.

4. The Lord Jesus was born of a pure virgin, lived, ministered, was betrayed, and cut off, precisely as Scripture foretold.

The Word of God promised that it would be so in all these cases. And so it was. The predictions of judgements on cities and nations have come to pass, though at the time they were first spoken they seemed incredible. Edom is a wilderness; Tyre is a rock for drying nets; Nineveh, that 'greater than great city', is laid waste, and has become a desolation; Babylon is a dry land and a wilderness — her extensive walls are utterly broken down. In all these cases the Word of God foretold that it should be so. And so it was.

The prediction of the Lord Jesus Christ that I impress on you this day will be fulfilled in the same way. Not one word of it will fail when it is due to be accomplished. 'Many will seek to enter and will not be able.'

There is a time coming when seeking God will be useless. Oh, if only men would remember that! Too many seem to believe that the hour will never arrive when they will seek and not find: but they are sadly mistaken. One day they will discover their mistake to their own confusion, unless they repent. When Christ comes, 'Many will seek to enter and will "not be able".'

There is a time coming when many will be shut out of heaven for ever. It will not be the lot of a few, but of a great multitude; it will not happen to one or two in this area, and one or two in another, it will be the miserable end of an immense crowd. '"Many" will seek to enter and will not be able.'

Knowledge will come to many too late. They will see at last the value of an immortal soul, and the happiness of its salvation. They will understand at last their own sinfulness and God's holiness, and the glorious fitness of the gospel of Christ. They will comprehend at last why ministers seemed so anxious, and preached so long, and implored them so earnestly to be converted. But, to their grief, they will know all this too late!

Repentance will come to many too late. They will discover their own surpassing wickedness and be thoroughly ashamed of their past folly. They will be full of bitter regret and hopeless wailing, of keen convictions and of piercing sorrows. They will weep, and wail, and mourn, when they reflect on their sins. The memory of their lives will be grievous to them; the burden of their guilt will seem intolerable. But, to their grief, like Judas Iscariot, they will repent too late!

Faith will come to many too late. They will no longer be able to deny that there is a God, and a devil, a heaven, and a hell. False religion, and scepticism, and unfaithfulness will be laid aside for ever; scoffing, and joking, and free-thinking will cease.

They will see with their own eyes and feel in their own bodies that the things of which ministers spoke were not cleverly devised fables, but great real truths. They will find out to their cost that evangelical religion was not lip service, extravagance, fanaticism and enthusiasm: they will discover that it was the one thing they needed, and that the lack of it will cause them to be lost for ever. Like the devil, they will finally believe and tremble, but too late!

A *desire of salvation* will come to many too late. They will long for forgiveness, and peace, and the favour of God, when they can have them no more. They will wish they might have one more Sunday over again, have one more offer of forgiveness, have one more call to prayer. But it will matter nothing what they think, or feel, or desire then: the day of grace will be over; the door of salvation will be bolted and barred. It will be too late!

I often think what a change there will be one day in the price and estimation at which things are valued. I look around this world in which my lot is cast; I note the current price of everything this world contains. I look forward to the coming of Christ, and the great day of God. I think of the new order of things, which that day will bring in; I read the words of the Lord Jesus, when he describes the master of the house rising up and shutting the door; and as I read, I say to myself, 'There will be a great change soon.'

What are the *dear things* now? Gold, silver, precious stones, banknotes, mines, ships, lands, houses, horses, cars, furniture, food, drink, clothes, and the like. These are the things that are thought valuable; these are the things that command a ready market; these are the things that you can never get below a certain price. Whoever has a lot of these things is counted a wealthy man. Such is the world!

And what are the *cheap things* now? The knowledge of God, the free salvation of the gospel, the favour of Christ, the grace of the Holy Spirit, the privilege of being God's son, the title to eternal life, the right to the tree of life, the promise of a room in the Father's house in heaven, the promises of an incorruptible inheritance, the offer of a crown of glory that does not fade away.

These are the things that no man hardly cares for. They are offered to the sons of men without money and without price: they may be had for nothing — freely and generously. Whoever will, may take his share. But, sadly, there is no demand for these things! They go begging. They are scarcely looked at. They are offered in vain. Such is the world!

But a day is coming upon us all when the value of everything will be altered. A day is coming when banknotes will be as useless as rags, and gold will be as worthless as the dust of the earth. A day is coming when thousands will care nothing for the things they once lived for, and will desire nothing as much as the things they once despised. The mansions and palaces will be forgotten in the desire for a 'house not made with hands'. The favour of the rich and great will be remembered no more, in the longing for the favour of the King of kings. The silks, and satins, and velvets, and laces, will be lost sight of in the anxious need for the robe of Christ's righteousness. All will be altered, all will be changed in the great day of the Lord's return. 'Many will seek to enter and will not be able.'

It was a weighty saying of some wise man, that 'hell is truth known too late'. I fear that thousands of those who profess to be Christians in this day will find this out by experience. They will discover the value of their souls when it is too late to obtain mercy, and see the beauty of the gospel when they can derive no benefit from it. Oh, that men would be wise early in life! I often think there are few passages of Scripture more awful than the one in the first chapter of Proverbs:

Because I have called and you refused,
I have stretched out my hand and no one regarded,

Because you disdained all my counsel,
And would have none of my rebuke,
I also will laugh at your calamity;
I will mock when your terror comes,
When your terror comes like a storm,
And your destruction comes like a whirlwind,
When distress and anguish come upon you.
Then they will call on me, but I will not answer;
They will seek me diligently, but they will not find me.
Because they hated knowledge
And did not choose the fear of the LORD,
They would have none of my counsel
And despised my every rebuke.
Therefore they shall eat the fruit of their own way,
And be filled to the full with their own fancies
(Proverbs 1:24-31).

There may be someone reading this who likes neither the faith nor the practice that the gospel of Christ requires. You think that we are extreme when we implore you to repent and be converted. You think we ask too much when we urge you to come out from the world, and take up the cross, and follow Christ. But take note that you will one day confess that we were right. Sooner or later, in this world or the next, you will acknowledge that you were wrong. Yes! It is a sad consolation for the faithful minister of the gospel, that all who hear him will one day acknowledge that his counsel was good. Mocked, despised, scorned, neglected as his testimony may be on earth, a day is coming that will prove that truth was on his side. The rich man who hears us and yet makes a god of this world; the tradesman who hears us and yet makes his ledger his Bible; the farmer who hears us and yet remains as cold as the clay on his land; the worker who hears us and feels no more for his soul than a stone — all, all will in time acknowledge before the world that they were wrong. All will in time earnestly desire that very mercy that we now set before them in vain. 'They will seek to enter and will not be able.'

There may be someone reading this who sincerely loves the Lord Jesus Christ. Such a person may well take comfort when he looks forward. You often suffer persecution now for Christianity's sake. You have to bear hard words and unkind insinuations. Your motives are often misrepresented, and your conduct slandered. The reproach of the cross has not ceased. But you may take courage when you look forward and think of the Lord's Second Coming. That day will make amends for all. You will see those who now laugh at you because you read the Bible, and pray, and love Christ, in a very different state of mind. They will come to you as the foolish virgins came to the wise, saying, 'Give us some of your oil, for our lamps are going out' (Matthew 25:8).

You will see those who now hate you and call you fools because, like Caleb and Joshua, you speak favourably of Christ's service. Some day they will say, 'Oh, if only we had taken part with you! You have been the truly wise, and we the foolish.' So do not fear the reproach of men. Confess Christ boldly before the world. Show your colours, and do not be ashamed of your Master. Time is short: eternity rushes on. The cross is only for a short time: the crown is for ever. 'Many will seek to enter and will not be able.'

Some words of application

And now let me offer every reader a few parting words to apply the whole subject to his soul. You have heard the words of the Lord Jesus unfolded and expounded. You have seen the picture of the way of salvation: it is a narrow door. You have heard the command of the King: 'Strive to enter'. You have been told of his solemn warning: 'Many will seek to enter and will not be able'. Bear with me a little longer while I try to impress the whole matter on your conscience. I still have something to say on God's behalf.

Have you entered in through the narrow gate?

For one thing, I will ask you a simple question. 'Have you entered in through the narrow gate or not?' Old or young, rich or poor, religious or atheist, I repeat my question, 'Have you entered in through the narrow gate?'

I do not ask whether you have heard of it, and believe there is a gate. I do not ask whether you have looked at it, and admired it, and hope one day to go through. I ask whether you have gone up to it, knocked on it, been admitted, and are now inside?

If you are not inside, what good have you got from your religion? You are not pardoned and forgiven. You are not reconciled to God. You are not born again, sanctified and suitable for heaven. If you die as you are, you will live in the same place of torment as the devil — for ever; and your soul will be eternally miserable.

Oh, think, think what a state this is to live in! Think, think above all things, what a state this is to die in! Your life is but a vapour. A few more years at most and you are gone. Your place in the world will soon be filled up; your house will be occupied by another. The sun will go on shining; the grass and daisies will soon grow thick over your grave; your body will be food for worms, and your soul will be lost for all eternity.

And all this time there stands open before you a gate of salvation. God invites you. Jesus Christ offers to save you. All things are ready for your deliverance. Only one thing is lacking, and that is that you should be willing to be saved. Oh, think of these things, and be wise!

Enter in without a day's delay

For another thing, I will give plain advice to all who are not yet inside the narrow gate. That advice is simply this: to enter in without a day's delay.

Tell me, if you can, of anyone who ever reached heaven except through 'the narrow gate'. I know of none. From Abel, the first who died, down to the end of the list of Bible names, I see none saved by any way but faith in Christ.

Tell me, if you can, of anyone who ever entered through the narrow gate without 'striving'. I know of none except those who die in infancy. He who would win heaven must be content to fight for it.

Tell me, if you can, of anyone who ever strove earnestly to enter, and failed to succeed. I know of none. I believe that however weak and ignorant men may be, they never seek life heartily and conscientiously, at the right door, and are left without an answer of peace.

Tell me, if you can, of anyone who ever entered through the narrow gate, and was sorry afterwards. I know of none. I believe the footsteps on the threshold of the gate are all one way. All have found it a good thing to serve Christ, and have never regretted taking up his cross.

If these things are true, seek Christ without delay, and enter through the gate of life while you can! Begin this very day. Go to that merciful and mighty Saviour in prayer, and pour out your heart before him. Confess to him your guilt and wickedness and sin. Open your heart freely to him; keep nothing back. Tell him that you put yourself and all your soul's affairs wholly in his hands, and ask him to save you according to his promise, and put his Holy Spirit within you.

There is everything to encourage you to do this. Thousands as bad as you have sought Christ in this way, and not one of them has been sent away and refused. They have found a peace of conscience they never knew before, and have gone on their way rejoicing. They have found strength for all the trials of life, and none of them have been allowed to perish in the wilderness. Why shouldn't you also seek Christ?

There is everything to encourage you to do what I tell you at once. I know no reason why your repentance and conversion should not be as immediate as that of others before you. The Samaritan woman came to the well an ignorant sinner, and returned to her home a new creature. The Philippian jailer turned from darkness to light, and became a professed disciple of Christ in a single day. And why shouldn't others do the same? Why shouldn't you give up your sins, and trust in Christ this very day?

I know that the advice I have given you is good. The great question is: Will you take it?

Tell others of the blessings you have found

The last thing I have to say will be a request to all who have really entered through the narrow gate. That request is that you will tell others of the blessings that you have found.

I want all converted people to be missionaries. I do not want them all to go out to foreign lands, and preach to the heathen; but I do want all to be of a missionary spirit, and to make every effort to do good at home. I want them to testify to all around them that the narrow gate is the way to happiness, and to persuade them to enter through it.

When Andrew was converted he found his brother Peter, and said to him, '"We have found the Messiah" (which is translated, the Christ). And he brought him to Jesus' (John 1:41-42). When Philip was converted he found Nathanael, and said to him, '"We have found him of whom Moses in the law, and also the prophets, wrote — Jesus of Nazareth, the son of Joseph." And Nathanael said to him, "Can anything good come out of Nazareth?" Philip said to him, "Come and see,"' (John 1:45-46). When the Samaritan woman was converted, she 'left her waterpot, went her way into the city, and said to the men, "Come, see a man who told me all things that I ever did. Could this be the Christ?"' (John 4:28-29). When Saul the Pharisee was converted, 'Immediately he preached the Christ in the synagogues, that he is the Son of God' (Acts 9:20).

I long to see this kind of spirit among Christians in the present day. I long to see more zeal to commend the narrow gate to all who are yet outside, and more desire to persuade them to enter through and be saved. Happy indeed is the church whose members not only desire to reach heaven themselves, but desire also to take others with them!

The great gate of salvation is still ready to open, but the hour draws near when it will be closed for ever. Let us work while it is called today, for 'night is coming when no one can work' (John 9:4). Let us tell our relatives and friends that we have accepted the way of life and found it pleasant, that we have tasted the bread of life and found it good.

I have heard it calculated that if every believer in the world were to bring one soul to Christ each year, the whole human race would be converted in less than twenty years. I make no comment on such a calculation. Whether such a thing might be or not, one thing is sure: that many more souls might probably be converted to God, if Christians were more zealous to do good.

This, at least, we may remember: that God is 'not willing that any should perish but that all should come to repentance' (2 Peter 3:9). He who endeavours to show his neighbour the narrow gate is doing a work that God approves. He is doing a work that angels look upon with interest, and with which the building of a pyramid will not compare in importance. What does the Scripture say? 'He who turns a sinner from the error of his way will save a soul from death and cover a multitude of sins' (James 5:20).

Let us all awaken to a deeper sense of our responsibility in this matter. Let us look around the circle of those among whom we live, and consider their state before God. Are there not many of them still outside the gate, unforgiven, unsanctified and not prepared to die? Let us watch for opportunities of speaking to them. Let us tell them of the narrow gate, and entreat them to 'strive to enter'.

Who can tell what 'a word spoken at the right time' may do? Who can tell what it may do when spoken in faith and prayer? It may be the turning point in some man's history. It may be the beginning of thought, prayer and eternal life. Oh, for more love and boldness among believers! Think what a blessing to be allowed to speak one converting word!

I do not know what the feelings of my readers may be on this subject. My heart's desire and prayer is that you may daily remember Christ's solemn words, 'Many, I say to you, will seek to enter and will not be able.' Keep these words in mind.

3.
Authentic religion

'Rejected silver' (Jeremiah 6:30).
'Nothing but leaves' (Mark 11:13).
'Let us not love in word or in tongue, but in deed and in truth' (1 John 3:18).
'You have a name that you are alive, but you are dead' (Revelation 3:1).

If we profess to have any religion at all, let us be careful that it is authentic. I say it emphatically, and I repeat the saying: Let us be careful that our religion is authentic.

What do I mean when I use the word 'authentic'? I mean that which is genuine, and sincere, and honest, and thorough. I mean that which is not inferior, and hollow, and formal, and false, and counterfeit, and sham, and nominal. 'Authentic' religion is not mere show, and pretence, and skin-deep feeling, and temporary profession, and works only on the outside. It is something inward, solid, substantial, intrinsic, living, lasting. We know the difference between counterfeit and authentic money — between solid gold and tinsel — between plated metal and silver — between authentic stone and plaster imitation. Let us think of these things as we consider the subject of this chapter. What is the character of our religion? Is it authentic? It may be weak, and feeble, and mingled with many defects. That is not the point before us now. Is our religion authentic? Is it true?

The times in which we live demand attention to this subject. A lack of authenticity is a striking feature of a vast amount of religion in the present day. Poets have sometimes told us that the world has passed through four different states or conditions. We have had a golden age, and a silver age, a brass age, and an iron age. How far this is true, I do not stop to ask. But I fear there is little doubt as to the character of the age in which we live now. It is universally an age of cheap metal and alloy. If we measure the religion of the age by its apparent quantity, there is much of it. But if we measure it by its quality, there is indeed very little. On every side we want *more authenticity*.

I ask for your attention, while I try to bring home to men's consciences the question in this chapter. There are two things that I propose to do.

> In the first place, I will show *the importance of authenticity in religion*.
> In the second place, I will supply *some tests by which we may prove whether our own religion is authentic*.

Do any of my readers have any desire to go to heaven when they die? Do you wish to have a religion that will comfort you in life, give you good hope in death, and survive the judgement of God at the last day? Then, do not turn away from the subject before you. Sit down, and consider calmly, whether your Christianity is authentic and true, or counterfeit and hollow.

The importance of authenticity in religion

The point is one which, at first sight, may seem to require very few remarks to establish it. All men, I am told, are fully convinced of the importance of authenticity. But is this true? Can it indeed be said that authenticity is rightly recognized among Christians? I deny this completely. The majority of people who profess to admire authenticity seem to think that everyone possesses it! They tell us that 'all have got good hearts', and that all are sincere and true for the most part, though they may make mistakes. They call us unchristian, and harsh, and censorious, if we doubt anybody's goodness of heart. In short, they destroy the value of authenticity by regarding it as something that almost everyone has.

This widespread delusion is precisely one of the causes why I take up this subject. I want men to understand that 'authenticity' is a far more rare and uncommon thing than is commonly supposed. I want men to see that 'unreality' is one of the great dangers of which Christians ought to beware.

What does the Scripture say? This is the only judge that can try the subject. Let us turn to our Bibles, and examine them fairly, and then deny, if we can, the importance of authenticity in religion, and the danger of not being authentic.

Firstly, then, let us look at the parables spoken by our Lord Jesus Christ. Observe how many of them are intended to put in strong contrast the true believer and the mere nominal disciple (in name only). The parables of the sower, the weeds, the net, the two sons, the wedding garment, the ten virgins, the talents, the great banquet, the ten minas, the two builders, all have one great point in common. They all bring out in striking contrast the difference between authenticity and unreality in religion. They all show the uselessness and danger of any Christianity that is not authentic, thorough and true.

Secondly, let us look at the language of our Lord Jesus Christ concerning the scribes and the Pharisees. Eight times in one chapter we find him denouncing them as 'hypocrites', in words of almost fearful severity: 'Serpents, brood of vipers! How can you escape the condemnation of hell?' (Matthew 23:33). What can we learn from these tremendously strong expressions? How is it that our gracious and merciful Saviour used such cutting words about people who at any rate were more moral and decent than the tax collectors and prostitutes? It is meant to teach us how exceedingly detestable false profession and mere outward religion is in God's sight. Open wickedness and wilful submission to fleshly lusts are no doubt ruinous sins, if not given up. But there seems nothing so displeasing to Christ as hypocrisy and unreality.

Thirdly, let us also look at the startling fact that there is hardly a grace in the character of a true Christian that does not have a corresponding counterfeit described in the Word of God. There is not a feature in a believer's countenance of which there is not an imitation. Give me your attention, and I will show you this in a few examples.

Is there not a false *repentance*? Without a doubt there is. Saul and Ahab, and Herod, and Judas Iscariot had many feelings of sorrow about sin. But they never really repented unto salvation.

Is there not a false *faith*? Without a doubt there is. It is written of Simon Magus, at Samaria, that he 'believed', and yet his heart was not right in the sight of God. It is even written of the devils that they 'believe — and tremble!' (Acts 8:13; James 2:19).

Is there not a false *holiness*? Without a doubt there is. Joash, king of Judah, appeared to everyone very holy and good, so long as Jehoiada the priest lived. But as soon as he died the religion of Joash died at the same time (2 Chronicles 24:2). Judas Iscariot's outward life was as correct as that of any of the Apostles up to the time that he betrayed his Master. There was nothing suspicious about him. Yet in reality he was 'a thief' and a traitor (John 12:6).

Is there not a false *love and kindness*? Without a doubt there is. There is a love that consists of words and tender expressions, and a great show of affection, and calling other people 'dear brethren', while the heart does not love at all. It is not for nothing that John says, 'Let us not love in word or in tongue, but in deed and in truth.'

It was not without reason that Paul said: 'Let love be without hypocrisy' (1 John 3:18; Romans 12:9).

Is there not a false *humility*? Without a doubt there is. There is a pretended meekness of demeanour, which often covers over a very proud heart. Paul warns us against a 'false humility', and speaks of having 'an appearance of wisdom, in self-imposed religion, false humility' (Colossians 2:18, 23).

Is there not a false *praying*? Without a doubt there is. Our Lord denounces it as one of the particular sins of the Pharisees — that for a 'pretence make long prayers' (Matthew 23:14). He does not charge them with not praying, or with praying short prayers. Their sin lay in the fact that their prayers were not authentic.

Is there not a false *worship*? Without a doubt there is. Our Lord said of the Jews: 'These people ... honour me with their lips, but their heart is far from me' (Matthew 15:8). They had plenty of formal services in their temples and their synagogues. But their fatal defect was their lack of authenticity and heart.

Is there not a lot of false *talking* about religion? Without a doubt there is. Ezekiel describes some professing Jews who talked and spoke like God's people 'but their hearts pursue their own gain' (Ezekiel 33:31). Paul tells us that we may 'speak with the tongues of men and of angels', and yet be no better than a resounding gong or a clanging cymbal (1 Corinthians 13:1).

What shall we say about these things? To say the least, they ought to set us thinking. To my own mind they seem to lead to only one conclusion. They show clearly the immense importance that Scripture attaches to authenticity in religion. They show clearly we need to be careful lest our Christianity turn out to be merely nominal, formal, unreal and inferior.

The subject is of deep importance in every age. There has never been a time, since the church of Jesus Christ was founded, when there has not been a vast amount of trivial and mere nominal religion among professing Christians. I am sure it is the case in the present day. Wherever I turn my eyes I see abundant cause for the warning, 'Beware of inferior religion. Be genuine. Be thorough. Be authentic. Be true.'

How much religion among some members of the church consists of *nothing but churchmanship*! They belong to the Established Church. They are baptized in her baptistry, married in her sanctuary, preached to on Sundays by her ministers. But the great doctrines and truths preached from her pulpits have no place in their hearts, and no influence on their lives. They neither think, nor feel, nor care, nor know anything about them. And is the religion of these people authentic Christianity? It is nothing of the kind. It is a cheap imitation. It is not the Christianity of Peter, and James, and John, and Paul. It is 'churchianity', and no more.

How much religion among some Independents consists of *nothing but disagreement*! They pride themselves on having nothing to do with the formal denomination church. They rejoice in having no ritual, no forms, no bishops. They glory in the exercise of their private judgement, and the absence of everything ceremonial in their public worship. But all this time they have neither grace, nor faith, nor repentance, nor holiness, nor spirituality of conduct or conversation. The experimental and practical piety of the old separatist is something of which they are utterly destitute. Their Christianity is as sapless and fruitless as a dead tree, and as dry and marrowless as an old bone. And is the Christianity of these people authentic? It is nothing of the kind. It is cheap imitation. It is not the Christianity of the Reformers of the past. It is 'nonconformity' and nothing more.

How much ritualistic religion is utterly false! You will sometimes see men boiling over with zeal about outward expressions of worship such as church music and order of service, while their hearts are manifestly in the world. Of the inward work of the Holy Spirit — of living faith in the Lord Jesus — of delight in the Bible and religious conversation — of separation from worldly silliness and entertainment — of zeal for the conversion of souls to Christ — of all these things they are profoundly ignorant. And is this kind of Christianity authentic? It is nothing of the kind. It is a mere name.

How much Evangelical religion is completely make-believe? You will sometimes see men professing great affection for the pure 'gospel', while they are, practically speaking, inflicting on it the greatest injury. They will talk loudly of soundness in the faith, and have a keen nose for heresy. They will run eagerly after popular preachers, and applaud Evangelical speakers at public meetings. They are familiar with all the phrases of Evangelical religion, and can converse fluently about its leading doctrines. To see their faces at public meetings, or in church, you would think they were eminently godly. To hear them talk you would suppose their lives were tied up in all kinds of religious activity. And yet these people will sometimes do things in private of which even some heathens would be ashamed. They are neither truthful, nor sincere, nor honest, nor just, nor good-tempered, nor unselfish, nor merciful, nor humble, nor kind! And is such Christianity as this authentic? It is not. It is a worthless fake, a wretched cheat and farce.

How much Revivalist religion in the present day is utterly false! You will find a crowd of false believers bringing discredit on the work of God wherever the Holy Spirit is poured out. How many people today will profess to be suddenly convinced of sin, to find peace in Jesus — to be overwhelmed with joys and ecstasies of soul — while in authenticity of religion they have no grace at all. Like the 'rocky-soil' hearers, they endure but for a short time. 'In time of temptation [they] fall away' (Luke 8:13). As soon as the first excitement has passed, they return to their old ways, and resume their former sins. Their religion is like Jonah's gourd, which came up in a night and perished in a night. They have neither root nor vitality. They only injure God's cause and give occasion to God's enemies to blaspheme. And is Christianity like this authentic? It is nothing of the kind. It is a cheap imitation from the devil's mint, and is worthless in God's sight.

I write these things with sorrow. I have no desire to bring any section of the church of Christ into contempt. I have no wish to cast any slur on any movement that begins with the Spirit of God. But the times demand very plain speaking about some points in the prevailing Christianity of our day. And one point I am quite sure demands attention is the abounding lack of authenticity which is to be seen on every side.

No reader, at any rate, can deny that the subject before him is of vast importance.

Some tests to try the reality of our religion

I now pass on to the second thing which I proposed to do. I will supply some tests by which we may try the reality of our religion. In approaching this part of my subject, I ask every reader to deal fairly, honestly and reasonably with his soul. Dismiss from your mind the common idea that of course all is right if you go to church. Cast away such vain notions for ever. You must look further, higher and deeper than this if you would find out the truth. Listen to me, and I will give you a few hints. Believe me, it is no light matter. It is your life.

The place it occupies in your soul

If you want to know whether your religion is authentic, try it by the place it occupies in your inner man. It is not enough that it is in your 'head'. You may know the truth, and assent to the truth, and believe the truth, and yet be wrong in God's sight. It is not enough that it is on your 'lips'. You may say 'Amen' to public prayer in church, and yet have nothing more than an outward religion. It is not enough that it is in your 'feelings'. You may weep under preaching one day, and be lifted to the third heaven by joyous excitement another day, and yet be dead to God. Your religion, if it is authentic, and given by the Holy Spirit, must be in your heart. It must hold the reins. It must sway the affections. It must lead the will. It must direct the tastes. It must influence the choices and decisions. It must fill the deepest, lowest, inmost seat in your soul. Is this your religion? If not, you may have good reason to doubt whether it is 'authentic' and true (Acts 8:21; Romans 10:10).

Your feelings towards sin

If you want to know whether your religion is authentic, try it by the feelings towards sin that it produces. The Christianity that is from the Holy Spirit will always have a very deep view of the sinfulness of sin. It will not merely regard sin as a blemish and misfortune, which makes men and women objects of pity and compassion. It will see in sin the abominable thing that God hates, the thing that makes man guilty and lost in his Maker's sight, the thing that deserves God's wrath and condemnation. It will look on sin as the cause of all sorrow and unhappiness, of strife and wars, of quarrels and contentions, of sickness and death — the curse that cursed God's beautiful creation, the cursed thing that makes the whole earth groan and struggle in pain. Above all, it will see in sin the thing that will ruin us eternally, unless we can find a ransom — lead us captive, unless we can get its chains broken — and destroy our happiness, both here and hereafter, unless we fight against it, even unto death. Is this your religion? Are these your feelings about sin? If not, you should doubt whether your religion is 'authentic'.

Your feelings towards Christ

If you want to know whether your religion is authentic, try it by the feelings towards Christ that it produces. Nominal religion may believe that such a person as Christ existed, and was a great helper to mankind. It may show him some external respect, attend the celebration of the Lord's Supper, and bow the head at his name. But it will go no further. Authentic religion will make a man glory in Christ, as the Redeemer, the Deliverer, the Priest, the Friend, without whom he would have no hope at all. It will produce confidence in him, love towards him, delight in him, comfort in him, as the mediator, the food, the light, the life, the peace of the soul. Is this your religion? Do you know anything of feelings like these towards Jesus Christ? If not, you have every reason to doubt whether your religion is 'authentic'.

The fruit it bears in your heart and life

If you want to know whether your religion is authentic, try it by the fruit it bears in your heart and life. The Christianity that is from above will always be known by its fruits. It will produce in the man who has it repentance, faith, hope, love, humility, spirituality, kindness, self-denial, unselfishness, forgiving spirit, moderation, truthfulness, hospitality and patience.

The degree to which these various graces appear may vary in different believers. The germ and seeds of them will be found in all who are the children of God. By their fruits they will be known. Is this your religion? If not, you should doubt whether it is 'authentic'.

Your feelings and habits about means of grace

If you want to know whether your religion is authentic, test it by your feelings and habits about means of grace. Prove it by your treatment of Sunday. Is that day a time of fatigue and pressure, or a delight and refreshment, and a sweet anticipation of the rest to come in heaven? Prove it by the public means of grace. What are your feelings about public prayer and public praise, about the public preaching of God's Word, and the administration of the Lord's Supper? Are they things to which you give a cold assent, and tolerate them as proper and correct? Or are they things in which you take pleasure, and without which you could not be happy? Prove it, finally, by your feelings about private means of grace. Do you find it essential to your comfort to read the Bible regularly in private, and to speak to God in prayer? Or do you find these practices boring, and either slight them, or neglect them altogether? These questions deserve your attention. If means of grace, whether public or private, are not as necessary to your soul as food and drink are to your body, you may well doubt whether your religion is 'authentic'.

I press on the attention of all my readers the five points that I have just named. There is nothing like getting down to details about these matters. If you want to know whether your religion is 'authentic', genuine and true, measure it by these five points. Measure it fairly; test it honestly. If your heart is right in the sight of God, you have no cause to flinch from examination. If it is wrong, the sooner you find it out the better.

Applying these truths to ourselves

And now I have done what I proposed to do. I have shown from Scripture the unspeakable importance of authenticity in religion, and the danger in which many stand of being lost for ever, for lack of it. I have given five plain tests by which a man may find out whether his Christianity is authentic. I will conclude with a direct application of the whole subject to the souls of all who read this. I will draw my bow and trust that God will bring an arrow home to the hearts and consciences of many.

1. *A question*

Is you own religion authentic or false? Genuine or fake? I do not ask what you think about others. Perhaps you may see many hypocrites around you. You may be able to point to many who have no 'authenticity' at all. This is not the question. You may be right in your opinion about others. But I want to know about yourself. Is your own Christianity authentic and true? Or nominal and counterfeit?

If you love life, do not turn away from the question that is now before you. The time must come when the whole truth will be known. The Judgement Day will reveal what sort of religion every man has. The parable of the wedding clothes will receive an awful fulfilment. Surely it is a thousand times better to find out *now* your condition, and to repent, than to find it out too late in the next world, when there will be no opportunity for repentance. If you have common sense, reason and judgement, consider what I say. Sit down quietly this day, and examine yourself. Find out the authentic character of your religion. With the Bible in your hand, and honesty in your heart, the answer is there. Then resolve to find out.

2. *A warning*

I address this to all who know, in their own consciences, that their religion is not authentic. I ask them to remember the greatness of their danger, and their exceeding guilt in the sight of God.

A false Christianity is especially offensive to that great God with whom we have to deal. He is continually spoken of in Scripture as the God of truth. Truth is particularly one of his

attributes. Can you doubt for a moment that he detests everything that is not genuine and true? It is better, I firmly believe, to
be found an ignorant heathen at the last day, than to be found
with nothing better than a nominal religion. If your religion is
like this, beware!

A false Christianity is sure to fail a man in the end. It will
wear out; it will break down; it will leave its possessor like a
wreck on a sandbank, high and dry and forsaken by the tide; it
will supply no comfort in the hour when comfort is most needed
— in the time of affliction, and on the deathbed. If you want a
religion to be of any use to your soul, beware of false Christianity! If you want to avoid being comfortless in death, and hopeless in the Judgement Day, be genuine, be authentic, be true.

3. *Advice*

I offer this to all who feel pricked in their conscience by the
subject before us. I advise them to cease from all trifling and
playing with religion, and to become honest, wholehearted followers of the Lord Jesus Christ.

Cry out without delay to the Lord Jesus, and ask him to
become your Saviour, your Physician, your Priest, and your
Friend. Do not let the thought of your unworthiness keep you
away: do not let the memory of your sins prevent your petition.
Never, never forget that Christ can cleanse you from any quantity of sins, if you only commit your soul to him. But one thing
he does ask of those who come to him: he asks them to be
authentic, honest and true.

Let authenticity be one great mark of your approach to Christ,
and there is everything to give you hope. Your repentance may
be feeble, but let it be authentic; your faith may be weak, but
let it be authentic; your desires after holiness may be mingled
with much weakness, but let them be authentic. Let there be
nothing of coldness, of double-dealing, of dishonesty, of sham,

of counterfeit, in your Christianity. Never be content to wear a cloak of religion. Be all that you profess. Though you may sin, be authentic. Though you may stumble, be true. Keep this principle continually before your eyes, and it will be well with your soul throughout your journey from grace to glory.

4. *Encouragement*

I address this to all who have courageously taken up the cross, and are honestly following Christ. I exhort them to persevere, and not to be moved by difficulties and opposition.

You may often find few with you, and many against you. You may often hear cruel things said of you. You may often be told that you go too far, and that you are extreme. Don't listen to it. Turn a deaf ear to remarks of this kind. Press on.

If there is anything that a man ought to do thoroughly, authentically, truly, honestly and with all of his heart, it is the matters concerning his soul. If there is any work which he ought never to slight, and do in a careless fashion, it is that great work of 'working out [his] own salvation' (Philippians 2:12). Believer in Christ, remember this! Whatever you do in religion, do it well. Be authentic. Be thorough. Be honest. Be true.

If there is anything in the world of which a man need not be ashamed, it is service to Jesus Christ. Of sin, of worldliness, of flippancy, of frivolousness, of time-wasting, of pleasure-seeking, of bad temper, of pride, of making an idol of money, clothes, hunting, sport, card-playing, reading novels, and the like — of all this a man should be ashamed. Living after this fashion he makes the angels sorrow, and the devils rejoice. But of living for his soul, caring for his soul, thinking of his soul, providing for his soul, making his soul's salvation the principal and chief thing in his daily life — of all this a man has no cause to be ashamed at all. Believer in Christ, remember this! Remember it in your Bible reading, and your private praying. Remember it on Sundays. Remember it in your worship of God. In all these things never be ashamed of being wholehearted, authentic, thorough and true.

The years of our life are fast passing away. Who knows, but this year may be the last in his life? Who can tell but that he may be called this very year to meet his God? If you would be found ready, be an authentic and true Christian. Do not be cheap imitation.

The time is fast coming when nothing but authenticity will stand the fire. Authentic repentance towards God; authentic faith towards our Lord Jesus Christ; authentic holiness of heart and life — these, these are the things which will alone stand the judgement at the last day. It is a solemn saying of our Lord Jesus Christ, 'Many will say to me in that day, "Lord, Lord, have we not prophesied in your name, cast out demons in your name, and done many wonders in your name?" And then I will declare to them, "I never knew you; depart from me, you who practise lawlessness!"' (Matthew 7:22-23).

4.
Prayer

'Men always ought to pray and not lose heart' (Luke 18:1).
'I desire therefore that the men pray everywhere, lifting up holy hands' (1 Timothy 2:8).

Prayer is the most important subject in practical religion. All other subjects are second to it. Reading the Bible, listening to sermons, attending public worship, going to the Lord's Table — all these are very important matters. But none of them are as important as private prayer.

I propose in this chapter to offer seven clear reasons why I use such strong language about prayer. I draw these reasons to the attention of every thinking man into whose hands this publication may fall. I venture to assert with confidence that they deserve serious consideration.

Absolutely necessary to a man's salvation

In the first place, prayer is absolutely necessary to a man's salvation. I use the words 'absolutely necessary' and do so deliberately. I am not speaking now of infants and those with learning difficulties. I remember that where little is given, little will be required. I speak especially of those who call themselves Christians, in a land like our own. Of these I say a man or woman who does not pray cannot expect to be saved.

I hold salvation by grace as strongly as anyone. I would gladly offer a free and full pardon to the greatest sinner that ever lived. I would not hesitate to stand by his dying bed, and say, 'Believe in the Lord Jesus, and you will be saved.' But that a man can have salvation without *asking* for it, I cannot see in the Bible. I cannot see that it states anywhere that a man who will not so much as lift up his heart inwardly, and say, 'Lord Jesus, give it to me,' will receive pardon for his sins. I can see that nobody will be saved by his prayers, but I cannot find that anybody will be saved without prayer.

It is not absolutely necessary to salvation that a man should *read* the Bible. A man may have no learning, or be blind, and yet have Christ in his heart. It is not absolutely necessary that a man should *hear* the public preaching of the gospel (though he must receive the Word by some means). He may live where the gospel is not preached publicly, or he may be bedridden, or deaf. But the same thing cannot be said about prayer. It is absolutely necessary to salvation that a man should *pray*.

There is no royal road either to health or learning. Princes and kings, poor men and peasants, all alike must attend to the wants of their own bodies and their own minds. No man can eat, drink, or sleep by proxy. No man can get the alphabet learned for him by another. All these are things that everybody must do for himself, or they will not be done at all.

Just as it is with the mind and body, so it is with the soul. There are certain things absolutely necessary to the soul's health and well-being. Each one must attend to these things for himself. Each must repent for himself. Each must submit to Christ for himself. And for himself each one must speak to God and pray. You must do it for yourself, for nobody else can do it for you.

How can we expect to be saved by an 'unknown' God? And how can we know God without prayer? We know nothing of men and women in this world, unless we speak with them. We cannot know God in Christ, unless we speak to him in prayer. If we wish to be with him in heaven, we must be his friends on earth. If we wish to be his friends on earth, 'We must pray.'

There will be many at Christ's right hand in the last day. The saints gathered from north and south, and east and west, will be 'a great multitude which no one could number' (Revelation 7:9). The song of victory that will burst from their mouths, when their redemption is finally complete, will be a glorious song indeed. It will be far above the noise of many waters, and of mighty thunders. But there will be no discord in that song. Those who sing will sing with one heart as well as one voice. Their experience will be one and the same. All will have believed. All will have been washed in the blood of Christ. All will have been born again. All will have prayed. Yes, we must pray on earth, or we will never praise in heaven. We must go through the school of prayer, or we will never be fit for the celebration of praise. In short, to be prayerless is to be without God — without Christ — without grace — without hope — and without heaven. It is to be on the road to hell.

One of the surest marks of a true Christian

In the second place, a habit of prayer is one of the surest marks of a true Christian. All the children of God on earth are alike in this respect. From the moment there is any life and reality in their religion, they pray. Just as the first sign of life in a newborn infant is the act of breathing, so the first act of men and women when they are born again is *praying*.

This is one of the common marks of all the elect of God: 'Men always ought to pray and not lose heart' (Luke 18:1). The Holy Spirit, who makes them new creatures, works in them the feeling of adoption, and makes them cry, 'Abba, Father' (Romans 8:15). The Lord Jesus, when he saves them, gives them a voice and a tongue, and says to them, 'Be silent no more.' God has no speechless children. It is as much a part of their new nature to pray, as it is of a child to cry. They see their need of mercy and grace. They feel their emptiness and weakness. They cannot do other than they do. They *must* pray.

I have looked carefully over the lives of God's saints in the Bible. I cannot find one of whom much history is told, from Genesis to Revelation, who was not a man of prayer. I find it mentioned as a characteristic of the godly, that they 'call on the Father', that they 'call on the name of Jesus Christ our Lord'. I find it recorded as a characteristic of the wicked, that they 'do not call on the Lord' (1 Peter 1:17; 1 Corinthians 1:2; Psalm 14:4).

I have read the lives of many great Christians who have been on earth since the days of the Bible. Some of them, I see, were rich, and some poor. Some were educated, and some uneducated. They came from various denominations and some were Independents. Some loved a very structured worship service, and some liked it rather informal. But one thing, I see, they all had in common. They have all been *men of prayer*.

I study the reports of missionaries in our own times. I rejoice that heathen men and women are receiving the gospel in various parts of the globe. There are conversions in Africa, in New Zealand and in America. The people converted are naturally unlike one another in every respect. But one striking thing I observe at all the missionary stations — the converted people *always pray*.

I do not deny that a man may pray without heart, and without sincerity. I do not for a moment pretend that the mere fact that a person prays proves everything about his soul. As in every other part of religion, so also in this, there is plenty of deception and hypocrisy. But this I do say — that *not* praying is a clear proof that a man is not yet a true Christian. He cannot really feel his sins. He cannot love God. He cannot feel himself in debt to God. He cannot long after holiness. He cannot desire heaven. He has yet to be born again. He has yet to be made a new creature. He may boast confidently of election, grace, faith, hope and knowledge, and deceive ignorant people. But you may rest assured it is all vain talk *if he does not pray.*

Furthermore, a habit of hearty private prayer is one of the most satisfactory evidences of the real work of the Spirit. A man may preach from false motives. A man may write books, and make fine speeches, and seem diligent in good works, and yet be a Judas Iscariot. But a man seldom goes into his room, and pours out his soul before God in secret, unless he is serious. The Lord himself has set his stamp on prayer as the best proof of true conversion. When he sent Ananias to Saul in Damascus, he gave him no other evidence of his change of heart than this: 'He is praying' (Acts 9:11).

I know that much may go on in a man's mind before he is brought to pray. He may have many convictions, desires, wishes, feelings, intentions, resolutions, hopes and fears. But all these things are very uncertain proofs. They are to be found in ungodly people, and often come to nothing. In many cases they are no more lasting than 'a morning cloud, and like the early dew it goes away' (Hosea 6:4). A real hearty prayer, flowing from a broken and repentant spirit, is worth all these things put together.

I know that the elect of God are chosen to salvation from all eternity. I do not forget that the Holy Spirit, who calls them in due time, in many instances leads them by very slow degrees to an awareness of Christ. But the *eye* of man can only judge by what it sees. I cannot call anyone justified until he believes. I dare not say that anyone believes until he prays. I cannot understand a silent and speechless faith. The first act of faith will be to speak to God. Faith is to the soul what life is to the body. Prayer is to faith what breath is to life. How a man can live and not breathe is past my comprehension; and how a man can believe and not pray is past my comprehension too.

Let no one be surprised if he hears ministers of the gospel dwelling much on the importance of prayer. This is the point we want to bring you to — we want to know that you pray. Your views of doctrine may be correct. Your love of evangelical religion may be warm and unmistakable. But still this may be nothing more than head knowledge and party spirit. The great point is this — whether you can speak *to* God as well as speak *about* God.

No duty so neglected as private prayer

In the third place, there is no duty in religion so neglected as private prayer. We live in days abounding in religious profession. There are more places of public worship now than there ever were before. There are more people attending them than there ever have been since we were a nation. And yet in spite of all this public religion, I believe there is a vast neglect of private prayer.

I would not have said that a few years ago. I once thought, in my ignorance, that most people said their prayers, and many people prayed. I have lived to think differently. I have come to the conclusion that the great majority of professing Christians do not pray at all.

I know that this sounds very shocking and will startle many. But I am convinced that prayer is just one of those things which is thought to be 'a private matter', and like many 'private matters' it is shamefully neglected. It is 'everybody's duty'; and, as often happens in such cases, it is a business carried on by very few. It is one of those private transactions between God and our souls which no eye sees, and therefore one which there is every temptation to pass over and leave undone.

I believe that thousands *never say a word of prayer at all.* They eat; they drink; they sleep; they rise; they go to their work; they return to their homes; they breathe God's air; they see

God's sun; they walk on God's earth; they enjoy God's mercies; they have dying bodies; they have judgement and eternity before them. But they *never speak to God*! They live like the animals that perish; they behave like creatures without souls; they have no words to say to the one in whose hand is their life, and breath, and all things, and from whose mouth they must one day receive their everlasting sentence. How dreadful this seems! But if the secrets of men were only known, how common!

I believe that there are tens of thousands *whose prayers are nothing but a mere form* — a set of words repeated by rote, without a thought about their meaning. Some say over a few hasty sentences picked up in the nursery when they were children. Many, even of those who use good forms, mutter their prayers after they have got into bed, or scramble over them while they wash or dress in the morning. Men may think what they please, but they can count on the fact that, in the sight of God, this is not praying. Words said without heart are as utterly useless to our souls as the drum-beating of the poor heathen before their idols. Where there is no heart, the lips may move and the tongue wag, but there is nothing that God listens to — there is *no prayer*. Saul, I have no doubt, said many a long prayer before the Lord met him on the way to Damascus. But it was not till his heart was broken that the Lord said, 'He is praying.'

Does this surprise any reader? Listen to me and I will show you that I am not speaking as I do without reason. Do you think that my assertions are extravagant and unwarranted? Listen to what I have to say, and I will soon show you that I am only telling you the truth.

Not natural

Have you forgotten that it is not natural to anyone to pray? The carnal mind has a hatred towards God. The desire of man's heart is to get far away from God, and to have nothing to do with him. His feeling towards him is not love but fear. Why, then, should a man pray when he has no real sense of sin, no real feeling of spiritual needs — no thorough belief in unseen things — no desire after holiness and heaven? Of all these things the vast majority of men know and feel nothing. The multitude are travelling on the wide road. I cannot forget this. Therefore I say boldly, I believe that few people pray.

Not fashionable

Have you forgotten that it is not fashionable to pray? It is just one of the things that many would be rather ashamed to admit is their practice. There are hundreds who would sooner storm a beach in battle than confess publicly that they make it a habit to pray. There are thousands who, if obligated by chance to sleep in the same room with a stranger, would lie down in bed without a prayer. To ride a horse well, to shoot well, to dress well, to go to dances and concerts, and theatres, to be thought clever and congenial — all this is fashionable; but not to pray. I cannot forget this. I cannot consider a habit is common when so many seem ashamed to admit to it. I believe that few pray.

How men live

Have you forgotten the lives that many live? Can we really suppose that people are praying against sin night and day, when we see them plunging right into it? Can we suppose they pray against the world, when they are entirely absorbed and taken up with its pursuits? Can we think they really ask God for grace to serve him, when they do not show the slightest desire to serve him at all? Oh, no! It is clear as daylight that the great majority of men either ask nothing of God, or 'do not mean what they say' when they do ask — which is just the same thing. Praying and sinning will never live together in the same heart. Prayer will consume sin, or sin will choke prayer. I cannot forget this. I look at men's lives. I believe that few pray.

How men die

Have you forgotten the deaths that many die? How many, when they draw near death, seem like entire strangers to God. Not only are they sadly ignorant of his gospel, but sadly devoid of the power of speaking to him. There is a terrible awkwardness, and shyness, and newness, and coldness, in their endeavours to approach him. They seem to be taking up something new. They appear as if they wanted an introduction to God, as if they had never talked with him before. I remember having heard of a lady who was anxious to have a minister to visit her in her last illness. She desired that he would pray with her. He asked her what he should pray for. She did not know and could not tell. She was utterly unable to name any one thing that she wished him to ask God for her soul. All she seemed to want was the form of a minister's prayers. I can quite understand this. Deathbeds are great revealers of secrets. I cannot forget what I have seen of sick and dying people. This also leads me to believe that few pray.

The greatest encouragement

In the fourth place, prayer is that act in religion to which there is the greatest encouragement. For his part, God does everything to make prayer easy, if men will only attempt it. 'All things are now ready' on his side (Luke 14:17). Every objection is antici-pated. Every difficulty is provided for. The crooked places are made straight, and the rough places are made smooth. There is no excuse left for the prayerless man.

There is a way by which any man, however sinful and un-worthy, may draw near to God the Father. Jesus Christ has opened that way by the sacrifice he made for us upon the cross. The holiness and justice of God need not frighten sinners and keep them back. Only let them cry to God in the name of Jesus — only let them plead the atoning blood of Jesus — and they will find God on a throne of grace, willing and ready to hear. The name of Jesus is a never-failing passport to our prayers. In that name a man may draw near to God with boldness, and ask with confidence. God has pledged to hear him. Think of this. Is this not encouragement?

There is *an advocate* and intercessor always waiting to present the prayers of those who will employ him. That advocate is Jesus Christ. He mingles our prayers with the incense of his own almighty intercession. So mingled they go up as a sweet savour before the throne of God. Poor as they are in them-selves, they are mighty and powerful in the hand of our High Priest and elder brother. The banknote without a signature at the bottom is nothing but a worthless piece of paper. A few strokes of a pen confer on it all its value. The prayer of a poor child of Adam is a feeble thing in itself, but once endorsed by the hand of the Lord Jesus it accomplishes much. There once was an officer in the city of Rome who was appointed to have his doors always open, in order to receive any Roman citizen who applied to him for help. In the same way, the ear of the Lord Jesus is ever open to the cry of all who want mercy and grace. It is his business to help them. Their prayer is his delight. Think of this. Is this not encouragement?

There is *the Holy Spirit* always ready to help our weakness in prayer. It is one part of his special functions to assist us in our endeavours to speak to God. We need not be cast down and distressed by the fear of not knowing what to say. The Spirit will give us words if we will only seek his aid. He will supply us with 'thoughts that breathe and words that burn'. The prayers

of the Lord's people are the inspiration of the Lord's Spirit —
the work of the Holy Spirit who dwells within them as the Spirit
of grace and supplications. Surely the Lord's people may well
hope to be heard. It is not that they merely pray, but the Holy
Spirit pleading in them (Romans 8:26). Think of this. Is this not
encouragement?

There are surpassing *promises* to those who pray. What did
the Lord Jesus mean when he spoke such words as these: 'Ask,
and it will be given to you; seek and you will find; knock, and it
will be opened to you. For everyone who asks receives, and he
who seeks finds, and to him who knocks it will be opened'
(Matthew 7:7-8). 'Whatever things you ask in prayer, believing,
you will receive' (Matthew 21:22). 'Whatever you ask in my
name, that I will do, that the Father may be glorified in the Son.
If you ask anything in my name, I will do it' (John 14:13-14).
What did the Lord mean when he spoke the parables of the
friend at midnight and the insistent widow? (Luke 11:5; 18:1).
Think over these passages. If this is not encouragement to pray,
then words have no meaning at all.

There are wonderful *examples* in Scripture of the power of
prayer. Nothing seems to be too great, too hard, or too difficult
for prayer to accomplish. It has obtained things that seemed
impossible and out of reach. It has won victories over fire, air,
earth and water. Prayer opened the Red Sea. Prayer brought
water from the rock and bread from heaven. Prayer made the
sun stand still. Prayer brought fire from the sky on Elijah's sacrifice. Prayer turned the counsel of Ahithophel into foolishness.
Prayer overthrew the army of Sennacherib. Mary Queen of Scots
rightly said: 'I fear John Knox's prayers more than an army of
ten thousand men.' Prayer has healed the sick. Prayer has raised
the dead. Prayer has procured the conversion of souls. 'The
child of many prayers', said an old Christian to Augustine's
mother, 'will never perish'. Prayer, pains and faith can do
anything. Nothing seems impossible when a man has the Spirit

of adoption. 'Leave me alone,' is the remarkable saying of God to Moses, when Moses was about to intercede for the children of Israel (Exodus 32:10). The Chaldee version renders it 'Stop praying.' As long as Abraham asked mercy for Sodom, the Lord went on giving. He never ceased to give till Abraham ceased to pray. Think of this. Is this not encouragement?

What more can a man want to lead him to take any step in religion than the things I have just told him about prayer? What more could be done to make the path to the mercy-seat easy, and to remove all causes of stumbling from the sinner's way? Surely if the devils in hell had such a door set open before them they would leap for gladness, and make the very pit ring with joy.

But in the end, where will the man who neglects such glorious encouragements hide his head? What can possibly be said for the man who dies without prayer? God forbid that any of my readers should be that man.

The secret of eminent holiness

In the fifth place, diligence in prayer is the secret of eminent holiness. Without question there is a vast difference among true Christians. There is an immense gap between the greatest and the weakest in the army of God.

They are all fighting the same good fight — but how much more valiantly some fight than others! They are all doing the Lord's work — but how much more some do than others! They are all light in the Lord — but how much more brightly some shine than others! They are all running the same race — but how much faster some run than others! They all love the same Lord and Saviour — but how much more some love him than others! I ask any true Christian whether this is not the case. Are these things not so?

There are some of the Lord's people who seem *never able to advance and grow* from the time of their conversion. They are born again, but they remain babies all their lives. They are learners in Christ's school, but they never seem to get beyond A B C. They have got inside the fold, but there they lie down and go no further. Year after year you see in them the same old habitual sins. You hear from them the same old experience. You note in them the same need of spiritual appetite — the same squeamishness about anything but the milk of the Word, and the same dislike of the strong meat of the Bible — the same childishness — the same feebleness — the same trivialness of mind — the same narrowness of heart — the same lack of interest in anything beyond their own little circle, that you noted ten years ago. They are indeed pilgrims, but they are like the Gibeonites of old; their bread is always dry and mouldy — their shoes always old and split, and their garments always ripped and torn (Joshua 9:4-5). I say this with sorrow and grief. But I ask any real Christian, 'Is it not true?'

There are others of the Lord's people who seem to be *always growing*. They grow like the grass after rain. They increase like Israel in Egypt. They press on like Gideon — though sometimes 'exhausted but still in pursuit' (Judges 8:4). They are ever adding to grace, and faith to faith, and strength to strength. Every time you meet them their hearts seem larger, and their spiritual stature bigger, taller and stronger. Every year they appear to see more, and know more, and believe more, and feel more in their religion. They not only have good works to prove the reality of their faith, but they are 'zealous' of them. They not only do well, but they do not 'grow weary' in well doing (Titus 2:14; Galatians 6:9). They attempt great things, and they do great things. When they fail they try again, and when they fall they are soon up again. And all this time they think of themselves poor unprofitable servants, and believe they do nothing at all! These are the people who make religion lovely and beautiful in the eyes of all. They obtain praise even from the unconverted, and win golden opinions even from the selfish men of the world. These are the people whom it does one good to see, to be with, and to hear. When you meet them, you could believe that, like Moses, they had just come out from the presence of God. When you part with them you feel warmed by their company, as if your soul had been near a fire. I know such people are rare. I only ask, 'Is it not true?'

Now, how can we account for the difference that I have just described? What is the reason that some believers are so much brighter and holier than others? I believe the difference in nineteen cases out of twenty arises from different habits of private prayer. I believe that those who are *not* eminently holy pray 'little', and those who *are* eminently holy pray 'much'.

I dare say this opinion will startle some readers. I have little doubt that many look on eminent holiness as a kind of special gift, which none but a few must pretend to aim at. They admire it at a distance, in books: they consider it beautiful to see an example for themselves. But as to its being something within the reach of any but a very few, such a notion never seems to enter their minds. In short, they consider it a kind of monopoly granted to a few favoured believers, but certainly not to all.

Now I believe that this is a most dangerous mistake. I believe that spiritual, as well as natural, greatness depends far more on the use of means within everybody's reach, than on anything else. Of course I do not say we have a right to expect a miraculous grant of intellectual gifts. But I do say this, that when a man is born again by Jesus Christ, whether he will be exceptionally holy or not depends mainly on his own diligence in the use of God's appointed means. And I confidently assert that the principal means by which most believers have become great in the church of Jesus Christ is the habit of 'diligent private prayer'.

Look through the lives of the brightest and best of God's servants, whether in the Bible or not. See what is written of

Moses, and David, and Daniel, and Paul. Note what is recorded about Luther and the Reformers. Observe what is related of the private devotions of Whitefield, and M'Cheyne. Tell me of one of all the godly fellowship of saints and martyrs who has not had this mark most prominently — he was a 'man of prayer'. Oh, depend on it, prayer is power!

Prayer obtains fresh and continued outpourings of the Spirit. He alone begins the work of grace in a man's heart; he alone can carry it forward and make it prosper. But the Holy Spirit loves to be petitioned. And those who ask most will always have most of his influence.

Prayer is the surest remedy against the devil and besetting sins. The sin that is heartily prayed against will never stand firm: the devil will never maintain influence over us when we ask the Lord to help us. But, then, we must cast our whole situation before our heavenly Physician, if he is to give us daily relief. We must drag our indwelling sins to the feet of Christ, and ask him to send them back to the pit.

Do we wish to grow in grace and be very holy Christians? Then let us never forget the value of prayer.

One great cause of backsliding

In the sixth place, neglect of prayer is one great cause of back-sliding. There is such a thing as going backwards in religion, after making a good profession. Men may run well for a season, like the Galatians, and then turn aside after false teachers. Men may profess loudly, while their feelings are warm, as Peter did; and then, in the hour of trial, deny their Lord. Men may lose their first love, as the Ephesians did. Men may cool down in their zeal to do good, like Mark, Paul's companion. Men may follow an apostle for a season, and then, like Demas, go back to the world — men may do all these things.

It is a miserable thing to be a backslider. Of all the unhappy things that can happen to a man, I suppose it is the worst. A stranded ship, a broken-winged eagle, a garden overrun with weeds, a harp without strings, a church in ruins — all these are sad sights; but a backslider is a sadder sight still. There is no doubt that if the person is truly a Christian then the true grace will never be extinguished, and true union with Christ will never be broken. But I do believe that a man may backslide so far that he will lose sight of his own grace, and despair of his own salvation. And if this is not hell, it is certainly the next thing to it! A wounded conscience, a mind sick of itself, a memory full of self-reproach, a heart pierced through with the Lord's arrows, a spirit broken with a load of inward accusation — all this is a 'taste of hell'. It is a hell on earth.

Now, what is the cause of most backsliding? I believe, as a general rule, one of the chief causes is neglect of private prayer. Of course the secret history of backsliding will not be known until the last day. I can only give my opinion as a minister of Christ and a student of the heart. That opinion is, that backsliding generally first begins with *neglect of private prayer*.

Bibles read without prayer, sermons heard without prayer, engagements to marriage without prayer, travel undertaken without prayer, homes chosen without prayer, friendships formed without prayer, the daily act of private prayer itself hurried over or gone through without heart — these are the kinds of downward steps by which many a Christian descends to a condition of spiritual paralysis, or reaches the point where God allows him to have a tremendous fall.

This is the process which forms the lingering Lots, the unstable Samsons, the wife-idolizing Solomons, the inconsistent Asas, the pliable Jehoshaphats, the over-careful Marthas, of whom so many are to be found in the church of Christ. Often the simple history of such cases is this — they became *careless about private prayer*.

We may be very sure that men fall in private long before they fall in public. They are backsliders on their knees long before they backslide openly in the eyes of the world. Like Peter, they first disregard the Lord's warning to watch and pray; and then, like Peter, their strength is gone, and in the hour of temptation they deny their Lord.

The world takes notice of their fall, and scoffs loudly. But the world knows nothing of the real reason. The heathen succeeded in making Origen, the old Christian Father, offer incense to an idol, by threatening him with a punishment worse than death. They then triumphed greatly at the sight of his cowardice and apostasy. But the heathen did not know the fact, which Origen himself tells us, that he had neglected his private time of prayer with the Lord.

If any of my readers is really a Christian then I trust he will never be a backslider. But if you do not wish to be a backsliding Christian, remember the hint I give you — mind your prayers.

One of the best ways to acquire happiness and contentment

In the seventh place, prayer is one of the best ways to acquire happiness and contentment. We live in a world where sorrow abounds. This has always been its state since sin came into the world. There cannot be sin without sorrow. And till sin is driven out from the world it is vain for anyone to suppose he can escape sorrow. Some, without doubt, have a larger cup of sorrow to drink than others. But few are to be found who live very long without sorrows or cares of one sort or another. Our bodies, our property, our families, our children, our relations, our friends, our neighbours, our worldly callings — each and all of these are fountains of care. Sicknesses, deaths, losses, disappointments, partings, separations, ingratitude, slander — all these are common things. We cannot get through life without them.

Some day they will find us out. The greater our affections, the deeper are our afflictions; and the more we love, the more we have to cry.

And what is the best way to acquire cheerfulness in such a world as this? How will we get through this valley of tears with the least pain? I know no better way than the habit of 'taking everything to God in prayer'.

This is the clear advice that the Bible gives both in the Old Testament and the New. What does God say? 'Call upon me in the day of trouble; I will deliver you, and you shall glorify me' (Psalm 50:15). 'Cast your burden on the LORD, and he shall sustain you; he shall never permit the righteous to be moved' (Psalm 55:22). What does the apostle Paul say? 'Be anxious for nothing, but in everything by prayer and supplication, with thanksgiving, let your requests be made known to God; and the peace of God, which surpasses all understanding, will guard your hearts and your minds through Christ Jesus' (Philippians 4:6-7). What does the apostle James say? 'Is anyone among you suffering? Let him pray' (James 5:13).

This was the practice of all the saints whose history we have recorded in the Scriptures. This is what Jacob did, when he feared his brother Esau. This is what Moses did, when the people were ready to stone him in the wilderness. This is what Joshua did, when Israel was defeated before Ai. This is what David did, when he was in danger at Keliah. This is what Hezekiah did, when he received the letter from Sennacherib. This is what the church did, when Peter was put in prison. This is what Paul did, when he was cast into the dungeon at Philippi.

The only way to be really happy, in such a world as this, is to be ever casting all our cares on God. It is the attempt of carrying their own burdens which so often makes believers sad. If they will only tell their troubles to God he will enable them to bear them as easily as Samson did the gates of Gaza. If they are resolved to keep them to themselves they will find one day that the very 'grasshopper is a burden' (Ecclesiastes 12:5).

There is a friend ever waiting to help us, if we will only tell him our sorrow — a friend who pitied the poor, and sick, and sorrowful, when he was on earth — a friend who knows the heart of a man, for he lived thirty-three years as a man among us — a friend who can weep with the weepers, for he was a man of sorrows and acquainted with grief — a friend who is able to help us, for there never was an earthly pain he could not cure. That friend is Jesus Christ. The way to be happy is to be always opening our hearts to him. Oh, if only we were all like that poor Black Christian who, when threatened and punished, only answered, 'I must tell the Lord.'

Jesus can make those who trust and call on him happy, whatever their outward condition. He can give them peace of heart in a prison, contentment in the midst of poverty, comfort in the midst of bereavements, joy on the brink of the grave. There is a mighty fulness in him for all his believing members — a fulness that is ready to be poured out on every one who will ask in prayer. Oh, if only men would understand that happiness does not depend on outward circumstances, but on the state of the heart!

Prayer can lighten crosses for us no matter how heavy they are. It can bring down to our side one who will help us to bear them. Prayer can open a door for us when our way seems hedged up. It can bring down one who will say, 'This is the way, walk in it.' Prayer can let in a ray of hope, when all our earthly prospects seem darkened. It can bring down one who will say, 'I will never leave you nor forsake you.' Prayer can obtain relief for us when those we love most are taken away, and the world feels empty. It can bring down one who can fill the gap in our hearts with himself, and say to the waves within, 'Peace: be still!' Oh, if only men were not so much like Hagar in the wilderness, blind to the well of living waters close beside them! (Genesis 21:19).

I want my readers to be really happy Christians. I am certain I cannot urge on them a more important duty than prayer.

Some final words

And now it is high time for me to bring this chapter to an end.
I trust I have brought before my readers things that will be seriously considered. I heartily pray to God that this consideration
may be blessed to their souls.

To those who do not pray

Let me speak a parting word to those who do not pray. I dare
not suppose that all who read these pages will be praying people.
If you are a prayerless person, permit me to speak to you on
God's behalf.

Prayerless friend, I can only warn you; but I do warn you most
solemnly. I warn you that you are in a position of dreadful danger.
If you die in your present state you are a lost soul. You will only
rise again to be eternally miserable. I warn you that of all professing Christians you are most utterly without excuse. There is not a
single good reason that you can show for living without prayer.

It is useless to say you *don't know how to pray*. Prayer is the
simplest act in all religion. It is simply speaking to God. It needs
neither learning, nor wisdom, nor book-knowledge to begin it.
It needs nothing but heart and will. The weakest infant can cry
when he is hungry. The poorest beggar can hold out his hand
for charity, and does not wait to find fine words. The most ignorant man will find something to say to God, if he has only a mind.

It is useless to say you *have no convenient place to pray in*.
Any man can find a place private enough, if he is inclined. Our
Lord prayed on a mountain; Peter on the housetop; Isaac in
the field; Nathanael under the fig tree; Jonah in the whale's
belly. Any place may become private, and a Bethel, and be to
us the presence of God.

It is useless to say you *have no time*. There is plenty of time,
if men will only utilize it. Time may be short, but time is always
long enough for prayer. Daniel had all the affairs of a kingdom

on his hands, and yet he prayed three times a day. David was
ruler over a mighty nation, and yet he says, 'Evening and morning and at noon I will pray, and cry aloud' (Psalm 55:17). When
time is really wanted, time can always be found.

It is useless to say you *cannot pray till you have faith and a
new heart*, and that you must sit still and wait for them. This is
to add sin to sin. It is bad enough to be unconverted and going
to hell. It is even worse to say, 'I know it, but I will not cry for
mercy.' This is a kind of argument for which there is no warrant
in Scripture. 'Seek the LORD while he may be found,' says Isaiah,
'Call upon him while he is near' (Isaiah 55:6). 'Take words with
you, and return to the LORD,' says Hosea (Hosea 14:2). 'Repent
therefore of this your wickedness, and pray God,' says Peter to
Simon Magus (Acts 8:22). If you want faith and a new heart,
go and cry to the Lord for them. The very attempt to pray has
often been the arousing of a dead soul. Yes, there is no devil so
dangerous as a speechless devil.

Oh, prayerless man, who and what are you that you will not
ask anything of God? Have you made a covenant with death
and hell? Are you at peace with the maggot and the fire? Have
you no sins to be pardoned? Have you no fear of eternal
torment? Have you no desire after heaven? Oh, that you would
awake from your present folly! Oh, if only you would consider
the coming end of your life! Oh, that you would rise up and call
upon God! Yes, there is a day coming when men will pray loudly,
'Lord, Lord, let us in,' but all will be too late; when many will
cry to the rocks to fall on them, and the hills to cover them, who
would never cry to God. In all affection I warn you. Beware lest
this be the end for your soul. Salvation is very near you. Do not
lose heaven because you failed to ask.

To those who have real desires for salvation

Let me speak, in the next place, to those who have real desires
for salvation, but do not know what steps to take or where to

begin. I can only hope that some readers may be in this state of mind, and if there is even one, I must offer him encouragement and advice.

In every journey there must be a first step. There must be a change from sitting still to moving forward. The journeyings of Israel from Egypt to Canaan were long and wearisome. Forty years passed before they crossed the Jordan. Yet there was someone who moved first when they marched from Rameses to Succoth. When does a man really take his first step in coming out from sin and the world? He does it on the day when he first prays with his heart.

In every building, the first stone must be laid, and the first blow must be struck. The ark was 120 years in building. Yet there was a day when Noah laid his axe to the first tree he cut down to form it. The temple of Solomon was a glorious building. But there was a day when the first huge stone was laid at the foot of Mount Moriah. When does the building of the Spirit really begin to appear in a man's heart? It begins, so far as we can judge, when he first pours out his heart to God in prayer.

If any of my readers desires salvation, and wants to know what to do, I advise him to go this very day to the Lord Jesus Christ, in the first private place he can find, and plead with him in prayer to save his soul.

Tell him that you have heard that he receives sinners, and has said, 'The one who comes to me I will by no means cast out' (John 6:37). Tell him that you are a poor wretched sinner, and that you come to him on the faith of his own invitation. Tell him you put yourself wholly and entirely in his hands — that you feel evil and helpless, and hopeless in yourself, and that unless he saves you, you have no hope to be saved at all. Plead with him to deliver you from the guilt, the power and the consequences of sin. Plead with him to pardon you and wash you in his own blood. Plead with him to give you a new heart, and plant the Holy Spirit in your soul. Plead with him to give you grace, and faith, and will, and power to be his disciple and servant from this day for ever. Yes; go this very day, and tell these things to the Lord Jesus Christ, if you really are serious about your soul.

Tell him in your own way and your own words. If a doctor came to see you when you were sick you could tell him where you felt pain. If your soul really feels its disease you can surely find something to tell Christ. Do not doubt his willingness to save you because you are a sinner. It is Christ's business to save sinners. He says himself, 'I have not come to call the righteous, but sinners, to repentance' (Luke 5:32).

Do not wait because you feel unworthy. Wait for nothing; wait for nobody. Waiting comes from the devil. Just as you are, go to Christ. The worse you are, the more you need to go to him. You will never mend yourself by staying away.

Do not fear because your prayer is stammering, your words feeble, and your language poor. Jesus can understand you. Just as a mother understands the first babblings of her infant, so does the blessed Saviour understand sinners. He can read a sign, and see a meaning in a groan.

Do not despair because you do not get an answer immediately. While you are speaking, Jesus is listening. If he delays in his answer, it is only for wise reasons, and to test if you are serious. Pray on, and the answer will surely come. Though it be delayed, wait for it: it will surely come at last.

If you have any desire to be saved, remember the advice I have given you this day. Act upon it honestly and heartily, and you will be saved.

To those who do pray

Let me speak, lastly, to those who do pray. I trust that some who are reading this know indeed what prayer is, and have the Spirit of adoption. To all these I offer a few words of brotherly counsel and exhortation. The incense offered in the tabernacle had to be made in a particular way. Not every kind of incense would do. Let us remember this, and be careful about the matter and manner of our prayers.

If I know anything of a Christian's heart, you to whom I now speak are often sick of your own prayers. You never enter into the Apostle's words, 'Evil is present with me, the one who wills to do good' (Romans 7:21), so thoroughly as you sometimes do upon your knees. You can understand David's words, 'I hate vain thoughts.' You can sympathize with that poor con-verted soul, who was overheard praying, 'Lord, deliver me from all my enemies; and, above all, from my own evil self!' There are few children of God who do not often find the season of prayer a season of conflict. The devil is especially angry towards us when he sees us on our knees. Yet I believe that prayers which cost us no trouble should be regarded with great suspi-cion. I believe we are very poor judges of the quality of our prayers, and that the prayer which pleases us least, often pleases God most.

Some words of exhortation

Permit me then, as a companion in the Christian warfare, to offer you a few words of exhortation. One thing, at least, we all feel — we must pray. We cannot give it up; we must go on.

Reverence and humility in prayer

I commend, then, to your attention the importance of rever-ence and humility in prayer. Let us never forget what we are, and what a solemn thing it is to speak with God. Let us beware of rushing into his presence with carelessness and flippancy. Let us say to ourselves, 'I am on holy ground. This is none other than the gate of heaven. If I do not mean what I say, I am trifling with God. If I hold sin in my heart, the Lord will not hear me.' Let us keep in mind the words of Solomon: 'Do not be rash with your mouth, and let not your heart utter anything hastily before God. For God is in heaven, and you on earth; therefore let your words be few' (Ecclesiastes 5:2). When Abraham spoke to God, he said, 'I who am but dust and ashes'. When Job spoke, he said, 'I am vile; what shall I answer you?' (Genesis 18:27; Job 40:4). Let us do likewise.

Praying 'spiritually'

I commend to you, in the next place, the importance of praying spiritually. By this I mean that we should labour always to have the direct help of the Spirit in our prayers, and, above all things, beware of formality. There is nothing so spiritual that it cannot become a routine, and this is especially true of private prayer. We may insensibly get into the habit of using the fittest possible words, and offering the most scriptural petitions; and yet we may do it all by rote, without feeling it, and walk daily round an old beaten path, like a horse in a mill. I wish to touch upon this point with caution and delicacy. I know that there are certain critical things we want every day, and that there is nothing nec-essarily formal in asking for these things with the same words. The world, the devil, and our hearts, are the same every day. Of necessity we must go over old ground each day. But I am saying that we must be very careful on this point. If the skeleton and outline of our prayers are by our habit almost a form, let us strive to make the clothing and filling of our prayers as much as possible of the Spirit.

As to praying a written prayer out of a book, it is a habit I cannot commend. If we can tell our doctors the state of our bodies without a book, we ought to be able to tell the state of our souls to God. I have no objection to a man using crutches, when he is first recovering from a broken limb. It is better to use crutches than not to walk at all. But if I saw him on crutches all his life, I would not consider it a matter for praise. I would like to see him strong enough to throw his crutches away.

A regular business of life

I commend to you, in the next place, the importance of making prayer a regular business of life. I might say something of the value of regular times in the day for prayer. God is a God of order. The hours of the morning and evening sacrifice in the Jewish temple were not established as they were without a meaning. Disorder is notably one of the fruits of sin. But I would not bring anyone under bondage. I only say that it is essential to your soul's health to make praying a part of the routine of every twenty-four hours in your life. Just as you allot time to eating, sleeping and business, so also allot time to prayer. Choose your own hours and periods. At the very least, speak with God in the morning, before you speak with the world; and speak with God at night, after you have finished with the world for that day. But settle it in your minds that prayer is one of the vital things of each day. Do not put it into a corner. Do not give it the scraps, and leftover minutes of your day. Whatever else you make a business of, make a business of prayer.

Perseverance in prayer

I commend to you now the importance of perseverance in prayer. Having once begun the habit, never give it up. Your heart will sometimes say, 'We have had family prayers; what great harm is it if we leave our private prayer unsaid?' Your body will sometimes say, 'You are sick, or sleepy, or weary; you do not need to pray.' Your mind will sometimes say, 'You have important business to attend to today; cut short your prayers.' Look on all such suggestions as coming directly from the devil. They are as good as saying, 'Neglect your soul.' I do not maintain that prayers should always be of the same length; but I do say, let no excuse make you give up prayer. Paul did not say without reason, 'Continue earnestly in prayer,' and 'Pray without ceasing' (Colossians 4:2; 1 Thessalonians 5:17). He did not mean that men should be always on their knees, as an old sect called the Euchitae supposed. But he did mean that our prayers should be like the continual burnt offering — something steadily persevered in every day; that it should be like seed-time and harvest, and summer and winter — something that should unceasingly come around at regular seasons; that it should be like the fire on the altar, not always consuming sacrifices, but never completely going out.

Never forget that you may tie together morning and evening devotions by an endless chain of short exclamatory prayers throughout the day. Even in the company of others, or while you work, or going down the street, you may be silently sending up little winged messengers to God, as Nehemiah did in the very presence of Artaxerxes (Nehemiah 2:4). And never think that time given to God is wasted. A nation does not become poorer because it loses one year of working days in seven by honouring the Lord's Day. A Christian never finds he is a loser in the long run by persevering in prayer.

Earnestness in prayer

I commend to you now the importance of earnestness in prayer. It is not necessary for a man to shout, or scream, or be very loud, in order to prove that he is serious. But it is desirable that we should be hearty, and fervent, and warm, and ask as if we were really interested in what we were doing. It is the prayer of a righteous man that is 'powerful and effective', and not the cold, sleepy, lazy, listless one. This is the lesson that is taught us by the expressions used in Scripture about prayer. It is called 'crying, knocking, wrestling, labouring, striving'. This is the lesson taught us by Scripture examples. Jacob is one. He said to the angel at Penuel, 'I will not let you go unless you bless me!' (Genesis 32:26). Daniel is another. Hear how he pleaded with God: 'O Lord, hear! O Lord, forgive! O Lord, listen and act! Do not delay for your own sake, my God' (Daniel 9:19). Our Lord Jesus Christ is another. It is written of him, 'In the days of his flesh, when he had offered up prayers and supplications, with vehement cries and tears' (Hebrews 5:7). Yet, how unlike many of our petitions this is! How tame and lukewarm they seem by comparison! How truly might God say to many of us, 'You do not really want what you pray for!' Let us try to amend this fault. Let us knock loudly at the door of grace, like Mercy in *Pilgrim's Progress*, as if we must perish unless heard. Let us settle it in our minds, that cold prayers are a sacrifice without fire. Let us remember the story of Demosthenes, the great orator, when one came to him, and wanted him to plead his cause. He paid little attention to him, while he told his story without earnestness. The man saw this, and cried out anxiously that it was all true. 'Ah!' said Demosthenes, 'I believe you now.'

Praying with faith

I commend to you now the importance of praying with faith. We should endeavour to believe that our prayers are always heard, and that if we ask things according to God's will, we will always be answered. This is the plain command of our Lord Jesus Christ: 'Whatever things you ask when you pray, believe that you receive them, and you will have them' (Mark 11:24). Faith is to prayer what the feather is to the arrow: without it prayer will not hit the target. We should cultivate the habit of pleading promises in our prayers. We should take with us some promise, and say, 'O LORD God, the word which you have spoken concerning your servant and concerning his house, establish it forever and do as you have said' (2 Samuel 7:25).

This was the habit of Jacob, and Moses, and David. Psalm 119 is full of things asked 'according to your word'. Above all, we should cultivate the habit of expecting answers to our prayers. We should do as the merchant who sends his ships to sea. We should not be satisfied unless we see some return. The church at Jerusalem prayed without ceasing for Peter in prison; but when the prayer was answered they would hardly believe it (Acts 12:15). It is a serious saying of old, 'There is no surer mark of trifling in prayer, than when men are careless what they get by prayer.'

Boldness in prayer

I commend to you now the importance of boldness in prayer. There is an unbecoming familiarity in some men's prayers, which I cannot praise. But there is such a thing as a holy boldness, which is greatly to be desired. I mean such boldness as that of Moses, when he pleads with God not to destroy Israel: 'Why should the Egyptians speak, and say, "He brought them out to harm them, to kill them in the mountains, and to consume them from the face of the earth"? Turn from your fierce wrath, and relent from this harm to your people' (Exodus 32:12). I mean such boldness as that of Joshua, when the children of Israel were defeated before Ai: 'Then what', he says, 'will you do for your great name?' (Joshua 7:9). This is the boldness for which Luther was distinguished. Someone who heard him praying said, 'What a spirit — what a confidence was in his very expression! With such a reverence he petitioned, as one begging of God, and yet with such hope and assurance, as if he spoke with a loving father or friend.' This is the boldness that distinguished Bruce, a great Scottish man of God of the seventeenth century. His prayers were said to be 'like thunderbolts shot up into heaven'. Here I also fear we sadly come short. We do not sufficiently realize the believer's privileges. We do not plead as often as we should, 'Lord, are we not your own people? Is it not for your glory that we should be made holy? Is it not for your honour that the gospel should be preached?'

The fulness of prayer

I commend to you, in the next place, the fulness of prayer. I do not forget that our Lord warns us against the example of the Pharisees, who for show uttered long prayers, and commands us, when we pray, not to use vain repetitions. But I cannot forget, on the other hand, that he has given his own sanction to long devotions, by continuing all night in prayer to God. In this day we are not likely to err on the side of praying 'too much'. Might it not rather be feared that many believers in this generation pray 'too little'? Is not the actual amount of time that many Christians give to prayer in total very small? I am afraid these questions cannot be answered satisfactorily. I am afraid the private devotions of many are most painfully few and limited — just enough to prove they are alive, and no more. They really seem to want little from God. They seem to have little to confess, little to ask for, and little to thank him for. Yes, this is completely wrong! Nothing is more common than to hear believers complaining that they do not grow in their faith. They tell us that they do not grow in grace, as they would desire. Is it not rather to be suspected that many have just as much grace as they ask for? Is it not true of many, that they have little, because they ask little? The cause of their weakness is to be found in their own stunted, dwarfish, clipped, contracted, hurried, little, narrow, diminutive prayers. *They do not have because they do not ask.* Oh, reader, we are not limited in Christ, but in ourselves. The Lord says, 'Open your mouth wide, and I will fill it.' But we are like the king of Israel who hit the ground three times and stopped, when he ought to have hit it five or six times (Psalm 81:10; 2 Kings 13:18-19).

Be specific in prayer

I commend to you, in the next place, the importance of being specific in prayer. We ought not be content with general petitions. We ought to specify our wants before the throne of grace. It should not be enough to confess we are sinners. We should name the sins of which our conscience tells us we are most guilty. It should not be enough to ask for holiness. We should name the graces in which we feel the most deficient. It should not be enough to tell the Lord we are in trouble. We should describe our trouble and all its circumstances. This is what Jacob did, when he feared his brother Esau. He tells God exactly what it is that he fears (Genesis 32:11). This is what Eliezer did, when he sought a wife for his master's son. He spreads before God precisely what he wants (Genesis 24:12). This is what Paul did, when he had a thorn in the flesh. He told the Lord (2 Corinthians 12:8). This is true faith and confidence. We should believe that nothing is too small to be named before God. What would we think of the patient who told his doctor he was ill, but never went into details? What would we think of the wife who told her husband she was unhappy, but did not specify the cause? What should we think of the child who told his father he was in trouble, but said nothing more? Let us never forget that Christ is the true Bridegroom of the soul — the true Physician of the heart — the real Father of all his people. Let us show we feel this by being completely open in our communications with him. Let us hide no secrets from him. Let us tell him everything that is in our hearts.

Intercession in our prayers

I commend to you, in the next place, the importance of intercession in our prayers. We are all selfish by nature, and our selfishness is very apt to stick with us, even when we are converted. There is a tendency in us to think only of our own souls, our own spiritual conflict, our own progress in religion, and to forget others. We need to watch and strive against this tendency, not least in our prayers. We should learn to be more open. We should stir ourselves up to name names other than our own before the throne of grace. We should try to bear in our hearts the whole world — the heathen — the Jew — the Roman Catholics — the body of true believers — the professing Protestant churches — the country in which we live — the congregation to which we belong — the family and home in which we live — the friends and relations we are connected with. For each and all of these we should plead. This is the highest love. He loves me best who loves me in his prayers. This is for our soul's health. It enlarges our sympathies and expands our hearts. This is for the benefit of the church. The wheels of all machinery for extending the gospel are oiled by prayer. Those who intercede like Moses on the mount do as much for the Lord's cause as those who fight like Joshua in the thick of the battle. This is to be like Christ. He bears the names of his people on his breast and shoulders as their High Priest before the Father. Oh, the privilege of being like Jesus! This is to be a true helper to ministers. If I must choose a congregation, give me a people who pray.

Thankfulness in prayer

I commend to you, in the next place, the importance of thankfulness in prayer. I know well that asking God is one thing, and praising God is another. But I see so close a connection between prayer and praise in the Bible that I dare not call prayer in which thankfulness has no part, *true* prayer. It is not without reason that Paul says, 'By prayer and supplication, with thanksgiving, let your requests be made known to God' (Philippians 4:6). 'Continue earnestly in prayer, being vigilant in it with thanksgiving' (Colossians 4:2). It is of mercy that we are not in hell. It is of mercy that we have the hope of heaven. It is of mercy that we live in a land with spiritual light. It is of mercy that we have been called by the Spirit, and not left to reap the fruit of our own ways. It is of mercy that we still live, and have opportunities of glorifying God actively or passively. Surely, these thoughts should come to mind whenever we speak with God. Surely, we should never open our lips in prayer without blessing God for that free grace by which we live, and for that loving-kindness which endures for ever. Never was there a celebrated saint who was not full of thankfulness. Men like Whitefield in the eighteenth century were ever running over with thankfulness. Oh, if we would be bright and shining lights in our day, we must cherish a spirit of praise! And above all, let our prayers be thankful prayers.

Be watchful over your prayers

I commend to you, in the last place, the importance of watchfulness over your prayers. Prayer is that point, above all others in religion, at which you must be on your guard. It is here that true religion begins; here it flourishes, and here it decays. Tell me what a man's prayers are, and I will soon tell you the state of his soul. Prayer is the spiritual pulse: by this the spiritual health may always be tested. Prayer is the spiritual barometer: by this we may always know whether it is fair or foul with our hearts. Oh, let us keep an eye continually upon our private devotions! Here is the essence, and substance, and backbone of our practical Christianity. Sermons, and books, and tracts, and committee meetings, and the company of good men are all good in their way; but they will never make up for the neglect of private prayer. Mark well the places, and society, and companions, that keep your hearts from communion with God, and tend to make your prayers difficult. *There be on your guard.*

Observe what friends and what occupations leave your soul in the most spiritual frame, and most ready to speak with God. *Cling and adhere to these, tightly.* If you will only take care of your prayers, I will promise that nothing will go wrong with your soul.

I offer these points for private consideration. I do it in all humility. I know no one who needs to be reminded of them more than I do myself. But I believe them to be God's own truth, and I would love to know and understand them more.

I want the times we live in to be praying times. I want the Christians of our day to be praying Christians. I want the church of our age to be a praying church. My heart's desire and prayer in sending out this publication is to promote a spirit of prayerfulness. I want those who have never yet prayed to rise and call upon God; and I want those who do pray, to improve their prayers every year, and to see that they are not becoming slack and praying in the wrong way.

5.
Bible reading

'Search the Scriptures' (John 5:39).
'What is your reading of it?' (Luke 10:26).

Next to praying there is nothing so important in practical religion as Bible reading. God has mercifully given us a book which is 'able to make you wise for salvation through faith which is in Christ Jesus' (2 Timothy 3:15). By reading this book we may learn what to believe, what to be, and what to do; how to live with comfort, and how to die in peace. Happy is the man who possesses a Bible! Happier still is he who reads it! Happiest of all is he who not only reads it, but also obeys it, and makes it the rule of his faith and practice!

Nevertheless it is a sorrowful fact that man has a sad ability to abuse God's gifts. His privileges, and power, and abilities are all ingeniously perverted to ends other than those for which they were granted. His speech, his imagination, his intellect, his strength, his time, his influence, his money — instead of being used as instruments for glorifying his Maker — are generally wasted, or employed for his own selfish ends. And just as man naturally badly uses his other mercies from God, so he does with the written Word. One sweeping charge may be brought against the whole of Christendom, and that charge is neglect and abuse of the Bible.

To prove this charge we have no need to look elsewhere: the proof lies at our own doors. I have no doubt that there are more Bibles in our country at this moment than there ever have been since the world began. There is more Bible-buying and Bible-selling, more Bible-printing and Bible-distributing than there ever has been since becoming a nation. We see Bibles in every bookstore: Bibles of every size, price and style; large Bibles, and small Bibles; Bibles for the rich, and Bibles for the poor. There are Bibles in almost every house in the land. But all this time I fear we are in danger of forgetting that to 'have' the Bible is one thing and to 'read' it quite another.

This neglected Book is the subject about which I wish to address my readers now. Surely it is no small thing what you are doing with the Bible. Surely, when the plague is spreading in other lands, you should search and see whether the plague-spot is on you. Spare me some time to supply you with a few plain reasons why every one who cares for his soul ought to value the Bible highly, to study it regularly, and to acquaint himself thoroughly with its contents.

It is unique

In the first place, there is no book in existence written in such a way as the Bible. It is 'given by inspiration of God' (2 Timothy 3:16). In this respect it is utterly unlike all other writings. God taught its writers what to say. He put thoughts and ideas into their minds. He guided their pens in writing down those thoughts and ideas. When you read it, you are not reading the self-taught compositions of poor imperfect men like yourself, but the words of the eternal God. When you hear it, you are not listening to the erring opinions of short-lived mortals, but to the unchanging mind of the King of kings. The men who were employed to write the Bible did not speak themselves. They 'spoke as they were moved by the Holy Spirit' (2 Peter 1:21). All other books in the world, however good and useful in their way, are more or less defective. The more you look at them the more you see their defects and blemishes. The Bible alone is absolutely perfect. From beginning to end it is 'the Word of God'.

I will not waste time by attempting any long and laboured proof of this. I say boldly that the Book itself is the best witness of its own inspiration. It is the greatest standing miracle in the world. He who dares to say the Bible is not inspired must give an explanation why he believes this, if he can. Let him explain the peculiar nature and character of the Book in a way that will satisfy any man with common sense. The burden of proof seems to my mind to lie on him.

It proves nothing against inspiration, as some have asserted, that the writers of the Bible each have a different style. Isaiah does not write like Jeremiah, and Paul does not write like John. This is perfectly true, and yet the works of these men are not a bit less equally inspired. The waters of the sea have many different shades. In one place they look blue, and in another green. And yet the difference is due to the depth or shallowness of the part we see, or to the nature of the bottom. The water in every case is the same salt sea. The breath of a man may produce different sounds according to the character of the instrument on which he plays. The flute, the bagpipe and the trumpet each have their peculiar note. And yet the breath that calls forth the notes is in each case one and the same. The light of the planets we see in heaven is extremely various. Mars, Saturn and Jupiter each have an individual colour. And yet we know that the light of the sun, which each planet reflects, is in each case one and the same. In just the same way the books of the Old and New Testaments are all inspired truth, and yet the aspect of that truth varies according to the mind through which the Holy Spirit makes it flow. The handwriting and style of the writers differ enough to prove that each had a distinct individual being; but the Divine Guide who dictates and directs the whole is always one. All are inspired. Every chapter, and verse, and word, is from God.

Oh, if only men who are troubled with doubts and thoughts about inspiration would calmly examine the Bible for themselves! Oh, if only they would take the advice which was the first step to Augustine's conversion, 'Pick it up and read it! Pick it up and read it!' How many difficulties and objections would vanish away at once like mist before the rising sun! How many would soon confess, 'The finger of God is here! God is in this Book, and I did not know it.'

This is the Book about which I address my readers. Surely it is no light matter what you are doing with this Book. It is no light thing that God should have caused this Book to be 'written for our learning', and that you should have before you 'the oracles of God' (Romans 15:4; 3:2). I charge you, I summon you, to give an honest answer to my questions. What are you doing with the Bible? Do you read it at all? *How do you read it?*

A knowledge of its truths are necessary for salvation

In the second place, there is no knowledge absolutely necessary to a man's salvation, except a knowledge of the things that are to be found in the Bible.

We live in days when the words of Daniel are fulfilled before our eyes: 'Many shall run to and fro, and knowledge shall increase' (Daniel 12:4). Schools are multiplying everywhere you look. New colleges are set up. Old universities are reformed and improved. New books are continually coming out. More is being taught, more is being learned, more is being read than there ever has been. It is all good. I rejoice in it. An ignorant population is a perilous and expensive burden to any nation. It is a ready prey to the first who may arise to entice it to do evil. But this I say — we must never forget that all the education a man can take in will not save his soul from hell, unless he knows the truths of the Bible.

A man *may have immense learning and yet never be saved.* He may be master of half the languages spoken around the globe. He may be acquainted with the highest and deepest things in heaven and earth. He may have read books till he is like a walking encyclopedia. He may be familiar with the stars of heaven, the birds of the air, the beasts of the earth, and the fishes of the sea. He may be able, like Solomon, to speak of 'trees, from the cedar tree of Lebanon even to the hyssop that springs out of the wall; he spoke also of animals, of birds, of creeping things, and of fish' (1 Kings 4:33). He may be able to lecture on all the secrets of fire, air, earth and water. And yet, if he dies ignorant of Bible truths, he dies a destitute man! Chemistry never silenced a guilty conscience. Mathematics never healed a broken heart. All the sciences in the world never soothed a dying man. No earthly philosophy ever supplied hope in death. No natural theology ever gave peace in the prospect of meeting a holy God. All these things are of the earth and can never raise a man above the earth's level. They may enable a man to strut and fret his little time here on earth with a more dignified manner of walking than his fellow-mortals, but they can never give him wings, and enable him to soar towards heaven. He who has the largest share of them will find in time that without Bible knowledge he has no lasting possession. Death will bring all his attainments to an end, and after death they will do him no good at all.

A man *may be a very ignorant man, and yet be saved.* He may be unable to read a word, or write a letter. He may know nothing of geography beyond the bounds of his own city or county, and be utterly unable to say which is nearest to England, Paris or New York. He may know nothing of arithmetic, and not see any difference between a million and a thousand. He may know nothing of history, not even of his own land, and be quite ignorant whether his country is headed up by a tribal chief or by Queen Elizabeth. He may know nothing of science and its discoveries — and whether Julius Caesar won his victories with gunpowder, or the Apostles had a printing press, or the sun orbits around the earth, may be matters about which he has no idea. And yet, if that very man has heard Bible truth with his ears and believed it with his heart, he knows enough to save his soul. He will be found in the end with Lazarus in heaven, while his scientific fellow-creature, who has died unconverted, is lost for ever.

There is much talk in these days about science and 'useful knowledge'. But knowledge of the Bible is the one type of knowledge that is necessary and eternally useful. A man may get to heaven without money, learning, health, or friends, but without Bible knowledge he will never get there at all. A man may have the mightiest of minds, and a memory stored with all that a strong mind can grasp — and yet, if he does not know the things of the Bible, his soul is damned for ever. Woe! Woe! Woe to the man who dies in ignorance of the Bible!

This is the Book about which I am addressing the readers of these pages now. It is no light matter what you do with such a book. It concerns the life of your soul. I summon you, I charge you to give an honest answer to my question. What are you doing with the Bible? Do you read it? *How do you read it?*

It contains such important matter

In the third place, no book in existence contains such important matter as the Bible. Time would fail me if I were to enter fully into all the great things that are to be found in the Bible, and only in the Bible. Its treasures cannot be displayed by any sketch or outline. It would be easy to fill a volume with a list of the exceptional truths it reveals, and still half of its riches would be left untold.

How glorious and soul-satisfying is the description it gives us of God's plan of salvation, and the way by which our sins can be forgiven! The coming into the world of Jesus Christ, the God-man, to save sinners; the redemption he has accomplished for man by his suffering, in our place, the just for the unjust; the complete payment he has made for our sins by his own blood; the justification of every sinner who simply believes on Jesus; the readiness of Father, Son and Holy Spirit to receive, pardon and save to the uttermost — how unspeakably grand and comforting are all these truths! We would know nothing of them without the Bible.

How comforting is the account it gives us of the great Mediator of the New Testament — the man Christ Jesus! Four times over, his picture is graciously drawn before our eyes. Four separate witnesses tell us of his miracles and his ministry, his sayings and his actions, his life and his death, his power and his love, his kindness and his patience — his ways, his words, his works, his thoughts, his heart. Blessed be God, there is one thing in the Bible that the most prejudiced reader can hardly fail to understand, and that is the character of Jesus Christ!

How encouraging are the examples the Bible gives us of good people! It tells us of many who were of similar passions to ourselves — men and women who had cares, crosses, families, temptations, afflictions, diseases, like ourselves — and yet 'through faith and patience inherit the promises', and got safely home (Hebrews 6:12). It keeps back nothing in the history of these people. Their mistakes, their weaknesses, their conflicts, their experience, their prayers, their praises, their useful lives, their happy deaths — all are fully recorded. And it tells us the God and Saviour of these men and women is still the same today as yesterday, and still waits to be gracious.

How instructive are the examples the Bible gives us of bad people! It tells us of men and women who had light and knowledge and opportunities like ourselves, and yet hardened their hearts, loved the world, clung to their sins, would have their own way, despised reproof, and ruined their own souls for ever. And it warns us that the God who punished Pharaoh, and Saul, and Ahab, and Jezebel, and Judas, is a God who never changes; and that there is a real hell.

How precious are the promises that the Bible contains for the use of those who love God! There is hardly any possible emergency or condition for which it does not have a word of hope and encouragement. And it tells men that God loves to be reminded of these promises, and that if he has said he will do something, his promise will certainly be fulfilled.

How blessed are the hopes that the Bible holds out to the believer in Christ Jesus! Peace in the hour of death, rest and happiness on the other side of the grave, a glorious body in the morning of the resurrection, a full and triumphant acquittal in the Day of Judgement, an everlasting reward in the kingdom of Christ, a joyful meeting with the Lord's people in the day of gathering together — these, these are the future prospects of every true Christian. They are all written in the book — in the book that is all true.

How striking is the light that the Bible throws on the character of man! It teaches us what men may be expected to be and do in every position and occupation of life. It gives us the deepest insight into the secret springs and motives of human actions, and the ordinary course of events under the control of human agents. It is the true 'discerner of the thoughts and intents of the heart' (Hebrews 4:12). How deep is the wisdom contained in the Books of Proverbs and Ecclesiastes! I can perfectly understand an old Christian saying, 'Give me a candle and a Bible and shut me up in a dark dungeon, and I will tell you everything that the whole world is doing.'

All these are things that men could find nowhere except in the Bible. We probably do not have the least idea how little we would know about these things if we did not have the Bible. We hardly know the value of the air we breathe, and the sun that shines on us, because we have never known what it is to be without them. We do not value the truths on which I have just been dwelling, because we do not realize the darkness of men to whom these truths have not been revealed. Surely no tongue can fully tell the value of the treasures this one volume contains. Well might old John Newton say that in his estimation some books were copper books, some were silver, and a few were gold, but the Bible alone was like a book all made up of banknotes.

This is the Book about which I address my readers now. Surely it is no light matter what you are doing with the Bible. It is no light matter how you are using this treasure. I charge you, I summon you to give an honest answer to my question: What are you doing with the Bible? Do you read it? *How do you read it?*

It affects mankind in general

In the fourth place, no book in existence has produced such wonderful effects on mankind at large as the Bible.

Changed the world in the days of the Apostles

Firstly, it is the Book whose doctrines turned the world upside down in the days of the Apostles. Many centuries have now passed by since God sent out a few Jews from a remote corner of the earth to do a work, which, according to man's judgement, must have seemed impossible. He sent them out at a time when the whole world was full of superstition, cruelty, lust and sin. He sent them out to proclaim that the established religions of the earth were false and useless, and must be forsaken. He sent them out to persuade men to give up old habits and customs, and to live different lives. He sent them out to do battle with the most perverted idolatry, with the vilest and most disgusting immorality, with a bigoted priesthood, with sneering philosophers, with an ignorant population, with bloody-minded emperors, with the whole influence of Rome. Never was there an enterprise for all appearances more unrealistic and less likely to succeed!

And how did he arm them for this battle? He gave them no worldly weapons. He gave them no worldly power to compel agreement, and no worldly riches to bribe belief. He simply put the Holy Spirit into their hearts, and the Scriptures into their hands. He simply commanded them to expound and explain, to compel and to publish the doctrines of the Bible. The preacher of Christianity in the first century was not a man with a sword and an army to frighten people, or a man with a licence to be sensual, to allure people, like the priests of the shameful idols of the Hindus. No, he was nothing more than one holy man with one holy book.

And how did these men of one book prosper? In a few generations they entirely changed the face of society by the doctrines of the Bible. They emptied the temples of the heathen gods. They starved out idolatry and left it high and dry like a stranded ship. They brought into the world a higher condition of morality between man and man. They raised the character and position of woman. They altered the standard of purity and decency. They put an end to man's cruel and bloody customs, such as the gladiatorial fights — there was no stopping the change. Persecution and opposition were useless. One victory after another was won. One bad thing after another melted away. Whether men liked it or not, they were slowly affected by the movement of the new religion and drawn within the whirlpool of its power. The earth shook, and their rotten shelters fell to the ground. The flood rose, and they found themselves obliged to rise with it. The tree of Christianity swelled and grew, and the chains they had thrown around it to arrest its growth snapped like string. And all this was done by the doctrines of the Bible! Talk about great victories! What are the victories of

Alexander, and Caesar, and Napoleon, compared with those I have just mentioned? For magnitude, for completeness, for results, for permanence, there are no victories like the victories of the Bible.

Changed the world during the Reformation

Secondly, it is the Book that turned Europe upside down in the days of the glorious Protestant Reformation. No man can read the history of Christendom as it was in the latter part of the fourteenth century, and not see that darkness covered the whole professing church of Christ, even a darkness that could be felt. So great was the change that had come over Christianity, that if an apostle had risen from the dead he would not have recognized it, and would have thought that heathenism had revived again. The doctrines of the gospel lay buried under a dense mass of human traditions. Penances, and pilgrimages, and indulgences, relic-worship, and image-worship, and saint-worship, and worship of the Virgin Mary, formed the sum and substance of most people's religion. The church was made an idol. The priests and ministers of the church usurped the place of Christ. And by what means was all this miserable darkness cleared away? By simply bringing forth once more the Bible.

It was not merely the preaching of Luther and his friends that established Protestantism in Germany. The great weapon that overthrew the Roman Catholic Church's power in that country was Luther's translation of the Bible into the German tongue. It was not merely the writings of English Reformers that threw down Roman Catholicism in England. The seeds of the work carried forward were first sown by Wycliffe's translation of the Bible many years before. It was not merely the quarrel of Henry VIII and the pope of Rome that loosened the pope's hold on English minds. It was the royal permission to have the Bible translated and set up in churches, so that every one who wanted might read it. Yes! It was the reading and circulation of Scripture that mainly established the cause of Protestantism in England, Germany and Switzerland. Without it the people would probably have returned to their former bondage when the first Reformers died. But by reading the Bible the public mind became gradually leavened with the principles of true religion. Men's eyes became thoroughly open. Their spiritual understandings became thoroughly enlarged. The abominations of Roman Catholicism became distinctly visible. The excellence of the pure gospel became a rooted idea in their hearts. It was then in vain for popes to thunder forth excommunications. It was useless for kings and queens to attempt to stop the course of Protestantism by fire and sword. It was all too late. The people knew too much. They had seen the light. They had heard the joyful sound. They had tasted the truth. The sun had risen on their minds. The scales had fallen from their eyes. The Bible had done its appointed work within them, and that work was not to be overthrown. The people would not return to Egypt. The clock could not be pushed back again. A mental and moral revolution had been effected, and mainly effected by God's Word. Those are the true revolutions that the Bible effects. What are all the revolutions which France and England have gone through, compared to these? No revolutions are so bloodless, none so satisfactory, none so rich in lasting results, as the revolutions accomplished by the Bible!

This is the Book upon which the well-being of nations has always hinged, and with which the best interests of everyone in Christendom at this moment are inseparably tied. By the same proportion that the Bible is honoured or not, light or darkness, morality or immorality, true religion or superstition, liberty or tyranny, good laws or bad will be found in a nation. Come with me and open the pages of history, and you will read the proof in times past.

Read it in the history of Israel in the Book of Kings. How great was the wickedness that then prevailed! But who can wonder? The law of the Lord had been completely lost sight of, and was found in the days of Josiah thrown aside in a corner of the temple (2 Kings 22:8). Read it in the history of the Jews in our Lord Jesus Christ's time. How awful the picture of scribes and Pharisees, and their religion! But who can wonder? The Scripture was made to have 'no effect by your tradition' (Matthew 15:6). Read it in the history of the church of Christ in the Middle Ages. What can be worse than the accounts we have of its ignorance and superstition? But who can wonder? The times when men did not have the light of the Bible were very dark.

This is the Book to which the civilized world is indebted for many of its best and most praiseworthy institutions. Probably few are aware how many good things men have adopted for public benefit, whose origin may be clearly traced to the Bible. It has left lasting marks wherever it has been received. Many of the best laws by which society is kept in order are drawn from the Bible. The standard of morality about truth, honesty and the relations of man and wife, which prevails among Christian nations, and which — however feebly respected in many cases — makes so great a difference between Christians and heathen, have all been obtained from *the Bible*. We are indebted to *the Bible* for that most merciful provision for the poor working man, the Lord's Day of rest — Sunday. We owe nearly every humane and charitable institution in existence to the influence of the Bible. The sick, the poor, the aged, the orphan, the insane, the retarded, the blind, were seldom or never thought of before the Bible influenced the world. You may search in vain for any record of institutions for their aid in the histories of Athens or of Rome. Yes! There are many who sneer at the Bible, and say the world would get on well enough without it, who do not realize how great are their own obligations to it. Little does the unbeliever think, as he lies sick in some of our great hospitals, that he owes all his present comforts to the very book he despises. Had it not been for the Bible, he might have died in misery, uncared for, unnoticed and alone. Truly the world we live in is unconscious of its debts. The Day of Judgement, I believe, will reveal the full amount of benefit conferred upon mankind by the Bible.

This wonderful Book is the subject about which I address my readers now. Surely it is no light matter what you are doing with the Bible. The swords of conquering generals, the ship in which Nelson led the fleets of England to victory, the hydraulic press which raised the tubular bridge at the Menai, each and every one of these are objects of interest as instruments of great power. The Book I speak of here is an instrument a thousand-fold mightier still. Surely it is no light matter whether you are paying it the attention it deserves. I charge you, I summon you to give me an honest answer this day: What are you doing with the Bible? Do you read it? *How do you read it?*

It affects everyone who reads it with an open heart

In the fifth place, no book in existence can do so much for everyone who reads it with an open heart, as the Bible.

The Bible does not profess to teach the wisdom of this world. It was not written to explain geology or astronomy. It will neither instruct you in mathematics, nor in natural philosophy. It will not make you a doctor, or a lawyer, or an engineer.

But there is another world to be thought of besides that world in which man now lives. There are other ends for which man was created, besides making money and working. There are other interests that he is meant to attend to, besides those of his body; and those are the interests of his soul. It is the interests of the immortal soul that the Bible is especially able to promote. If you want to know law, you may study Blackstone or Sugden. If you would know astronomy or geology, you may study Herschel and Lyell. But if you want to know how to have your soul saved, you must study the written Word of God.

Makes you wise for salvation

The Bible is able to make you wise for salvation through faith which is in Christ Jesus (2 Timothy 3:15). It can show you the way that leads to heaven. It can teach you everything you need to know, point out everything you need to believe, and explain everything you need to do. It can show you what you are — a sinner. It can show you what God is — perfectly holy. It can show you the great giver of pardon, peace and grace — Jesus Christ. I have read of an Englishman who visited Scotland in the days of Blair, Rutherford and Dickson, three famous preachers, and heard all three in succession. He said that the first showed him the majesty of God, the second showed him the beauty of Christ, and the third showed him everything in his heart. It is the glory and beauty of the Bible that it is always teaching these three things more or less, from its first chapter to its last.

The means by which souls are converted

The Bible applied to the heart by the Holy Spirit is the grand instrument by which souls are first converted to God. That mighty change is generally begun by some text or doctrine of the Word, brought home to a man's conscience. In this way the Bible has worked moral miracles by the thousand. It has made drunkards become sober, immoral people become pure, thieves become honest and violent-tempered people become meek. It has wholly altered the course of men's lives. It has caused their old things to pass away, and made all their ways new. It has taught worldly people to seek first the kingdom of God. It has taught lovers of pleasure to become lovers of God. It has taught the stream of men's affections to run upwards instead of running downwards. It has made men think of heaven, instead of always thinking of earth, and live by faith, instead of living by sight. It has done all this in every part of the world. It is still all being accomplished. What are the Roman Catholic miracles that weak men believe compared to all this, even if they were true? Those are the truly great miracles that are constantly being worked by the Word.

The means by which men are built up

The Bible applied to the heart by the Holy Spirit is the chief means by which men are built up and strengthened in the faith, after their conversion. It is able to make them pure, to sanctify them, to train them in righteousness, and to thoroughly equip them for every good work (Psalm 119:9; John 17:17; 2 Timothy 3:16-17). The Spirit ordinarily does these things by the written Word: sometimes by the Word read, and sometimes by the Word preached, but seldom, if ever, without the Word. The Bible can show a believer how to walk in this world to please God. It can teach him how to glorify Christ in all the relationships of life, and can make him a good leader, employee, subordinate, husband, father, or son. It can enable him to bear misfortunes and loss without murmuring, and say, 'It is well'. It can enable him to look down into the grave, and say, 'I will fear no evil' (Psalm 23:4). It can enable him to think about judgement and eternity, and not feel afraid. It can enable him to bear persecution without flinching and to give up liberty and life rather than deny Christ's truth.

Is he weary in soul? It can awaken him.
Is he mourning? It can comfort him.
Is he erring? It can restore him.
Is he weak? It can make him strong.
Is he in the company of the unbeliever? It can keep him
    from evil.
Is he alone? It can talk with him (Proverbs 6:22).

The Bible can do all this for all believers; for the least as well as the greatest; for the richest as well as the poorest. It has done it for thousands already, and is doing it for thousands every day.

The man who has the Bible, and the Holy Spirit in his heart, has everything that is absolutely necessary to make him spiritually wise. He needs no priest to break the bread of life for him. He needs no ancient traditions, no writings of the Fathers, no voice of the church, to guide him into all truth. He has the well of truth open before him, and what more can he want? Yes! Though he is shut up alone in a prison, or cast on a desert island — though he never sees a church or minister again — if he only has the Bible, he has got the infallible guide, and needs no other. If he only has the will to read that Bible properly, it will certainly teach him the road that leads to heaven. It is here alone that infallibility resides. It is not in the church. It is not in the councils. It is not in ministers. It is only in the written Word.

No saving power?

I know well that many say they have found no saving power in the Bible. They tell us they have tried to read it, and have learned nothing from it. They can see in it nothing but difficult and abstract things. They ask us what we mean by talking of its power.

I reply that the Bible no doubt contains some difficult things, or else it would not be the book of God. It contains things hard to comprehend, but only hard because we do not have the understanding of mind to comprehend them. It contains things above our reasoning powers, but nothing that might not be explained if the eyes of our understanding were not feeble and dim. But is not an acknowledgement of our own ignorance the very cornerstone and foundation of all knowledge? Do we not have to take many things for granted at the beginning of every science, before we can proceed one step towards any understanding of it? Do we not require our children to learn many things of which they cannot see the meaning at first? And ought we not then to expect to find 'deep things' when we begin studying the Word of God, and yet believe that if we persevere in reading it the meaning of many of them will one day be made clear? No doubt we ought to expect, and so believe this. We must read with humility. We must take much on trust. We must believe that what we don't know now, we will know later, partly in this world, and completely in the world to come.

But I ask the man who has given up reading the Bible because it contains hard topics, whether he did not find many things in it easy and plain? I put it to his conscience whether he did not see great landmarks and principles in it all the way through? I ask him whether the things necessary for salvation did not stand out boldly before his eyes, like lighthouses. What would we think of the captain of a ship who came, at night, into the entrance of the Channel, and claimed that he did not know every parish, and village, and creek, along the British coast? Would we not think him a lazy coward, when the lights on the Lizard, and Eddystone, and the Start, and Portland, and St Catherine's, and Beachy Head, and Dungeness, and the Forelands, were shining forth like so many lamps, to guide him up to the river? Would we not ask, 'Why did you not steer by the great leading lights?' And what would we say to the man who gives up reading the Bible because it contains hard things, when his own state, and the path to heaven, and the way to serve God, are all written down clearly and unmistakably, as if with a sunbeam? Surely we ought to tell that man that his objections are no better than lazy excuses, and do not deserve to be heard.

Of no effect?

I know well that many raise the objection that thousands read the Bible and are not a bit better off for doing so. And they ask us, when this is the case, what becomes of the Bible's boasted power?

I reply that the reason why so many read the Bible without any benefit is plain and simple — they do not read it in the right way. There is generally a right way and a wrong way of doing everything in the world; and just as it is with other things, so it is in the matter of reading the Bible. The Bible is not so entirely different from all other books as to make it of no importance in what spirit and manner you read it. It does not do any good to merely run our eyes over the print as a matter of course, any more than baptism and the Lord's Supper do any good by the mere virtue of our receiving them. It does not ordinarily do any good, unless it is read with humility and earnest prayer. The best engine that was ever built is useless if a man does not know how to operate it. The best sundial that was ever constructed will not tell its owner the time of day if he is so ignorant as to put it in the shade. Just as it is with that engine, and that sundial, so it is with the Bible. When men read it without benefit, *the fault is not in the Book, but in themselves.*

I tell the man who doubts the power of the Bible, because many read it and are no better for doing so, that the abuse of a thing is no argument against the use of it. I tell him boldly that the man or woman who read that book never did so in a child-like persevering spirit — like the Ethiopian eunuch, and the Bereans (Acts 8:28; 17:11) — and miss the way to heaven. Yes, many will be exposed to shame in the Day of Judgement; but there will not rise up one soul who will be able to say that he went thirsting to the Bible, and found in it no living water — he searched for truth in the Scriptures, but in searching did not find it. The words that speak of wisdom in the Proverbs are strictly true of the Bible: 'If you cry out for discernment and lift up your voice for understanding, if you seek her as silver and search for her as for hidden treasures; then you will understand the fear of the LORD, and find the knowledge of God' (Proverbs 2:3-5).

This wonderful Book is the subject about which I address my readers now. Surely it is no light matter what you are doing with the Bible. What would you think of the man who, when he had cholera, rejected a sure remedy for preserving the health of his body? What must we think of someone who rejects the only sure remedy for the everlasting health of their soul? I charge you, I entreat you, to give an honest answer to my question. What do you do with the Bible? Do you read it? *How do you read it?*

The only standard

In the sixth place, the Bible is the only standard by which all questions of doctrine or of duty can be tested.

The Lord God knows the weakness and infirmities of our poor fallen understandings. He knows that, even after conversion, our perceptions of right and wrong are extremely vague. He knows how artfully Satan can overlay error with an appearance of truth, and can dress up wrong with plausible arguments, till it looks like right. Knowing all this, he has mercifully provided us with an unerring standard of truth and error, right and wrong, and has taken care to make that standard a written book — the Scriptures.

No one can look around the world, and not see the wisdom of such a provision. No one can live long, and not find out that he is constantly in need of a counsellor and adviser — of a rule of faith and practice, on which he can depend. Unless he lives like a beast, without a soul and conscience, he will find himself constantly assailed by difficult and puzzling questions. He will often ask himself: 'What must I believe? And what must I do?'

Points of doctrine

The world is full of difficulties about points of doctrine. The house of error lies close alongside the house of truth. The door of one is so like the door of the other that there is continual risk of mistakes.

Does a man read or travel much? He will soon find exact opposite opinions prevailing among those who are called Christians. He will discover that different persons give completely different answers to the important question: 'What must I do to be saved?' The Roman Catholic, the Protestant and the Mormon each will assert that he alone has the truth. Each will tell him that safety is only to be found in his quarter. Each says, 'Come with us.' All this is puzzling. What will a man do?

Does he settle down quietly in some church here at home? He will soon find that even in our own land the most conflicting views are held. He will soon discover that there are serious differences among Christians as to the comparative importance of the various parts and articles of the faith. One man thinks of nothing but church government; another of nothing but sacraments, services and forms; a third of nothing but preaching the gospel. Does he ask ministers for a solution? He will perhaps find one minister teaching one doctrine, and another minister, another. All this is puzzling. What will a man do?

There is only one answer to this question. A man must make the Bible alone his rule. He must receive nothing and believe nothing that is not according to the Word. He must try all religious teaching by one simple test: Does it square with the Bible? What does the Scripture say?

I pray to God that the eyes of the Christians of this country were more open on this subject. I pray to God that they would learn to weigh sermons, books, opinions and ministers, in the scales of the Bible, and to value all according to their conformity to the Word. I pray to God that they would see that it matters little who says a thing. The question is: Is what is said scriptural? If it is, it ought to be received and believed. If it is not, it ought to be refused and cast aside. I fear the consequences of a submissive acceptance of everything that 'the preacher' says, which is so common among many Christians. I am afraid that they may be led where they do not know, like the blinded Syrians, and awake some day to find themselves in the power of Rome (2 Kings 6:20). Oh, if men would only remember for what purpose the Bible was given to them!

I tell Christians that it is nonsense to say, as some do, that it is arrogant to judge a minister's teaching by the Word. When one doctrine is proclaimed in one church, and another in another, people must read and judge for themselves. Both doctrines cannot be right, and both ought to be tried by the Word. I charge them, above all things, never to suppose that any true minister of the gospel will dislike his people measuring all he teaches by the Bible. On the contrary, the more they read the Bible, and prove all he says by the Bible, the better he will be pleased. A false minister may say, 'You have no right to use your private judgement: leave the Bible to we who are ordained.' A true minister will say, 'Search the Scriptures, and if I do not teach you what is scriptural, do not believe me.' A false minister may cry, 'Listen to the church,' and 'Listen to me.' A true minister will say, 'Listen to the Word of God.'

Points of practice

But the world is not only full of difficulties about points of doctrine, it is equally full of difficulties about points of practice.

Every professing Christian who wishes to act conscientiously must know that it is so. The most puzzling questions are continually arising. He is tested on every side by doubts as to the line of duty, and can often hardly see what is the right thing to do.

He is tested by questions connected with the management of his *worldly calling*, if he is in business or in trade. He sometimes sees things going on that are of a very doubtful character — things that can hardly be called fair, straightforward, truthful, and things that you would not want done to you. But then everybody in business does these things. They have always been done in the most respectable houses. There would be no carrying on of a profitable business if they were not done. They are not things distinctly named and prohibited by God. All this is very puzzling. What is a man to do?

He is tested by questions about *worldly amusements*. Horse races, and dances, and operas, and theatres, and gambling dens, are all very doubtful methods of spending time. But then he sees numbers of great people taking part in them. Are all these people wrong? Can there really be such mighty harm in these things? All this is very puzzling. What is a man to do?

He is tried by questions about the *education of his children*. He wishes to train them up morally and religiously, and to re-member their souls. But he is told by many sensible people that young people will be young — that it is not right to check and restrain them too much, and that he ought to attend shows, and children's parties, and hold children's dances himself. He is informed that this noble person, or that lady of rank, always does so, and yet they are considered religious people. Surely it cannot be wrong. All this is very puzzling. What is he to do?

There is only one answer to all these questions. A man must make the Bible his rule of conduct. He must make its leading principles the compass by which he steers his course through life. By the letter or spirit of the Bible he must test every difficult point and question. 'To the law and to the testimony! What does the Scripture say?' He ought to care nothing for what other people may think right. He ought not to set his watch by the clock of his neighbour, but by the watch of the Word.

I charge my readers solemnly to act on the maxim I have just laid down, and to adhere to it rigidly all the days of their lives. You will never repent of it. Make it a leading principle never to act contrary to the Word. Do not worry about the charge of being overly strict, and a person of needless preci-sion. Remember you serve a strict and holy God. Do not listen to the common objection that the rule you have laid down is impossible, and cannot be observed in such a world as this. Let those who make such an objection speak out plainly, and tell us for what purpose the Bible was given to man. Let them remember that by the Bible we will all be judged at the last day, and let them learn to judge themselves by it here, lest they be judged and condemned by it on Judgement Day.

This mighty rule of faith and practice is the book about which I am addressing my readers now. Surely it is no light matter 'what you are doing with the Bible'. Surely when danger is near on the right hand and on the left, you should consider what you are doing with the safeguard that God has provided. I charge you, I beg you, to give an honest answer to my question. What are you doing with the Bible? Do you read it? *How do you read it?*

The Book to live by

In the seventh place, the Bible is the book that all true servants of God have always lived by and loved.

Every living thing that God creates requires food. The life that God imparts needs sustaining and nourishing. It is true with animal and vegetable life — with birds, beasts, fishes, reptiles, insects and plants. It is equally true with spiritual life. When the Holy Spirit raises a man from the death of sin and makes him a new creature in Christ Jesus, the new principle in that man's heart requires food, and the only food that will sustain it is the Word of God.

There never was a man or woman truly converted, from one end of the world to the other, who did not love the revealed will of God. Just as a child born into the world naturally desires the milk provided for its nourishment, so a 'born again' soul desires the sincere milk of the Word. This is a common mark of all the children of God — they 'delight in the law of the LORD' (Psalm 1:2).

Show me a person who despises Bible-reading, or thinks little of Bible preaching, and I believe it is a certain fact that he is not yet 'born again'. He may be zealous about forms and ceremonies. He may be diligent in attending church and the taking of the Lord's Supper. But if these things are more precious to him than the Bible, I cannot believe that he is a converted man. Tell me what the Bible is to a man and I will generally tell you what he is. This is the pulse to try — this is the barometer to look at — if we would know the state of the heart. I have no notion of the Spirit dwelling in a man and not giving clear evidence of his presence. And I believe it to be clear evidence of the Spirit's presence when the Word is really precious to a man's soul.

Love of the Word is one of the characteristics we see in Job. Little as we know of this patriarch and his age this at least stands out clearly. He says, 'I have treasured the words of his mouth more than my necessary food' (Job 23:12).

Love of the Word is a shining feature in the character of David. Note how it appears all through that wonderful part of Scripture, Psalm 119. He said, 'Oh, how I love your law!' (Psalm 119:97).

Love of the Word is a striking point in the character of Paul. What were he and his companions but men mighty in the Scriptures? What were his sermons but expositions and applications of the Word?

Love of the Word appears pre-eminently in our Lord and Saviour Jesus Christ. He read it publicly. He quoted it continually. He expounded it frequently. He advised the Jews to 'search' it. He used it as his weapon to resist the devil. He said repeatedly, 'The Scripture must be fulfilled.' Almost the last thing he did was to '[open] their understanding, that they might comprehend the Scriptures' (Luke 24:45). I am afraid that a man who does not have something of his Master's mind and feeling towards the Bible cannot be a true servant of Christ.

Love of the Word has been a prominent feature in the history of all the saints, of whom we know anything, since the days of the Apostles. This is the lamp that Athanasius and Chrysostom and Augustine followed. This is the compass that kept the Vallenses and Albigenses from making shipwreck of the faith. This is the well that was reopened by Wycliffe and Luther, after it had been long stopped up. This is the sword with which Latimer, and Jewell, and Knox won their victories. This is the manna that fed Baxter and Owen, and the noble host of the Puritans, and made them strong in battle. This is the armoury from which Whitefield and Wesley drew their powerful weapons. This is the mine from which Bickersteth and M'Cheyne brought forth rich gold. Differing as these holy men did in some matters, on one point they were all agreed — they all delighted in the Word.

Love of the Word is one of the first things that appears in the converted heathen, at the various missionary stations throughout the world. In hot climates and in cold — among savage people and among civilized — in New Zealand, in the South Sea Islands, in Africa, in India — it is always the same. They enjoy hearing it read. They long to be able to read it themselves. They wonder why Christians did not send it to them before. How striking is the picture that Moffat draws of Africaner, the fierce South African chieftain, when first brought under the power of the gospel! 'Often have I seen him', he says, 'under the shadow of a great rock nearly the whole day, eagerly perusing the pages of the Bible.' How touching is the expression of a poor converted Black, speaking of the Bible! He said, 'It is never old and never cold.' How affecting was the language of another old Black man, when some would have discouraged him from learning to read, because of his old age. 'No!' he said, 'I will never give it up till I die. It is worth all the labour to be able to read that one verse, "God so loved the world that he gave his only begotten Son, that whoever believes in him should not perish but have everlasting life"' (John 3:16).

Love of the Bible is one of the grand points of agreement among all converted men and women in our own land. People from many Evangelical denominations all unite in honouring the Bible, as soon as they are real Christians. This is the manna that all the tribes of our new Israel feed upon, and find satisfying food. This is the fountain around which all the various portions of Christ's flock meet together, and from which no sheep goes away thirsty. Oh, if only believers in this country would learn to cleave more closely to the written Word! Oh, if only they would see that the more the Bible, and only the Bible, is the substance of men's religion, the more they agree! There was probably never an uninspired book more universally admired than Bunyan's *Pilgrim's Progress*. It is a book that all denominations of Christians delight to honour. It has won praise from all parties. Now what a striking fact it is that the author was pre-eminently a man of one book! He had read hardly anything but the Bible.

It is a blessed thought that there will be 'many people' in heaven in the end. Few as the Lord's people undoubtedly are at any one given time or place, yet all gathered together in the end, they will be 'a great multitude which no one could number' (Revelation 7:9; 19:1). They will be of one heart and mind. They will have passed through the same experience. They will all have repented, believed, lived holy, prayerful and humble lives. They will all have washed their robes and made them white in the blood of the Lamb. But one thing besides all this they will have in common: they will all love the texts and doctrines of the Bible. The Bible will have been their food and delight in the days of their pilgrimage on earth. And the Bible will be a common subject of joyful meditation and retrospect, when they are gathered together in heaven.

This Book, which all true Christians live upon and love, is the subject about which I am addressing my readers now. Surely it is no light matter what you are doing with the Bible. Surely it is matter for serious inquiry, whether you know anything of this love of the Word, and have this mark of following 'in the footsteps of the flock' (Song of Solomon 1:8). I charge you, I entreat you to give me an honest answer. What are you doing with the Bible? Do you read it? *How do you read it?*

The only comfort

In the last place, the Bible is the only book that can comfort a man in the last hours of his life.

Death is an event that in all probability is before us all. There is no avoiding it. It is the river that each of us must cross. I who write, and you who read, have to die one day. It is good to remember this. We are all sadly apt to keep away from the subject. 'Each man thinks each man mortal but himself.' I want everyone to do his duty in life, but I also want everyone to think of death. I want everyone to know how to live, but I also want everyone to know how to die.

Death is a solemn event to everyone. It is the winding up of all earthly plans and expectations. It is a separation from all we have loved and live with. It is often accompanied by much bodily pain and distress. It brings us to the grave, the maggot and corruption. It opens the door to judgement and eternity — to heaven or to hell. It is an event after which there is no change, or space for repentance. Other mistakes may be corrected or retrieved, but not a mistake on our deathbeds. As the tree falls, there it must lie. No conversion in the coffin! No new birth after we have ceased to breathe! And death is before us all. It may be close at hand. The time of our departure is quite uncertain. But sooner or later we must each lie down alone and die. All these are serious considerations.

Death is a solemn event even to the believer in Christ. For him no doubt the 'sting of death' is taken away (1 Corinthians 15:56). Death has become one of his privileges, for he is Christ's. Living or dying, he is the Lord's. If he lives, Christ lives in him; and if he dies, he goes to live with Christ. To him, 'to live is

Christ and to die is gain' (Philippians 1:21). Death frees him from many trials — from a weak body, a corrupt heart, a tempting devil, and an ensnaring or persecuting world. Death admits him to the enjoyment of many blessings. He rests from his labours — the hope of a joyful resurrection is changed into a certainty; he has the company of holy redeemed spirits — he is 'with Christ'. All this is true, and yet, even to a believer, death is a solemn thing. Flesh and blood naturally shrink from it. To part from all we love is a strain and trial to the feelings. The world we go to is a world unknown, even though it is our home. Friendly and harmless as death is to a believer, it is not an event to be treated lightly. It must always be a very solemn thing.

It is good for every thoughtful and sensible man to consider calmly how he is going to meet death. Be strong, like a man, and look the subject in the face. Listen to me while I tell you a few things about the end to which we are coming.

The good things of the world cannot comfort a man when he draws near death. All the gold of California and Australia will not provide light for the dark valley of death. Money can buy the best medical advice and attendance for a man's body; but money cannot buy peace for his conscience, heart and soul.

Relatives, lovers, friends and co-workers cannot comfort a man when he draws near death. They may minister affectionately to his bodily wants. They may watch by his bedside tenderly, and anticipate his every wish. They may smooth down his dying pillow, and support his sinking frame in their arms. But they cannot 'minister to a mind diseased'. They cannot stop the aching of a troubled heart. They cannot screen an uneasy conscience from the eye of God.

The pleasures of the world cannot comfort a man when he draws near death. The brilliant ballroom, the merry dance, the midnight frolic, the party at the races, the card table, the box at the opera, the voices of singing men and singing women — all these are, in the end, distasteful things. To hear of hunting and shooting engagements gives him no pleasure. To be invited to feasts, and regattas, and fancy-fairs, gives him no relief. He cannot hide from himself that these are hollow, empty, power- less things. They are noise to the ear of his conscience. They are out of harmony with his condition. They cannot stop one gap in his heart, when the last enemy is coming in like a flood. They cannot make him calm in the prospect of meeting a holy God.

Books and newspapers cannot comfort a man when he draws near death. The most brilliant writings of Dickens will be gloom to his ear. The most able article in *The Times* will fail to interest him. The *Edinburgh* and *Quarterly Reviews* will give him no pleasure. The *Illustrated News*, and the latest new novel, will lie unopened and unheeded. Their time will be past. Their calling will be gone. Whatever they may be in health, they are useless in the hour of death.

There is but one fountain of comfort for a man drawing near to his end, and that is the Bible. Chapters from the Bible, texts from the Bible, statements of truth taken from the Bible, books containing matter drawn from the Bible — these are a man's only chance of comfort when he comes to die. I am not saying that, as a matter of course, the Bible will do good to a dying man if he has not valued it before. Unhappily, I have attended too many deathbeds to say that. I do not say whether it is prob- able that he who has not believed and neglected the Bible in life will at once believe and derive comfort from it in death. But I do say positively, that no dying man will ever get real comfort, except from the contents of the Word of God. All comfort from any other source is a house built upon sand.

I lay this down as a rule of universal application. I make no exception in favour of any class on earth. Kings and poor men, learned and unlearned — all are equal in this matter. There is not a bit of real consolation for any dying man, unless he gets it

from the Bible. Chapters, passages, texts, promises and doctrines of Scripture heard, received, believed and rested on —
these are the only comforters I dare promise to anyone when
he leaves the world. Taking communion will do a man no more
good than the Roman Catholic sacrament of 'extreme unction',
as long as the Word is not received and believed. The Roman
Catholic priest's absolution will no more ease the conscience
than the incantations of a heathen magician, if the poor dying
sinner does not receive and believe Bible truth. I tell everyone
reading this that although men may seem to get on comfortably without the Bible while they live, they may be sure that
without the Bible they cannot comfortably die. It was a true
confession of the learned Selden, 'There is no book upon which
we can rest in a dying moment but the Bible.'

I could easily confirm all I have just said by examples and
illustrations. I could describe for you the deathbeds of men who
have despised the Bible. I could tell you how Voltaire and Paine,
the famous atheists, died in misery, bitterness, rage, fear and
despair. I could show you the happy deathbeds of those who
have loved the Bible and believed it, and the blessed effect the
sight of their deathbeds had on others. Cecil, a minister whose
name should be honoured in all churches, says, 'I will never
forget standing by the bedside of my dying mother. "Are you
afraid to die?" I asked. "No!" she replied. "But why does the
uncertainty of another state give you no concern?" "Because
God has said, 'When you pass through the waters, I will be
with you; and through the rivers, they shall not overflow you'"'
(Isaiah 43:2). I could easily multiply illustrations of this kind.
But I think it better to conclude this part of my subject by giving
the result of my own observations as a minister.

I have seen many dying persons in my time. I have seen
great varieties of character and behaviour among them. I have
seen some die bad-tempered, silent and comfortless. I have
seen others die ignorant, unconcerned and apparently without

much fear. I have seen some die so worn out with a long illness that they were quite willing to depart, and yet they did not seem to me at all in a fit state to go before God. I have seen others die with professions of hope and trust in God, without leaving satisfactory evidences that they were on the rock. I have seen others die who, I believe, were 'in Christ', and safe, and yet they never seemed to enjoy much tangible comfort. I have seen a few dying in the full assurance of hope and, like Bunyan's 'Standfast', giving glorious testimony to Christ's faithfulness, even in the river. But one thing I have never seen. I have never seen anyone enjoy what I would call real, solid, calm, reasonable peace on his deathbed, who did not draw his peace from the Bible. And this I say boldly, that the man who thinks he can go to his deathbed without having the Bible for his comforter, his companion and his friend is one of the greatest madmen in the world. There are no comforts for the soul but Bible comforts, and he who does not have a hold of these, does not have a hold of anything at all, unless it is a broken reed.

The only comforter for a deathbed is the book about which I address my readers now. Surely it is no light matter whether you read that book or not. Surely a dying man, in a dying world, should seriously consider whether he has got anything to comfort him when his turn comes to die. I charge you, I entreat you, for the last time, to give an honest answer to my question. What are you doing with the Bible? Do you read it? *How do you read it?*

I have now given the reasons why I press on every reader the duty and importance of reading the Bible. I have shown that no book is written in such a manner as the Bible,

  that knowledge of the Bible is absolutely necessary to
     salvation
  that no book contains such matter
  that no book has done so much for the world generally

    that no book can do so much for everyone who reads it

    that this Book is the only rule of faith and practice

    that it is, and always has been, the food of all true servants
        of God

    and that it is the only Book which can comfort men when
        they die.

All these are ancient things. I do not pretend to say anything new. I have only gathered together old truths, and tried to mould them into a new shape. Let me finish everything by addressing a few plain words to the conscience of every group of readers.

Some words of application

This publication may fall into the hands of some who *can read, but never do read the Bible at all*.

Are you one of them? If you are, I have something to say to you. I cannot comfort you in your present state of mind. It would be mockery and deceit to do so. I cannot speak to you of peace and heaven, while you treat the Bible as you do. You are in danger of losing your soul.

You are in danger, because *your neglected Bible is plain evidence that you do not love God*. The health of a man's body may generally be known by his appetite. The health of a man's soul may be known by his treatment of the Bible. Now you are manifestly living with a serious disease. Will you not repent?

I know I cannot reach your heart. I cannot make you see and feel these things. I can only enter my solemn protest against your present treatment of the Bible, and lay that protest before your conscience. I do so with all my soul. Oh, beware lest you repent too late! Beware lest you put off reading the Bible till you send for the doctor in your last illness, and then find the Bible a sealed book, and dark, as the cloud between the hosts of Israel and Egypt, to your anxious soul! Beware lest you go on saying all your life, 'Men get along very well without all this Bible-reading' and find in time, to your cost, that men without the Bible do very poorly, and end up in hell! Beware lest the day come when you will feel, 'Had I but honoured the Bible as much as I have honoured the newspaper, I would not have been left without comfort in my last hours!' Bible-neglecting reader, I give you a plain warning. Judgement is outside your door, ready to come in and destroy you. May the Lord have mercy upon your soul!

This publication may fall into the hands of someone who is *willing to begin reading the Bible, but wants advice on how to begin*. Are you that man? Listen to me, and I will give a few short hints.

1. *Begin reading your Bible this very day*

The way to do a thing is to do it, and the way to read the Bible is actually to read it. It is not meaning, or wishing, or resolving, or intending, or thinking about it, which will not advance you one step. You must positively read. There is no royal road in this matter, any more than in the matter of prayer. If you cannot read yourself, you must persuade somebody else to read to you. But one way or another, through eyes or ears, the words of Scripture must actually pass before your mind.

2. *Read the Bible with an earnest desire to understand it*

Do not think for a moment that the great object is to turn over a certain quantity of printed paper, and that it does not matter at all whether you understand it or not. Some ignorant people seem to believe that all is done if they read so many chapters every day, though they may have no idea what they are all about, and only know that they have pushed on their bookmark

so many pages. This is turning Bible-reading into a mere form.
It is almost as bad as the Roman Catholic habit of buying indulgences, by saying an almost incredible number of 'Hail Marys'
and 'Our Fathers'. Settle it in your mind as a general principle
that a Bible that is not understood is a Bible that does no good.
Say to yourself often as you read, 'What is all this about?' Dig
for the meaning like a man digging for gold. Work hard, and do
not give up the work in a hurry.

3. Read the Bible with childlike faith and humility

Open your heart as you open your book, and say, 'Speak,
Lord, for your servant is listening.' Resolve to believe implicitly
whatever you find there, however much it may run counter to
your own prejudices. Resolve to receive heartily every statement of truth, whether you like it or not. Beware of that miserable habit of mind into which some readers of the Bible fall.
They receive some doctrines because they like them; they reject others because they condemn themselves, or some lover,
or relation, or friend. With this attitude the Bible is useless. Are
we to be judges of what ought to be in the Word? Do we know
better than God? Be convinced in your own mind that you will
receive everything and believe everything, and that what you
cannot understand you will take on trust. Remember, when
you pray, you are speaking to God and God hears you. But,
remember, when you read, God is speaking to you, and you
are not to 'talk back' but to listen.

4. Read the Bible in a spirit of obedience and self-application

Sit down to study it with a daily determination that *you* will live
by its rules, rest on its statements, and act on its commands.
Consider, as you travel through every chapter: 'How does this
affect *my* view and course of conduct? What does this teach

me?' It is improper to read the Bible out of mere curiosity, and for speculative purposes, in order to fill your head and your mind with opinions, while you do not allow the book to influence your heart and life. The Bible that is read best is put into practice in our daily lives.

5. *Read the Bible every day*

Make it a part of every day's business to read and meditate on some portion of God's Word. Private means of grace are just as needful every day for our souls as food and clothing are for our bodies. Yesterday's meal will not feed the worker today, and today's meal will not feed the worker tomorrow. Do as the Israelites did in the wilderness. Gather your manna fresh every morning. Choose your own periods and hours. Do not hurry your reading. Give your Bible the best and not the worst part of your time. But whatever plan you pursue, let it be a rule of your life to visit the throne of grace and the Bible every day.

6. *Read all the Bible, and read it in an orderly way*

I fear there are many parts of the Word that some people never read at all. This is a very arrogant habit. 'All Scripture is given by inspiration of God, and is profitable for doctrine' (2 Timothy 3:16). This habit produces that lack of a broad, well-proportioned view of truth, which is so common in this day. Some people's Bible-reading is a system of perpetual dipping and picking. They do not seem to have any idea of regularly going through the whole book. This is also a great mistake. No doubt in times of sickness and affliction it is acceptable to search out seasonable portions. But with this exception, I believe it is by far the best plan to begin the Old and New Testaments at the same time, to read each straight through to the end, and then begin again. This is a matter in which everyone must be persuaded in his own mind. I can only say it has been my own plan for nearly forty years, and I have never seen cause to alter it.

7. *Read the Bible fairly and honestly*

Determine to take everything in its plain, obvious meaning, and regard all forced interpretations with great suspicion. As a general rule, whatever a verse of the Bible seems to mean, it does mean. Cecil's rule is a very valuable one: 'The right way of interpreting Scripture is to take it as we find it, without any attempt to force it into any particular system.' Hooker well said, 'I hold it for a most infallible rule in the exposition of Scripture, that when the literal construction will stand, the furthest from the literal is commonly the worst.'

8. *Read the Bible with Christ continually in view*

The primary object of all Scripture is to testify about Jesus:

Old Testament ceremonies are shadows of Christ
Old Testament judges and deliverers are types of Christ
Old Testament history shows the world's need of Christ
Old Testament prophecies are full of Christ's sufferings
Old Testament prophecies are full of Christ's glory yet to
    come

The first and second coming, the Lord's humiliation, the Lord's kingdom, the Lord's cross and crown — all these shine forth everywhere in the Bible. Remember this clue, if you would read the Bible right.

I might easily add to these hints, if space permitted. Few and short as they are, you will find them worth your attention. Act upon them, and I firmly believe you will never be allowed to miss the way to heaven. Act upon them, and you will find light continually increasing in your mind. No book of evidence can be compared with that internal evidence obtained by the one who daily uses the Word in the right way. Such a man does not need the books of learned men — he has the witness in himself. The book satisfies and feeds his soul. A poor Christian woman once said to an unbeliever, 'I am no scholar. I cannot argue like you. But I know that honey is honey, because it leaves a sweet taste in my mouth. And I know the Bible to be God's book, because of the taste it leaves in my heart.'

This publication may fall into the hands of someone who *loves and believes the Bible, and yet reads it only a little*. I fear there are many such people in this day. It is a day of hustle and hurry. It is a day of talking, and committee meetings, and public work. These things are all very well in their way, but I fear that they sometimes clip and cut short the private reading of the Bible. Does your conscience tell you that you are one of the persons I am speaking of? Listen to me, and I will say a few things that deserve your serious attention.

You are the man who is likely to *get little comfort from the Bible in time of need*. Trials come at various times. Affliction is a searching wind, which strips the leaves off the trees, and exposes the birds' nests. Now I fear that your stores of Bible consolations may one day run very low. I am afraid that you may find yourself on very short allowance in the end, and come into the harbour weak, worn and thin.

You are the man who is likely *never to be established in the truth*. I will not be surprised to hear that you are troubled with doubts and questions about assurance, grace, faith, perseverance and the like. The devil is an old and cunning enemy. Like the Benjamites, he can 'sling a stone at a hair's breadth and not miss' (Judges 20:16). He can quote Scripture easily enough when he pleases. Now you are not sufficiently ready with your weapons to be able to fight a good fight with him. Your armour does not fit well. Your sword sits loosely in your hand.

You are the man who is likely to *make mistakes in life*. I will not wonder if I am told that you have erred about your own marriage, erred about your children's education of spiritual things, erred about the conduct of your household, erred about the company you keep. The world you steer through is full of rocks, and reefs, and sandbars. You are not sufficiently familiar either with the searchlights or your charts.

You are the man who is likely to *be carried away by some deceptive false teacher for a time*. It will not surprise me if those clever, eloquent men, who can 'make the lie appear to be the truth', is leading you into many foolish notions. You are out of balance. No wonder if you are tossed to and fro, like a cork on the waves.

All these are uncomfortable things. I want every one of my readers to escape them all. Take the advice I offer you this day. Do not merely read your Bible 'a little', but read it a great deal. 'Let the word of Christ dwell in you richly' (Colossians 3:16). Do not be a mere babe in spiritual knowledge. Seek to become 'well instructed in the kingdom of heaven', and to be continually adding new things to old. A religion of feeling is an uncertain thing. It is like the tide, sometimes high, and sometimes low. It is like the moon, sometimes bright, and sometimes dim. A religion of deep Bible knowledge is a firm and lasting possession. It enables a man not merely to say, 'I feel hope in Christ,' but 'I know whom I have believed' (2 Timothy 1:12).

This volume may fall into the hands of someone who *reads the Bible a lot, and yet believes he is no better because of his reading*. This is a crafty temptation of the devil. At one stage he says, 'Do not read the Bible at all.' At another he says, 'Your reading does you no good: give it up.' Are you that man? I feel for you from the bottom of my soul. Let me try to do you good.

Do not think you are getting no good from the Bible, merely because you do not see that good day by day. The greatest effects are often silent, quiet and hard to detect at the time they are being produced. Think of the influence of the moon upon the earth, and of the air upon the human lungs. Remember how silently the dew falls, and how unperceptively the grass grows. There may be far more going on in your soul from your Bible-reading than you think .

The Word may be gradually producing deep 'impressions' on your heart, of which you are not presently aware. Often when the memory is retaining no facts, the character of a man is receiving some everlasting impression. Is sin becoming more hateful to you every year? Is Christ becoming more precious every year? Is holiness becoming more lovely and desirable in your eyes every year? If these things are so, take courage. The Bible is doing you good, though you may not be able to trace it out day by day.

The Bible may be restraining you from some sin or delusion into which you would otherwise run. It may be daily keeping you back, and hedging you up, and preventing many a false step. Yes, you might soon find this out to your cost, if you were to cease reading the Word! The very familiarity of blessings sometimes makes us insensible to their value. Resist the devil. Settle it in your mind as an established rule, that, whether you feel it at the moment or not, you are inhaling spiritual health by reading the Bible, and unknowingly becoming more strong.

This volume may fall into the hands of some who *really love the Bible, live upon the Bible, and read it regularly.* Are you one of these? Give me your attention, and I will mention a few things, which we will do well to lay to heart for time to come.

Let us resolve to *read the Bible more and more* every year we live. Let us try to get it rooted in our memories, and engraved into our hearts. Let us be thoroughly well provisioned with it against the voyage of death. Who knows but we may have a very stormy passage? Sight and hearing may fail us, and we may be in deep waters. Oh, to have the Word 'hidden in our hearts' in such an hour as that! (Psalm 119:11).

Let us resolve to *be more watchful over our Bible reading* every year that we live. Let us be jealously careful about the time we give to it, and the manner that time is spent. Let us beware of omitting our daily reading without sufficient cause. Let us not be gaping, and yawning, and dozing over our book, while we read. Let us read like a London merchant studying the city article in *The Times* — or like a wife reading a husband's letter from a distant land. Let us be very careful that we never exalt any minister, or sermon, or book, or tract, or friend above the Word. Cursed be that book, or tract, or human counsel, which creeps in between us and the Bible, and hides the Bible from our eyes! Once more I say, let us be very watchful. The moment we open the Bible the devil sits down by our side. Oh, to read with a hungry spirit, and a simple desire for edification!

Let us resolve to *honour the Bible more in our families.* Let us read it morning and evening to our children and spouses, and not be ashamed to let men see that we do so. Let us not be discouraged by seeing no good arise from it. The Bible-reading in a family has kept many a one from jail and prison, and from the eternal fires of hell.

Let us resolve to *meditate more on the Bible.* It is good to take two or three texts with us when we go out into the world, and to turn them over and over in our minds whenever we have a little leisure. It keeps out many vain thoughts. It tightens the nail of daily reading. It preserves our souls from stagnating and breeding corrupt things. It sanctifies and quickens our memories, and prevents them becoming like those ponds where the frogs live but the fish die.

Let us resolve to *talk more to believers about the Bible* when we meet them. Unfortunately, the conversation of Christians, when they do meet, is often sadly unprofitable! How many frivolous, and trifling, and uncharitable things are said! Let us bring out the Bible more, and it will help to drive the devil away, and keep our hearts in tune. Oh, that we may all strive so to walk together in this evil world, that Jesus may often draw near, and go with us, as he went with the two disciples journeying to Emmaus!

Last of all, let us resolve *to live by the Bible more and more* every year we live. Let us frequently take account of all our opinions and practices, of our habits and tempers, of our behaviour in public and in private, in the world and in our own homes. Let us measure everything by the Bible, and resolve, by God's help, to conform to it. Oh, that we may learn increasingly to 'cleanse [our] way, by taking heed according to your word' (Psalm 119:9).

I commend all these things to the serious and prayerful attention of every one into whose hands this book may fall. I want the ministers of my beloved country to be Bible-reading ministers; the congregations, Bible-reading congregations; and the nation, a Bible-reading nation. To bring about this desirable end I cast in my resources into God's treasury. May the Lord grant that it may prove not to have been in vain!

6.
The Lord's Supper

*'But let a man examine himself, and so let him eat of the
bread and drink of the cup'* (1 Corinthians 11:28).

The words that form the title of this chapter refer to a subject of
vast importance. That subject is the Lord's Supper.

Perhaps no part of the Christian religion is so thoroughly
misunderstood as the Lord's Supper. On no point have there
been so many disputes, strife and controversies for over 2000
years. On no point have mistakes done so much harm. The
very ordinance that was meant for our peace and profit has
become the cause of discord and the occasion of sin. These
things ought not to be!

I make no excuse for including the Lord's Supper among
the leading points of 'practical' Christianity. I firmly believe that
ignorant views or false doctrine about this ordinance lie at the
root of some of the present divisions of professing Christians.
Some neglect it altogether; some completely misunderstand it;
some exalt it to a position it was never meant to occupy, and
turn it into an idol. If I can throw a little light on it, and clear up
the doubts in some minds, I will feel very thankful. It is hopeless, I fear, to expect that the controversy about the Lord's
Supper will ever be finally closed until the Lord comes. But it is
not too much to hope that the fog and mystery and obscurity
with which it is surrounded in some minds may be cleared away
by plain Bible truth.

In examining the Lord's Supper I will be content with asking four practical questions, and offering answers to them.

1. Why was the Lord's Supper ordained?
2. Who ought to go to the Table and be communicants?
3. What may communicants expect from the Lord's Supper?
4. Why do many so-called Christians never go to the Lord's Table?

I think it will be impossible to handle these four questions fairly, honestly and impartially, without seeing the subject more clearly, and getting some distinct and practical ideas about some leading errors of our day. I emphasize the word 'practical'. My chief aim in this volume is to promote practical Christianity.

Why was the Lord's Supper ordained?

In the first place, why was the Lord's Supper ordained? It was ordained for the continual remembrance of the sacrifice of the death of Christ, and of the benefits that we receive from it. The bread that in the Lord's Supper is broken, given and eaten is meant to remind us of Christ's body given on the cross for our sins. The wine that is poured out and received is meant to remind us of Christ's blood shed on the cross for our sins. He who eats that bread and drinks that wine is reminded, in the most striking and forcible manner, of the benefits Christ has obtained for his soul, and of the death of Christ as the hinge and turning point on which all those benefits depend.

Now, is the view stated here the doctrine of the New Testament? If it is not, let it be rejected, cast aside, and refused by men for ever. If it is, let us never be ashamed to hold it close, profess our belief in it, pin our faith on it, and steadfastly refuse to hold any other view, no matter who teaches it. In subjects like this we must call no man master. It matters little what great theologians and learned preachers have thought fit to put forth about the Lord's Supper. If they teach more than the Word of God contains they are not to be believed.

I take down my Bible and turn to the New Testament. There I find no less than four separate accounts of the first appointment of the Lord's Supper. Matthew, Mark, Luke and Paul all describe it: all four agree in telling us what our Lord did on this memorable occasion. Only two tell us the reason why our Lord commanded his disciples to eat the bread and drink the cup. Paul and Luke both record the remarkable words, 'Do this in remembrance of me.' Paul adds his own inspired comment: 'For as often as you eat this bread and drink this cup, you proclaim the Lord's death till he comes' (Luke 22:19; 1 Corinthians 11:25-26). When Scripture speaks so clearly, why can't men be content with it? Why should we mystify and confuse a subject that in the New Testament is so simple? The 'continual remembrance of Christ's death' was the one grand object for which the Lord's Supper was ordained. Whoever goes further than this is adding to God's Word, and does so to the great peril of his soul.

Now, is it reasonable to suppose that our Lord would appoint an ordinance for so simple a purpose as 'remembering his death'? It most certainly is. Of all the facts in his earthly ministry none are equal in importance to that of his death. It was the great settlement for man's sin, which had been appointed in God's promise from the foundation of the world. It was the great redemption of almighty power, to which every sacrifice of animals, from the fall of man, continually pointed. It was the grand end and purpose for which the Messiah came into the world. It was the cornerstone and foundation of all man's hopes of pardon and peace with God. In short, Christ would have lived, and taught, and preached, and prophesied, and performed miracles in vain, if he had not 'crowned it all by dying for our sins as our Substitute on the cross'! His death was our life. His death was the payment of our debt to God. Without his death we would have been the most miserable of all creatures. No wonder an ordinance was specially appointed to remind us of our Saviour's death! It is the one thing of which poor, weak, sinful man needs to be continually reminded.

Does the New Testament authorize men to say that the Lord's Supper was ordained to be a sacrifice, and that in it Christ's literal body and blood are present under the forms of bread and wine? Most certainly not! When the Lord Jesus said to the disciples, 'This is my body,' and 'This is my blood,' he clearly meant, 'This bread in my hand is a symbol of my body, and this cup of wine in my hand contains a symbol of my blood.' The disciples were accustomed to hearing him use such language. They remembered him saying, 'The field is the world, the good seeds are the sons of the kingdom, but the tares are the sons of the wicked one' (Matthew 13:38). It never entered their minds that he meant to say he was holding his own body and his own blood in his hands, and literally giving them his literal body and blood to eat and drink. Not one of the writers of the New Testament ever speaks of the Lord's Supper as a sacrifice, or calls the Lord's Table an altar, or even hints that a Christian minister is a sacrificing priest. The universal doctrine of the New Testament is that after the one offering of Christ there remains no further need of sacrifice.

If anyone believes that Paul's words to the Hebrews, 'We have an altar' (Hebrews 13:10), are a proof that the Lord's Table is an altar, I remind him 'Christians have an altar where they partake. That altar is Christ our Lord, who is Altar, Priest, and Sacrifice, all in One.'[1]

Throughout the Communion Service the one idea of the ordinance continually pressed on our attention is that of a 're-membrance' of Christ's death. As to any presence of Christ's natural body and blood under the forms of bread and wine, the clear answer is that 'The natural body and blood of Christ are in heaven, and not here.' Those Roman Catholics who delight in talking of the 'altar', the 'sacrifice', the 'priest', and the 'real presence' in the Lord's Supper, would do well to remember that they are using language which is entirely nonbiblical.

The point before us is one of vast importance. Let us lay hold upon it firmly, and never let it go. It is the very point on which our Reformers had their sharpest controversy with the Roman Catholics, and went to the stake, rather than give way. Sooner than admit that the Lord's Supper was a sacrifice, they cheerfully laid down their lives. To bring back the doctrine of the 'real presence', and to turn the communion into the Roman Catholic 'mass', is to pour contempt on our martyrs, and to upset the first principles of the Protestant Reformation. No, rather, it is to ignore the plain teaching of God's Word, and to dishonour the priestly office of our Lord Jesus Christ. The Bible teaches expressly that the Lord's Supper was ordained to be 'a remembrance of Christ's body and blood', and not an offering. The Bible teaches that Christ's substituted death on the cross was the perfect sacrifice for sin, which never needs to be repeated. Let us stand firm in these two great principles of the Christian faith. A clear understanding of the intention of the Lord's Supper is one of the soul's best safeguards against the delusions of false doctrine.

Who ought to receive the Lord's Supper?

In the second place, let me try to show who ought to be communicants. What kind of people were meant to go to the Table and receive the Lord's Supper?

I will first show who ought not to be partakers of this ordinance. The ignorance that prevails on this, as on every part of the subject, is vast, lamentable and appalling. If I can contribute anything that may throw light upon it, I will feel very thankful.

The principal giants whom John Bunyan describes in *Pilgrim's Progress* as dangerous to Christian pilgrims were Pope and Pagan. If the good old Puritan had foreseen the times we live in, he would have said something about the giant Ignorance.

Not all professing believers should come to the Table

Firstly, it is not right to urge all professing Christians to go to the Lord's Table. There is such a thing as fitness and preparedness for the ordinance. It does not work like a medicine, independently of the state of mind of those who receive it. The teaching of those who urge the whole congregation to come to the Lord's Table, as if it must necessarily do everyone good, is entirely without warrant in Scripture. No, rather, it is a teaching that is calculated to do immense harm to men's souls, and to turn the reception of the Lord's Supper into a mere form. Ignorance can never be the mother of acceptable worship, and an ignorant communicant who comes to the Lord's Table without knowing why he comes is in the wrong place altogether: 'But let a man examine himself, and so let him eat of the bread and drink of the cup'. 'Discerning the Lord's body', that is, understanding what the elements of bread and wine represent, and why they are appointed, and what is the particular use of remembering Christ's death, is an essential qualification of a true communicant. God commands all people everywhere to repent and believe the gospel (Acts 17:30), but he does not in the same way, or in the same manner, command everyone to come to the Lord's Table. No; this is not to be taken lightly, or carelessly! It is a solemn ordinance, and ought to be used solemnly.

Unrepentant sinners should not come

Secondly, sinners living in open sin, and determined not to give it up, ought never to come to the Lord's Table. To do so is a positive insult to Christ, and to pour contempt on his gospel. It is nonsense to profess we desire to remember Christ's death, while we cling to the accursed thing that made it necessary for Christ to die. The mere fact that a man is continuing in sin is clear evidence that he does not care for Christ, and feels no gratitude for the offer of redemption.

The ignorant Roman Catholic who goes to the priest's confessional and receives absolution may think he is fit to go to the Roman Catholic mass, and after mass may return to his sins. He never reads the Bible, and knows no better! But the professing Christian who habitually breaks any of God's commandments, and yet goes to the Lord's Table, as if it would do him good and wipe away his sins, is very guilty indeed. So long as he chooses to continue his wicked habits he cannot receive the slightest benefit from the Lord's Table, and is only adding sin to sin. To carry unrepented sin to the Lord's Table, and there receive the bread and wine, knowing in our own hearts that we and wickedness are still friends, is one of the worst things man can do, and one of the most hardening to the conscience. If a man must have his sins, and can't give them up, let him by all means stay away from the Lord's Supper. There is such a thing as 'eating and drinking in an unworthy manner' and to our own 'judgement'. To no one do these words apply so thoroughly as to an unrepentant sinner.

The self-righteous should not come

Thirdly, self-righteous people who think that they will be saved by their own works have no business to come to the Lord's Table. Strange as it may sound at first, these persons are the least qualified of all to receive the ordinance. They may be outwardly correct, moral and respectable in their lives, but so long as they trust in their own goodness for salvation they are entirely in the wrong place at the Lord's Supper. For what do we declare at the Lord's Supper? We publicly profess that we have no goodness, righteousness, or worthiness of our own, and that all our hope is in Christ.

We publicly profess that we are guilty, sinful, corrupt, and naturally deserve God's wrath and condemnation. We publicly profess that Christ's merit and not ours, Christ's righteousness and not ours, is the only cause why we look for acceptance with God. Now what has a self-righteous man to do with an ordinance like this? Clearly nothing at all.

One thing, at any rate, is very clear: a self-righteous man has no business to receive the Lord's Supper. The Communion Service of the church bids all communicants declare that 'They do not presume to come to the Table trusting in their own righteousness, but in God's numerous and great mercies.' It tells them to say, 'We are not worthy so much as to gather up the crumbs under Your table'; 'The memory of our sins is grievous to us; the burden of them is intolerable.' How many self-righteous professing Christians can ever go to the Lord's Table and take these words into his mouth is beyond my understanding! It only shows that many professing Christians use the 'forms' of worship without taking the trouble to consider what they mean.

The plain truth is that the Lord's Supper was not meant for dead souls, but for living ones. The careless, the ignorant, the wilfully wicked, the self-righteous, are no more fit to come to the Lord's Table than a dead corpse is fit to sit down at a king's feast. To enjoy a spiritual feast we must have a spiritual heart, and taste, and appetite. To suppose that the Lord's Table can do any good to an unspiritual man is as foolish as to put bread and wine into the mouth of a dead person. So long as the careless, the ignorant and the wilfully wicked continue in that state, they are utterly unfit to come to the Lord's Supper. To urge them to partake is not to do them good but harm. The Lord's Supper is not a converting or justifying ordinance. If a man goes to the Table unconverted or unforgiven, he will be no better when he comes away (actually worse due to the associated judgements for coming unworthily).

But, in the end, having cleared the ground of error, the question still remains to be answered: What sort of people ought to receive the Lord's Supper? My reply would be, people who have 'examined themselves to see whether they have truly repented of their former sins, steadfastly purposing to lead a new life; who have a true faith in God's mercy through Christ, with a thankful remembrance of his death; and who have a love for all men'. In a word, I find that a worthy communicant is one who possesses three simple marks and qualifications — repentance, faith and love. Does a man truly repent of sin and hate it? Does a man put his trust in Jesus Christ as his only hope of salvation? Does a man live in love towards others? The one who can truly answer each of these questions, 'I do,' is scripturally qualified for the Lord's Supper. Let him come boldly. Let no barrier be put in his way. He comes up to the Bible standard of communicants. He may draw near with confidence, and feel assured that the great Master of the banquet is not displeased.

Such a man's repentance may be very imperfect. Never mind! Is it real? Is he truly repentant? His faith in Christ may be very weak. Never mind! Is it real? A penny is as much true currency as a one hundred pound note. His love may be very defective in quantity and degree. Never mind! Is it genuine? The grand test of a man's Christianity is not the quantity of holiness he has, but whether he has any at all.

The first twelve communicants, when Christ himself gave the bread and wine, were weak indeed — weak in knowledge, weak in faith, weak in courage, weak in patience, weak in love! But eleven of them had something about them that outweighed all defects: they were real, genuine, sincere and true.

Let this great principle be for ever rooted in our minds —
the only worthy communicant is the man who has demonstrated
repentance towards God, faith towards our Lord Jesus Christ,
and practical love towards others. Are you that man? Then you
may draw near to the Table, and take the ordinance for your
comfort. Anything less than this I dare not change in my standard of a communicant. I will never encourage someone to receive
the Lord's Supper who is careless, ignorant and self-righteous.
I will never tell anyone to keep away till he is perfect, and to
wait till his heart is as unruffled as an angel's. I will not do so,
because I believe that neither my Master nor his Apostles would
have done so. Show me a man who really feels his sins, really
leans on Christ, really struggles to be holy, and I will welcome
him in my Master's name. He may feel weak, erring, empty,
feeble, doubting, wretched and poor. But what does that matter?
Paul, I believe, would have received him as a right communicant, and I will do likewise.

What benefit may communicants expect?

In the third place, let us consider what benefit communicants
may expect to get by receiving the Lord's Supper. This is a
point of grave importance, and one on which many mistakes
abound. On no point, perhaps, connected with this ordinance
are the views of Christians so vague and indistinct and
undefined.

One common idea among men is that 'receiving the Lord's
Supper must do them some good'. Why, they can't explain.
What good, they can't exactly say. But they have a loose general
notion that it is the right thing to be a communicant, and that
somehow or other it is of value to their souls! This is of course
nothing better than ignorance. It is unreasonable to suppose
that such communicants can please Christ, or receive any real

benefit from what they do. If there is any principle clearly laid down in the Bible about any act of religious worship, it is that it must be with understanding. The worshipper must at least understand something about what he is doing. Mere bodily worship, unaccompanied by mind or heart, is utterly worthless. The man who eats the bread and drinks the wine, as a mere matter of form, because it is the 'right' thing to do, without any clear idea of what it all means, derives no benefit. He might just as well stay at home!

Another common idea among men is that 'taking the Lord's Supper will help them get to heaven, and take away their sins'. To this false idea you may trace the habit in some churches of going to the Lord's Table once a year, in order, as an old farmer once said, 'to wipe off the year's sins'. To this idea again, you may trace the too common practice of sending for a minister in time of sickness, in order to receive the ordinance before death. Yes, how many take comfort over their relatives, after they have lived a most ungodly life, for no better reason than that they took the Lord's Supper when they were dying! Whether they repented and believed and had new hearts, they neither seem to know nor care. All they know is that 'They took the Lord's Supper before they died.' My heart sinks within me when I hear people resting on such evidence as this.

Ideas like these are sad proofs of the ignorance that fills the minds of men about the Lord's Supper. They are ideas for which there is not the slightest warrant in Scripture. The sooner they are cast aside and given up, the better for the church and the world.

Let us be firmly convinced in our minds that the Lord's Supper was not given to be a means either of justification or of conversion. It was never meant to give grace where there is no grace already, or to provide pardon when pardon is not already enjoyed. It cannot possibly provide what is lacking in repentance to God, and faith towards the Lord Jesus Christ. It is an ordinance for the penitent, not for the impenitent; for the believing, not for the unbelieving; for the converted, not for the unconverted. The unconverted man, who believes that he can find a 'shortcut' to heaven by taking the Lord's Supper, without treading the well-worn steps of repentance and faith, will find to his cost one day that he is totally deceived. The Lord's Supper was meant to increase and help the grace that a man has, but not to impart the grace that he does not have. It was certainly never intended to make our peace with God, to justify, or to convert.

The simplest statement of the benefit that a truehearted communicant may expect to receive from the Lord's Supper is the strengthening and refreshing of our souls. Clearer views of Christ and his atonement, clearer views of all the offices which Christ fills as our Mediator and Advocate, clearer views of the complete redemption Christ has obtained for us by his substituted death on the cross, clearer views of our full and perfect acceptance in Christ before God, fresh reasons for deep repentance for sin, fresh reasons for lively faith — these are among the leading returns that a believer may confidently expect to get from his attendance at the Lord's Table. Whoever eats the bread and drinks the wine in a right spirit will find himself drawn into closer communion with Christ, and will feel that he knows him more, and understands him better.

Firstly, it will have a *humbling* effect on the soul. The sight of the bread and wine as emblems of Christ's body and blood reminds us how sinful sin must be, if nothing less than the death of God's own Son could make satisfaction for it, or redeem us from its guilt. Never should we be so 'clothed with humility', as when we receive the Lord's Supper.

Secondly, it will have a *cheering* effect on the soul. The sight of the bread broken, and the wine poured out, reminds us how full, perfect and complete is our salvation. Those vivid emblems remind us what an enormous price has been paid for our redemption. They press on us the mighty truth that, believing on Christ we have nothing to fear, because a sufficient payment has been made for our debt. The 'precious blood of Christ' answers every charge that can be brought against us. God can be 'just and the justifier of the one who has faith in Jesus' (Romans 3:26).

Thirdly, it will have a *sanctifying* effect on the soul. The bread and wine remind us how great is our debt of gratitude to our Lord, and how thoroughly we are bound to live for the one who died for our sins. They seem to say to us, 'Remember what Christ has done for you, and ask yourself whether there is anything too great to do for him.'

Fourthly, it will have a *restraining* effect on the soul. Every time a believer receives the bread and the wine he is reminded what a serious thing it is to be a Christian, and what an obligation is laid on him to lead a consistent life. Bought with such a price as that bread and wine remind him, ought he not to glorify Christ in body and spirit, which are his? The man who goes regularly and intelligently to the Lord's Table finds it increasingly hard to yield to sin and conform to the world.

This is a brief account of the benefits that a right-hearted communicant may expect to receive from the Lord's Supper. In eating that bread and drinking that cup, such a man will have his repentance deepened, his faith increased, his knowledge enlarged, his habit of holy living strengthened. He will realize more of the 'real presence' of Christ in his heart. Eating that bread by faith, he will feel closer communion with the body of Christ. Drinking that wine by faith, he will feel closer communion with the blood of Christ. He will see more clearly what Christ is to him, and what he is to Christ. He will understand more thoroughly what it is to be 'one with Christ, and Christ one with him'. He will feel the roots of his soul's spiritual life watered, and the work of grace in his heart established, built up and carried forward. All these things may seem and sound like foolishness to a natural man, but to a true Christian these things are light, and health, and life, and peace. No wonder that a true Christian finds the Lord's Supper a source of blessing!

Remember, I do not pretend to say that all Christians experience the full blessing of the Lord's Supper, which I have just attempted to describe. Nor do I say that the same believer will always find his soul in the same spiritual frame, and always receive the same amount of benefit from the ordinance. But I boldly say this: you will rarely find a true believer who will not say that he believes the Lord's Supper is one of his best helps and highest privileges. He will tell you that if he were deprived of the Lord's Supper on a regular basis he would find its loss a great detriment to his soul. There are some things of which we never know the value until they are taken from us. So I believe it is with the Lord's Supper. The weakest and humblest of God's children gets a blessing from this ordinance, to an extent of which he is not aware.

Why do so many so-called Christians never go to the Lord's Table?

In the last place, I have to consider why it is that so many so-called Christians never come to the Lord's Supper. It is a simple matter of fact that myriads of persons who call themselves Christians never come to the Table of the Lord. They would not tolerate being told that they deny the faith, and are not in communion with Christ. When they worship, they attend a place of Christian worship; when they hear religious teaching, it is the teaching of Christianity; when they are married, they use a Christian service. Yet all this time they never come to the Lord's Supper! They often live on in this state of mind for many years, and to all appearance are not ashamed. They often die in this condition without ever having received the ordinance, and yet profess to feel hope at the last, and their friends express a hope about them. And yet they live and die in open disobedience to a plain command of Christ! These are simple facts. Let anyone look around him, and deny them if he can.

Now why is this? What explanation can we give? Our Lord Jesus Christ's last injunctions to his disciples are clear, plain and unmistakable. He says to all, 'Eat, drink: do this in remembrance of me.' Did he leave it to our discretion whether we would obey his injunction or not? Did he mean that it was not significant whether his disciples did or did not keep up the ordinance he had just established? Certainly not. The very idea is absurd, and one certainly never dreamed of in apostolic times. Paul evidently takes it for granted that every Christian would go to the Lord's Table when it was available. A class of Christian worshippers who never came to the Table was a class whose existence was unknown to him. What, then, are we to say of that number which fail to receive the Lord's Supper, unabashed, unhumbled, not afraid, not the least ashamed? Why is it? How is it? What does it all mean? Let us look these questions fairly in the face, and endeavour to answer them.

Ignorance

For one thing, many fail to go to the Table because they are utterly careless and thoughtless about religion, and ignorant of very first principles of Christianity. They go to church, as a matter of form, but they neither know, nor care anything about what is done at church! The faith of Christ has no place either in their hearts, or heads, or consciences, or wills, or understandings. It is a mere affair of 'words and names', about which they know no more than Festus or Gallio. There were very few such false Christians in Paul's times, if indeed there were any. There are far too many in these last days of the world. They are the dead weight of the churches, and the scandal of Christianity. What

such people need is light, knowledge, grace, a renewed conscience, a changed heart. In their present state they have no
part of Christ; and dying in this state they are thrown into hell.
Do I wish them to come to the Lord's Supper? Certainly not, till
they are converted. No one can enter the kingdom of God
unless he is born again.

Unrepented sin or neglect

For another thing, many false Christians do not receive the
Lord's Supper because they know they are living in the habitual practice of some sin, or in the neglect of some Christian
duty. Their conscience tells them that so long as they live in this
state, and do not turn away from their sins, they are unfit to
come to the Table of the Lord. Well; so far they are quite right!
I wish no man to be a communicant if he cannot give up his
sins. But I warn these people not to forget that if they are unfit
for the Lord's Supper they are unfit to die, and that if they die
in their present condition they will be lost eternally. The same
sins that disqualify them from the ordinance, most certainly
disqualify them from heaven. Do I want them to come to the
Lord's Supper as they are? Certainly not! But I do want them
to repent and be converted, to cease to do evil, and to break
off from their sins. Let it be for ever remembered that the man
unfit for the Lord's Supper is unfit to die.

Increased responsibility

For another thing, some do not come to the Table because they
believe that it will add to their responsibility. They are not, like
many, ignorant and careless about religion. They even attend
church regularly and listen to the preaching of the gospel. But
they say they dread coming to the Lord's Table and making a
confession and a profession. They fear that they might

afterwards fall away, and bring scandal on the cause of Christianity. They think it wisest to be on the safe side, and not commit themselves at all. Such people would do well to remember that if they avoid responsibility of one kind by not coming to the Lord's Table, they incur responsibility of another kind, quite as grave, and quite as injurious to the soul. They are responsible for open disobedience to a command from Christ. They are shrinking from doing what their Master continually commands his disciples — confessing him before men. No doubt it is a serious step to come to the Lord's Table and receive the bread and the wine. It is a step that none should take lightly and without self-examination. But it is *no less a serious step to walk away and refuse the ordinance*, when we remember who invites us to receive it, and for what purpose it was appointed! I warn the people I am now dealing with to be careful what they are doing. Let them not flatter themselves that it can ever be a wise, prudent, safe line of conduct to neglect a plain command of Christ. They may find at length, to their cost, that they have only increased their guilt and forsaken their mercies.

Unworthy

Also, some false Christians stay away from the Lord's Supper because they believe they are not yet worthy. They wait and stand still, under the mistaken notion that no one is qualified for the Lord's Supper unless he feels within him something like perfection. They pitch their idea of a communicant so high that they despair of attaining it. Waiting for inward perfection they live, and waiting for it they die. Now such persons would do well to understand that they are completely mistaken in their estimate of what 'worthiness' really is. They are forgetting that the Lord's Supper was not intended for unsinning angels, but for men and women subject to weakness, living in a world full of temptations, and needing mercy and grace every day they live.

A sense of our own utter unworthiness is the best worthiness that we can bring to the Lord's Table. A deep feeling of our own entire indebtedness to Christ for all we have and hope for is the best feeling we can bring with us. The people I now have in view ought to consider seriously whether the ground they have taken up is defensible, and whether they are not standing in their own light. If they are waiting till they feel in themselves perfect hearts, perfect motives, perfect feelings, perfect repentance, perfect love, perfect faith, they will wait for ever. There never were such communicants in any age — certainly not in the days of our Lord and of the Apostles — there never will be as long as the world stands. No, rather, the very thought that we feel literally worthy is a symptom of secret self-righteousness, and proves us unfit for the Lord's Table in God's sight. Sinners we are when we first come to the throne of grace — sinners we shall be till we die; converted, changed, renewed, sanctified, but sinners still (though not like before — sin is not the pattern of a believer's new life). In short, no man is really worthy to receive the Lord's Supper who does not deeply feel that he is a 'miserable sinner'.

Bad example of others

In the last place, some object going to the Lord's Table because they see others partaking who are not worthy, and not in a right state of mind. Because others eat and drink unworthily, they refuse to eat and drink at all. Of all the reasons taken up by those refusing to come to the Lord's Supper to justify their own neglect of Christ's ordinance, I must plainly say, I know none which seems to me so foolish, so weak, so unreasonable, and so unscriptural as this. It is as good as saying that we will never receive the Lord's Supper at all! When will we ever find a body of communicants on earth of which all the members are converted and living perfect lives? It is setting up ourselves in

the most unhealthy attitude of judging others. 'Who are you
that you judge another person?' 'What is that to you? You follow me' (John 21:22). It is depriving ourselves of a great privilege because others profane it and use it wrongly. It is pretend-
ing to be wiser than our Master himself. It is taking up ground
for which there is no warrant in Scripture. Paul rebukes the
Corinthians sharply for the irreverent behaviour of some of the
communicants; but I cannot find him giving a single hint that
when some came to the Table unworthily, others ought to draw
back or stay away. Let me advise the non-communicants I have
now in mind to beware of being wise above that which was
written. Let them study the parable of the wheat and tares, and
notice how both were to 'grow together until the harvest'
(Matthew 13:30).

Perfect churches, perfect congregations, perfect bodies of
communicants, are all unattainable in this world of confusion
and sin. Let us covet the best gifts, and do all we can to check
sin in others; but let us not starve ourselves because others are
ignorant sinners, and turn their food into poison. If others are
foolish enough to eat and drink unworthily, let us not turn our
backs on Christ's ordinance, and refuse to eat and drink at all.

These are the five common excuses why myriads in the present
day, though professing to be Christians, never come to the Lord's
Supper. One common remark may be made about them: there
is not a single reason among the five that deserves to be called
'good', and which does not condemn the man who gives it. I
challenge anyone to deny this. I have said repeatedly that I
want no one to come to the Lord's Table who is not properly
qualified. But I ask those who stay away never to forget that
the very reasons they give for their conduct are their condemnation. I tell them that they stand convicted before God of either
being very ignorant of what a communicant is, and what the
Lord's Supper is; or else of being persons who are not living

right, and are unfit to die. In short, to say 'I am a non-communicant' is as good as saying one of three things: 'I am living in sin, and cannot come'; 'I know Christ commands me, but I will not obey him'; 'I am an ignorant man, and do not understand what the Lord's Supper means.'

Some necessary warnings

I do not know in what state of mind this book may find my reader, or what his opinions may be about the Lord's Supper. But I will conclude the whole subject by offering to all some warnings, which I venture to believe are highly required by the times.

1. *Do not neglect the Lord's Supper*

The man who coolly and deliberately refuses to use an ordinance that the Lord Jesus Christ appointed for his profit may be very sure that his soul is in a very wrong state. There is a judgement to come; there is an account to be rendered of all our conduct on earth. How anyone can look forward to that day, and expect to meet Christ with comfort and in peace, if he has refused all his life to commune with Christ at his Table, is something that I cannot understand. Does this hit home to you? Be careful what you are doing.

2. *Do not receive the Lord's Supper carelessly, irreverently and as a matter of form*

The man who goes to the Lord's Table, and eats the bread and drinks the wine while his heart is far away, is committing a great sin, and robbing himself of a great blessing. In this, as in every other means of grace, everything depends on the state of mind in which the ordinance is used. He who draws near without repentance, faith and love, and with a heart full of sin and the world, will certainly be nothing better, but rather worse. Does this hit home to you? Be careful what you are doing.

3. *Do not make an idol of the Lord's Supper*

The man who tells you that it is the first, foremost, chief and principal precept in Christianity is telling you something he will find hard to prove. In the great majority of the books of the New Testament the Lord's Supper is not even named. In the letter to Timothy and Titus, about a minister's duties, the subject is not even mentioned. To repent and be converted, to believe and be holy, to be born again and have grace in our hearts — all these things are of far more importance than to be a communicant. Without them we cannot be saved. Without the Lord's Supper we can. Are you tempted to make the Lord's Supper override and overshadow everything in Christianity, and place it above prayer and preaching? Be careful. Pay attention to what you are doing.

4. *Do not use the Lord's Supper irregularly*

Never be absent when the Lord's Supper is administered. Make every effort to attend. Regular habits are essential to the maintenance of the health of our bodies. Regular use of the Lord's Supper is essential to the well-being of our souls. The man who finds it a burden to attend on every occasion when the Lord's Table is spread may well doubt whether all is right within him, and whether he is ready for the Marriage Supper of the Lamb. If Thomas had not been absent when the Lord appeared the first time to the assembled disciples, he would not have said the foolish things he did. Absence made him miss a blessing. Does this hit home to you? Be careful what you are doing.

5. *Do not do anything to bring discredit on your profession*

The man who, after attending the Lord's Table, runs into sin does more harm perhaps than any sinner. He is a walking sermon on behalf of the devil. He gives opportunity to the enemies of the Lord to blaspheme. He helps to keep people away from Christ. Lying, drinking, adulterous, dishonest, passionate communicants are the helpers of the devil, and the worst enemies of the gospel. Does this hit home to you? Be careful what you are doing.

6. *Do not despair and be cast down, if with all your desires you do not feel that you get a lot of good from the Lord's Supper*

Very likely you are expecting too much. Very likely you are a poor judge of your own state. Your soul's roots may be strengthening and growing, while you think you are not. Very likely you are forgetting that earth is not heaven, and that here we walk by sight and not by faith, and must expect nothing perfect. Lay these things to heart. Do not think harsh things about yourself without cause.

To every reader into whose hands this may fall, I commend its whole subject as deserving serious and solemn consideration. I am nothing better than a poor fallible man myself. But if I have made up my mind on any point it is this — there is no truth that demands such plain speaking as truth about the Lord's Supper.

Note

1. *Waterland's works*, volume V, p. 268, Oxford edition.

7.

Love

'And now abide faith, hope, love, these three;
but the greatest of these is love' (1 Corinthians 13:13).

Love is rightly called 'the Queen of Christian graces'. 'Now the purpose of the commandment', says Paul, 'is love' (1 Timothy 1:5). It is a grace that all people profess to admire. It seems a plain practical thing that everybody can understand. It is none of 'those troublesome doctrinal points' about which Christians disagree. Thousands, I suspect, would not be ashamed to tell you that they know nothing about justification, or regeneration, or about the work of Christ, or of the Holy Spirit. But nobody, I believe, would like to say that he knows nothing about love! If men possess nothing else in religion, they always flatter themselves that they possess 'love'.

A few plain thoughts about love will be very useful. There are false notions about love that need to be dispelled. There are mistakes about it which require to be rectified. In my admiration of love I yield to none. But I am confident that in many minds the whole subject seems completely misunderstood. I therefore wish to show the following four points.

Let me show, firstly, *the place the Bible gives to love.*
Let me show, secondly, *what the love of the Bible really is.*
Let me show, thirdly, *where true love comes from.*
Let me show, lastly, *why love is 'the greatest' of the graces.*

I ask for the sincere attention of my readers to the subject. My heart's desire and prayer to God is that the growth of love may be promoted in this sin-burdened world. In nothing does the fallen condition of man show itself so strongly as in the scarcity of Christian love. There is little faith on earth, little hope, little knowledge of divine things. But nothing, after all, is as scarce as real love.

The place the Bible gives to love

Let me show, firstly, the place the Bible gives to love. I begin with this point in order to establish the immense practical importance of my subject. I do not forget that there are many Christians in this present day who almost refuse to look at anything practical in Christianity. They can talk of nothing but two or three favourite doctrines. Now I want to remind my readers that the Bible contains much about practice as well as doctrine, and that one thing to which it attaches great weight is 'love'.

I turn to the New Testament, and ask men to observe what it says about love. In all religious inquiries there is nothing like letting the Scripture speak for itself. There is no surer way of finding out truth than the old way of turning to simple Bible texts. Texts were our Lord's weapons, both in answering Satan, and in arguing with the Jews. Texts are the guides we must never be ashamed to refer to in the present day: What does the Scripture say? What is written? How do you read it?

Let us hear what Paul says to the Corinthians: 'Though I speak with the tongues of men and of angels, but have not love, I have become sounding brass or a clanging cymbal. And though I have the gift of prophecy, and understand all mysteries and all knowledge, and though I have all faith, so that I could remove mountains, but have not love, I am nothing. And though I bestow all my goods to feed the poor, and though I give my body to be burned, but have not love, it profits me nothing' (1 Corinthians 13:1-3).

Let us hear what Paul says to the Colossians: 'But above all these things put on love, which is the bond of perfection' (Colossians 3:14).

Let us hear what Paul says to Timothy: 'Now the purpose of the commandment is love from a pure heart, from a good conscience, and from sincere faith' (1 Timothy 1:5).

Let us hear what Peter says: 'And above all things have fervent love for one another, for "love will cover a multitude of sins"'(1 Peter 4:8).

Let us hear what our Lord Jesus Christ himself says about that love: 'A new commandment I give to you, that you love one another; as I have loved you, that you also love one another. By this all will know that you are my disciples, if you have love for one another' (John 13:34-35). Above all, let us read our Lord's account of the last judgement, and note that the lack of love will condemn millions: 'Then he will also say to those on the left hand, "Depart from me, you cursed, into the everlasting fire prepared for the devil and his angels: for I was hungry and you gave me no food; I was thirsty and you gave me no drink"' (Matthew 25:41-42).

Let us hear what Paul says to the Romans: 'Owe no one anything except to love one another, for he who loves another has fulfilled the law' (Romans 13:8).

Let us hear what Paul says to the Ephesians: 'And walk in love, as Christ also has loved us and given himself for us, an offering and a sacrifice to God for a sweet-smelling aroma' (Ephesians 5:2).

Let us hear what John says: 'Beloved, let us love one another, for love is of God; and everyone who loves is born of God and knows God. He who does not love does not know God, for God is love' (1 John 4:7-8).

I shall make no comment upon these texts. I think it best to place them before my readers in their naked simplicity, and to let them speak for themselves. If anyone should think that the subject of this chapter is an insignificant matter, I will only ask him to look at these texts, and to think again. He who would take down 'love' from the high and holy place it occupies in the Bible, and treat it as a matter of secondary importance, must settle his account with God's Word. I certainly shall not waste time in arguing with him.

To my own mind the evidence of these texts appears clear, plain and incontrovertible. They show the immense importance of love as one of the 'things that accompany salvation'. They prove that it has a right to demand the serious attention of all who call themselves Christians, and that those who despise the subject are only exposing their own ignorance of Scripture.

What the love of the Bible really is

Let me show, secondly, what the love of the Bible really is. I consider it extremely important to have clear views on this point. It is precisely here that mistakes about love begin. Out of a downright ignorance of Scripture, thousands delude themselves with the idea that they have 'love', when they don't. Their love is not the love described in the Bible.

What love is not

Firstly, the love of the Bible does not consist in *giving to the poor*. It is a common delusion to suppose that it does. Yet Paul tells us plainly that a man may 'bestow all my goods to feed the poor' (1 Corinthians 13:3), and not have love. That a loving man will 'remember the poor', there can be no question (Galatians 2:10). That he will do all he can to assist them, relieve them and lighten their burdens, I don't deny for a moment. All I say is that this does not make up 'love'. It is easy to spend a fortune in giving away money, and soup, and bread, and blankets, and clothing, and yet to be utterly destitute of Bible love.

Secondly, the love of the Bible does not consist in *never disapproving anybody's conduct*. Here is another very common delusion! Thousands pride themselves on never condemning others, or saying they are wrong, whatever they may do. They convert the precept of our Lord, 'Do not judge,' into an excuse for having no unfavourable opinion at all of anybody. They pervert his prohibition of rash and censorious judgements into a prohibition of all judgement whatsoever. Your neighbour may be a drunkard, a liar, a violent man. Never mind! 'It is not love', they tell you, 'to pronounce him wrong.' You are to believe that, basically, he has a good heart! This idea of love is, unhappily, a very common one. It is full of mischief. To throw a veil over sin, and to refuse to call things by their right names — to talk of 'hearts' being good, when 'lives' are completely wrong — to shut our eyes against wickedness, and excuse their immorality — this is not scriptural love.

Thirdly, the love of the Bible does not consist in *never disapproving anybody's religious opinions*. Here is another most serious and growing delusion. There are many who pride themselves on never pronouncing others mistaken, whatever views they may hold. Your neighbour, for example, may be a Roman Catholic, or a Mormon. But the 'love' of many says that you have no right to think him wrong! If he is sincere, it is 'unloving' to think unfavourably of his spiritual condition! From such love may I ever be delivered! In that case the Apostles were wrong in going out to preach to the Gentiles! In that case there is no use in missions! In that case we had better close our Bibles, and shut up our churches! Everybody is right, and nobody is wrong! Everybody is going to heaven, and nobody is going to hell!

Such love is a monstrous caricature. To say that all are equally right in their opinions, though their opinions flatly contradict one another; to say that all are equally on their way to heaven, though their doctrinal sentiments are as opposite as black and

white — this is not scriptural love. Love like this pours contempt
on the Bible, and talks as if God had not given it as a written
test of truth. Love like this confuses all our notions of heaven
and would fill it with a discordant inharmonious rabble. True
love does not think everybody is right in their doctrines. True
love cries, 'Do not believe every spirit, but test the spirits, whether
they are of God; because many false prophets have gone out
into the world.' 'If anyone comes to you and does not bring
this doctrine, do not receive him into your house nor greet him'
(1 John 4:1; 2 John 10).

I leave the negative side of the question here. I have dwelt
upon it at some length because of the days in which we live
and the strange notions that abound. Let me now turn to the
positive side. Having shown what love is not, let me now show
what it is.

What love is

Love is the 'love' that Paul places first among those fruits brought
forth in the heart of a believer. 'The fruit of the Spirit is love'
(Galatians 5:22). Love to God, such as Adam had before the
Fall, is its first feature. He who has love desires to love God
with heart, and soul, and mind, and strength. Love to man is
its second feature. He who has love desires to love his neighbour as himself. This is indeed the view in which the word
'love' in Scripture is more especially regarded. When I speak of
a believer having 'love' in his heart, I mean that he has love to
both God and man. When I speak of a believer having 'love',
I mean more particularly that he has love towards man.

The love of the Bible will show itself in a believer's *actions*. It
will make him ready to do kind acts to everyone within his
reach — both to their bodies and souls. It will not let him be
content with soft words and kind wishes. It will make him diligent in doing all within his power to lessen the sorrow and

increase the happiness of others. Like his Master, he will care more for ministering than for being ministered to, and will look for nothing in return. Like his Master's great apostle he will very willingly 'spend and be spent' for others, even though they repay him with hatred, and not with love. True love does not want rewards. Its work is its reward.

The love of the Bible will show itself in a believer's *readiness to bear* evil as well as to do good. It will make him patient under provocation, forgiving when injured, meek when unjustly attacked, quiet when slandered. It will make him bear much, put up with much and look over much, submit often and deny himself often, all for the sake of peace. It will make him control his temper, and check his tongue. True love is not always asking, 'What are my rights? Am I treated as I deserve?' but, 'How can I best promote peace? How can I do what is most edifying to others?'

The love of the Bible will show itself in the *general spirit and demeanour* of a believer. It will make him kind, unselfish, good-natured, good-tempered and considerate of others. It will make him gentle, friendly and courteous, in all the daily relations of private life, thoughtful for others' comfort, tender for others' feelings, and more anxious to give pleasure than to receive. True love never envies others when they prosper, nor rejoices in the calamities of others when they are in trouble. At all times it will believe, and hope, and try to put to good use the actions of others. And even at worst, it will be full of pity, mercy and compassion.

Would we like to know where the true pattern of love like this can be found? We have only to look at the life of our Lord Jesus Christ, as described in the Gospels, and we will see it perfectly exemplified. Love radiated forth in everything he did. His daily life was an incessant 'going about' doing good. Love radiated forth in his whole manner. He was continually hated, persecuted, slandered, misrepresented. But he patiently endured it all. No angry word ever fell from his lips. No ill temper ever appeared in his demeanour. 'When he was reviled, did not revile in return; when he suffered, he did not threaten' (1 Peter 2:23). Love radiated forth in all his spirit and deportment. The law of kindness was ever on his lips. Among weak and ignorant disciples, among sick and sorrowful petitioners for help and relief, among publicans and sinners, among Pharisees and Sadducees, he was always one and the same — kind and patient to all.

And yet, remember our blessed Master never flattered sinners, or turned a blind eye to sin. He never shrunk from exposing wickedness in its true colours, or from rebuking those who would cling to it. He never hesitated to denounce false doctrine regardless of who held to it, or to expose false practice in its true colours and the certain end to which it is heading. He called things by their right names. He spoke as freely of hell and the unquenchable fire, as of heaven and the kingdom of glory. He has left on record an everlasting proof that perfect love does not require us to approve everybody's life or opinions, and that it is quite possible to condemn false doctrine and wicked practice, and yet to be full of love at the same time.

Some practical thoughts

I have now set before my readers the true nature of scriptural love. I have given a slight and very brief account of what it is not, and what it is. I cannot pass on without suggesting two practical thoughts, which weigh heavily on my mind, and I hope may press home to others.

You have heard of love. Think, for a moment, how deplorably little love there is upon earth! How conspicuous is the absence of true love among Christians! I am not speaking of the heathen, I am now speaking of Christians. What angry tempers, what passions, what selfishness, what bitter tongues are to be found in private families! What strife, what quarrels, what spitefulness, what malice, what revenge, what envy between neighbours and fellow church members! What jealousies and contentions between those of varying doctrines! 'Where is love?' we may well ask. 'Where is love? Where is the mind of Christ?' when we look at the spirit that reigns in the world. No wonder Christ's cause stands still, and sin abounds, when men's hearts know so little of love! Surely we can say, 'When the Son of Man comes, will he find love on the earth?'

Think, for another thing, what a happy world this would be if there was more love. It is the lack of love that causes half the misery there is upon earth. Sickness, and death, and poverty will not account for more than half the sorrows. The rest come from ill-temper, ill-nature, strife, quarrels, lawsuits, malice, envy, revenge, fraud, violence, wars and the like. It would be one great step towards doubling the happiness of mankind, and halving their sorrows, if all men and women were full of scriptural love.

Where the love of the Bible comes from

Let me show, thirdly, where the love of the Bible comes from. Love, such as I have described, is certainly not natural to man. Naturally, we are all more or less selfish, envious, ill-tempered, spiteful, ill-natured and unkind. We have only to observe children, when left to themselves, to see the proof of this. Let boys and girls grow up without proper training and education, and you will not see one of them possessing Christian love. See how some of them think first of themselves, and their own comfort and advantage! Note how others are full of pride, passion and evil tempers! How can we account for it? There is but one reply. The natural heart knows nothing of true love.

The love of the Bible will never be found except in a heart prepared by the Holy Spirit. It is a tender plant, and will never grow except in one soil. You may as well expect grapes on thorns, or figs on thistles, as look for love when the heart is not right.

The heart in which love grows is a heart changed, renewed and transformed by the Holy Spirit. The image and likeness of God, which Adam lost at the Fall, has been restored, however feeble and imperfect the restoration may appear. It is to be 'partakers of the divine nature' by union with Christ and Sonship to God; and one of the first features of that nature is love (2 Peter 1:4).

Such a heart is deeply convinced of sin, hates it, flees from it, and fights with it from day to day. And one of the prime elements of sin, which it daily labours to overcome, is selfishness and lack of love.

Such a heart is deeply aware of its mighty debt to our Lord Jesus Christ. It feels continually that it owes all its present comfort, hope and peace to the one who died for us on the cross. How can it show forth its gratitude? What can it render to its Redeemer? If it can do nothing else, it strives to be like him, to walk in his footsteps, and, like him, to be full of love. The fact that 'God has poured out his love into our hearts by the Holy Spirit' is the surest fountain of Christian love. Love will produce love.

I ask my readers to pay special attention to this point. It is one of great importance in the present day. There are many who profess to admire love, while they care nothing about vital Christianity. They like some of the fruits and results of the gospel, but not the root from which these fruits alone can grow, or the doctrines with which they are inseparably connected.

Hundreds who hate to be told of man's corruption, of the blood of Christ, and of the inward work of the Holy Spirit will praise love. Many a parent would like his children to grow up unselfish and good-tempered, but would not be very pleased if someone pressed upon their children the need for conversion, repentance and faith.

Now I wish to protest against the notion that you can have the fruits of Christianity without the roots; that you can produce Christian dispositions without teaching Christian doctrines; that you can have love that will wear and endure without grace in the heart.

I grant, most freely, that every now and then one sees a person who seems very loving and amiable, without any distinctive doctrinal religion. But such cases are so rare and remarkable, that, like exceptions, they only prove the truth of the general rule. And often, too often, it may be feared in such cases the apparent love is only external, and in private completely fails. I firmly believe, as a general rule, you will only find such love as the Bible describes in the soil of a heart thoroughly endowed with Bible religion. Holy practice will not flourish without sound doctrine. What God has joined together it is useless to expect to have separate and apart.

The delusion that I am trying to combat is promoted most mischievously by the vast majority of novels, romances and tales of fiction. Who does not know that the heroes and heroines of these works are constantly described as patterns of perfection? They are always doing the right thing, saying the right thing, and showing the right disposition! They are always kind, and amiable, and unselfish, and forgiving! And yet you never hear a word about their religion! In short, to judge by works of fiction in general, it is possible to have excellent practical religion without doctrine, the fruits of the Spirit without the grace of the Spirit, and the mind of Christ without union with Christ!

Here, in short, is the great danger of reading most novels, romances and works of fiction. The majority of them give a false or incorrect view of human nature. They paint their model men and women as they ought to be, and not as they really are. The readers of such writings get their minds filled with wrong conceptions of what the world is. Their notions of mankind become visionary and unreal. They are constantly looking for such men and women as they never meet, and expecting what they never find.

Let me entreat my readers, once and for all, to draw their ideas of human nature from the Bible, and not from novels. Be convinced in your mind that there cannot be true love without a heart renewed by grace. A certain degree of kindness, courtesy, amiability and good nature may undoubtedly be seen in many who have no vital religion. But the glorious plant of Bible love, in all its fulness and perfection, will never be found without union with Christ and the work of the Holy Spirit. Teach this to your children, if you have any. Hold it up in schools, if you are connected with any. Lift up love. Make much of love. Give way to no one in exalting the grace of kindness, love, good nature, unselfishness, good temper. But never, never forget that there is but one school in which these things can be thoroughly learned, and that is the school of Christ. Real love comes down from above. True love is the fruit of the Spirit. He who would have it must sit at Christ's feet and learn of him.

Why love is called the 'greatest' of the graces

Let me show, lastly, why love is called the 'greatest' of the graces. The words of Paul on this subject are distinct and unmistakable. He winds up his wonderful chapter on love in the following manner: 'And now abide faith, hope, love, these three; but the greatest of these is love' (1 Corinthians 13:13).

This expression is very remarkable. Of all the writers in the New Testament, none, certainly, exalts 'faith' as highly as Paul. The Epistles to the Romans and Galatians abound in sentences showing its vast importance. By faith the sinner lays hold of Christ and is saved. Through it we are justified, and have peace with God. Yet here the same Paul speaks of something that is even greater than faith. He puts before us the three leading Christian graces, and pronounces the following judgement on them: 'The greatest of these is love.' Such a sentence from such a writer demands special attention. What are we to understand when we hear of love being greater than faith and hope?

We are not to suppose for a moment that love can atone for our sins, or make our peace with God. Nothing can do that for us but the blood of Christ, and nothing can give us an interest in Christ's blood but faith. It is unscriptural ignorance not to know this. The office of justifying and joining the soul to Christ belongs to faith alone. Our love, and all our other graces, are all more or less imperfect, and could not stand the severity of God's judgement. When we have done all, we are 'unprofit-able servants' (Luke 17:10).

We are not to suppose that love can exist independently of faith. Paul did not intend to set up one grace in rivalry to the other. He did not mean that one man might have faith, another hope, and another love, and that the best of these was the man who had love. The three graces are inseparably joined together. Where there is faith, there will always be love; and where there is love, there will be faith. Sun and light, fire and heat, ice and cold, are no more intimately united than faith and love.

The reasons why love is called the greatest of the three graces appear to me plain and simple. Let me show what they are.

Firstly, love is called the greatest of the graces because it is the one in which there is *some likeness between the believer and his God*. God has no need of faith. He is dependent on no one. There is none superior to the one in whom we must trust. God has no need of hope. To him all things are certain, whether past, present, or to come. But 'God is love' and the more love his people have, the more they are like their Father in heaven.

Secondly, love is called the greatest of the graces because it is *most useful to others*. Faith and hope, beyond doubt, how-ever precious, have special reference to a believer's own pri-vate individual benefit. Faith unites the soul to Christ, brings peace with God and opens the way to heaven. Hope fills the soul with cheerful expectation of things to come, and, amid the

many discouragements of things seen, comforts with visions of
the things unseen. But love is pre-eminently the grace that makes
a man useful. It is the spring of good works and kindnesses. It is
the root of missions, schools and hospitals. Love made apostles spend and be spent for souls. Love raises up workers for
Christ and keeps them working. Love smoothes quarrels, and
stops strife, and in this sense 'will cover a multitude of sins'
(1 Peter 4:8). Love adorns Christianity and recommends it to
the world. A man may have real faith, and feel it, and yet his
faith may be invisible to others. But a man's love cannot be
hidden.

Thirdly, love is the greatest of the graces because it is the
one that *endures the longest*; in fact, it will never die. Faith will
one day be swallowed up in sight, and hope in certainty. Their
office will be useless on the morning of the resurrection, and
like old almanacs, they will be laid aside. But love will live on
through the endless ages of eternity. Heaven will be the home
of love. The inhabitants of heaven will be full of love. One
common feeling will be in all their hearts, and that will be love.

Conclusion

I leave this part of my subject here and pass on to a conclusion.
It would be easy to enlarge on each of the three points of comparison between love and the other graces I have just named.
But time and space both forbid me to do so. If I have said
enough to guard men against mistakes about the right meaning
of the 'greatness' of love, I am content. Love, may it ever be
remembered, cannot justify and put away our sins. It is neither
Christ, nor faith. But love makes us somewhat like God. Love
is of mighty use to the world. Love will live and flourish when
faith's work is done. Surely, with such points as these, love well
deserves the crown.

1. *Have you love?*

And now let me ask every one of my readers a simple question. Let me press home on your conscience the whole subject of this chapter. Do you know anything of the grace of which I have been speaking? Have you love?

The strong language of the apostle Paul must surely convince you that the inquiry is not one that ought to be lightly put aside. The grace without which that holy man could say, 'I am nothing', the grace which the Lord Jesus says expressly is the great mark of being his disciple — such a grace as this demands the serious consideration of every one who is in earnest about the salvation of his soul. It should set him thinking, 'How does this affect me? Do I have love?'

You may have some knowledge of religion. You know the difference between true and false doctrine. You can, perhaps, even quote texts and defend the opinions you hold. But remember, the knowledge that is barren of practical results in life and temperament is a useless possession. The words of the Apostle are very plain: 'And though I ... understand all mysteries and all knowledge ... but have not love, I am nothing' (1 Corinthians 13:3).

You think you have faith, perhaps. You trust you are one of God's elect, and rest in that. But surely you should remember that there is a faith of devils, which is utterly unprofitable, and that the faith of God's elect is a 'faith expressing itself through love'. It was when Paul remembered the 'love' of the Thessalonians, as well as their faith and hope, that he said 'knowing ... your election by God' (1 Thessalonians 1:4).

Look at your own daily life, both at home and away, and consider what place the love of Scripture has in it. What is your temperament? What are your ways of behaving towards all around you in your own family? What is your manner of speaking, especially in times of irritation and provocation? Where is your good nature, your courtesy, your patience, your meekness, your gentleness, your tolerance? Where are your practical actions of love in your dealing with others? What do you know of the mind of the one who 'went around doing good'; who loved everyone, though especially his disciples; who returned good for evil, and kindness for hatred, and had a heart wide enough to feel for everyone?

What would you do in heaven, I wonder, if you got there without love? What comfort could you have in a home where love was the law, and selfishness and ill nature completely shut out? Yes! I fear that heaven would be no place for an unloving and ill-tempered man! Note what a little boy said one day. 'If grandfather goes to heaven, I hope that I and my brother will not go there.' 'Why do you say that?' he was asked. He replied, 'If he sees us there, I am sure he will say, as he does now, "What are these boys doing here? Let them get out of the way." He does not like to see us on earth, so I suppose he would not like to see us in heaven.'

Give yourself no rest till you know something by experience of real Christian love. Go and learn from the one who is meek and lowly of heart, and ask him to teach you how to love. Ask the Lord Jesus to put his Spirit within you, to take away the old heart, to give you a new nature, to make you know something of his mind. Cry to him night and day for grace, and give him no rest until you feel something of what I have been describing. Happy indeed will your life be when you really understand 'walking in love'.

2. Practise and teach the grace of love

I do not forget that I am writing to some who are not ignorant of the love of Scripture, and who long to feel more of it every year. I will give you two simple words of exhortation. These are: 'Practise and teach the grace of love.'

Practise love diligently. It is one of those graces, above all, which grows by constant exercise. Strive more and more to carry it into every little detail of daily life. Watch over your own tongue and temper throughout every hour of the day, and especially in your dealing with children and near relatives. Remember the character of the excellent woman: 'She opens her mouth with wisdom, and on her tongue is the law of kindness' (Proverbs 31:26). Remember the words of Paul: 'Let all that you do be done with love' (1 Corinthians 16:14). Love should be seen in little things as well as in great ones. Remember, not least, the words of Peter: 'Have fervent love for one another', not a love which just barely is a flame, but a burning, shining fire, which everyone around us can see (1 Peter 4:8). It may cost pain and trouble to keep these things in mind. There may be little encouragement from the example of others. But persevere. Love like this brings its own reward.

Finally, teach love to others. Press it, above all, on children, if you have any. Remind them constantly that kindness, good nature, and good disposition are among the first evidences which Christ requires in children. If they cannot know much, or explain doctrines, they can understand love. A child's religion is worth very little if it only consists in repeating texts and hymns. Useful as they are, they are often learned without thought, remembered without feeling, repeated without consideration of their meaning, and forgotten when childhood is gone. By all means let children be taught texts and hymns; but let not such teaching be made everything in their religion. Teach them to keep their tempers, to be kind to one another, to be unselfish, good-natured, obliging, patient, gentle, forgiving. Tell them never to forget to their dying day, if they live as long as Methuselah, that without love the Holy Spirit says, 'We are nothing.' Tell them 'above all these things put on love, which is the bond of perfection' (Colossians 3:14).

8.
Zeal

'It is good to be zealous in a good thing always'
(Galatians 4:18).

Zeal is a subject, like many others in religion, that is most sadly misunderstood. Many would be ashamed to be thought zealous Christians. Many are ready to say of zealous people what Festus said of Paul: 'Paul, you are beside yourself!' he shouted. 'Much learning is driving you mad!' (Acts 26:24).

But zeal is a subject that no reader of the Bible has any right to pass over. If we make the Bible our rule of faith and practice, we cannot turn away from it. We must look it in the face. What does the apostle Paul say to Titus? '[Christ] gave himself for us, that he might redeem us from every lawless deed and purify for himself his own special people, zealous for good works' (Titus 2:14). What does the Lord Jesus say to the Laodicean church? 'Be zealous and repent' (Revelation 3:19).

My object in this chapter is to plead the cause of zeal in religion. I believe we ought not to be afraid of it, but rather to love and admire it. I believe it is a mighty blessing to the world and the origin of countless benefits to mankind. I want to remind Christians that 'Zealot' was a name given to one of our Lord Jesus Christ's Apostles, to persuade them to be zealous men.

I ask every one of my readers to pay attention while I tell him something about zeal. Listen to me for your own sake —

for the sake of the world — for the sake of the church of our
Christ. Listen to me and by God's help I will show you that to
be 'zealous' is to be wise, using the following three questions.

Let me show, in the first place, what is zeal in religion.
Let me show, in the second place, when a man can be
   correctly called zealous in religion.
Let me show, in the third place, why it is a good thing for a
   man to be zealous in religion.

What is zeal in religion?

First of all, I propose to consider this question: What is zeal in
religion? Zeal in religion is a burning desire to please God, to
do his will, and to advance his glory in the world in every possible way. It is a desire that is not natural to man. It is a desire
that the Spirit puts in the heart of every believer when he is
converted; however, a desire that some believers feel so much
more strongly than others that they alone deserve to be called
'zealous' men.

This desire is so strong, when it really reigns in a man, that it
impels him to make any sacrifice, to go through any trouble, to
deny himself to any amount, to suffer, to work, to labour, to
toil, to spend himself and be spent, and even to die — if only
he can please God and honour Christ.

A zealous man in religion is pre-eminently a man of one
thing. It is not enough to say that he is earnest, strong, uncompromising, meticulous, wholehearted, fervent in spirit. He only
sees one thing, he cares for one thing, he lives for one thing, he
is swallowed up in one thing; and that one thing is to please
God. Whether he lives, or whether he dies; whether he has
health, or whether he has sickness; whether he is rich, or whether
he is poor; whether he pleases man, or whether he gives offence;

whether he is thought wise, or whether he is thought foolish; whether he gets blame, or whether he gets praise; whether he gets honour, or whether he gets shame; for all this the zealous man cares nothing at all. He burns for one thing, and that one thing is to please God and to advance God's glory. If he is consumed in the very burning, he does not care — he is content. He feels that, like a lamp, he is made to burn; and if consumed in burning, he has but done the work for which God has appointed him. Such a person will always find a sphere for his zeal. If he cannot preach, and work, and give money, he will cry, and sigh, and pray. Yes; if he is only a pauper, on a perpetual bed of sickness, he will make the activity of sin around him slow to a standstill, by continually interceding against it. If he cannot fight in the valley with Joshua, he will do the work of Moses, Aaron and Hur, on the hill (Exodus 17:9-13). If he is cut off from working himself, he will give the Lord no rest till help is raised up from another quarter, and the work is done. This is what I mean when I speak of zeal in religion.

We all know the habit of mind that makes men great in this world — that makes such men as Alexander the Great, or Julius Caesar, or Oliver Cromwell, or Peter the Great, or Napoleon. We know that with all their faults they were all men of one thing. They threw themselves into one grand pursuit. They cared for nothing else. They put everything else aside. They counted everything else as second-rate and of subordinate importance, compared to the one thing that they put before their eyes every day they lived. I say that the same habit of mind applied to the service of the Lord Jesus Christ becomes religious zeal.

We know the habit of mind that makes men great in the sciences of this world — that makes such men as Archimedes, or Sir Isaac Newton, or Galileo, or Ferguson the astronomer, or James Watt. All these were men of one purpose. They brought the powers of their minds into one single focus. They cared for nothing else besides. And this was the secret of their success. I say that this same habit consecrated to the service of God becomes religious zeal.

We know the habit of mind that makes men rich, that makes men amass mighty fortunes, and leave millions behind them. What kind of people were the bankers, and merchants, and tradesmen, who have left a name behind them as men who acquired immense wealth and became rich from being poor? They were all men who threw themselves entirely into their business, and neglected everything else for the sake of that business. They gave their first attention, their first thoughts, the best of their time, and the best part of their mind, to pushing forward the transactions in which they were engaged. They were men of one purpose. Their hearts were not divided. They devoted themselves, body, soul and mind, to their business. They seemed to live for nothing else. I say that if you turn that habit of mind to the service of God and his Christ it makes religious zeal.

All the Apostles

Now this habit of mind — this zeal — was the characteristic of all the Apostles. See for example the apostle Paul. Hear him when he speaks to the Ephesian elders for the last time: 'Nor do I count my life dear to myself, so that I may finish my race with joy, and the ministry which I received from the Lord Jesus, to testify to the gospel of the grace of God' (Acts 20:24). Hear him again, when he writes to the Philippians: 'One thing I do ... I press toward the goal for the prize of the upward call of God in Christ Jesus' (Philippians 3:13-14). See him from the day of his conversion, giving up his brilliant prospects — forsaking all for Christ's sake — and going forth to preach that very Jesus whom he had once despised. See him going to and fro throughout the world from that time — through persecution — through oppression — through opposition — through prisons — through bonds — through afflictions — through things next to death itself, up to the very day when he sealed his faith with his blood and died at Rome, a martyr for the gospel that he had so long proclaimed. This was true religious zeal.

The early Christians

This zeal was also the characteristic of the early Christians. They were men that were 'spoken against everywhere' (Acts 28:22). They were driven to worship God in dens and caves of the earth. They often lost everything in the world for their religion's sake. They generally gained nothing but the cross, persecution, shame and reproach. But they seldom, very seldom, went back. If they could not debate, at least they could suffer. If they could not convince their adversaries by argument, at least they could die and prove that they themselves were in earnest. Look at Ignatius cheerfully travelling to the place where he was to be devoured by lions, and saying as he went, 'Now do I begin to be a disciple of my Master, Christ.' Hear old Polycarp before the Roman Governor, saying boldly, when called upon to deny Christ, 'Four score and six years have I served Christ, and he has never offended me in anything, and how can I then revile my King?' This was true zeal.

Martin Luther

This zeal was also the characteristic of Martin Luther. He boldly defied the most powerful hierarchy that the world has ever seen. He unveiled the corruptions with an unflinching hand. He preached the long-neglected truth of justification by faith, in spite of curses and excommunications that were thickly poured upon him. See him pleading his cause before the Emperor, and a host of the children of this world. Hear him saying, when men were persuading him from going, and reminding him of the fate of John Huss, 'Though there were a devil under every tile on the roofs of this building, in the name of the Lord I shall go forward.' This was true zeal.

Our own English Reformers

This zeal was also the characteristic of our own English Reformers. You have it in our first Reformer, Wickliffe, when he rose up on his sickbed and said to the friars who wanted him to retract all he had said against the pope, 'I shall not die, but live to declare the wickedness of the friars.' You have it in Cranmer, dying at the stake rather than deny Christ's gospel, holding out first to be burned the hand which, in a moment of weakness, had signed a recantation; and saying as he held it in the flames, 'This unworthy hand!' You have it in old Latimer, standing boldly on his kindling wood for the fire, at the age of seventy years, and saying to Ridley, 'Courage, brother Ridley! We shall light such a candle this day that, by God's grace, shall never be put out.' This was zeal.

All the greatest missionaries

This zeal was also the characteristic of all the greatest missionaries. You see it in Dr Judson, in Carey, in Morrison, in Schwartz, in Williams, in Brainerd, in Elliott. You see it in none more brightly than in Henry Martyn. Here was a man who had reached the highest scholastic honours that Cambridge could bestow. Whatever profession he chose to follow, he had the most dazzling prospects of success. He turned his back upon it all. He chose to preach the gospel to poor unreasonable heathen. He went forth to an early grave, in a foreign land. He said when he got there and saw the condition of the people, 'I would be willing to be torn in pieces, if I could only hear the sobs of repentance — I could see the eyes of faith directed to the Redeemer!' This was zeal.

Our Lord and Saviour Jesus Christ

But let us look away from all earthly examples — remember that zeal was pre-eminently the characteristic of our Lord and Saviour Jesus Christ himself. It was written of him hundreds of years before he came upon earth that he 'was clad with zeal as a cloak', and 'zeal for your house has eaten me up'. And his own words were 'My food is to do the will of him who sent me, and to finish his work' (Isaiah 59:17; Psalm 69:9; John 4:34).

Where shall we begin, if we try to give examples of his zeal? Where should we end, once we had begun? Trace all the narratives of his life in the four Gospels. Read all the history of what he was from the beginning of his ministry to the end. Surely if there ever was one who was all zeal, it was our great Example — our Head — our High Priest — the great Shepherd of our profession, the Lord Jesus Christ.

If these things are true, we should not only beware of running down zeal, but we should also beware of allowing zeal to be run down in our presence. It may be badly directed, and then it becomes a curse — but it may be turned to the highest and best ends, and then it is a mighty blessing. Like fire, it is one of the best of servants — but, like fire also, if not well directed, it may be the worst of masters. Do not listen to those people who talk of zeal as weakness and enthusiasm. Do not listen to those who see no beauty in missions, who laugh at all attempts at the conversion of souls, who call societies for sending the gospel to the world useless, and who look upon city missions, visiting and open-air preaching, as nothing but foolishness and fanaticism. Beware, lest in joining a cry of that kind you condemn the Lord Jesus Christ himself. Beware lest you speak against the one who has 'suffered for us, leaving us an example, that you should follow his steps' (1 Peter 2:21).

Yes! I fear there are many professing Christians who, if they had lived in the days when our Lord and his Apostles walked upon earth, would have called him and all his followers zealots and fanatics. There are many, I fear, who have more in common with Annas and Caiaphas, with Pilate and Herod, with Festus and Agrippa, with Felix and Gallio, than with Paul and the Lord Jesus Christ.

When is a man truly zealous in religion?

I now pass on to the second thing I proposed to speak of. When is a man truly zealous in religion?

There never was a grace of which Satan has not made a counterfeit. There never was a coin issued from the mint that forgers did not at once coin something very similar. It was one of Nero's cruel practices first to sew Christians into the skins of wild beasts, and then bait them with dogs. It is one of Satan's devices to place distorted copies of the believer's graces before the eyes of men, and so bring the true graces into contempt. No grace has suffered so much in this way as zeal. Of none perhaps are there so many shams and counterfeits. We must therefore clear the ground of all rubbish on this question. We must find out when zeal in religion is really good, and true, and of God.

According to knowledge

If zeal is true zeal, it will be zeal according to knowledge. It must not be a blind, ignorant zeal. It must be a calm, reasonable, intelligent principle, which can show the warrant of Scripture for every step it takes. The unconverted Jews had zeal. Paul says, 'I bear them witness that they have a zeal for God, but not according to knowledge' (Romans 10:2). Saul had zeal when he was a persecuting Pharisee. He says himself, in one of his addresses to the Jews, 'I was zealous toward God as you all are today' (Acts 22:3). Manasseh had zeal in the days when he was an idolater. The man who threw his own children into the fire, who gave up the fruit of his body to Moloch, to atone for the sin of his soul — that man had zeal. James and John had zeal when they would have called down fire on a Samaritan village. But our Lord rebuked them. Peter had zeal when he drew his sword and cut off the ear of Malchus. But he was quite wrong. Bonner and Gardiner had zeal when they burned Latimer and Cranmer. Were they not earnest? Let us do them justice. They were zealous, though it was for a false religion.

The members of the Inquisition in Spain had zeal when they tortured men, and put them to horrible deaths because they would not forsake the gospel. Yes! They marched men and women to the stake in solemn procession and called it 'an act of faith', and believed they were doing a service for God. The Hindus, who used to lie down before the car of Juggernaut and allow their bodies to be crushed under its wheels: did they not have zeal? The Indian widows, who used to burn themselves on the funeral pile of their deceased husbands; the Roman Catholics, who persecuted to death the Vaudois and Albigenses, and cast down men and women from rocks and precipices because they were heretics: did they not have zeal? The Saracens, the Crusaders, the Jesuits, the Anabaptists of Munster — did they not all have zeal? Yes! Yes! I do not deny it. All these had zeal beyond question. They were all zealous. They were all very fervent. But their zeal was not such zeal as God approves — it was not zeal according to knowledge.

From true motives

If zeal is true, it will be a zeal from true motives. Such is the subtlety of the heart that men will often do right things from wrong motives. Amaziah and Joash, kings of Judah, are striking proofs of this. In the same way a man may have zeal about things that are good and right but from second-rate motives, and not from a desire to please God. And such zeal is worth nothing. It is impure silver. It is utterly inadequate when placed in the balance of God. Man looks only at the action: God looks at the motive. Man only thinks of the quantity of work done: God considers the doer's heart.

There is such a thing as zeal from *party spirit*. It is quite possible for a man to be unwearied in promoting the interest of his own church or denomination, and yet to have no grace in his own heart; to be ready to die for the peculiar opinions of his brand of Christianity, and yet have no real love for Christ. Such was the zeal of the Pharisees. They 'travel land and sea to win one proselyte, and when he is won, you make him twice as much a son of hell as yourselves' (Matthew 23:15). This zeal is not true zeal.

There is such a thing as zeal from *mere selfishness*. There are times when it is in men's interest to be zealous in religion. Power and patronage are sometimes given to godly men. The good things of the world are sometimes to be attained by wearing a cloak of religion. And whenever this is the case there is no lack of false zeal. Such was the zeal of Joab, when he served David.

There is such a thing as zeal from the *love of praise*. Such was the zeal of Jehu, when he was putting down the worship of Baal. Remember how he met Jonadab the son of Rechab, and said, 'Come with me, and see my zeal for the LORD' (2 Kings 10:16). Such is the zeal that Bunyan refers to in *Pilgrim's Progress*, when he speaks of some who went 'for praise' to mount Zion. Some people feed on the praise of their fellow-creatures. They would rather have it from Christians than have none at all.

It is a sad and humbling proof of man's corruption that there is no degree of self-denial and self-sacrifice to which men may not go from false motives. It does not follow that a man's religion is true because he 'gives his body to be burned', or because he 'gives his goods to feed the poor'. The apostle Paul tells us that a man may do this and yet not have true love (1 Corinthians 13:1 etc.) It does not follow that, because men go into a wilderness and become hermits, they know what true self-denial is. It does not follow that, because people enclose themselves in monasteries and nunneries, or become 'sisters of charity' and 'sisters of mercy', they know what true crucifixion of the flesh and self-sacrifice is in the sight of God. All these things people may do from wrong principles. They may do them from wrong motives — to satisfy a secret pride and love of notoriety — but not from the true motive of zeal for the glory of God. All such zeal, let us understand, is false. It is of the earth, and not of heaven.

According to God's mind, and sanctioned in God's Word

If zeal is true, it will be a zeal about things according to God's mind, and sanctioned by plain examples in God's Word. Take, for one instance, that highest and best kind of zeal — I mean zeal *for our own growth in personal holiness.* Such zeal will make a man feel incessantly that sin is the mightiest of all evils, and conformity to Christ the greatest of all blessings. It will make him feel that there is nothing that ought not to be done, in order to keep up a close walk with God. It will make him willing to cut off the right hand, or pluck out the right eye, or make any sacrifice, if only he can attain a closer communion with Jesus. Isn't this just what you see in the apostle Paul? He says, 'I discipline my body and bring it into subjection, lest, when I have preached to others, I myself should become disqualified'; 'I do not count myself to have apprehended; but one thing I do, forgetting those things which are behind and reaching forward to those things which are ahead, I press toward the goal' (1 Corinthians 9:27; Philippians 3:13-14).

Take, for another instance, zeal *for the salvation of souls.* Such zeal will make a man burn with desire to enlighten the darkness that covers the souls of multitudes, and to bring every man, woman and child he sees to the knowledge of the gospel. Isn't this what you see in the Lord Jesus? It is said that he neither gave himself nor his disciples much spare time and at times they didn't even have a chance to eat (Mark 6:31). Isn't this what you see in the apostle Paul? He says, 'I have become all things to all men, that I might by all means save some' (1 Corinthians 9:22).

Take, for another instance, zeal *against evil practices*. Such zeal will make a man hate everything that God hates, such as drunkenness, slavery, or infanticide, and long to sweep it from the face of the earth. It will make him jealous of God's honour and glory, and look on everything that robs him of it as an offence. Isn't this what you see in Phinehas, the son of Eleazar? Or in Hezekiah and Josiah, when they put down idolatry?

Take, for another instance, zeal *for maintaining the doctrines of the gospel*. Such zeal will make a man hate unscriptural teaching, just as he hates sin. It will make him regard religious error as a pestilence that must be checked, whatever the cost may be. It will make him scrupulously careful about every word in the counsel of God, lest by some omission the whole gospel should be spoiled. Isn't this what you see in Paul at Antioch, when he withstood Peter to his face and said he was to be blamed? (Galatians 2:11). These are the kind of things that true zeal is made of. Such zeal, let us understand, is honourable before God.

Tempered with love

Furthermore, if zeal is true, it will be a zeal tempered with love. It will not be a bitter zeal. It will not be a fierce hatred of people. It will not be a zeal that is ready to take the sword and to lash out with carnal weapons. The weapons of true zeal are not carnal, but spiritual. True zeal will hate sin, and yet love the sinner. True zeal will hate heresy, and yet love the heretic. True zeal will long to smash the idol, but deeply pity the idolater. True zeal will detest every kind of wickedness, but labour to do good even to the vilest of sinners.

True zeal will warn as Paul warned the Galatians and yet feel tenderly, as a nurse or a mother over erring children. It will expose false teachers, as Jesus did the Scribes and Pharisees, and yet weep tenderly as Jesus did over Jerusalem when he came near to it for the last time. True zeal will be decisive, as a surgeon dealing with a diseased limb; but true zeal will be gentle, as one who is dressing the wounds of a brother. True zeal will speak truth boldly, like Athanasius against the world, and not care who is offended; but in its voice true zeal will endeavour to 'speak the truth in love'.

Joined to a deep humility

If zeal is true, it will be joined to a deep humility. A truly zealous man will be the last to discover the greatness of his own attainments. All that he is and does will come so immensely short of his own desires, that he will be filled with a sense of his own weakness and amazed to think that God should work through him at all. Like Moses, when he came down from the Mount, he will not know that his face shines. Like the righteous in the twenty-fifth chapter of Matthew, he will not be aware of his own good works. Dr Buchanan is someone who is highly respected in all the churches. He was one of the first to take up the cause of the perishing heathen. He literally spent himself, body and mind, in labouring to arouse sleeping Christians to see the importance of missions. Yet he says in one of his letters, 'I do not know that I ever had what Christians call zeal.' Whitefield was one of the most zealous preachers of the gospel the world has ever seen. Fervent in spirit, instant in season and out of season, he was a burning and shining light, and turned thousands to

God. Yet he says after preaching for thirty years, 'Lord, help me to begin to begin.'

M'Cheyne was one of the greatest blessings that God ever gave to the Church of Scotland. He was a minister who insatiably desired the salvation of souls. Few men ever did so much good as he did, though he died at the age of twenty-nine. Yet he says in one of his letters, 'No one but God knows what an abyss of corruption is in my heart. It is perfectly wonderful that God could ever bless such a ministry.' We may be very sure that where there is self-conceit there is little true zeal.

I ask my readers to particularly remember the description of true zeal that I have just given. Zeal according to knowledge; zeal from true motives; zeal warranted by scriptural examples; zeal tempered with love; zeal accompanied by deep humility; this is true genuine zeal — this is the kind of zeal which God approves. You and I need never be afraid of having too much of such zeal.

I ask you to remember the description because of the times in which you live. Beware of supposing that sincerity alone can ever make up true zeal — that earnestness, however ignorant, makes a man a really zealous Christian in the sight of God. There is a generation in these days that makes an idol of what it is pleased to call seriousness in religion. These men will not accept there is any fault in a man who is serious. Whatever his theological opinions may be — if he is a serious man, that is enough for these people, and we are to ask no more. They tell you we should have nothing to do with minute points of doctrine and with questions of words and names, about which Christians are not agreed. Is the man a serious man? If he is, we ought to be satisfied. Seriousness in their eyes covers over a multitude of sins. I warn you solemnly to beware of this dubious doctrine. In the name of the gospel, and in the name of the Bible, I enter my protest against the theory that mere seriousness can make a man a truly zealous and pious man in the sight of God.

These idolaters of seriousness would make us believe that God has not given us a standard of truth and error, or that the true standard, the Bible, is so obscure that no man can find out what truth is by simply reading it. They pour contempt upon the Word, the written Word, and therefore they must be wrong.

These idolaters of seriousness would make us condemn every witness for the truth, and every opponent of false teaching from the time of the Lord Jesus down to this day. The Scribes and Pharisees were serious, and yet our Lord opposed them. And shall we dare even to hint the thought that they ought to have been let alone? Queen Mary was serious in restoring the Roman Catholic religion and trying to put down Protestantism, and yet godly brothers who believed in Christ in truth and seriousness opposed her to the death. And shall we dare to say that since both parties were 'serious' both were in the right? The devil-worshippers and idolaters of today are serious and yet our missionaries labour to expose their errors. And shall we dare say that seriousness would take them to heaven, and that missionaries to heathens and Roman Catholics should stay at home? Are we really going to admit that the Bible does not show us what is truth? Are we really going to put a mere vague thing called seriousness in the place of Christ and maintain that no serious man can be wrong? God forbid that we should give way to such doctrine! I shrink with horror from such theology. I warn men solemnly to beware of being carried away by it for it is common and most seductive in this day. Beware of it, for it is only a new form of an old error — that old error which says that a man who lives a serious and righteous life can't be wrong.

Admire zeal. Seek after zeal. Encourage zeal. But see that your own zeal is true. See that the zeal that you admire in others is a zeal based on knowledge — a zeal from right motives — a zeal that can bring chapter and verse out of the Bible for its foundation. Any zeal but this is but a false fire. It is not ignited by the Holy Spirit.

Why is it good for a man to be zealous?

I now pass on to the third thing I proposed to speak of. Let me show why it is good for a man to be zealous. It is certain that God never gave man a commandment that was not in man's interest to obey. He never gave his believing people a teaching that they would not find their highest happiness to follow after. This is true of all the instructions about the Christian character. Perhaps it is pre-eminently true in the case of zeal.

Zeal is good for a Christian's own soul

We all know that exercise is good for the health, and that regular exercise of our muscles and limbs promotes our bodily comfort, and increases bodily strength. None have so much enjoyment of Christ as those who are ever zealous for his glory, watchful over their own walk, sensitive to their own consciences, full of concern about the souls of others, and ever watching, working, labouring and striving to expand the knowledge of Jesus Christ on earth. Such men live in the full light of the sun, and therefore their hearts are always warm. Such men water others and therefore they are watered themselves. Their hearts are like a garden daily refreshed by the dew of the Holy Spirit. They honour God, and so God honours them.

I want to be sure that everyone understands what I am saying. I do not want to appear to speak thoughtlessly of any believer. I know that 'the Lord takes pleasure in his people' (Psalm 149:4). There is not one, from the least to the greatest — from the smallest child in the kingdom of God, to the oldest warrior in the battle against Satan — there is not one in whom the Lord Jesus Christ does not take great pleasure. We are all his children — and however weak and feeble some of us may be, as a father has compassion on his children, so the LORD has compassion on those who fear him (Psalm 103:13). We are all the plants of his own planting; and though many of us are poor, weak exotic plants, scarcely staying alive in foreign soil — yet as the gardener loves that which his hands have raised, so does the Lord Jesus love the poor sinners that trust in him. But while I say this, I do also believe that the Lord takes special pleasure in those who are zealous for him, in those who give their body, soul and spirit to extend his glory in this world. To them he reveals himself, in a way different than to others. To them he shows things that other men never see. He blesses the work of their hands. He commends them with spiritual contentment that others have only heard about. They are men after his own heart, for they are men more like himself than others. No one has such joy and peace in believing, no one has such tangible contentment in their religion, no one has so much of heaven on earth, no one sees and feels so much of the compassion of the gospel as those who are zealous, serious, devoted Christians. For the sake of our own souls, if there were no other reason, it is good to be zealous, to be very zealous in our religion.

Zeal is good for the professing church

As zeal is good for ourselves individually, so it is good for the professing church of our Lord Jesus Christ generally. Nothing is so effective in keeping true religion alive as the yeast of zealous Christians scattered throughout the church. Like salt, they prevent the whole body from falling into a state of decay. Only men like this can revive churches that are about to die. It is impossible to overestimate the debt that all Christians owe to zeal. The greatest mistake the leaders of a church can make is to drive zealous men out of its congregation. By doing so they drain out the life-blood of the system, and advance the church's decline and death.

God delights in honouring zeal. Look through the list of Christians who have been used most mightily by God. Who are the men that have left the deepest and most indelible marks on the church of their day? Who are the men that God has generally honoured to build up the walls of his Zion, and also to fight the enemy at the gate? He does not use men of learning and literary talent as readily as men of zeal.

Latimer was not such a deeply-read scholar as Cranmer or Ridley. He could not quote from memory about the early church, as they did. He refused to be drawn into arguments about church history. He stuck to his Bible. Yet it is clear that no English Reformer left such a lasting impression on the nation as Latimer did. And what was the reason? His simple zeal.

Baxter, the Puritan, was not equal to some of his contemporaries in intellectual gifts. He in no way could stand on a level with Manton or Owen. Yet few men probably exercised so wide an influence on the generation in which he lived. And what was the reason? His burning zeal.

Whitefield, and Wesley, and Berridge, and Venn were inferior in mental attainments to Butler and Watson. But they produced effects on the people of this country which fifty Butlers and Watsons would probably never have produced. They saved the Church of England from ruin. And what was one secret of their power? Their zeal.

These men stood up front at turning points in the history of the church. They remained unmoved during storms of opposition and persecution. It could be said that:

They were not afraid to stand alone.
They did not care if their motives were misinterpreted.
They considered everything a loss for the sake of the truth.
Each one of them were eminently men of one thing: and that one thing was to advance the glory of God, and to declare his truth in the world.

They were all on fire, and so they lighted others.

They were wide awake, and so awakened others.

They were always working, and so shamed others into working too.

They came down upon men, like Moses from the mountain.

They shone as if they had been in the presence of God.

They carried with them, everywhere they walked in the world, something of the atmosphere and savour of heaven itself.

There is a sense in which it may be said that zeal is contagious. Nothing is more useful to the professors of Christianity than to see a real live Christian, a thoroughly zealous man of God. They may speak reproachfully to him; they may criticize him; they may pick holes in his conduct; they may look at him suspiciously; they may not understand him any more than men understand a new phenomena in the heavens when it appears; but by degrees so slight as to be virtually imperceptible, a zealous man does them good. He opens their eyes. He makes them feel their own indifference. He makes their own great darkness visible. He compels them to see their own emptiness. He compels them to think, whether they like it or not: What are we doing? Are we nothing better than a vegetable that grows out of the ground?

It may be a sad truth that one sinner destroys many good people; but it is also a blessed truth that one zealous Christian can do a lot of good. Yes; one single zealous man in a town, one zealous man in a congregation, one zealous man in a community, one zealous man in a family, may be a great blessing.

How many useful ministries does such a man get going! How much Christian activity he often calls into being that would otherwise have remained dormant! How many fountains he opens that would have otherwise been sealed! Truly there is a deep mine of truth in the words of the apostle Paul to the Corinthians: 'Your zeal has stirred up the majority' (2 Corinthians 9:2).

Zeal is good for the world

As zeal is good for the church and for individuals, so zeal is good for the world. Where would the missionary work be if it was not for zeal? Where would our city missions and school missions be if it was not for zeal? Where would our evangelistic outreach programme be without zeal? Without zeal, who would be willing to go and root out sin and ignorance, and find the dark places of the earth, and recover poor lost souls? Where would all these glorious instruments for good be if it was not for Christian zeal? Zeal called many of these institutions into being, and zeal keeps them at work when they have begun. Zeal gathers a few despised men, and makes them the nucleus of many a powerful ministry. Zeal prevents man from becoming lazy and sleepy when the ministry is large and begins to receive favour from the world. Zeal raises up men to go out, putting their lives in their hands. Zeal supplies their replacements when their lives are taken from them and they go home to heaven.

What would become of the ignorant masses who crowd the streets and alleys of our overgrown cities if it were not for Christian zeal? Governments can do nothing with them: they cannot make laws that will confront the evil. The vast majority of professing Christians have no eyes to see it; like the priest and the Levite, they pass by on the other side. But zeal has eyes to see, and a heart to feel, and a head to devise, and a tongue to plead, and hands to work, and feet to travel, in order to rescue poor souls and raise them from their fallen state.

Zeal does not stand poring over difficulties, but simply says, 'Here are some souls that are perishing, and we will do something.' Zeal does not shrink back because there are Anakites in the way: it looks over their heads, like Moses on Pisgah, and says, 'We will possess the land.' Zeal does not wait for company and delay until good works are fashionable: it goes forward like one who is deserted, and trusts that others will follow eventually. Yes, the world knows very little what a debt it owes to Christian zeal. How much crime it has restrained! How much disobedience it has prevented! How much public discontent it has calmed! How much obedience to the law and love of order it has produced! How many souls it has saved! Yes! and I believe we know very little of what might be accomplished if every Christian was a zealous man! How much if more ministers were zealous! How much if more laymen were more zealous! Oh, for the world's sake, as well as your own, resolve, work, strive to be a zealous Christian!

Let every one who professes to be a Christian beware of suppressing zeal. Seek it. Cultivate it. Try to enlarge the fire in your own heart, and the hearts of others, but never, never stop it. Beware of throwing cold water on zealous souls, whenever you meet with them. Beware of nipping this precious gift in the bud when it first shoots up. If you are a parent, beware of suppressing it in your children. If you are a husband, beware of stopping it in your wife. If you are a brother, beware of restraining it in your sisters — and if you are a minister, beware of checking it in the members of your congregation. It is a shoot of heaven's own planting. Beware of crushing it, for Christ's sake.

Zeal may make mistakes. Zeal may need directing. Zeal may lack guiding, controlling and advising. Like the elephants on ancient fields of battle, it may sometimes injure its own side. But zeal does not need damping in a wretched, cold, corrupt, miserable world like this. Zeal, like John Knox tearing down the Scottish monasteries, may hurt the feelings of narrow-minded and sleepy Christians. It may offend the prejudices of those old-fashioned religionists who hate everything new, and (like those who wanted soldiers and sailors to go on wearing pigtails) abhor all change. But zeal in the end will be justified by its results. Zeal, like John Knox, in the long run will do infinitely more good than harm. There is little danger of there ever being too much zeal for the glory of God. God forgive those who think there is! You know little of human nature. You forget that sickness is far more contagious than health, and that it is much easier to catch a cold than to give warmth.

Depend on it, the church seldom needs a bridle, but often needs a spur. It seldom needs to be restrained; it often needs to be urged on.

Applying these truths to ourselves

And now, in conclusion, let me try to apply this subject to the conscience of every person reading this.

It is a warning subject, an arousing subject, an encouraging subject, according to the state of our hearts. I hope, by God's help, to give every reader his portion.

A warning

First of all, let me offer a warning to all who sit in church and yet have not made a clear profession of Christianity. There are millions, I fear, in this condition. If you are one, the subject before you is full of solemn warning. Oh, that the Lord in mercy may incline your heart to receive it!

I ask you, then, with all love, 'Where is your zeal in Christianity?' With the Bible opened before me I ask boldly. But with your life before me, I tremble at what your answer will be. I ask again: 'Where is your zeal for the glory of God? Where is your zeal for sharing Christ's gospel to an evil world?' Zeal, which was the characteristic of the Lord Jesus — zeal, which is the characteristic of the angels — zeal, which shines forth in all the brightest Christians — where is your zeal, unconverted reader?

Where your zeal? You know it is nowhere at all; you know you
see no value in it; you know it is scorned and rejected as evil by
you and your companions; you know it has no place, no share,
no home in the religion of your soul. It is not that you don't
know what it is to be zealous. You have zeal, but it is all
misapplied. It is all earthly: it is all about the things of this age.
It is not zeal for the glory of God; it is not zeal for the salvation
of souls. Yes, many a man has zeal for the newspaper, but not
for the Bible — zeal for the daily reading of the news, but no
zeal for the daily reading of God's blessed Word. Many a man
has zeal for his chequebook and other business books, but no
zeal about the Book of Life and the last great accounting at the
Great White Judgement Throne; zeal about gold, but no zeal
about the unsearchable riches of Christ. Many a man has zeal
about his earthly concerns — his family, his pleasures, his daily
pursuits; but no zeal about God, and heaven, and eternity.

If this is the state of anyone who is reading this, awake, I do
implore you, to see your gross folly. You cannot live for ever.
You are not ready to die. You are utterly unfit for the company
of saints and angels. Awake, be zealous and repent! Awake to
see the harm you are doing! You are putting arguments in the
hands of unbelievers by your shameful coldness. You are pull-
ing down as fast as ministers build. You are helping the devil.
Awake, be zealous, and repent! Awake to see your childish inconsistency! What can be more worthy of zeal than eternal
things, than the glory of God, than the salvation of souls?

Surely it is good to labour for rewards that are temporal, but
it is a thousand times better to labour for those that are eternal.
Awake, be zealous, and repent! Go and read that long-neglected
Bible. Take up the blessed Book that you have, and perhaps
never use. Read that New Testament through. Do you find
nothing there to make you zealous — to make you serious about
your soul? Go and look at the cross of Christ. Go and see how

the Son of God there shed his precious blood for you — how he suffered and groaned and died for you — how he poured out his soul as an offering for sin, in order that you, sinful brother or sister, might not perish but have eternal life. Go and look at the cross of Christ and never rest until you feel some zeal for your own soul, some zeal for the glory of God, some zeal for sharing the gospel throughout the world. Once more I say: Awake, be zealous and repent!

Where is our zeal?

Let me, in the next place, say something to arouse those who make a profession of being committed Christians, and yet are lukewarm in their practice.

There are too many, I regret to say, in this state. If you are one, there is a lot in this subject that ought to lead you to a thorough searching of your heart.

Let me speak to your conscience. I also desire to put the question to you with all brotherly affection: Where is your zeal? Where is your zeal for the glory of God, and for the spreading of the gospel throughout the world? You know better than any-one else that your zeal is almost non-existent. You know that your zeal is nothing more than a feeble glimmering spark that just sits there and does no more — it is like a something 'ready to die' (Revelation 3:2). Surely, there is a fault somewhere, if this is the case. This state of things ought not to be. You, the child of God — you, redeemed at so glorious a price — you, ransomed with such precious blood — you, who are an heir of glory such as the world has never seen or spoken of — surely you ought to be a man of great zeal. Surely your zeal should not be so weak.

I feel deeply that this is a painful subject to talk about. I do it reluctantly, constantly remembering my own weakness.

Nevertheless, I must speak the truth. The plain truth is that many believers today seem so afraid of doing some harm that they hardly ever do anything good. There are many who are quick to object to something, but never take any action; they are truly lacking anything even like Christian fire. They are like the Dutch government officials recorded in the history of the eighteenth century who would never allow Marlborough to risk anything, and by their extreme caution prevented many victories from being won. Truly, in looking around the church of our Lord Jesus Christ, a man might sometimes think that God's kingdom had come, and God's will was being done upon earth, so small is the zeal that some believers show. It is vain to deny it. I do not need to go far for evidence. I point to the many missionary agencies that are trying to reach the heathen in foreign lands and even the lost of our own country, struggling and paralysed because of the lack of workers and funds. I ask you, 'Is this zeal?' I point to the false doctrine that is allowed to flourish in our churches and homes without any effort being made to stop it, while so-called believers look on, and are content with wishing that it wasn't that way. I ask, 'Is this zeal?' Would the apostles have been satisfied with such a state of things? We know they would not.

If the conscience of anyone who is reading this pleads guilty to being any part of the weaknesses I have just spoken of, I call on him in the name of the Lord, to wake up, be zealous, and repent. Don't let zeal be confined to those who are busy making money in the marketplace or the stock markets. Let us not be so zealous to pursue riches or to make new discoveries in the world but indifferent to send the gospel to the heathen, or to pluck Roman Catholics out of the coming fires of hell, or to share the gospel to those in our own country. Never has there been so many doors of opportunity opened — never has there been so many possibilities for doing good. I detest the squeamishness that refuses to help Christian ministries if there is an imperfection in the methods used to carry out the work. At this rate we would never do anything at all. Let us resist the feeling, if we are tempted by it. It is one of Satan's schemes. It is better to work with weak instruments than not to work at all. At all times try to do something for God and Christ — something against ignorance and sin. Give, teach, admonish, visit, pray, according as God enables you. Only make up your mind that everyone *can* do something and resolve that you, at any rate, *will* do something. If you have only one talent do not bury it in the ground. Try to live your life so as to be missed when you are gone. You can do more in twelve hours than most people have ever done on any day in their lives.

Think of *the precious souls* that are perishing while you are sleeping. Go ahead, if you want, and be taken up with your inward conflicts. Go on and analyse your own feelings and lament over your own vices, if you are so determined. But remember, all this time souls are going to hell, and you might be able to do something to save them by working, by giving, by writing, by begging, and by prayer. Oh, awake! Be zealous, and repent!

Think of *the shortness of time*. You will soon be gone. You will not have any opportunity for works of mercy in another world. In heaven there will be no uneducated people to instruct, and no unconverted to save. Whatever you do must be done now. Oh, when are you going to begin? Awake! Be zealous, and repent.

Think of *the devil*, and his zeal to destroy people. It was a solemn saying of Bernard when he stated that 'Satan would rise up in judgement against some people at the last day, because he had shown more zeal to ruin souls than they had to save them.' Awake! Be zealous, and repent.

Think of *your Saviour*, and all his zeal for you. Think of him in Gethsemane and on Calvary, shedding his blood for sinners.

Think of his life, death and sufferings. All this he has done for you. What are you doing for him? Oh, resolve that for the time to come you will spend and be spent for Christ! Awake! Be zealous and repent.

An encouragement

Last of all, let me encourage all my readers who are truly zealous Christians.

I have but one request to make, and that is that you will persevere. I do implore you to maintain your zeal and never let it go. I do urge you never to stop doing the things you did at first, never to leave your first love, never let it be said of you that the things you did in the first part of your Christian life were better than the things you did in your latter years. Beware of cooling down. All you have to do is to be lazy, and to sit still, and you will soon lose all your zeal. You will soon become another man from what you are now. Oh, don't think that this is a needless exhortation!

It may be true that wise young believers are very rare. But it is just as true that zealous old believers are also very rare. Never allow yourself to think that you can do too much — that you can work too hard and long for the cause of Christ. For every man who does too much I will show you a thousand who don't do enough. Instead think that 'the night is coming when no one can work' (John 9:4). Give, teach, visit, work and pray, as if you were doing it for the last time.

Take to heart the words of a zealous Christian, who said, when told that he ought to rest a little, 'What should we rest for? Don't we have all eternity to rest?'

Do not fear the reproach of men. Do not faint because you are sometimes abused. Don't let it bother you if you are sometimes called a bigot, a zealot, a fanatic, a crazy person, and a fool. There is nothing disgraceful in these titles. They have often been given to the best and wisest of men. If you are only zealous when you receive praise for it, if the wheels of your zeal must be oiled by the world's commendation, your zeal will be short-lived. Do not care for the praise or the frown of man. There is only one thing worth caring for, and that is the praise of God. There is only one question worth asking about our actions: 'How will they appear in the Day of Judgement?'

9.
Freedom

'Therefore if the Son makes you free, you shall be free indeed'
(John 8:36).

The subject before us now deserves our attention. It should ring in the ears of every person like the sound of a trumpet. We live in a land that is the very cradle of freedom. But are we free ourselves?

The question is one that demands special attention to the present state of public opinion. The minds of many are absorbed in politics. Yet there is a freedom, within the reach of us all, which few, I am afraid, ever think of — a freedom independent of all political changes — a freedom which neither the prevailing government, nor the cleverest politician can bestow. This is the freedom about which I now write. Do we know anything of it? Are we free?

In opening this subject, there are three points that I wish to present.

I will show, in the first place, *the general excellence of freedom.*

I will show, in the second place, *the best and truest kind of freedom.*

I will show, in the last place, *the way in which the best kind of freedom may become your own.*

Let no reader think for a moment that this is going to be a political paper. I am no politician: I have no politics but those of the Bible. The only party I care for is the Lord's side: show me where that is, and it will have my support. The only election I am anxious about is the election of grace. My one desire is that sinners should make their own calling and election sure. The liberty I desire above all things to make known, and further, is the glorious liberty of the children of God. The government I care to support is the government that is on the shoulder of my Lord and Saviour Jesus Christ. I want every knee to bow before Christ, and every tongue to confess that he is Lord. I ask for your attention while I discuss these subjects closely. If you are not free, I want to guide you into true liberty. If you are free, I want you to know the full value of your freedom.

The general excellence of freedom

The first thing I have to show is the general excellence of freedom. On this point some readers may think it needless to say anything: they imagine that all men know the value of freedom, and that to dwell on it is merely a waste of time. I do not agree with such people at all. I believe that myriads of our countrymen know nothing of the blessings that they enjoy in their own land: they have grown up from infancy to manhood in the midst of freedom. They do not have the least idea of the state of things in other countries: they are similarly ignorant of those two worst kinds of tyranny — the crushing tyranny of a cruel military dictator, and the intolerant tyranny of an unreasoning mob. In short, many of us know nothing of the value of liberty, merely because we have been born in the middle of it, and have never been without it for a moment.

I call on every one who is reading this to remember that liberty is one of the greatest earthly blessings that man can have this side of the grave.

We live in a land where *our bodies* are free. So long as we don't hurt someone's body, or property, or character, no one can touch us: the poorest man's house is his castle.

We live in a land where *our actions* are free. So long as we support ourselves, we are free to choose what we will do, where we will go, and how we will spend our time.

We live in a land where *our consciences* are free. So long as we are quiet about our beliefs, and do not interfere with others, we are free to worship God as we please, and no man can compel us to take his way to heaven.

We live in a land where *no foreigner rules over us.* Our laws are made and altered by people like ourselves, and our leaders live by our side, bone of our bone and flesh of our flesh.

In short, we have every kind of freedom to an extent that no other nation on earth can equal. We have personal freedom, civil freedom, religious freedom and national freedom. We have free bodies, free consciences, free speech, free thought, free action, free Bibles, a free press and free homes. How vast is this list of privileges! How endless are the comforts that it contains! Their full value perhaps can never be known. It was well said by the Jewish rabbis of long ago, 'If the sea were ink and the world parchment, it would never serve to describe the praises of liberty.'

The desire for this freedom has been the most fertile cause of misery to nations in every age of the world. What reader of the Bible can fail to remember the sorrows of the children of Israel, when they were slaves under Pharaoh in Egypt, or under the Philistines in Canaan? What student of history needs to be reminded of the woes inflicted on the Netherlands, Poland, Spain and Italy by the hands of foreign oppressors, or the Inquisition? Who, even in our own time, has not heard of that enormous fountain of wretchedness, the slavery of the Negro race? Certainly no misery is so great as the misery of slavery.

To win and preserve freedom has been the aim of many national struggles that have deluged the earth with blood. Liberty has been the cause for which myriads of Greeks, and Romans, and Germans, and Poles, and Swiss, and Englishmen, and Americans have willingly laid down their lives. No price has been thought too great to pay in order that nations might be free.

The champions of freedom in every age have been justly esteemed among the greatest benefactors of mankind. Such names as Moses and Gideon in Jewish history, the Spartan Leonidas, the Roman Horatius, the German Martin Luther, the Swedish Gustavus Vasa, the Swiss William Tell, the Scots Robert Bruce and John Knox, the English Alfred and Hampden and the Puritans, and the American George Washington are deservedly embalmed in history, and will never be forgotten. To be the mother of many patriots is the highest praise of a nation.

The enemies of freedom in every age have been rightly regarded as the pests and nuisances of their times. Such names as Pharaoh in Egypt, Dionysius at Syracuse, Nero at Rome, Charles IX in France, bloody Mary in England, are names that will never be rescued from disgrace. The public opinion of mankind will never cease to condemn them, on the one ground that they would not let people be free.

But why should I dwell on these things? There would not be enough time and space to attempt to say a tenth of what might be said in praise of freedom. What are the annals of history but a long record of conflicts between the friends and foes of liberty? Where is the nation on the earth that has attained greatness, and left its mark on the world, without freedom? Which are the countries on the face of the globe at this very moment that are making the most progress in trade, in arts, in sciences, in civilisation, in philosophy, in morals, in social happiness? Precisely those countries in which there is the greatest amount of true freedom. Which are the countries this very day where there is the greatest amount of internal misery, where we hear continually of secret plots, and murmuring, and discontent, and attempts on life and property? Precisely those countries where freedom does not exist or exists only in name — where men are treated as slaves, and are not allowed to think and act for themselves. No wonder that Patrick Henry, a mighty American statesman of the eighteenth century, declared on a great occasion to his assembled countrymen: 'Is life so dear, or peace so sweet, as to be purchased at the price of chains and slavery? Forbid it, Almighty God! I do not know what course others may take; but as for me, give me liberty or give me death!'

Let us beware of *undervaluing* the liberty we enjoy in this country of ours. I am sure this warning is necessary. There is, perhaps, no country on earth where there is so much grumbling and fault-finding as there is here. Men look at the perceived evils that they see around them, and exaggerate both their number and their intensity. They refuse to look at the countless blessings and privileges that surround us, or underrate their advantages. They forget that comparison should be applied to everything. With our faults and defects there is at this time no country on earth where there is so much liberty and happiness for all sections of the community, as there is here. They forget that as long as human nature is corrupt, it is vain to expect perfection here below. No laws or government whatever can possibly prevent a certain quantity of abuses and corruptions.

Once more then, I say, let us beware of undervaluing our liberty, and eagerly following every one who proposes sweeping changes. Changes are not always improvements. The old shoes may have some holes and defects, but the new shoes may pinch so much that we cannot walk at all. No doubt we might have better laws and government than we have: but I am quite sure we might easily have worse. At this very time there is no country on the face of the globe where there is so much care taken of the life, and health, and property, and character, and personal liberty of the poorest inhabitant, as there is in our country. Those who want to have more liberty would soon find, if they crossed the seas, that there is no country on earth where there is so much real liberty as our own.

But while I bid men not to undervalue our liberty, so also on the other hand I charge them not to *overvalue* it. Never forget that earthly slavery is not the only slavery, and earthly freedom is not the only freedom. What will you gain from being a citizen of a free country, if your soul is not free? What is the use of living in a free land like ours, with free thought, free speech, free action, free conscience, if you are a slave to sin, and a captive to the devil? Yes, there are tyrants whom no eye can see, as real and destructive as Pharaoh or Nero! There are chains that no hands can touch, as true and heavy and soul-withering as ever crushed the limbs of a slave! These are the tyrants I want you to remember now. These are the chains from which I want you to be free. By all means value your earthly liberty; but do not overvalue it. Look higher, further, than any earthly freedom. In the highest sense let us take care that 'we are free'.

The best and truest kind of freedom

The second thing I have to show is the truest and best kind of freedom. The freedom I speak of is a freedom that is within the reach of every child of Adam who is willing to have it. No power on earth can prevent a man or woman having it, if they have but the will to receive it. Tyrants may threaten and cast in prison, but they can do nothing to stop a person having this liberty. And, once our own, nothing can take it away. Men may torture us, banish us, hang us, behead us, burn us, but they can never tear from us true freedom. The poorest may have it no less than the richest; the most unlearned may have it as well as the most learned; and the weakest as well as the strongest. Laws cannot deprive us of it; the Roman Catholic Church cannot rob us of it. Once it is ours, it is an everlasting possession.

Now, what is this glorious freedom? Where is it to be found? What is it like? Who has obtained it for man? Who has it at this moment to bestow? I ask my readers to give me their attention, and I will supply a plain answer to these questions.

The true freedom I speak of is spiritual freedom — freedom of the soul. It is the freedom that Christ bestows freely on all true Christians. Those whom the Son makes free are free indeed: 'Where the Spirit of the Lord is, there is liberty' (2 Corinthians 3:17). Let men say what they please of the comparative freedom of monarchies and republics; let them struggle, if they will, for universal liberty, fraternity, and equality: we will never know the highest style of liberty until we are enrolled as citizens in the kingdom of God. We are ignorant of the best kind of freedom if we have not been set free by Christ.

Free from the guilt of sin

Those set free by Christ are free from the guilt of sin. That heavy burden of unforgiven sin, which lies so heavy on many consciences, no longer presses them down. Christ's blood has cleansed it all away. They feel pardoned, reconciled, justified and accepted in God's sight. They can look back to their old sins, however black and many, and say, 'You cannot condemn me.' They can look back on long years of carelessness and worldliness and say, 'Who can hold me accountable for anything in my past?' This is true liberty. This is to be free.

Free from the power of sin

Those set free by Christ are free from the power of sin. It no longer rules and reigns in their hearts, and overtakes them like a flood. Through the power of Christ's Spirit they restrain the deeds of their bodies, and crucify their flesh with its affections and lusts. Through his grace working in them they get the victory over their evil inclinations. The flesh may fight, but it does not conquer them; the devil may tempt and harass, but does not overcome them: they are no longer the slave of lusts and appetites, and passions, and moods. In all these things they are more than conquerors through him who loved them. This is true liberty. This is to be free.

Free from the cringing fear of God

Those set free by Christ are free from the cringing fear of God. They no longer look at him with dread and apprehension, as an offended Maker; they no longer hate him, and hide from him, like Adam did among the trees of the garden; they no longer tremble at the thought of his judgement. Through the Spirit of adoption that Christ has given them, they look on God as a reconciled Father, and rejoice in the thought of his love. They no longer feel his anger. They feel that when God the Father looks down upon them, he sees them in Christ and, unworthy as they are in themselves, is well pleased. This is true liberty. This is to be free.

Free from the fear of man

Those set free by Christ are free from the fear of man. They are no longer afraid of man's opinions, or care much what man thinks of them; they are also indifferent to his favour or hatred, his smile or his frown. They look away from man who can be seen, to Christ who is not seen, and having the favour of Christ, they care little for the condemnation of man. 'The fear of man' was once a snare to them. They trembled at the thought of what man would say, or think, or do: they dared not run counter to the fashions and customs of those around them; they shrank from the idea of standing alone. But the snare is now broken and they are delivered. This is true liberty. This is to be free.

Free from the fear of death

Those set free by Christ are free from the fear of death. They no longer look forward to it with silent dismay, as something horrible that they don't care to think of. Through Christ they can look this last enemy calmly in the face, and say, 'You cannot harm me.' They can look forward to all that comes after death — decay, resurrection, judgement and eternity — and yet not feel cast down. They can stand by the side of an open grave, and say, 'O death, where is your sting? O grave, where is your victory?' They can lay down on their deathbeds, and say, 'Though I walk through the valley of the shadow of death, I will fear no evil' (Psalm 23:4). 'Not a hair of my head will perish.' This is true liberty. This is to be free.

Free for ever

Best of all, those set free by Christ are free for ever. Once enrolled in the list of heavenly citizens, their names shall never be erased. Once presented with the freedom of Christ's kingdom, they will possess it for evermore. The highest privileges of this world's freedom can only endure for a lifetime; the freest citizen on earth must submit eventually to death, and lose his privilege for ever: but the privilege of Christ's people is eternal. They carry it down to the grave, and it still lives; they will rise again with it at the last day, and enjoy its privileges for evermore. This is true liberty. This is to be free.

Does anyone ask how and in what way Christ has obtained these mighty privileges for his people? You have a right to ask the question, and it is one that can never be answered too clearly. Give me your attention, and I will show you how Christ has made his people free.

The freedom of Christ's people has been procured, like all other freedoms, at a mighty cost and by a mighty sacrifice. Great was the bondage in which they were naturally held, and great was the price necessary to be paid to set them free: mighty was the enemy who claimed them as his captives, and it needed mighty power to release them out of his hands. But, blessed be God, there was enough grace, and enough power ready in Jesus Christ. He provided to the uttermost everything that was required to set his people free. The price that Christ paid for his people was nothing less than his own lifeblood. He became their Substitute, and suffered for their sins at the cross: he redeemed them from the curse of the law, by being made a curse for them (Galatians 3:13). He paid all their debt in his own person, by allowing the punishment that would bring them peace to be laid on him (Isaiah 53:5). He satisfied every possible demand of the law against them, by fulfilling its righteousness to the uttermost. He cleared them from every accusation of sin, by becoming sin for them (2 Corinthians 5:21). He fought their battle with the devil, and triumphed over him on the cross. As their Champion, he disarmed principalities and powers, and made a show of them openly on Calvary. In a word Christ, having given himself for us, has purchased the full right of redemption for us. Nothing can touch those to whom he gives freedom: their debts are paid, and paid a thousand times over; their sins are atoned for by a full, perfect and sufficient atonement. A divine Substitute's death meets completely the justice of God, and provides completely redemption for man.

Let us take a good look at this glorious plan of redemption, and take care to understand it. Ignorance on this point is one great secret of faint hopes, little comfort, and ceaseless doubts in the minds of Christians. Too many are content with a vague idea that Christ will somehow save sinners: but how or why they cannot tell. I protest against this ignorance. Let us set fully before our eyes the doctrine of Christ dying in our place — his substituted death — and rest our souls upon it. Let us grasp firmly the mighty truth that Christ on the cross:

> stood in the place of his people
> died for his people
> suffered for his people
> was counted a curse and sin for his people
> paid the debts of his people
> made restitution for his people
> became the insurance of his people
> became the representative of his people

And in this way Christ procured his people's freedom. Let us understand this clearly, and then we will see what a mighty privilege it is to be made free by Christ.

This is freedom that, above all others, is worth having. We can never value it too highly: there is no danger of overvaluing it. All other freedom is unsatisfying at the best, and a poor uncertain possession at any time. Christ's freedom alone can never be overthrown. It is secured by a covenant ordered in all things and sure: its foundations are laid in the eternal councils of God, and no foreign enemy can overthrow them. They are cemented and secured by the blood of the Son of God himself, and can never be destroyed. The freedom of nations often lasts no longer than a few centuries; the freedom that Christ gives to any one of his people is a freedom that will outlive this material universe.

This is the truest, highest kind of freedom. This is the freedom that in a changing, dying world, I want men to possess.

How the best kind of freedom can be ours

I have now to show, in the last place, the way in which the best kind of freedom is made our own. This is a point of vast importance, on account of the many mistakes that prevail about it. Thousands, perhaps, will agree that there is such a thing as spiritual freedom, and that Christ alone has purchased it for us; but when they come to the application of redemption, they go astray. They cannot answer the question, 'Who are those that Christ truly sets free?' And because they are lacking in any real knowledge about the answer, they sit still in their chains. I ask every reader to give me his attention once more, and I will try to throw a little light on the subject. The redemption that Christ has obtained is indeed useless, unless you know how the fruit of that redemption can become your own. You have read of the freedom by which Christ makes people free in vain, unless you understand how you yourself may have an interest in it.

We are not born Christ's freemen. The inhabitants of many a city enjoy privileges by virtue of their birthplace. Paul, who drew his first life-breath at Tarsus in Cilicia, could say to the Roman commander, 'I was born free.' But this is not the case with Adam's children, with regard to spiritual things. We are born slaves and servants of sin: we are by nature 'children of wrath' and destitute of any claim to heaven.

We are not made Christ's freemen by baptism. Every year there are many who are solemnly baptized in the name of the Trinity, who serve sin like slaves, and neglect Christ all of their days. Wretched indeed is that man's state of soul who can give no better evidence of his citizenship of heaven than the mere naked fact of his baptism!

We are not made Christ's freemen by mere membership of Christ's church. There are companies and corporations whose members are entitled to vast privileges, without any respect to their personal character, as long as their names are on the list of members. The kingdom of Christ is not a corporation like this. The grand test of belonging to it is personal character.

Let these things sink into our minds. Far be it from me to narrow the extent of Christ's redemption: the price he paid on the cross is sufficient for the whole world. Far be it from me to undervalue baptism or church membership: neither the ordinance that Christ appointed, nor the church that he maintains in the midst of a dark world, ought to be considered lightly. All I am contending is the absolute necessity of not being content with either baptism or church membership. If our religion stops short here it is unprofitable and unsatisfying. It needs something more than this to give us an interest in the redemption that Christ has purchased.

There is no other way to become Christ's freemen than that of simply believing. It is by faith, simple faith in him as our Saviour and Redeemer, that men's souls are made free. It is by receiving Christ, trusting Christ, committing ourselves to Christ, placing our whole weight on Christ — it is by this, and by no other plan, that spiritual liberty is made our own. Mighty as the privileges which Christ's freemen possess are, they all become a man's property on the day that he first believes. He may not yet know their full value, but they are all his own. He who believes in Christ is not condemned; rather he is justified, is born again, is an heir of God, and has everlasting life.

The truth before us is one of priceless importance. Let us cling to it openly and never let it go. If you desire peace of conscience, if you want inward rest and consolation, then lock on to the truth that faith is the grand secret of an interest in Christ's redemption. Take the simplest view of faith: beware of confusing your mind by complicated ideas about it. Follow holiness as closely as you can: seek the fullest and clearest evidence of the inward work of the Spirit. But in the matter of an interest in Christ's redemption, remember that faith stands alone. It is by believing, simply believing, that souls become free.

There is no more perfect doctrine than this to ideally suit the ignorant and the unlearned! Visit the poorest and humblest person who knows nothing of theology, tell him the story of the cross, and the good news about Jesus Christ, and his love to sinners; show him that there is freedom provided for him, as well as for the most learned in the land — freedom from guilt, freedom from the devil, freedom from condemnation, freedom from hell. And then tell him plainly, boldly, broadly, unreservedly, that this freedom may be all his own, if he will but trust Christ and believe.

There is no more perfect doctrine than this to ideally suit the sick and dying! Go to the bedside of the vilest sinner when death is coming near, and tell him lovingly that there is a hope even for him, if he can receive it. Tell him that Christ came into the world to save sinners, even the worst of them; tell him that Christ has done it all, paid it all, performed all, purchased all that the soul of man can possibly need for salvation. And then assure him that he, even he, may be freed at once from all his guilt, if he will only believe. Yes, say to him, in the words of Scripture, 'If you confess with your mouth the Lord Jesus and believe in your heart that God has raised him from the dead, you will be saved' (Romans 10:9).

Let us never forget that this is the point to which we must turn our own eyes, if we want to know whether we have a saving interest in Christ's redemption. Do not waste your time speculating whether you are elect, and converted, and a vessel of grace. Do not stand poring over the unprofitable question whether Christ died for you or not. Settle your thoughts on these simple questions: 'As a humble sinner, do I really trust in Christ? Do I throw myself at his feet? Do I believe?' Do not look to anything else. Look at this alone. Do not be afraid to rest your soul on plain texts and promises of Scripture. If you believe, you are free.

Conclusion

Now as I bring this chapter to a conclusion, let me affectionately press upon every reader the question that naturally grows out of the whole subject. Let me ask one plain question: 'Are you free?'

Are you free?

I do not know who or what type of person is reading this book. But this I do know, there never was a time when the question I press upon you was more completely necessary. Political freedom, civil freedom, commercial freedom, freedom of the press — all these, and a hundred other related subjects, are swallowing up men's attention. Few, very few, find time to think of spiritual freedom. Many, too many, forget that no man is so thoroughly a slave, whatever his position, as the man who serves sin.

Yes! There are thousands in this country who are slaves of beer and alcohol, slaves of lust, slaves of ambition, slaves of political party, slaves of money, slaves of gambling, slaves of fashion, or slaves of temper!

You may not see their chains with the naked eye, and they themselves may boast of their freedom; but, for all that, they are slaves through and through. Whether men like to hear it or not, the gambler and the drunkard, the covetous and the passionate, the glutton and the sensualist, are not free, but slaves. They are tied hand and foot by the devil. 'Whoever commits sins is a slave of sin' (John 8:34). He who boasts of freedom, while he is enslaved by lusts and passions, is going down to hell with a lie in his right hand.

Wake up and see these things, while health, and time, and life are granted to you. Don't let political struggles and party strife make you forget your precious soul. Take any side in politics you please, and honestly follow your conscientious convictions; but never, never forget that there is a freedom far higher and more lasting than any that politics can give you. Don't rest till liberty is your own. Don't rest till *your soul is free.*

Do you feel any desire to be free?

Do you find any longing within you for a higher, better freedom than this world can give — a freedom that will not die at your death, but will go with you beyond the grave? Then take the advice I give you this day. Seek Christ, repent, believe, and be free. Christ has a glorious liberty to bestow on all who humbly cry to him for freedom. Christ can take burdens off your heart, and remove the chains from your inner soul. 'If the Son makes you free, you shall be free indeed' (John 8:36).

Freedom like this is the secret of true happiness. None go through the world with such ease and contentment as those who are citizens of a heavenly country. Earth's burdens press lightly upon their shoulders; earth's disappointments do not crush them down as they do others; earth's duties and anxieties do not drink up their spirit. In their darkest hours they always have this sustaining to fall back on, 'I have something which makes me independent of this world: I am spiritually free.'

Freedom like this is the secret of being a good politician. In every age Christ's freemen have been the truest friends to law and order, and to measures for the benefit of the whole of mankind. Never, never let it be forgotten that hundreds of years ago the despised Puritans did more for the cause of real liberty than all the governments that ever ruled this land. The root of the most genuine patriotism is to be one of those whom Christ has made free.

Are you spiritually free?

Then rejoice, and be thankful for your freedom. Don't worry about the scorn and contempt of man: you don't have any reason to be ashamed of your religion or your Master. He whose citizenship is in heaven (Philippians 3:20), who has God for his

Father, and Christ for his Elder Brother, angels for his daily
guards, and heaven itself for his home, is one that is well provided for. No change of laws can add to his greatness: no ex-
tension of right or privilege can raise him higher than he stands
in God's sight. 'The lines have fallen to me in pleasant places;
yes, I have a good inheritance' (Psalm16:6). Grace now, and
the hope of glory hereafter, are more lasting privileges than the
power of voting in countries.

Are you free? Then stand firm in your liberty, and don't be
entangled again in the yoke of bondage. Don't listen to those
who by good words and fair speeches would draw you back to
the Roman Catholic Church. Beware of anyone who would try
to persuade you of the following points.

> Beware of anyone who would try to persuade you that there
> is any mediator but the one Mediator, Christ Jesus.
> Beware of anyone who would try to persuade you that there
> is any sacrifice but the one Sacrifice offered on Calvary.
> Beware of anyone who would try to persuade you that there
> is any priest but the great High Priest Emmanuel.
> Beware of anyone who would try to persuade you that there
> are any additions needed in worship but the savour of
> the name of the one who was crucified.
> Beware of anyone who would try to persuade you that there
> is any rule of faith and practice but God's Word.
> Beware of anyone who would try to persuade you that there
> is any confessional but the throne of grace.
> Beware of anyone who would try to persuade you that there
> is any effectual absolution but that which Christ bestows
> on the hearts of his believing people.
> Beware of anyone who would try to persuade you that there
> is any purgatory (place where man is to pay for his sins)
> but the one fountain open for all sins, the blood of Christ,
> to be used only while we are alive.

On all these points stand firm, and be on your guard. Scores of misguided teachers are trying to rob Christians of gospel liberty, and to bring back among us exploded superstitions. Resist them completely, and do not give way for a moment. Remember what the Roman Catholic Church was before the blessed Reformation. Remember at what mighty cost our martyred Reformers brought spiritual freedom to light by the gospel. Stand firm for this freedom like a man, and labour to hand it down to your children, whole and unimpaired.

Are you free? Then every day you live, think of the millions of your fellow creatures who are still bound hand and foot in spiritual darkness. Think of the millions of heathens who have not yet heard of Christ and salvation. Think of the Jews, scattered over the face of the earth, who are still waiting for their Messiah. Think of the millions of Roman Catholics who are still in captivity under the pope, and know nothing of true liberty, light and peace. Think of the myriads of your own fellow countrymen in our great cities, who, without the influence of Christ, are in reality heathens, and whom the devil is continually leading captive at his will. Think of them all, and feel for them. Think of them all, and say often to yourself: 'What can I do for them? How can I help to set them free?'

What! Shall it be proclaimed at the last day that Pharisees and Jesuits have travelled the sea and land to make proselytes? that politicians have united and laboured night and day to obtain worldly freedom and free trade? that philanthropists have travailed in soul for years to procure suppression of Negro slavery? And shall it appear at the same time that Christ's freemen have done little to rescue men and women from hell? Forbid it! Forbid it! Surely if the children of this world are zealous to promote earthly freedom, the children of God ought to be much more zealous to promote spiritual freedom. In the past, suffice it to say, we have been selfish and lazy in this matter. For the rest of our days let us use every effort to promote spiritual freedom. If we have tasted the blessings of freedom, let us spare no pains to make others free.

Are you free? Then look forward in faith and hope for good things yet to come. Free as we are from guilt and power of sin if we believe on Christ, we must surely feel every day that we are not free from its presence and the temptations of the devil. Redeemed as we are from the eternal consequences of the Fall, we must often feel that we are not yet redeemed from sickness and infirmity, from sorrow and from pain. No, indeed! Where is the freeman of Christ on earth who is not often painfully reminded that we are not yet in heaven? We are still in the body; we are still travelling through the wilderness of this world: we are not at home. We have shed many tears already, and probably we shall have to shed many more; we still have within us a poor weak heart: we are still liable to be assaulted by the devil. Our redemption has begun indeed, but it is not yet completed. We have redemption now in the root, but we do not have it in flower.

But let us take courage: there are better days still to come. Our great Redeemer and Liberator has gone before us to prepare a place for his people, and when he comes again our redemption will be complete. The great jubilee year is yet to come:

a few more Christmases and New Year's Days
a few more meetings and partings
a few more births and deaths
a few more weddings and funerals
a few more tears and struggles
a few more sicknesses and pains
a few more Sundays, baptisms, and Lord's Suppers
a few more preachings and prayings
a few more, and the end will come!

Our Master will come back again. The dead saints will be raised.
The living saints will be changed. Then, and not till then, will
we be completely free. The liberty that we enjoyed by faith will
be changed into the liberty of sight, and the freedom of hope
into the freedom of certainty.

Come, then, and let us resolve to wait, and watch, and hope,
and pray, and live like men who have something laid up for
them in heaven. The night is far spent, and the day is at hand.
Our King is not far off: our full redemption draws near. Our full
salvation is nearer than when we first believed. The signs of the
times are strange, and demand every Christian's serious attention. The kingdoms of this world are in confusion: the powers
of this world are everywhere reeling and shaken to their foundations. Happy, thrice happy, are those who are citizens of
Christ's eternal kingdom, and ready for anything that may come.
Blessed indeed are those men and women who know and feel
that they are free!

10.
Happiness

'Happy are the people whose God is the LORD!'
(Psalm 144:15).

An atheist was once addressing a crowd of people in the open air. He was trying to persuade them that there was no God and no devil, no heaven, and no hell, no resurrection, no judgement, and no life to come. He advised them to throw away their Bibles, and not to pay attention to what preachers said. He recommended that they think as he did, and be like him. He talked boldly. The crowd listened eagerly. It was 'the blind leading the blind'. Both were falling into the ditch (Matthew 15:14).

In the middle of his address a poor old woman suddenly pushed her way through the crowd, to the place where he was standing. She stood before him. She looked him full in the face. 'Sir,' she said, in a loud voice, 'are you happy?' The atheist looked scornfully at her, and gave her no answer. 'Sir,' she said again, 'I ask you to answer my question. Are you happy? You want us to throw away our Bibles. You tell us not to believe what preachers say about Christ. You advise us to think as you do, and be like you. Now before we take your advice we have a right to know what good we will gain from it. Do your fine new ideas give you a lot of comfort? Do you yourself really feel happy?'

The atheist stopped, and attempted to answer the old woman's question. He stammered, and shuffled, and fidgeted, and endeavoured to explain his meaning. He tried hard to return to the subject. He said he 'had not come to preach about happiness'. But it was of no use. The old woman stuck to her point. She insisted on her question being answered, and the crowd took her side. She pressed him hard with her inquiry, and would accept no excuse. And at last the atheist was obliged to leave, and sneak off in the confusion. His conscience would not let him stay: he dared not say that he was happy.

The old woman showed great wisdom in asking the question that she did. The argument she used may seem very simple, but in reality it is one of the most powerful that can be employed. It is a weapon that has more effect on some minds than the most elaborate reasoning by some of our great apologists. Whenever a man begins to speak against and despise old Bible Christianity, thrust home at his conscience the old woman's question. Ask him whether his new views make him feel comfortable within himself. Ask him whether he can say, with honesty and sincerity, that he is happy. The grand test of a man's faith and religion is, 'Does it make him happy?'

Let me now warmly invite every reader to consider the subject before us now. Let me warn you to remember that the salvation of your soul, and nothing less, is closely bound up with the subject. The heart that knows nothing of happiness cannot be right in the sight of God. The man or woman who feels nothing of peace within cannot have a safe state of soul.

There are three things that I intend to do, in order to clear up the subject of happiness. I ask that particular attention be paid to each one of them. And I pray the Spirit of God will apply it to the souls of all my readers.

Firstly, let me point out some things that are absolutely essential to happiness.

Secondly, let me expose some common mistakes about the way to be happy.

Thirdly, let me show the way to be truly happy.

Some essentials for true happiness

First of all I have to point out some things that are absolutely essential to true happiness. Happiness is what all mankind wants to obtain: the desire of it is deeply planted in the human heart. All men naturally dislike pain, sorrow and discomfort. All men naturally like ease, comfort and bliss. All men naturally hunger and thirst after happiness. Just as the sick man longs for health, and the prisoner of war for liberty; just as the parched traveller in hot countries longs to see the cooling fountain, or the ice-bound polar voyager the sun rising above the horizon — in just the same way poor mortal man longs to be happy. But how few consider what they really mean when they talk of happiness! How vague and indistinct and undefined are the ideas of most men on the subject! They consider some to be happy who in reality are miserable; they think some are gloomy and sad who in reality are truly happy. They dream of a happiness that in reality would never satisfy their nature's wants. Let me try now to throw a little light on the subject.

Not freedom from sorrow

True happiness *is not perfect freedom from sorrow and discomfort.* Let that never be forgotten. If it were, there would be no such thing as happiness in the world. Such happiness is for angels who have never fallen, and not for man. The happiness I am inquiring about is the kind that a poor, dying, sinful creature may hope to attain. Our whole nature is defiled by sin. Evil abounds in the world. Sickness, and death, and change are daily doing their sad work on every side. In such a state of things the highest happiness man can attain to on earth must of necessity be mixed. If we expect to find any literally perfect happiness on this side of the grave, we expect what we will not find.

Not laughter and smiles

True happiness *does not consist of laughter and smiles*. The face is very often a poor index of the inward man. There are thousands who laugh loud and are merry in the company of others, but are wretched and miserable in private, and almost afraid to be alone. There are hundreds who are solemn and serious in their demeanour, whose hearts are full of solid peace. A poet once wrote that our smiles are not worth very much; he said, 'A man may smile and smile and be a villain.'

The eternal Word of God teaches us that 'Even in laughter the heart may sorrow' (Proverbs 14:13). Don't tell me of smiling and laughing faces: I want to hear of something more than that when I ask whether a man is happy. A truly happy man no doubt will often show his happiness in his face; but a man may have a very merry face and yet not be happy at all.

Of all deceptive things on earth nothing is so deceptive as mere fun and cheerfulness. It is a hollow empty show, utterly devoid of substance and reality. Listen to the brilliant talker in society, and note the applause that he receives from an admiring company: follow him to his own private room, and you will very likely find him plunged in sad despondency. I know a man who confessed that even when he was thought to be most happy he often wished that he was dead. Look at the smiling beauty at the party, and you might suppose she never knew what it was like to be unhappy; see her the next day at her own home, and you may probably find her angry at herself and everybody else besides. No, worldly fun is not real happiness! There is a certain pleasure about it, I do not deny. There is an animal excitement about it, I make no question. There is a temporary elevation of spirits about it, I freely concede. But don't call it by the sacred name of happiness. The most beautiful cut flowers stuck in the ground do not make a garden. When ordinary glass is called diamond, and tinsel is called gold, then, and not till then, can people who can laugh and smile be called happy men. Once there was a man who consulted a physician about his depression. The physician advised him to keep up his spirits by going to hear the great comic actor of the day. 'You should go and hear Matthews. He will make you feel good.' 'Sorry to say, sir,' was the reply, 'I am Matthews himself!'

A man's highest needs must be met

To be truly happy *the highest wants of a man's nature must be met and satisfied.* The requirements of his curiously wrought constitution must all be met. There must be nothing about him that cries, 'Give, give,' but cries in vain and gets no answer. Animals are happy as long as they are warm and fed. The little infant looks happy when it is clothed, and fed, and well, and in its mother's arms. And why? Because it is satisfied. And so it is with man. His highest wants must be met and satisfied before he can be truly happy. All needs must be met. There must be no void, no empty places, no unsupplied cravings. Till then he is never truly happy.

And what are 'man's principal wants'? Does he only have a body? No; he has something more! He has a soul. Does he only have the five senses? Can he do nothing but hear, and see, and smell, and taste, and feel? No; he has a thinking mind and a conscience! Does he have any consciousness of any world but that in which he lives and moves? He has. There is still a small voice within him that often makes itself heard: 'This is not all there is to life! There is world unseen: there is a life beyond the grave.' Yes! It is true. We are fearfully and wonderfully made. All men know it: all men feel it, if they would only speak the truth. It is utter nonsense to pretend that food and clothing and earthly material wealth alone can make men happy. The soul has needs. There are needs of the conscience. There can be no true happiness until these wants are satisfied.

Independence from the world

To be truly happy *a man must have sources of happiness which are not dependent on anything in this world.* There is nothing on earth that is not stamped with the mark of instability and uncertainty. All the good things that money can buy are but for a moment: they either leave us or we are obliged to leave them. All the sweetest relationships in life are liable to come to an end: death may come any day and cut them off. The man whose happiness depends entirely on things here below is like the one who builds his house on sand.

Don't tell me of your happiness if it daily depends on the uncertainties of the earth. Your home may be rich in comforts; your wife and children may be all you could desire; your incomes may be amply sufficient to meet all your wants. But oh, remember, if you have nothing more than this to look to, you are standing on the edge of a cliff! Your joy may be deep and earnest, but it is fearfully short-lived. It has no root. It is not true happiness.

Must be comfortable about his life

To be really happy *a man must be able to look at every part of his life without uncomfortable feelings.* He must be able to look at the past without guilty fears; he must be able to look around him without discontent; he must be able to look forward without anxious dread. He must be able to sit down and think calmly about things past, present, and to come, and feel prepared. The man who has a weak side in his condition — a side that he does not like looking at or considering — is not really happy.

Do not talk to me of your happiness if you are unable to look steadily either before or behind you. Your present position may be easy and pleasant. You may find many sources of joy and gladness in your profession, your dwelling-place, your family and your friends. Your health may be good, your spirits may be cheerful. But stop and think quietly over your past life. Can you reflect calmly on all the omissions and commissions of bygone years? How will they bear God's inspection? How will you answer for them at the last judgement? And then look forward and think on the years yet to come. Think of the certain end towards which you are heading; think of death; think of judgement; think of the hour when you will meet God face to face. Are you ready for it? Are you prepared? Can you look forward to these things without alarm? Oh, be very sure if you cannot look comfortably at any time in your life but the present, then your boasted happiness is poor and unreal! It is but a fancy and decorated coffin — fair and beautiful on the outside, but nothing but bones and decay within. It is a mere thing of a day, like Jonah's gourd. It is not real happiness.

I ask my readers to fix in their minds this account of things essential to happiness that I have attempted to give. Dismiss from your thoughts the many mistaken notions on this subject, they are like counterfeit money. To be truly happy, the wants of your soul and conscience must be satisfied; to be truly happy, your joy must be founded on something more than this world can give you; to be truly happy, you must be able to look on every side — above, below, behind, before — and feel that all is right. This is real, genuine happiness: this is the happiness I have in view when I urge your attention to this subject.

Some common mistakes about the way to be happy

In the next place, let me expose some common mistakes about the way to be happy. There are several roads thought by many to lead to happiness. In each of these roads thousands and tens of thousands of men and women are continually travelling. Each believes that if he could only attain all he wants he would be happy. Each believes that if he does not succeed, the fault is not in the road he is on, but in his own lack of luck and good fortune. And everyone seems ignorant of the fact that they are chasing after shadows. They have started in a wrong direction: they are seeking that which can never be found in the place where they seek it.

I will mention by name some of the principal delusions about happiness. I do it in love, and kindness and compassion to men's souls. I believe it is a public duty to warn people against cheats, quacks and impostors. Oh, how much trouble and sorrow it might save my readers, if they would only believe what I am going to say!

Position and fame alone

It is an utter mistake to suppose that position and fame alone can give happiness. The kings, presidents and rulers of this world are not necessarily happy men. They have troubles and crosses, which none know but themselves. They see a thousand evils, which they are unable to remedy; they are slaves working in golden chains, and have less real liberty than anyone in the world. They have burdens and responsibilities laid upon them, which are a daily weight on their hearts. The Roman Emperor Antonine often said that 'the imperial power was an ocean of miseries'. When Queen Elizabeth heard a milkmaid singing, she wished that she had been born to *her* lot, instead of her own. The poet never wrote a truer word than when he said, 'Uneasy lies the head that wears a crown.'

Riches alone

It is an utter mistake to suppose that riches alone can give happiness. They can enable a man to command and possess everything but inward peace. They cannot buy a cheerful spirit and a light heart. There is anxiety in getting them, and anxiety in keeping them; anxiety in using them, and anxiety in disposing of them; anxiety in gathering, and anxiety in scattering them. He is a wise man who said that 'money' was only another name for 'trouble'.

Learning and science alone

It is an utter mistake to suppose that learning and science alone can give happiness. They may occupy a man's time and attention, but they cannot really make him happy. Those who increase knowledge often 'increase sorrow': the more they learn, the more they discover their own ignorance (Ecclesiastes 1:18). The heart wants something as well as the head: the conscience needs food as well as the intellect. All the secular knowledge in the world will not give a man joy and gladness when he thinks about sickness, and death, and the grave. Those who have climbed the highest have often found themselves solitary, dissatisfied and empty of peace. The learned Selden, at the close of his life, confessed that all his learning did not give him such comfort as four verses of Titus (2:11-14):

> 'For the grace of God that brings salvation has appeared to all men, teaching us that, denying ungodliness and worldly lusts, we should live soberly, righteously, and godly in the present age, looking for the blessed hope and glorious appearing of our great God and Saviour Jesus Christ, who gave himself for us, that he might redeem us from every lawless deed and purify for himself his own special people, zealous for good works.'

Idleness alone

It is an utter mistake to suppose that idleness alone can give happiness. The labourer who gets up at five in the morning, and goes out to work all day in a cold clay ditch, often thinks, as he walks past the rich man's house, 'What a fine thing it must be to have no work to do.' Poor fellow! He doesn't know what he is saying. The most miserable creature on earth is the man who has nothing to do. Work for the hands or work for the mind is absolutely essential to human happiness. Without it the mind feeds upon itself, and the whole inward man becomes diseased. The machinery within *will* work, and without something to work upon, will often wear itself to pieces. There was no idleness in the Garden of Eden. Adam and Eve had to 'tend and keep it'. There will be no idleness in heaven: God's 'servants shall serve him'. Oh, be very sure the idlest man is the man most truly unhappy! (Genesis 2:15; Revelation 22:3).

Pleasure-seeking and amusement alone

It is an utter mistake to suppose that pleasure-seeking and amusement alone can give happiness. Of all roads that men can take in order to be happy, this is the one that is most completely wrong. Of all weary, flat, dull and unprofitable ways of spending life, this exceeds them all. To think of a dying creature, with an immortal soul, expecting happiness in feasting and revelling — in dancing and singing — in dressing and visiting — in party-going and gambling — in races and fairs — in hunting and shooting — in crowds, in laughter, in noise, in music, in wine! Surely it is a sight that is enough to make the devil laugh and the angels weep. Even a child will not play with its toys all day long. It must have food. But when grown-up men and women think they will find happiness in a constant round of amusement they sink far below a child.

I place before every one of my readers these common mistakes about the way to be happy. I ask you to mark them well. I warn you plainly against these pretended short cuts to happiness, however popular they may be. I tell you that if you believe that any one of them can lead you to true peace you are entirely

deceived. Your conscience will never feel satisfied; your immortal soul will never feel easy: your whole inward man will
feel uncomfortable and unhealthy. Take any one of these roads,
or take all of them, and if you have nothing besides to look to,
you will never find happiness. You may travel on and on and
on, and the object wished for will seem as far away at the end
of each stage of life as when you started. You are like one pour-
ing water into a sieve, or putting money into a bag with holes.
You might as well try to make an elephant happy by feeding
him with a grain of sand a day, as try to satisfy that heart of
yours with position, riches, learning, idleness, or pleasures.

Do you doubt the truth of all that I am saying to you? I dare
say you do. Then let us turn to the great Book of human experience, and read over a few lines from its solemn pages. You
will have the testimony of a few competent witnesses on the
great subject I am bringing to your attention.

A king will be our first witness: I mean Solomon, King of
Israel. We know that he had power, and wisdom, and wealth,
far exceeding that of any ruler of his time. We know from his
own confession that he tried the great experiment of seeing
how far the good things of this world can make men happy. We
know, from the record of his own hand, the result of this curious experiment. He writes it by the inspiration of the Holy Spirit,
for the benefit of the whole world, in the book of Ecclesiastes.
Never, surely, was the experiment tried under such favourable
circumstances: never was anyone so likely to succeed as the
Jewish king. Yet what is Solomon's testimony? You have it in
his melancholy words: 'I have seen all the works that are done
under the sun; and indeed, all is vanity and grasping for the
wind' (Ecclesiastes 1:14).

A famous French lady will be our next witness: I mean Madam
De Pompadour. She was the friend and favourite of Louis the
Fifteenth. She had unbounded influence at the Court of France.
She had everything that money could buy. Yet what does she
have to say?

What a situation is that of those who are great! They only live in the future, and are only happy in hope. There is no peace in ambition. I am always gloomy, and so often very unreasonable. The kindness of the King, the respect of the court officials, the devotion of my servants, and the faithfulness of a large number of friends — motives like these, which ought to make me happy, no longer affect me. I no longer have feelings for those things and persons which once pleased me. I have magnificently furnished my house in Paris: well; it pleased me for two days!

My residence in the French countryside is charming; and yet I cannot endure being there alone. Kindhearted people relate to me all the news and adventures of Paris: they think I listen, but when they are done I ask them what they said. In a word, I do not live: I am dead before my time. I have no interest in the world. Everything conspires to make my life bitter. My life is a continual death.

To such testimony I do not need to add a single word.[1]

Our next witness will be a famous German writer: Goethe. It is well known that he was almost idolized by many during his life. His works were read and admired by thousands. His name was known and honoured, wherever German was read, all over the world. And yet the praise of man, of which he reaped such an abundant harvest, was utterly unable to make Goethe happy. 'He confessed, when about eighty years old, that he could not remember being in a really happy state of mind even for a few weeks together; and that when he wished to feel happy, he had to veil his self-consciousness'.[2]

Our next witness will be an English poet: Lord Byron. If ever there was one who ought to have been happy according to the standard of the world, Lord Byron was the man. He began life with all the advantages of English rank and position. He had splendid abilities and powers of mind, which the world soon discovered and was ready to honour. He had sufficient means to gratify every lawful wish. Humanly speaking, there seemed nothing to prevent him from enjoying life and being happy. Yet it is a notorious fact that Byron was a miserable man. Misery stands out in his poems; misery creeps out in his letters. Weariness, boredom, disgust and discontent appear in all of his ways. He is an awful warning that rank, and title, and literary fame, alone, are not sufficient to make a man happy.

Our next witness will be a man of science: Sir Humphrey Davy. He was eminently successful in the line of life that he chose, and deservedly so. A distinguished philosopher — the inventor of the famous safety-lamp which bears his name, and has preserved many a poor miner from death by fiery explosion. A member of the ruling class in England and President of the Royal Society — his whole life seemed a continual career of prosperity. If education alone was the road to happiness, this man at least ought to have been happy. Yet what was the true record of Davy's feelings? We have it in his own sad journal at the latter part of his life. He describes himself in two painful words: 'Very miserable'.

Our next witness will be a man of humour and pleasure: Lord Chesterfield. He will speak for himself: his testimony will be a letter written in his own words.

I have seen the silly cycle of business and pleasure, and have no use for any of it. I have enjoyed all the pleasures of the world, and consequently know their futility, and do not regret their loss. I appraise them at their real value, which in truth is very low; whereas those who lack experience always overrate them. They only see their gay outside, and are dazzled with their glare; but I have been behind the scenes. I have seen all the coarse pulleys and dirty ropes that exhibit and move the gaudy machine, and I have seen and smelt the burning lard candles which illuminate the whole decoration, to the astonishment and admiration of the ignorant audience. When I reflect on what I have seen, what I have heard, and what I have done, I cannot persuade myself that all that frivolous hurried movement and pleasure of the world had any reality. I look on all that is past as one of those romantic dreams which the drug opium can bring about, and I do by no means wish to repeat the nauseous dose for the sake of the evading dream.

These sentences speak for themselves. I need not add one single word to them.

The statesmen and politicians who have swayed the destinies of the world ought by all rights to be our last witnesses. But I refrain, in Christian love, from putting them forward. It makes my heart ache when I run my eye over the list of names famous in history, and think how many have worn out their lives in a breathless struggle after office and distinction. How many of our greatest men have died of broken hearts — disappointed, disgusted and tried with constant failure! How many have left on record some humbling confession that in the plenitude of their power they were grieving for rest, as the caged eagle for liberty! How many whom the world is applauding as 'masters of the situation' are in reality little better than galley slaves, chained to the oar and unable to get free! Yes, there are many sad proofs, both among the living and the dead, that to be great and powerful is not necessarily to be happy.

I think it is very likely that men do not believe what I am saying. I know something of the deceitfulness of the heart on the subject of happiness. There are few things that man is so slow to believe as the truths I am now putting forth about the way to be happy. Bear with me then while I say something more.

Come and stand with me some afternoon in the heart of the city. Let us watch the faces of most of the wealthy men whom we will see leaving their places of business at the close of the day. Some of them are worth hundred of thousands: some of them are worth millions. But what is written in the faces of these grave men we see swarming out from the Bank of England and the Stock Exchange? What is the meaning of those deep lines that wrinkle so many a cheek and so many a brow? What is the meaning of that air of anxious thoughtfulness that is worn by five out of every six we meet? Yes, these things tell a serious tale. They tell us that it needs something more than gold and banknotes to make men happy.

Come next and stand with me near the Houses of Parliament, in the middle of a busy session. Let us scan the faces of the politicians, whose names are familiar or well known all over the civilized world. There, on some fine evening, you may see the mightiest statesmen in England hurrying to a debate, like eagles to the carcass. Each has the power of good or evil in his tongue, which is fearful to contemplate. Each may say things before tomorrow's sun dawns, which may affect the peace and prosperity of nations, and convulse the world. There you may see the men who hold the reins of power and government already; there you may see the men who are daily watching for an opportunity to snatch those reins out of their hands, and governing in their stead. But what do their faces tell us as they rush to their posts? What may be read in many of their wrinkled foreheads — so absent-looking and sunk in thought? They teach us a solemn lesson. They teach us that it needs something more than political greatness to make men happy.

Come next and stand with me in the most fashionable part of London, in the height of the season. Let us visit Regent Street or Pall Mall, Hyde Park or Mayfair. How many beautiful faces and splendid clothes we will see! How many we will count in an hour who seem to possess the choicest gifts of this world — beauty, wealth, position, fashion and a throng of friends. But how few we will see who appear happy! In how many faces we will read weariness, dissatisfaction, discontent, sorrow, or un-happiness, as clearly as if it was written with a pen! Yes, it is a humbling lesson to learn; but a very wholesome one! It needs something more than position, and fashion, and beauty, to make people happy.

Come next and walk with me through some quiet country village in merry England. Let us visit some secluded corner, far away from the great cities, and fashionable indulgence and political strife. There are many such villages to be found in the land. There are even rural places where there is neither street, nor shop, nor bar — where there is work for all the labourers, a church for all the population, a school for all the children, and a minister of the gospel to look after the people. Surely, you will say, we will find happiness here! Surely such places must be the very habitats of peace and joy! Go into these quiet-looking cottages, one by one, and you will soon be shocked. Learn the inner history of each family, and you will soon alter your mind. You will soon discover that backbiting, and lying, and slander-ing, and envy, and jealousy, and pride, and laziness, and drinking, and extravagance, and lust, and petty quarrels, can murder happiness in the country just as much as in the town. No doubt a rural village sounds pretty in poetry, and looks beautiful in pictures; but in sober reality human nature is the same evil thing everywhere. Yes, it needs something more than a residence in a quiet country village to make any child of Adam a happy man!

I know these are ancient things. They have been said a thou-sand times before without effect, and I suppose they will be said without effect again. I want no greater proof of the corrup-tion of human nature than the determination with which we seek happiness where happiness cannot be found. Century after century, wise men have left on record their experience about the way to be happy. Century after century, the children of men will declare that they know the way to happiness perfectly well, and need no teaching. They cast to the winds our warnings; they rush, every one, on his own favourite path; they walk in a worthless shadow, and trouble themselves in vain, and wake up when it is too late, to find that their whole life has been a great mistake. Their eyes are blinded: they will not see that their visions are as baseless and disappointing as the mirage of the African desert. Like the tired traveller in those deserts, they think they are approaching a lake of cooling waters; like the same traveller, they find to their dismay that this imaginary lake was a splendid optical delusion, and that they are still helpless in the midst of burning sands.

Are you a young person? I implore you to accept the tender warning of a minister of the gospel, and not to seek happiness where happiness cannot be found. Don't seek it in riches; don't seek it in power and position; don't seek it in pleasure; don't seek it in learning. All these are bright and splendid fountains: their waters taste sweet. A crowd is standing around them, which will not leave them, but oh, remember that God has written over each of these fountains, 'Whoever drinks of this water will thirst again' (John 4:13). Remember this and you will be wise.

Are you poor? Are you tempted to daydream that if you were in the rich man's place you would be quite happy? Resist the temptation, and cast it behind you. Do not envy your wealthy neighbours: be content with the things that you have. Happiness does not depend on houses or land; silk and fine clothes cannot shut out sorrow from the heart; mansions and villas cannot prevent anxiety and care coming in through their doors. There is as much misery riding and driving about in cars as there is walking about on foot: there is as much unhappiness in elegant houses as in humble cottages. Oh, remember the common misconceptions about happiness, and be wise!

The way to be really happy

Let me now, in the last place, point out the way to be really happy. There is a sure path that leads to happiness, if men will only take it. There never lived a person who travelled in that path and missed the object that he sought to attain.

It is a path open to all. It needs neither wealth, nor position, nor learning in order to walk in it. It is for the servant as well as for the master; it is for the poor as well as for the rich. None are excluded but those who exclude themselves. Where is this path? Where is this road? Read on, and you will see.

The way to be happy is *to be a real, thoroughgoing true-hearted Christian*. Scripture declares it; experience proves it. The converted man, the believer in Christ, the child of God — he, and he alone, is the happy man.

It sounds too simple to be true: it seems at first sight so simple a statement that it is not believed. But the greatest truths are often the simplest. The secret that many of the wisest on earth have utterly failed to discover is revealed to the humblest believer in Christ. I repeat it deliberately, and defy the world to disprove it: the true Christian is the only happy man.

What do I mean when I speak of a true Christian? Do I mean everybody who goes to a church? Do I mean everybody who professes an orthodox creed, and bows his head at the belief? Do I mean everybody who professes to love the gospel? No, indeed! I mean something very different. All are not Christians who are called Christians. The man I have in view is *the Christian in heart and life*. He who has been taught by the Spirit to really feel his sins; he who really rests all his hopes on the Lord Jesus Christ, and his payment for man's sins on the cross; he who has been born again and really lives a spiritual, holy life; he whose religion is not merely a Sunday show, but a mighty constraining principle governing every day of his life — he is the man I mean, when I speak of a true Christian.

What do I mean when I say the true Christian is happy? Has he no doubts and no fears? Has he no anxieties and no troubles? Has he no sorrows and no cares? Does he never feel pain, and shed no tears? Far be it from me to say anything of the kind. He has a weak and frail body like other men; he has affections and passions like everyone born of a woman; he lives in a changing world. But deep down in his heart he has a mine of solid peace and substantial joy that is never exhausted. This is true happiness.

Do I say that all true Christians are equally happy at all times? No, not for a moment! All have their ebbs and flows of peace, like the sea. Their bodily health is not always the same; their earthly circumstances are not always the same; the souls of those they love fill them at times with particular anxiety: they themselves are sometimes overcome by a fault, and walk in darkness. They sometimes give way to inconsistencies and besetting sins, and lose their sense of forgiveness. But, as a general rule, the true Christian has a deep pool of peace within him, which even at its lowest is never entirely dry.

I use the words 'as a general rule' advisedly. When a believer falls into such a horrible sin as that of David (adultery and murder), it would be monstrous to talk of his feeling inward peace. If a man professing to be a true Christian talked to me of being happy in such a case — before giving any evidence of the deepest, most heart-abasing repentance — I would feel great doubts whether he ever had any grace at all.

The true Christian is the only happy man, because *his conscience is at peace.* That mysterious witness for God, which is so mercifully placed within us, is fully satisfied and at rest. It sees in the blood of Christ a complete cleansing away of all its guilt. It sees in the priesthood and mediation of Christ a complete answer to all its fears. It sees that through the sacrifice and death of Christ, God can now be just, and yet be the justifier of the ungodly. It no longer bites and stings, and causes fear within

himself. The Lord Jesus Christ has amply met all its requirements. Conscience is no longer the enemy of the true Christian, but his friend and adviser. Therefore he is happy.

The true Christian is the only happy man, because *he can sit
down quietly and think about his soul.* He can look behind him
and ahead of him, he can look within him and around him,
and feel, 'All is well.' He can think calmly on his past life, and
however many and great his sins, take comfort in the thought
that they are all forgiven. The righteousness of Christ covers all,
as Noah's flood covered the highest mountain. He can think
calmly about things to come, and yet not be afraid. Sickness is
painful; death is solemn; the Judgement Day is an awful thing:
but having Christ for him, he has nothing to fear. He can think
calmly about the holy God, whose eyes are on all his ways,
and feel, 'He is my Father, my reconciled Father in Christ Jesus.
I am weak; I am unprofitable: yet in Christ he regards me as his
dear child, and is well pleased'. Oh, what a blessed privilege it
is to be able to 'think', and not be afraid! I can well understand
the mournful complaint of the prisoner in solitary confinement.
He had warmth, and food, and clothing, and work, but he was
not happy. And why? He said, 'He was obliged to think.'

The true Christian is the only happy man, because *he has
sources of happiness entirely independent of this world.* He has
something that cannot be affected by sickness and by death, by
private losses and public calamities — he has the 'peace of
God, which transcends all understanding'. He has a hope laid
up for him in heaven; he has a treasure that moth and rust
cannot corrupt; he has a house that can never be torn down.
His loving wife may die, and his heart feel torn in two; his dar-
ling children may be taken from him, and he may be left alone
in this cold world; his earthly plans may be crossed; his health
may fail; but all this time he has a part of him that can never be
hurt. He has a Friend who never dies; he has possessions beyond the grave, of which nothing can deprive him: his springs

of water on this earth may dry up, but his springs of living water never run dry. This is real happiness.

The true Christian is happy, because *he is in his right position*. All the powers of his being are directed to right ends. His affections are not set on things here on earth, but on things in heaven; his will is not bent on self-indulgence, but is submissive to the will of God; his mind is not absorbed in wretched perishable insignificant things. He desires useful employment: he enjoys the luxury of doing good. Who does not know the misery of disorder? The heart of an unconverted man is like a house in a mess. Grace puts everything in that heart in its right position. The things of the soul come first, and the things of the world come second. Anarchy and confusion cease: unruly passions no longer do what seems right in their own eyes. Christ reigns over the whole man, and each part of him does his proper work. The new heart is the only real happy heart, for it is the only heart that is in order. The true Christian has found his place. He has laid aside his pride and self-will; he sits at the feet of Jesus, and is in his right mind: he loves God and loves man, and so he is happy. In heaven all are happy because all do God's will perfectly. The nearer a man gets to this standard the happier he will be.

The plain truth is that without Christ there is no happiness in the world. He alone can give the Comforter who abides for ever. He is the sun; without him men never feel warm. He is the light; without him men are always in the dark. He is the bread; without him men are always starving. He is the living water; without him men are always thirsty. Give them what you like — place them where you please — surround them with all the comforts you can imagine — it makes no difference. Separate from Christ, the Prince of Peace, a man cannot be happy.

Give a man a sensible interest in Christ, and he will be happy *in spite of poverty*. He will tell you that he wants nothing that is really good. He is provided for: he has riches in possession, and riches in restoration; he has food to eat that the world does not know of; he has friends who never leave him nor forsake him. The Father and the Son come to him, and make their home with him: the Lord Jesus Christ has supper with him, and he with Christ (Revelation 3:20).

Give a man a sensible interest in Christ, and he will be happy *in spite of sickness*. His flesh may groan, and his body worn out with pain, but his heart will rest and be at peace. One of the happiest people I ever saw was a young woman who had been hopelessly ill for many years with disease of the spine. She lay in an attic without the warmth of a fire; the roof was less than two feet above her face. She did not have the slightest hope of recovery. But she was always rejoicing in the Lord Jesus. The spirit triumphed mightily over the flesh. She was happy, because Christ was with her.

Give a man a sensible interest in Christ, and he will be happy *in spite of abounding public calamities*. The government of his country may be thrown into confusion; rebellion and disorder may turn everything upside down; laws may be trampled underfoot; justice and equity may be outraged; liberty may be cast down to the ground; might may prevail over right: but still his heart will not fail. He will remember that the kingdom of Christ will one day be set up. He will say, like the old minister who lived throughout the turmoil of the French revolution: 'It is all right: it will be well with the righteous.'

I know well that Satan hates the doctrine that I am endeavouring to impress upon you. I have no doubt he is filling your mind with objections and reasoning, and persuading you that I am wrong. I am not afraid to meet these objections face to face. Let us bring them forward and see what they are.

You may tell me that you *know many very religious people who are not happy at all*. You see them diligent in attending public worship. You know that they are never missing at the Lord's Supper. But you see in them no marks of the peace that I have been describing.

But are you sure that these people you speak of are true believers in Christ? Are you sure that, with all their appearance of religion, they are born again and converted to God? Isn't it more likely that they have nothing but the name of Christianity, without the reality; and a form of godliness, without the power? Yes! You have yet to learn that people may do many religious acts, and yet possess no saving religion! It is not a mere formal, ceremonial Christianity that will ever make people happy. We want something more than going to church, and going to the Lord's Table, to give us peace. There must be a real, vital union with Christ. It is not the formal Christian but the true Christian who is the happy man.

You may tell me that *you know really spiritually-minded and converted people who do not seem happy*. You have heard them frequently complaining of their own hearts, and groaning over their own weaknesses. They seem to you all doubts, and anxieties, and fears; and you want to know where is the happiness in these people of which I have been saying so much.

I do not deny that there are many saints of God such as these whom you describe, and I am sorry for it. I concede that there are many believers who live far below their privileges, and seem to know nothing of the joy and peace in believing. But did you ever ask any of these people whether they would give up their Christianity, and go back to the world? Did you ever ask them, after all their groaning, and doubting, and fearing, whether they think they would be happier if they ceased to follow after Christ? 'Did you ever ask those questions?' I am certain that if you did, the weakest and lowest believers would all give you one answer. I am certain they would tell you that they would rather cling to their little scrap of hope in Christ, than possess the world. I am sure they would all answer, 'Our faith is weak, if we have any; our grace is small, if we have any; our joy in Christ is next to nothing at all: but we cannot give up what we have got. Though the Lord slay us, we must cling to him.' The root of happiness lies deep in many a poor weak believer's heart, when neither leaves nor blossoms are to be seen!

But you will tell me, in the last place, that *you cannot believe most believers are happy, because they are so solemn and serious.* You think that they do not really possess this happiness I have been describing, because their faces do not show it. You doubt the reality of their joy, because it is so little seen.

I might easily repeat what I told you at the beginning of this chapter — that a merry face is no sure proof of a happy heart. But I will not do so. I will rather ask you whether you yourself may not be the cause why believers look grave and serious when you meet them? If you are not converted yourself, you surely cannot expect them to look at you without sorrow. They see you on the broad road to hell, and that alone is enough to give them pain; they see thousands like you, hurrying on to weeping and wailing and endless torment. Now, is it possible that such a daily sight would not give them grief? Your company, very likely, is one cause why they are solemn. Wait till you are a converted man yourself, before you pass judgement on the seriousness of converted people. See them in the company of those who are all of one heart, and all love Christ, and as far as my own experience goes, you will find no people so truly happy as true Christians.

I repeat my assertion in this part of my subject. I repeat it boldly, confidently, deliberately. I say that there is no happiness among men that will at all compare with that of the true Christian. All other happiness compared to this is moonlight compared to sunshine, and brass by the side of gold. Boast, if you will, of the laughter and merriment of irreligious men; sneer, if you will, at the concern and seriousness that appear in the demeanour of many Christians. I have looked the whole subject in the face, and am not moved. I say that the true Christian alone is the truly happy man, and the way to be happy is to be a true Christian.

Some words of application

Now I am going to close with a few words of plain application. I have endeavoured to expose the fallacy of many views that prevail upon the subject. I have endeavoured to point out, in plain and unmistakable words, where true happiness alone can be found. Permit me to close by an affectionate appeal to the consciences of all who are reading this.

Are you happy?

Firstly, let me entreat every reader to apply to his own heart the solemn question that deserves an answer: 'Are you happy?'

High or low position, rich or poor, master or servant, farmer or labourer, young or old, here is a question that deserves an answer: *Are you really happy?*

Man of this world, who cares about nothing but the things of this world, neglecting the Bible, making a god of business or money, providing for everything but the Day of Judgement, scheming and planning about everything but eternity: are you happy? *You know that you are not.*

Foolish woman, who is throwing life away in flippancy and fickleness, spending hour after hour on that poor frail body that must soon be fed to the worms, making an idol of dress and fashion, and excitement, and human praise, as if this world was all there was: Are you happy? *You know that you are not.*

Young man, who is bent on pleasure and self-indulgence, fluttering from one idle pastime to another, like the moth about the candle — believing yourself clever and knowing, and too wise to be led by preachers, and ignorant that the devil is leading you captive, like the animal that is led to the slaughter: are you happy? *You know that you are not.*

Yes; each and every one of you, you are not happy! And in your own consciences you know it well. You may not admit it, but it is sadly true. There is a great empty place in each of your hearts, and nothing will fill it. Pour into it money, learning, position and pleasure, and it will still be empty. There is a sore place in each of your consciences, and nothing will heal it. Immorality cannot; freethinking cannot; Roman Catholicism cannot; they are all quack medicines. Nothing can heal it, but that which at present you have not used — the simple gospel of Christ. Yes; you are indeed a miserable people!

Take warning this day, that you will never be happy till you are converted. You might as well expect to feel the sun shine on your face when you turn your back to it, as to feel happy when you turn your back on God and on Christ.

Your folly

In the second place, let me warn all who are not true Christians of the folly of living a life that cannot make them happy. I pity you from the bottom of my heart, and eagerly persuade you to open your eyes and be wise. I stand as a watchman on the tower of the everlasting gospel. I see you sowing misery for yourselves, and I call upon you to stop and think, before it is too late. Oh, that God may show you your folly!

You are hewing out for yourselves cisterns, broken cisterns, which can hold no water. You are spending your time, and strength, and affections on that which will give you no return for your labour — 'you spend money for what is not bread, and your wages for what does not satisfy' (Isaiah 55:2). You are building up Babels of your own contriving, ignorant that God will pour contempt on your schemes for procuring happiness, because you attempt to be happy without him.

Awake from your dreams, I beg you, and prove yourselves to be men. Think of the uselessness of living a life that you will be ashamed of when you die, and of having a religion, in name only, which will fail you just when it is most wanted.

Open your eyes and look around the world. Tell me who was ever really happy without God and Christ and the Holy Spirit. Look at the road on which you are travelling. See the footsteps of those who have gone before you: how many have turned away from it, and confessed that they were wrong. I warn you plainly, that if you are not a true Christian you will miss happiness in the world that now is, as well as in the world to come. Oh, believe me, the way of happiness, and the way of salvation are one and the same! He who will have his own way, and refuses to serve Christ, will never be really happy. But he who serves Christ has the promise of both lives. He is happy on earth, and will be happier still in heaven.

If you are neither happy in this world nor the next, it will be all your own fault. Oh, think about this! Do not be guilty of such enormous folly. Who does not mourn over the folly of the drunkard, the drug addict and the person who commits suicide? But there is no folly like that of the unrepentant child of the world.

The way to happiness

In the next place, let me entreat all my readers who are not yet happy, to seek happiness where alone it can be found.

The keys of the way to happiness are in the hands of the Lord Jesus Christ. He is sealed and appointed by God the Father, to give the bread of life to those who hunger, and to give the water of life to those who thirst. The door that riches and position and learning have so often tried to open, and tried in vain, is now ready to open to every humble, praying believer. Oh, if you want to be happy, come to Christ!

Come to him, confessing that you are weary of your own ways, and want rest; that you have found you have no power and might to make yourself holy or happy or fit for heaven, and have no hope but in him. [Believe and trust in Christ, repent of your sins, and submit to his Lordship.] Tell him this unreservedly. This is coming to Christ.

Come to him, imploring him to show you his mercy, and grant you his salvation; to wash you in his own blood, and take your sins away; to speak peace to your conscience, and heal your troubled soul. Tell him all this unreservedly. This is coming to Christ.

You have everything to encourage you. The Lord Jesus himself invites you. He proclaims to you as well as to others, 'Come to me, all you who labour and are heavy-laden, and I will give you rest. Take my yoke upon you and learn from me; for I am gentle and lowly in heart, and you will find rest for your souls. For my yoke is easy and my burden is light' (Matthew 11:28-30). Wait for nothing. You may feel unworthy. You may feel as if you did not repent enough. But wait no longer. Come to Christ.

You have everything to encourage you. Thousands have walked in the way you are invited to enter, and have found it good. Once, like yourself, they served the world, and plunged deeply into folly and sin. Once, like yourself, they became weary of their wickedness, and longed for deliverance and rest. They heard of Christ, and his willingness to help and save: they came to him by faith and prayer, after many a doubt and hesitation; they found him a thousand times more gracious than they had expected. They rested on him and were happy: they carried his cross and tasted peace. Oh, walk in their steps!

I implore you, by the mercies of God, to come to Christ. If you ever hope to be happy, I entreat you to come to Christ. Do not delay. Awake from your sleep: arise and be free! Come to Christ this day.

Some help to promote happiness

In the last place, let me offer a few hints to all true Christians for the increase and promotion of their happiness. I humbly offer these hints. I desire to apply them to my own conscience as well as to yours. You have found Christ's service happy. I have no doubt that you feel such sweetness in Christ's peace that you would desire to know more of it. I am sure that these hints deserve attention.

Believers, if you would have an increase of happiness in Christ's service, *Labour every year to grow in grace.* Beware of standing still. The holiest men are always the happiest. Let your aim be to be more holy every year — to know more, to feel more, to see more of the fulness of Christ. Do not rest on old grace; do not be content with the degree of Christianity that you have attained. Search the Scriptures more earnestly; pray more fervently; hate sin more; mortify self-will more; become more humble the nearer you draw to your end; seek more direct personal communion with the Lord Jesus; strive to be more like Enoch — daily walking with God; keep your conscience clear of little sins; do not grieve the Spirit; avoid arguments and disputes about the lesser matters of religion: take a firmer hold of those great truths without which no man can be saved. Remember and practise these things, and you will be more happy.

Believers, if you wish to have greater happiness in serving Christ, *Labour every year to be more thankful.* Pray that you may know more and more what it is to 'rejoice in the Lord' (Philippians 3:1). Learn to have a deeper sense of your own wretched sinfulness and corruption, and to be more deeply grateful that by the grace of God you are what you are. Yes, there is too much complaining and too little thanksgiving among the people of God! There is too much murmuring and pondering over the things that we don't have. There is too little praising and blessing for the many undeserved mercies that we have. Oh, that God would pour out upon us a great spirit of thankfulness and praise!

Believers, if you would have an increase of happiness in Christ's service, *Labour every year to do more good.* Look around the circle in which you live your life, and determine to be useful. Strive to be of the same character as God: he is not only good, but '[does] good' (Psalm 119:68). Alas, there is far too much selfishness among believers in the present day! There is far too much lazy sitting by the fire nursing our own spiritual diseases, and growling over the state of our own hearts. Get up; and be useful in your day and generation! Is there no one in the whole world that you can read the Bible to? Is there no one that you can speak to about Christ? Is there no one that you can write to about Christ? Is there literally nothing that you can do for the glory of God, and the benefit of your fellow men? Oh, I cannot believe it! I cannot believe it. There is much that you might do, if only you had the will. For your own happiness' sake, arise and do it, without delay. The bold, outspoken, working Christians are always the happiest. The more you do for God, the more God will do for you.

The compromising lingering Christian must never expect to taste perfect peace. *The most energetic Christian will always be the happiest man.*

Notes

1. Sinclair's *Anecdotes and Aphorisms*, p. 33.

2. Sinclair's *Anecdotes and Aphorisms*, p. 280.

II.
Formalism

'Having a form of godliness but denying its power'
(2 Timothy 3:5).
*'For he is not a Jew who is one outwardly, nor is circumcision
that which is outward in the flesh; but he is a Jew who is one
inwardly; and circumcision is that of the heart, in the Spirit,
not in the letter; whose praise is not from men but from God'*
(Romans 2:28-29).

The texts above deserve serious attention at any time. But they deserve special notice in this age of the church and the world. Never since the Lord Jesus Christ left the earth was there so much formalism and false profession as there is in the present day. Now, more than ever, we ought to examine ourselves, and search our religion, that we may know what it really is. Let us try to find out whether our Christianity is a mere formality, or of the heart.

I know of no better way of unfolding the subject than by turning to a plain passage of the Word of God. Let us listen to what Paul says about it. He lays down the following great principles in his Epistle to the Romans: 'For he is not a Jew who is one outwardly, nor is circumcision that which is outward in the flesh; but he is a Jew who is one inwardly; and circumcision is that of the heart, in the Spirit, not in the letter; whose praise is not from men but from God' (Romans 2:28-29). Three most instructive lessons appear to me to stand out on the face of that passage. Let us see what they are.

We learn, firstly, that formal religion is not true religion, and
a formal Christian is not a true Christian in God's sight.
We learn, secondly, that the heart is the seat of true religion,
and that the true Christian is the Christian in heart.
We learn, thirdly, that true religion must never expect to be
popular. It will not have the 'praise of man, but praise
from God'.

Let us thoroughly consider these great principles. Hundreds of
years have passed since a mighty Puritan preacher said, 'Formalism, formalism, formalism is the great sin of this day, under
which the whole country groans. There is more light than there
was, but less life; more profession, but less holiness' (Thomas
Hall, on 2 Timothy 3:5, 1658). What would this good man
have said if he lived in our times?

Formal religion is not religion

We learn, firstly, that formal religion is not true religion, and a
formal Christian is not a Christian in God's sight. What do I
mean when I speak of formal religion? This is a point that must
be made clear. Thousands, I suspect, know nothing about it.
Without a distinct understanding of this point my whole dis-
course will be useless. My first step will be to paint, describe
and define.

When a man is a Christian in name only, and not in reality
— in outward things only, and not in his inward feelings — in
profession only, and not in practice — when his Christianity, in
short, is a mere matter of form, or fashion, or custom, without
any influence on his heart or life — the man has what I call a
'formal religion'. He possesses indeed the *form*, or shell, or surface of religion, but he does not possess its substance or its *power*.

Look, for example, at those thousands of people whose
whole religion seems to consist in keeping religious ceremonies

and ordinances. They regularly attend public worship. They regularly go to the Lord's Table. But they never get any further. They know nothing of true heartfelt Christianity. They are not familiar with the Scriptures, and take no delight in reading them. They do not separate themselves from the ways of the world. They draw no distinction between godliness and ungodliness in their friendships, or marriages. They care little or nothing about the distinctive doctrines of the gospel. They appear utterly indifferent as to what they hear preached. You may be in their presence for weeks, and from what you hear or see on any weekday, you might easily assume they were atheists. What can be said about these people? They clearly profess to be Christians; and yet there is neither heart nor life in their Christianity. There is but one thing to be said about them — they are formal Christians. Their religion is only a *form*.

Look in another direction at those hundreds of people whose religion seems to consist of a lot of talk and profession. They know the theory of the gospel with their heads, and profess to delight in Evangelical doctrine. They can say a lot about the 'soundness' of their own views, and the 'ignorance' of all who disagree with them. But they never get any further! When you examine their inner lives you find that they know nothing of practical godliness. They are neither truthful, nor loving, nor humble, nor honest, nor kind, nor gentle, nor giving, nor honourable. What shall we say of these people? They claim to be Christians, and yet there is neither substance nor fruit in their Christianity. There is but one thing to be said: they are formal Christians. Their religion is only an empty *form*.

This is the formal religion against which I wish to raise a warning voice this day. Here is the rock on which multitudes of people from every part of the world are making catastrophic shipwreck of their souls. One of the most wicked things that was ever said was: 'Don't worry about your religion, only its appearance.'

Such notions are from the earth. No, rather, they are from beneath the earth: they smell of the pit. Beware of them, and stand on your guard. If there is anything about which the Scripture speaks expressly, it is the sin and uselessness of *formalism*.

Listen to what Paul tells the Romans: 'For he is not a Jew who is only one outwardly, nor is circumcision that which is outward in the flesh' (Romans 2:28). These are strong words indeed! A man might be a son of Abraham according to the flesh; a member of one of the twelve tribes; circumcized the eighth day; keeper of all the feasts; a regular worshipper in the temple — and yet in God's sight not be a Jew! In the same way, a man may be a Christian by outward profession; a member of a Christian church; baptized with Christian baptism; faithful in receiving the Lord's Supper — and yet in God's sight, not a Christian at all.

Hear what the prophet Isaiah says:

'To what purpose is the multitude of your sacrifices to me?' says the LORD. 'I have had enough of burnt offerings of rams and the fat of fed cattle. I do not delight in the blood of bulls, or of lambs or goats. When you come to appear before me, who has required this from your hand, to trample my courts? Bring no more futile sacrifices; incense is an abomination to me. The New Moons, the Sabbaths, and the calling of assemblies — I cannot endure iniquity and the sacred meeting. Your New Moons and your appointed feasts my soul hates; they are a trouble to me, I am weary of bearing them. When you spread out your hands, I will hide my eyes from you; even though you make many prayers, I will not hear. Your hands are full of blood' (Isaiah 1:11-15).

These words, when examined, are extraordinary. The sacrifices that are here declared to be useless were appointed by God himself! The feasts and ordinances that God says he 'hates' had been prescribed by him! God himself pronounces his own institutions to be useless when they are used formally and without heart by the worshipper! In fact, they are worse than useless; they are even offensive and hurtful. Words cannot be imagined more distinct and unmistakable. They show that formal religion is worthless in God's sight. It is not worth calling it religion at all.

Hear, lastly, what our Lord Jesus Christ says. We find him saying of the Jews of his day: 'These people draw near to me with their mouth, and honour me with their lips, but their heart is far from me. And in vain they worship me, teaching as doctrines the commandments of men' (Matthew 15:8-9). We see him repeatedly denouncing the formalism and hypocrisy of the scribes and Pharisees, and warning his disciples against it. Eight times in one chapter (Matthew 23:13) he says to them, 'Woe to you, scribes and Pharisees, hypocrites!' For the worst of sinners he always had a word of kindness, and held out to them an open door. But formalism, he would have us know, is a desperate disease, and must be exposed in the severest language. To the eye of an ignorant man, a formalist may seem to have a very decent *quantity* of religion, though not perhaps of the best *quality*. In the eye of Christ, however, the situation is very different. In his sight, formalism is not a true religion at all.

What shall we say to these testimonies of Scripture? It would be easy to add to them. They do not stand alone. If words mean anything, they are a clear warning to all who profess and call themselves Christians. They teach us plainly that as we dread and avoid sin, so we ought to dread and avoid formalism. Formalism may take your hand with a smile, and look like a brother, while sin comes against us with drawn sword, and strikes at us like an enemy. But both have one end in view. Both want to ruin our souls; and of the two, formalism is the one most likely to do it. If we love life, let us beware of formalism in religion.

Common

Nothing is *so common*. It is one of the great family diseases of
the whole race of mankind. It is born with us, grows with us,
and is never completely cast out of us till we die. It meets us in
church, it meets us among the rich, and it meets us among the
poor. It meets us among educated people, and it meets us among
the uneducated. It meets us among the Roman Catholics, and
it meets us among Protestants. It meets us among the leaders
of the church, and it meets us among the newest member. It
meets us among Evangelicals, and it meets us among those
who go through many rituals, like the Liberals. Go wherever
we will, and join whatever church we may, we are never beyond
the risk of its infection. We will find it among Quakers and Ply-
mouth Brethren, as well as among the Roman Catholics. The man
who thinks that there is no formal religion in his church is a very
blind and ignorant person. If you love life, beware of formalism.

Dangerous

Nothing is *so dangerous* to a man's own soul. Familiarity with
the form of religion, while we neglect its reality, has a fearfully
deadening effect on the conscience. It brings up by degrees a
thick crust of insensibility over the whole inner man. None seem
to become so desperately hard as those who are continually
repeating holy words and handling holy things, while their hearts
are running after sin and the world. Leaders in our society, who
go to church just for show, to make everyone think they are
religious; fathers who have family prayers formally, to keep up
a good appearance in their homes; unconverted ministers, who
every week are reading prayers and lessons of Scripture, in
which they feel no real interest; unconverted church members,
who are constantly reading responses and saying 'Amen', without feeling what they say; unconverted singers, who sing the

most spiritual hymns every Sunday, merely because they have good voices, while their affections are entirely on things below — all, all, all are in awful danger. They are gradually hardening their hearts, and searing the skin of their consciences. If you love your own soul, beware of formalism.

Foolish

Nothing, finally, is *so foolish*, senseless and unreasonable. Can a formal Christian really suppose that the mere outward Christianity he professes will comfort him in the day of sickness and the hour of death? That is impossible. A painting of a fire cannot warm, a painted banquet cannot satisfy hunger, and a formal religion cannot bring peace to the soul. Does he suppose that God does not see the heartlessness and deadness of his Christianity? Though he may deceive neighbours, acquaintances, fellow worshippers and ministers with a form of godliness, does he think that he can deceive God? The very idea is absurd. 'He who formed the eye, shall he not see?' He knows the very secrets of the heart. He will 'judge the secrets of men' at the last day. He who said to each of the seven churches, 'I know your works' has not changed. He who said to the man without the wedding garment, 'Friend, how did you come in here?' will not be deceived by a little cloak of outward religion. If you don't want to be put to shame at the last day, once more I say, beware of formalism (Psalm 94:9; Romans 2:16; Revelation 2:2; Matthew 22:12).

The heart is the seat of true religion

I move on to the second thing that I want you to consider. The heart is the seat of true religion, and the true Christian is the one who is a Christian in their heart. The heart is the real test of

a man's character. A man may not always be known by what
he says or what he does. He may say and do things that are
right, from false and unworthy motives, while his heart is altogether wrong. The heart is the man. 'As he thinks in his heart,
so is he' (Proverbs 23:7).

The heart is the right test of a man's religion. It is not enough
that a man holds to correct doctrine, and maintains a proper
outward form of godliness. What is in his heart? That is the
great question. That is what God looks at. 'Man looks at the
outward appearance, but the LORD looks at the heart' (1 Samuel
16:7). This is what Paul lays down distinctly as the standard
measure of the soul: 'But he is a Jew who is one inwardly; and
circumcision is that of the heart' (Romans 2:29). Who can doubt
that this mighty sentence was written for Christians as well as
for Jews? The apostle would have us know that a true Christian
is one inwardly, and baptism is of the heart.

The heart is the place where saving religion must begin. It is
naturally irreligious, and must be renewed by the Holy Spirit. 'I
will give you a new heart,' your old heart is naturally hard, and
must be made tender and be broken. 'I will take the heart of
stone out of your flesh and give you a heart of flesh.' 'The
sacrifices of God are a broken spirit, a broken and a contrite
heart — these, O God, you will not despise.' Man's heart is
naturally closed and shut against God, and must be opened.
The Lord 'opened the heart' of Lydia (Ezekiel 36:26; Psalm
51:17; Acts 16:14).

The heart is the seat of true saving faith. 'For with the heart
one believes unto righteousness' (Romans 10:10). A man may
believe that Jesus is the Christ, as the demons do, and yet remain in his sins. He may believe that he is a sinner, and that
Christ is the only Saviour, and occasionally wish that he was a
better man. But no one ever lays hold of Christ, and receives
pardon and peace, until he believes with the heart. It is heart-
faith that justifies.

The heart is the origin of true holiness and the source for continued obedience. True Christians are holy because their hearts are committed to Christ. They obey from the heart. They do the will of God from the heart. Weak, and feeble, and imperfect as all their deeds are, they please God, because they are done from a loving heart. He who commended the widow's offering of a few pennies more than all the offerings of the wealthy Jews regards quality far more than quantity. What he likes to see is a thing done from 'a noble and good heart' (Luke 8:15). There is no real holiness without a right heart towards Christ.

The things I am saying may sound strange. Perhaps they run counter to all the notions of some into whose hands this publication may fall. Perhaps you have thought that if a man's religion is correct outwardly, he must be one with whom God is well pleased. You are completely mistaken. You are rejecting the whole tenor of Bible teaching. Outward correctness without a right heart is neither more nor less than living like a Pharisee. The outward things of Christianity — baptism, the Lord's Supper, church membership, giving, Bible reading and the like — will never take any man's soul to heaven, unless his heart is right. There must be inward things as well as outward — and it is on the inward things that God's eyes are chiefly fixed.

Hear how Paul teaches us about this matter in three most striking texts:

'Circumcision is nothing and uncircumcision is nothing, but keeping the commandments of God is what matters' (1 Corinthians 7:19).

'Neither circumcision nor uncircumcision avails anything, but a new creation' (Galatians 6:15).

'For in Christ Jesus neither circumcision nor uncircumcision avails anything, but faith working through love' (Galatians 5:6).

Did the Apostle only mean in these texts that circumcision was no longer needed under the gospel? Was that all? No indeed! I believe that he meant much more. He meant that under Christ Jesus, everything depended on being born again — on having true saving faith — on being holy in life and conduct. He meant that these are the things we ought to look at chiefly, and not outward forms. 'Am I a new creature? Do I really believe in Christ? Am I a holy person?' These are the great questions that we must seek to answer.

When the heart is wrong all is wrong in God's sight. Many right things may be done. The forms and ordinances that God himself has appointed may seem to be honoured. But so long as the heart is at fault, God is not pleased. He will have man's heart or nothing.

The ark was the most sacred thing in the Jewish tabernacle. On it was the mercy seat. Within it were the tablets of the law, written by God's own finger. The High Priest alone was allowed to go into the place where it was kept, within the veil, and even then, only once every year. The presence of the ark within the camp was thought to bring a special blessing. And yet this very ark could do the Israelites no more good than any common wooden box, when they trusted in it like an idol, with their hearts full of wickedness. They brought it into the camp on a special occasion, saying, 'Let us bring the ark of the covenant of the LORD from Shiloh to us, that when it comes among us it may save us from the hand of our enemies' (1 Samuel 4:3). When it came into the camp they showed it all reverence and honour, 'They shouted so loudly that the earth shook.' But it was all in vain. They were slaughtered by the Philistines, and the ark of God was captured. And why was this? It was because their religion was a mere form. They honoured the ark, but did not give the God of the ark their hearts.

There were some kings of Judah and Israel who did many things that were right in God's sight, and yet were never written in the list of godly and righteous men. Rehoboam started off well, and for three years was noted as '[walking] in the way of David and Solomon' (2 Chronicles 11:17). But afterwards 'he did evil, because he did not prepare his heart to seek the LORD' (2 Chronicles 12:14). Abijah, according to the Book of Chronicles, said many things that were right, and fought successfully against Jeroboam. Nevertheless, the general verdict is against him. We read, in Kings, that 'his heart was not loyal to the LORD his God' (1 Kings 15:3). Amaziah, we are expressly told, 'did what was right in the sight of the LORD, but not with a loyal heart' (2 Chronicles 25:2). Jehu, King of Israel, was raised up, by God's command, to put down idolatry. He was a man of special zeal in doing God's work. But unhappily it is written of him: 'Jehu took no heed to walk in the law of the LORD God of Israel with all his heart; for he did not depart from the sins of Jeroboam, who had made Israel sin' (2 Kings 10:31). In short, one general remark applies to all these kings. They were all wrong inwardly, they were rotten in their hearts.

There are places of worship in our country today where all the outward things of religion are done to perfection. The building is beautiful. The service is beautiful. The singing is beautiful. The forms of devotion are beautiful. There is everything to gratify the senses. Eye, ear and natural sentimentality are all pleased. But all the time God is not pleased. One thing is missing, and the lack of that one thing spoils everything. What is that one thing? It is heart! Under all this outward show, God sees the form of religion put in the place of substance, and is displeased. He sees nothing favourable in the building, the service, the minister, or the people. If he does not see converted, renewed, broken, penitent hearts, then he is not pleased! Bowed heads, bended knees, loud amens, eyes lifted to heaven, all, all are nothing in God's sight without right hearts.

When the heart is right God can look over many things that are defective. There may be faults in judgement, and weakness in practice. There may be many deviations from the best course in the outward things of religion. But if the heart is sound, God is gentle in pointing out that which is amiss. He is merciful and gracious, and will pardon much that is imperfect, when he sees a true heart and an eye fixed on his glory.

Jehoshaphat and Asa were kings of Judah, who were defective in many things. Jehoshaphat was a timid, irresolute man, who did not know how to say 'No,' and joined affinity with Ahab, the most wicked king that ever reigned over Israel. Asa was an unstable man, who at one time trusted in the King of Syria more than in God, and at another time was angry with God's prophet for rebuking him (2 Chronicles 16:10). Yet both of them had one great redeeming point in their characters. With all their faults they had right *hearts*.

The Passover kept by Hezekiah was one at which there were many irregularities. The proper forms were not kept by many. They ate the Passover 'contrary to what was written'. But they did it with true and honest *hearts*. And we read that 'Hezekiah prayed for them, saying, "May the good LORD provide atonement for everyone who prepares his heart to seek God, the LORD God of his fathers, though he is not cleansed according to the purification of the sanctuary." And the LORD listened to Hezekiah and healed the people' (2 Chronicles 30:18-20).

The Passover kept by Josiah must have been far smaller and worse attended than the numerous Passovers in the days of David and Solomon, or even in the reign of Jehoshaphat and Hezekiah. How then can we account for the strong language used in Scripture about it? 'There had been no Passover kept in Israel like that since the days of Samuel the prophet; and none of the kings of Israel had kept such a Passover as Josiah kept, with the priests and the Levites, all Judah and Israel who were present, and the inhabitants of Jerusalem' (2 Chronicles 35:18). There is but one explanation. There never was a Passover at which the *hearts* of the worshippers were so truly in the feast. The Lord does not look at the quantity of worshippers so much as the quality. The glory of Josiah's Passover was the state of people's hearts.

There are many assemblies of Christian worshippers on earth this very day in which there is literally nothing to attract the natural man. They meet in miserable, dirty, so-called chapels, or in wretched upper-rooms and cellars. They sing out of tune. They have feeble prayers and feeble sermons. And yet the Holy Spirit is often in the midst of them! Sinners are often converted in them, and the Kingdom of God prospers far more than in any Roman Catholic cathedral, or any gorgeous Protestant churches. How is this? How can it be explained? The cause is simply this, that in these humble assemblies heart-religion is taught and held. Heart-work is aimed at. Heart-work is honoured. And the consequence is that God is pleased and grants his blessing.

I leave this part of my subject here. I ask my readers to consider carefully the things that I have been saying. I believe that they will bear examination, and are all true. Resolve this day, whatever church you belong to, to be a Christian in 'heart'. Do not be content with a mere form of godliness, without the power. Be firmly convinced in your mind that formal religion is not saving religion, and that heart-religion is the only religion that leads to heaven.

I only give one word of caution. Do not suppose, because formal religion will not save, that forms of religion are of no use at all. Beware of any such senseless extreme. The misuse of a thing is no argument against the right use of it. The blind idolatry of forms that prevails in some quarters is no reason why you should throw away all forms. The ark, when made an idol by Israel and put in the place of God, was unable to save them from the Philistines, and when irreverently and improperly handled, brought death on Uzza. And yet the same ark, when honoured and reverenced, brought a blessing on the house of Obed-edom. The words of one of our ministers are strong, but true: 'He that has but a form of religion is a hypocrite; but he that does not have a form of religion is an Atheist' (*Hall's sermons*, No. 28). Forms cannot save us, but they are not therefore to be despised. A light is not a man's home, and yet it helps a man find his house when he is travelling home on a dark night. Use the forms of Christianity diligently, and you will find them a blessing. Only remember the great principle, that the first thing in religion is the state of the heart.

True religion must never expect to be popular

I now come to the last thing that I want you to consider. True religion must never expect to be popular. It will not have the praise of man, but of God.

I dare not turn away from this part of my subject, however painful it may be. Anxious as I am to commend heart-religion to everyone reading this, I will not try to conceal what heart-religion entails. I will not gain a recruit for my Master's army under false pretences. I will not promise anything that the Scripture does not warrant. The words of Paul are clear and unmistakable. Heart-religion is a religion whose 'praise is not from men but from God' (Romans 2:29).

God's truth and scriptural Christianity are never really popular. They never have been. They never will be as long as the world stands. No one can calmly consider what human nature is, as described in the Bible, and reasonably expect anything else. As long as man is what man is, the majority of mankind will always like a religion of form far better than a religion of heart.

Formal religion just suits an unenlightened conscience. Man must have some religion. Atheism and downright unbelief, as a general rule, are never very popular. But a man must have a religion that does not require very much, trouble his heart very much, interfere with his sins very much. Formal Christianity satisfies him. It seems to be the thing that he wants.

Formal religion gratifies the secret self-righteousness of man. All of us, more or less, are Pharisees. We all naturally cling to the idea that the way to be saved is to do so many things, and go through so many religious observances, and as a result we will get to heaven. Formalism meets us here. It seems to show us a way by which we can make our own peace with God.

Formal religion pleases the natural laziness of man. It attaches an excessive importance to that which is the easiest part of Christianity — the shell and the form. Man likes this. He hates exertion in religion. He wants something that will not meddle with his conscience and inner life. Only leave his conscience alone, and it will want to do works or actions. Formalism seems to open a wider gate, and a more easy way to heaven.

Facts speak louder than assertions. Facts are stubborn things. Look over the history of religion in every age of the world, and observe what has always been popular. Look at the history of Israel from the beginning of Exodus to the end of the Acts of the Apostles, and see what has always found favour. Formalism was one main sin against which the Old Testament prophets were continually protesting. Formalism was the great plague that had overcome the Jews, when our Lord Jesus Christ came into the world. Look at the history of the church of Christ after the days of the apostles. How soon formalism ate out the life and vitality of the primitive Christians! Look at the Middle Ages, as they are called. Formalism so completely covered the face of Christendom that the gospel laid there as if dead. Look, lastly, at the history of Protestant churches in the last three centuries. How few are the places where religion is a living thing! How many are the countries where Protestantism is nothing more than a form! There is no getting past these things. They speak with a voice of thunder. They all show that formal religion is a popular thing. It has the praise of man.

But why should we look at facts in history? Why shouldn't we look at the facts under our own eyes, and by our own doors? Can anyone deny that a mere outward religion, a religion of downright formalism, is the religion that is popular today? Is it for nothing that John says of certain false teachers, 'They are of the world. Therefore they speak as of the world, and the world hears them' (1 John 4:5). Only say your prayers, and go to church regularly, and receive the Lord's Supper occasionally, read your Bible occasionally, and the vast majority of our nation will call you a good Christian person. 'What more would you have to do?' they say. 'If this is not Christianity, what is?' To require more of anyone is thought to be unfair, fanaticism and to be too enthusiastic! To insinuate that such a man as this may not go to heaven is called unloving! It is vain to deny that formal religion is popular. It is popular. It always was popular. It always will be popular till Christ comes again. It always has had and always will have the 'praise of man'.

Turn now to the religion of the heart, and you will hear a very different report. As a general rule it has never been liked by mankind. It has brought upon its professors laughter, ridicule, scorn, contempt, seclusion, imprisonment and even death. Its lovers have been faithful and zealous — but they have always been few in number. It has never had, comparatively, 'the praise of man'.

Heart-religion is too humbling to be popular. It leaves natural man no room to boast. It tells him that he is a guilty, lost, hell-deserving sinner, and that he must flee to Christ for salvation. It tells him that he is dead, and must be made alive again, and born of the Spirit. The pride of man rebels against such words as these. He hates to be told that he is that bad.

Heart-religion is too holy to be popular. It will not leave natural man alone. It interferes with his worldliness and his sins. It requires of him things that he hates and despises — conversion, faith, repentance, spiritual-mindedness, Bible-reading and prayer. It commands him to give up what he loves and clings to, and refuses to lay aside. It would be strange indeed if he liked it. It crosses his path as a killjoy and a troublemaker, and it is absurd to expect that he will be pleased with it.

Was heart-religion popular in Old Testament times? We find David complaining: 'Those who sit in the gate speak against me, and I am the song of the drunkards' (Psalm 69:12). We find the prophets persecuted and ill-treated because they preached against sin, and required men to give their hearts to God. Elijah, Micaiah, Jeremiah, Amos, are all cases in point. To formalism and ceremonialism the Jews never seem to have objected. What they disliked was serving God with their hearts.

Was heart-religion popular in New Testament times? The whole history of our Lord Jesus Christ's ministry and the lives of his apostles are a sufficient answer. The scribes and Pharisees would have willingly received a Messiah who encouraged formalism, and a gospel that exalted ceremonialism. But they could not tolerate a religion of which the first principles were humiliation and sanctification of the heart.

Has heart-religion ever been popular in the professing church of Christ? Hardly ever, except in the early centuries when the primitive church had not left her first love. Soon, very soon, the men who protested against formalism and sacramentalism were fiercely denounced as 'troublers of Israel'. Long before the Reformation, things came to this, that anyone who preached heart-holiness and condemned formalism was treated as a common enemy. He was either silenced, excommunicated, imprisoned, or put to death like John Huss. In the time of the Reformation itself, the work of Luther and his companions was carried on under an incessant storm of defamation and slander. And what was the cause? It was because they protested against formalism, ceremonialism, the false Roman Catholic priesthood, monks, and taught the necessity of heart-religion.

Has heart-religion ever been popular in our own country in the past? Never, except for a short time. It was not popular in the days of Queen Mary, when Latimer and his fellow martyrs were burned at the stake. It was not popular in the days when to be a Puritan was worse than to be a drunkard or a blasphemer.

It was not popular in the middle of the eighteenth century, when Wesley and Whitefield were shut out of the established church. The cause of our martyred Reformers, of the early Puritans, and of the Methodists, was essentially one and the same. They were all hated because they preached the uselessness of formalism, and the impossibility of salvation without repentance, faith, regeneration, spiritual-mindedness and holiness of heart.

Is heart-religion popular in our country today? I answer sorrowfully that I do not believe it is. Look at its followers among the congregations. They are always comparatively few in number. They stand alone in their respective congregations. They have put up with many difficult things, harsh words, censure, harsh treatment, laughter, ridicule, slander and petty persecution. This is not popularity! Look at the teachers of heart-religion in the pulpit. They are loved and liked, no doubt, by the few hearers who agree with them. They are sometimes admired for their talents and eloquence by the many who do not agree with them. They are even called 'popular preachers', because of the crowds who listen to their preaching. But none know so well as the faithful teachers of heart-religion that few really like them. Few really help them. Few sympathize with them. Few stand by them in any time of need. They find, like their divine Master, that they must work almost alone. I write these things with sorrow, but I believe they are true. Real heart-religion today, no less than in days gone by, does not have 'the praise of man'.

But in the end it is not important what man thinks, and what man praises. He who judges us is the Lord. Man will not judge us at the last day. Man will not sit on the great white throne, examine our religion, and pronounce our eternal sentence. Only those whom God commends will be commended at the judgement seat of Christ. Here lies the value and glory of heart-religion. It may not have the praise of man, but it has 'the praise of God'.

God approves and honours heart-religion in this life. He looks down from heaven, and reads the hearts of all the children of men. Wherever he sees heart-repentance for sin, heart-faith in Christ, heart-holiness of life, heart-love to his Son, his law, his will and his Word — wherever God sees these things he is well pleased. He writes a book of remembrance for that man, however poor and uneducated he may be. He gives his angels special charge over him. He maintains in him the work of grace, and gives him daily supplies of peace, hope and strength. He regards him as a member of his own dear Son, as one who is witnessing for the truth, as his Son did. Weak as the man's heart may seem to himself, it is the living sacrifice that God loves, and the heart that he has solemnly declared he will not despise. Such praise is worth more than the praise of man!

God will proclaim his approval of heart-religion before the assembled world at the last day. He will command his angels to gather together his saints, from every part of the globe, into one glorious company. He will raise the dead and change the living, and place them at the right hand of his beloved Son's throne. Then all who have served Christ with the heart shall hear him say, 'Come, you blessed of my Father; inherit the kingdom prepared for you from the foundation of the world.' 'You were faithful over a few things, I will make you ruler over many things. Enter into the joy of your lord.' 'Whoever confesses me before men, him the Son of Man also will confess before the angels of God.' 'But you are those who have continued with me in my trials. And I bestow upon you a kingdom, just as my Father bestowed one upon me' (Matthew 25:21-34; Luke 12:8; 22:28-29). These words will be addressed to none but those who have given Christ their hearts! They will not be addressed to the formalist, the hypocrite, the wicked and the ungodly. They will, indeed, see the fruits of heart-religion, but they will not eat of them. We will never know the full value of heart-religion until the last day. Then, and only then, will we fully understand how much better it is to have the praise of God than the praise of man.

If you take up heart-religion I cannot promise you the praise of man. Pardon, peace, hope, guidance, comfort, consolation, grace according to your need, strength according to your day, joy which the world can neither give nor take away — all this I can boldly promise to the man who comes to Christ, and serves him with his heart. But I cannot promise him that his religion will be popular with man. I would rather warn him to expect mockery and ridicule, slander and unkindness, opposition and persecution. There is a cross belonging to heart-religion, and we must be content to carry it. 'We must through many tribulations enter the kingdom of God'. 'All who desire to live godly in Christ Jesus will suffer persecution' (Acts 14:22; 2 Timothy 3:12). But if the world hates you, God will love you. If the world forsakes you, Christ has promised that he will never forsake and never fail. Whatever you may lose by heart-religion, be sure that the praise of God will make up for it.

Words of application

And now I close this chapter with three plain words of application. I want it to strike and stick to the conscience of every one into whose hands it falls. May God make it a blessing to many a soul, both in time and eternity!

Is your religion a matter of form?

In the first place, is your religion a matter of form and not of heart? Answer this question honestly, and as in the sight of God. If it is, *consider solemnly the immense danger in which you stand.*

You have nothing to comfort your soul in the day of trial, nothing to give you hope on your deathbed, nothing to save you at the last day. Formal religion never took any man to heaven. Like cheap metal, it will not stand the fire. Continuing in your present state you are in imminent danger of being lost for ever.

I earnestly beseech you this day to be aware of your danger, to open your eyes and repent. Whether you go to a fancy big city church or to a plain small church in the country, if you are a Christian in name only, and possess a form of godliness without the power — awake and repent. Awake, above all, if you are an Evangelical formalist. 'There is no devil', said the quaint old Puritans, 'like a white devil.' There is no formalism so dangerous as Evangelical formalism.

I can only warn you. I do so with all affection. God alone can apply the warning to your soul. Oh, that you would see the folly as well as the danger of a heartless Christianity! It was sound advice that a dying man once gave to his son: 'Son,' he said, 'whatever religion you have, never be content with wearing a cloak.'

Does your heart condemn you?

In the second place, if your heart condemns you, and you wish to know what to do, *consider seriously the only course that you can safely take.*

Cry out to the Lord Jesus Christ without delay, and spread before him the state of your soul. Confess before him your formalism of the past, and ask him to forgive it. Seek from him the promised grace of the Holy Spirit, and beg him to quicken and renew your inward man.

The Lord Jesus is appointed and commissioned to be the Physician of man's soul. There is no case too hard for him. There is no condition of soul that he cannot cure. There is no devil he cannot cast out. Seared and hardened as the heart of a formalist may be, there is medicine that can heal him, and a Physician who is mighty to save. Go and call on the Lord Jesus Christ this very day. 'Ask, and it will be given to you; seek, and you will find; knock, and it will be opened to you' (Luke 11:9).

Does your heart not condemn you?

In the last place, if your heart does not condemn you, and you have real well-grounded confidence towards God, *consider seriously the many responsibilities of your position.*

Praise him daily who has called you out of darkness into light, and made you to be different. Praise him daily, and ask him never to forsake the work of his own hands.

Watch with a jealous watchfulness every part of your inward man. Formalism is ever ready to come in upon us, like the Egyptian plague of frogs, which even went into the king's bedroom. Watch and be on your guard. Watch over your Bible-reading, your praying, your temper and your tongue, your family life and your Sunday religion. There is nothing so good and spiritual that we may not fall into formal habits about it. There is no one so spiritual that they cannot fall into formalism. Watch, therefore, and be on your guard.

Look forward, finally, and hope for the coming of the Lord. Your best things are yet to come. The second coming of Christ will soon be here. The time of temptation will soon be past and gone. The judgement and reward of the saints shall soon make amends for everything. Rest in the hope of that day. Work, watch, and look forward. There is one thing, at any rate, that day will make abundantly clear. It will show that there was never an hour in our lives in which we had our hearts too thoroughly focused on Christ.

12.
The world

'Come out from among them and be separate, says the Lord'
(2 Corinthians 6:17).

The text above touches a subject of vast importance in Christianity. That subject is the great duty of separation from the world. This is the point that Paul had in view when he wrote to the Corinthians, 'Come out from among them and be separate.'

The subject is one that demands the absolute attention of all who profess and call themselves Christians. In every age of the church, separation from the world has always been one of the great evidences of a work of grace in the heart. He who has been really born of the Spirit, and made a new creature in Christ Jesus, has always endeavoured to 'come out from the world', and live a separate life. Those who only wore the name 'Christian', without the reality, have always refused to 'come out and be separate' from the world.

The subject perhaps was never more important than it is today. There is a widespread desire to make things pleasant in Christianity — to saw off the corners and edges of the cross, and to avoid, as far as possible, self-denial. Everywhere we hear professing Christians declaring loudly that we must not be 'too narrow and exclusive', and that there is no harm in many things that the holiest saints of old thought would be bad for their souls. That we may go anywhere, and do anything, and spend our time in anything, and read anything, and keep any company, and plunge into anything, and all the while still be good Christians — this is what thousands are saying. In a day like this I think it is good to raise a warning voice and bring attention to the teaching of God's Word. It is written in that Word, 'Come out from among them and be separate.'

There are four points that I will try to show my readers, in examining this great subject.

Firstly, I will try to show that the world is a source of great danger to the soul.

Secondly, I will try to show what is *not* meant by separation from the world.

Thirdly, I will try to show what real separation from the world entails.

Fourthly, I will try to show the secret of victory over the world.

And now, before I go a single step further, let me warn every one of my readers that he will never understand this subject unless he first understands what a true Christian is. If you are one of those unhappy people who thinks that everybody who goes to a place of worship is a Christian, no matter how he lives, or what he believes, I fear you will care little about separation from the world. But if you read your Bible, and are serious about your soul, you will know that there are two classes of (those who call themselves) 'Christians' — converted and unconverted. You will know that what the Jews were among the nations of the Old Testament, the true Christian is meant to be under the New. You will understand what I mean when I say that, in the same way, true Christians are meant to be a 'peculiar people' under the gospel, and that there must be a difference between believers and unbelievers. To you, therefore, I make a special appeal this day. While many avoid the subject of separation from the world, many absolutely hate it, and many are puzzled by it, give me your attention while I try to show it to you 'as it is'.

The world is a source of great danger to the soul

First of all, let me show that the world is a source of great danger to the soul. Remember that by 'the world', I do not mean the material world on the face of which we are living and moving. He who pretends to say that anything that God has created in the heavens above, or the earth beneath, is in itself harmful to man's soul, is being unreasonable and absurd. On the contrary, the sun, moon and stars; the mountains, the valleys and the plains; the seas, the lakes and rivers; the animal and vegetable creation — all are in themselves 'very good' (Genesis 1:31). All are full of lessons of God's wisdom and power, and all proclaim daily, 'The hand that made us is divine.' The idea that 'matter' is in itself sinful and corrupt is a foolish heresy.

When I speak of 'the world' in this publication, I mean those people who think only, or chiefly, of this world's things, and neglect the world to come — the people who are always think-ing more of earth than of heaven, more of time than of eternity, more of body than of soul, more of pleasing man than of pleas-ing God. It is of them and their ways, habits, customs, opin-ions, practices, tastes, aims, spirit and tone that I am speaking when I speak of 'the world'. This is the world from which Paul tells us to 'Come out and be separate.'

Now 'the world', in this sense, is an enemy to the soul. There are three things that a baptized Christian must renounce and give up, and three enemies that he must fight with and resist. These three are the flesh, the devil and 'the world'. All three are terrible foes, and all three must be overcome if we would be saved.

Let us turn to the testimony of the Holy Scriptures. If the texts I am about to quote do not prove that the world is a source of danger to the soul, then words have no meaning.

1. This is what the apostle Paul says:

'Do not be conformed to this world, but be transformed by the renewing of your mind' (Romans 12:2).

'Now we have received, not the spirit of the world, but the Spirit who is from God' (1 Corinthians 2:12).

'[Christ] gave himself for our sins, that he might deliver us from this present evil age [world]' (Galatians 1:4).

'You ... who were dead in trespasses and sins, in which you once walked according to the course of this world' (Ephesians 2:1-2).

'for Demas has forsaken me, having loved this present world' (2 Timothy 4:10).

2. This is what James says:

'Pure and undefiled religion before God and the Father is this: to visit orphans and widows in their trouble, and to keep oneself unspotted from the world' (James 1:27).

'Do you not know that friendship with the world is enmity with God? Whoever therefore wants to be a friend of the world makes himself an enemy of God' (James 4:4).

3. This is what John says:

'Do not love the world or the things in the world. If anyone loves the world, the love of the Father is not in him. For all that is in the world — the lust of the flesh, the lust of the eyes, and the pride of life — is not of the Father but is of the world. And the world is passing away, and the lust of it; but he who does the will of God abides for ever' (1 John 2:15-17).

'Therefore the world does not know us, because it did not know him' (1 John 3:1).

'They are of the world. Therefore they speak as of the world, and the world hears them' (1 John 4:5).

'For whatever is born of God overcomes the world' (1 John 5:4).

'We know that we are of God, and the whole world lies under the sway of the wicked one' (1 John 5:19).

4. Lastly, this is what the Lord Jesus Christ says:

'Now he who received seed among the thorns is he who hears the word, and the cares of this world and the deceitfulness of riches choke the word, and he becomes unfruitful' (Matthew 13:22).

'You are of this world; I am not of this world' (John 8:23).

'... the Spirit of truth, whom the world cannot receive, because it neither sees him nor knows him' (John 14:17).

'If the world hates you, you know that it hated me before it hated you' (John 15:18).

'If you were of the world, the world would love its own. Yet because you are not of the world, but I chose you out of the world, therefore the world hates you' (John 15:19).

'In the world you will have tribulation; but be of good cheer,
I have overcome the world' (John 16:33).

'They are not of the world, just as I am not of the world'
(John 17:16).

I make no comment on these texts. They speak for themselves.
If anyone can read them carefully, and fail to see that 'the world'
is an enemy to the Christian's soul, and that there is an utter
opposition between the friendship of the world and the friendship of Christ, he is past the reach of argument, and it is a
waste of time to reason with him. To my eyes they contain a
lesson as clear as the noonday sun.

I turn from Scripture to matters of fact and experience. I
appeal to any mature Christian who keeps his eyes open, and
knows what is going on in the churches. I ask him whether it is
true that nothing damages the cause of Christianity so much as
'the world'? It is not open sin, or open unbelief, which robs
Christ of his professing servants, so much as the love of the
world, the fear of the world, the cares of the world, the business of the world, the money of the world, the pleasures of the
world, and the desire to keep in with the world. This is the
great rock on which thousands of young people are continually
being crushed against and destroyed. They don't object to any
of the truths of the Christian faith. They do not deliberately
choose evil, and openly rebel against God. They hope somehow to get to heaven in the end; and they think it is right to
have some religion. But they cannot give up their idol: they
must have the world. And so, after running well and longing
for heaven while boys and girls, they turn aside when they
become men and women, and go down the broad way that
leads to destruction. They begin with Abraham and Moses,
and end with Demas and Lot's wife.

The last day alone will prove how many souls 'the world' has slain. Hundreds will be found to have been trained in Christian homes, and to have known the gospel from their very childhood, and yet missed heaven. They left the harbour of home with bright prospects, and launched forth on the ocean of life with a father's blessing and a mother's prayers, and then turned from the right course through the seductions of the world, and ended their voyage on the reef and in misery. It is a sorrowful story to tell; but it is all too common! I can clearly see why Paul says, 'Come out from among them and be separate.'

What does *not* constitute separation from the world

Let me now try to show what does not constitute separation from the world. This is a point that requires clearing up. There are many mistakes made about it. You will sometimes see sincere and well-meaning Christians doing things that God never intended them to do, in the matter of separation from the world, and honestly believing that they are in the very will of God. Their mistakes often cause them great harm. They give the wicked the opportunity to ridicule all Christianity, and supply them with an excuse for having no part of it. Because of them, people speak evil of the way of truth, and so they add to the offence of the cross. I consider it my plain duty to make a few remarks on the subject. We must never forget that it is possible to be very dedicated, and to think we are 'doing God service', when in reality we are making some great mistakes. There is such a thing as having a 'zeal for God, but not according to knowledge' (Romans 10:2); for example, 'The time is coming that whoever kills you will think that he offers God service' (John 16:2). There are few things about which it is so important to pray for sound judgement and sanctified common sense, than separation from the world.

Do not give up your professions

When Paul said, 'Come out from among them and be separate', he did not mean that Christians ought to give up all worldly
callings, trades, professions and business. He did not forbid
men to be soldiers, sailors, lawyers, doctors, merchants, bankers, shopkeepers, or tradesmen. There is not a word in the New
Testament to justify such a line of conduct. Cornelius the
centurion, Luke the physician and Zenas the lawyer are examples to the contrary. Idleness is in itself a sin. A lawful calling is
a remedy against temptation. 'If anyone will not work, neither
shall he eat' (2 Thessalonians 3:10). To give up any business of
life that is not necessarily sinful to the wicked and the devil,
from fear of being harmed by it, is lazy, cowardly conduct. The
right plan is to carry our Christianity into our business, and not
to give up business under the false pretence that it interferes
with our Christianity.

Do not disassociate from the unconverted

When Paul said, 'Come out from among them and be separate', he did not mean that Christians ought to decline all asso-
ciation with unconverted people, and refuse to go into their
circles. There is no warrant for such conduct in the New Testament. Our Lord and his disciples did not refuse to go to a marriage feast, or to sit at dinner in the home of a Pharisee. Paul
does not say, 'If any of those who do not believe invites you to
dinner', you must not go, but tells us how to behave if we *do* go
(1 Corinthians 10:27). Moreover, it is a dangerous thing to begin
judging people too closely, and deciding who are converted
and who are not, and what society is godly and what ungodly.
We are sure to make mistakes. Above all, such a course of life
would deprive us of many opportunities of doing good. If we
carry our Master with us wherever we go, who can tell but we

may 'save some', and not come to any harm? 'To the weak I
became as weak, that I may win the weak. I have become all
things to all men, that I might by all means save some'
(1 Corinthians 9:22).

Acquaint yourself with the world

When Paul says, 'Come out from among them and be separate,' he did not mean that Christians ought to take no interest
in anything on earth except religion. To neglect science, art,
literature and politics; to read nothing which is not directly spiritual; to know nothing about what is going on among mankind,
and never to look at a newspaper; to care nothing about the
government of one's country, and to be utterly indifferent as to
the people who guide it, counsel and make its laws — all this
may seem very right and proper in the eyes of some people.
But I think that it is an idle, selfish neglect of duty. Paul knew
the value of good government as one of the main aids to our
'[leading] a quiet and peaceable life in all godliness and rever-
ence' (1 Timothy 2:2). Paul was not ashamed to read heathen
writers, and to quote their words in his speeches and writings.
He did not think it beneath him to show he was acquainted
with the laws and customs and callings of the world, in the
illustrations he gave from them. Christians who pride themselves on their ignorance of secular things are precisely the
Christians who bring Christianity into contempt. I knew the case
of a blacksmith who would not come to hear his clergyman
preach the gospel, until he found out that he knew the properties
of iron. Then he came.

Dress moderately

When Paul said, 'Come out from among them and be separate,' he did not mean that Christians should be strange and

odd in their dress, manners, demeanour and voice. Anything that attracts attention to these matters is most objectionable, and ought to be carefully avoided. To wear clothes of such a colour, or made in such a fashion that when you go into company every eye is fixed on you, and you are the object of general observation, is an enormous mistake. It gives the wicked the opportunity to ridicule Christianity, and looks self-righteous and unnatural. There is not the slightest proof that our Lord and his apostles, and Priscilla, and Persis, and their companions, did not dress and behave just like others in their own ranks of life. On the other hand, one of the many charges our Lord brings against the Pharisees was that they 'make their phylacteries broad and enlarge the borders of their garments', so as to be 'seen by men' (Matthew 23:5). True sanctity and sanctimoniousness are entirely different things. Those who try to show their unworldliness by wearing conspicuously ugly clothes, or by speaking in a whining, snuffling voice, or by affecting an unnatural slavishness, humility and gravity of manner miss their mark altogether, and only give cause to the enemies of the Lord to blaspheme.

Do not become reclusive

When Paul said, 'Come out from them and be separate,' he did not mean that Christians ought to retire from the company of mankind, and shut themselves up in solitude. It is one of the crying errors of the Roman Catholic Church to suppose that eminent holiness is to be attained by such practices. It is the unhappy delusion of the whole army of monks, nuns and hermits. Separation of this kind is not according to the mind of Christ. He said distinctly in his last prayer, 'I do not pray that you should take them out of the world, but that you should keep them from the evil one' (John 17:15). There is not a word in Acts or the Epistles to recommend such a separation. True believers are always represented as mixing in the world, doing their duty in it, and glorifying God by patience, meekness, purity and courage in their many positions, and not by cowardly deserting them.

Besides, it is foolish to suppose that we can keep the world and the devil out of our hearts by going into holes and corners. True Christianity and unworldliness are best seen, not in timidly forsaking the post which God has allotted to us, but in boldly standing our ground, and showing the power of grace to overcome evil.

Do not withdraw from a church with unbelievers

Last, but not least, when Paul said, 'Come out from among them and be separate,' he did not mean that Christians ought to withdraw from every church in which there are unconverted members, or to refuse to worship in company with any who are not believers, or to keep away from the Lord's Table if any ungodly people go up to it. This is a very common but grievous mistake. There is not a text in the New Testament to justify it, and it ought to be condemned as a pure invention of man. Our Lord Jesus Christ deliberately allowed Judas Iscariot to be an apostle for three years, and gave him the Lord's Supper. He has taught us, in the parable of the wheat and tares, that converted and unconverted will be together till the harvest, and cannot be divided (Matthew 13:30). In his Epistles to the Seven Churches, and in all Paul's Epistles, we often see faults and corruption mentioned and reproved; but we are never told that they justify desertion of the assembly, or the neglect of the Lord's Table. In short, we must not look for a perfect church, a perfect congregation, and a perfect company of communicants until the Marriage Supper of the Lamb. If others are unworthy churchgoers or unworthy partakers of the Lord's Supper, the sin is theirs and not ours: we are not their judges. But to separate ourselves from church assemblies, and deprive ourselves of the Lord's Supper because others use them unworthily, is to take up a foolish, unreasonable and unscriptural position. It is not the mind of Christ, and it certainly is not Paul's idea of separation from the world.

I commend these six points to the calm consideration of all who wish to understand the subject of separation from the world. Far more might be said about each and every one of them than I have space to say here. I have seen so many mistakes made about each one, and so much misery and unhappiness caused by those mistakes, that I want to put Christians on their guard. I want them not to take up positions carelessly, in the zeal of their first love, which they will afterwards be obliged to give up.

I leave this part of my subject with two pieces of advice, which I offer especially to young Christians.

I advise them, for one thing, if they really desire to come out from the world, they should remember that the shortest path is not always the path of duty. To argue with our unconverted relatives, to 'avoid' all our old friends, to withdraw entirely from mixed society, to live an exclusive life, to give up every act of courtesy and civility in order that we may devote ourselves to the direct work of Christ — all this may seem very right, and may satisfy our consciences and save us trouble. But I venture a doubt as to whether it is not often a selfish, lazy, self-pleasing line of conduct, and whether the true cross and true line of duty may not be to deny ourselves, and adopt a very different course of action.

I advise them, for another thing, if they really want to come out from the world, they should guard against a sour, morose, ungenial, gloomy, unpleasant, surly demeanour, and never forget that there is such a thing as 'winning without the Word' (1 Peter 3:1: 'Wives, likewise, be submissive to your own husbands, that even if some do not obey the word, they, without a word, may be won by the conduct of their wives'). Let them

strive to show unconverted people that their principles, whatever may be thought of them, make them cheerful, amiable,
good-tempered, unselfish, considerate for others, and ready to
take an interest in everything that is innocent and of good report. In short, let there be no needless separation between us
and the world. In many things, as I will soon show, we must be
separate; but let us take care that it is the right sort of separation. If the world is offended by such separation we cannot help
it. But let us never give the world occasion to say that our separation is foolish, senseless, ridiculous, unreasonable, uncharitable and unscriptural.

What true separation from the world really is

In the third place, I will try to show what true separation from
the world really is. I take up this branch of my subject with a
very deep sense of its difficulty. It is very evident that there is a
certain line of conduct that all true Christians ought to pursue
with respect to 'the world, and the things of the world'. The
texts already quoted make that plain. The key to the solution of
that question lies in the word 'separation'. But in what separation
consists it is not easy to show. On some points it is not hard to lay
down particular rules, on others it is impossible to do more than
state general principles, and leave everyone to apply them according to his position in life. This is what I will attempt to do.

Do not be guided by the world's standards

First and foremost, he who desires to 'come out from among
the world, and be separate' must steadily and habitually refuse
to be guided by the world's standard of right and wrong.
    The rule of the mass of mankind is to go with the flow, to do
as others, to follow the fashion, to keep in with common opinion,

and to set your watch by the town clock. The true Christian will never be content with such a rule as that. He will simply ask, 'What does the Scripture say? What is written in the Word of God?' He will maintain firmly that nothing that God says is wrong can be right, that the customs and opinions of his neighbours can never make what God calls serious an unimportant matter, or that what God calls sin, cannot be called anything else. He will never think lightly of such sins as drinking, swearing, gambling, lying, cheating, swindling, or dishonouring the Lord's Day, because they are common, and of which many say, 'Where is the harm?' That miserable argument, 'Everybody thinks this way, everybody says so, everybody does it, everybody will be there,' means nothing to him. Is it condemned or approved by the Bible? That is his only question. If he stands alone in the town, or congregation, he will not go against the Bible. If he has to come out from the crowd, and take a position by himself, he will not flinch from it rather than disobey the Bible. This is genuine scriptural separation.

Be careful how you spend your leisure time

He who desires to 'come out from among the world, and be separate' must be very careful how he spends his leisure time. This is a point that at first sight appears of little importance. But the longer I live, the more I am persuaded that it deserves most serious attention. Honourable occupation and lawful business are a great safeguard to the soul and the time that is spent upon them is comparatively the time of our least danger. The devil finds it hard to get a hearing from a busy man. But when the day's work is over and leisure time arrives, then with it comes the hour of temptation.

I do not hesitate to warn every man who wants to live a Christian life to be very careful how he spends his evenings. Evening is the time when we are naturally disposed to relax after the labours of the day; and evening is the time when the Christian is too often tempted to lay aside his armour, and consequently brings trouble on his soul. 'Then comes the devil,' and with the devil the world. Evening is the time when the poor man is tempted to go to the bar and fall into sin. Evening is the time when the workman too often sits for hours hearing and seeing things that do him no good. Evening is the time that the higher classes choose for dancing, gambling and the like; and consequently never get to bed till late at night. If we love our souls, and would not become worldly, let us be careful how we spend our evenings. Tell me how a man spends his evenings, and I can generally tell what his character is.

The true Christian will do well to make it a settled rule never to 'waste' his evenings. Whatever others may do, let him resolve always to make time for quiet, calm thought — for Bible-reading and prayer. The rule will prove a hard one to keep. It may bring on him the charge of being unsociable and overly strict. Let him not mind this. Anything of this kind is better than habitual late hours in company, hurried prayers, slovenly Bible reading, and a bad conscience. Even if he stands alone in his church or town, let him not depart from his rule. He will find himself in a minority, and be thought an eccentric man. But this is genuine scriptural separation.

Determine not to be swallowed up and absorbed with the world's affairs

He who desires to 'come out from among the world, and be separate' must steadily and habitually determine not to be swallowed up and absorbed in the business of the world. A true Christian will strive to do his duty in whatever situation or position he finds himself, and to do it well. Whether statesman, or merchant, or banker, or lawyer, or doctor, or tradesman, or farmer, he will try to do his work so that no one can find cause for fault in him. But he will not allow it to get between him and Christ. If he finds his business beginning to eat up his Sundays, his Bible-reading, his private prayer time, and to bring clouds between him and heaven, he will say, 'Stand back! There is a limit. This is as far as you can go, and no further. I cannot sell my soul for position, fame or gold.' Like Daniel, he will make time for communion with God, whatever the cost may be. He will deny himself anything rather than lose his Bible-reading and his prayers. In all this he will find he stands almost alone. Many will laugh at him, and tell him they get along just fine without being so strict and particular. He will not listen. He will resolutely hold the world at arms' length, whatever present loss or sacrifice it may seem to entail. He will choose, rather, to be less rich and prosperous in this world, than not to prosper about his soul. To stand alone in this way, to run counter to the ways of others, requires immense self-denial. But this is genuine scriptural separation.

Abstain from all sinful amusements and recreations

He who desires to 'come out from among the world, and be separate' must steadily abstain from all amusements and recreations that are inseparably connected with sin. This is a hard subject to handle, and I approach it with pain. But I do not think I would be faithful to Christ, and faithful to my office as a minister, if I did not speak very plainly about it, when considering such a matter as separation from the world.

Let me, then, say honestly, that I cannot understand how anyone who makes any pretence to real vital Christianity can allow himself to attend horse races and theatres. Conscience no doubt is a strange thing, and every man must judge for himself and use his liberty. One man sees no harm in things that another regards with abhorrence as evil. I can only give my own opinion for what it is worth, and entreat my readers to consider seriously what I say.

No sensible man will pretend to deny that to look at horses running at full speed is in itself perfectly harmless. It is equally undeniable that many plays, such as Shakespeare's, are among the finest productions of the human intellect. But all this is beside the point. The question is whether horse racing and theatres, as they are conducted, are downright wicked. I assert without hesitation that they are. I assert that the breach of God's commandments so invariably accompanies the race and the play, that you cannot go there without helping sin.

I entreat all professing Christians to remember this, and to take heed what they do. I warn them plainly that they have no right to shut their eyes to facts that every intelligent person knows, for the mere pleasure of seeing a horse race, or listening to good actors or actresses. I warn them that they must not talk of separation from the world, if they can lend their sanction to amusements that are invariably connected with gambling, betting, drunkenness and fornication. These are the things 'God will judge', and which result 'in death'! (Hebrews 13:4; Romans 6:21).

These are hard words! But are they not true? It may seem to your relatives and friends very strait-laced, strict and narrow, if you tell them you cannot go to the races or the theatre with them. But we must fall back on first principles. Is the world a danger to the soul, or is it not? Are we to come out from the world, or are we not? These are questions that can only be answered in one way.

If we love our souls we must have nothing to do with entertainment that is bound up with sin. Nothing short of this can be called genuine scriptural separation from the world.

I would like to note here that thoughtful and intelligent readers will probably observe that, under the heading of worldly entertainment, I have said nothing about dancing and playing cards. They are delicate and difficult subjects, but I am quite willing to give my opinion, all the more because I can speak of them from experience in the days of my youth.

Concerning *dancing* (or going to 'balls'), I only ask Christians to judge this entertainment by its tendencies and accomplishments. To say there is anything morally wrong in the mere bodily act of dancing would be absurd. David danced before the ark. Solomon said, 'There is a time to dance' (Ecclesiastes 3:4). Just as it is natural to lambs and kittens to frisk about, so it seems natural to young people, all over the world, to jump about to a lively tune of music. If dancing were taken up for mere exercise, if dancing took place at early hours, and men only danced with men, and women with women, it would be needless and absurd to object to it. But everybody knows that this is not what is meant by modern dancing (going to balls and dances). This is entertainment that involves very late hours, extravagant dressing, and an immense amount of frivolity, vanity, jealousy, unhealthy excitement and vain conversation. Who would like to be found in a modern dance-hall when the Lord Jesus Christ comes the second time? Whoever has taken much part in balls and dancing, as I myself once did before I knew better, can deny that they have a most dissipating effect on the mind, like using drugs and the drinking of alcoholic beverages does on the body? I cannot withhold my opinion that dancing and going to balls is one of those worldly amusements which 'wars against the soul', and which it is wisest and best to give up. And as for those parents who urge their sons and daughters, against their wills and inclinations, to go to such places, I can only say that they are taking on themselves a most dangerous responsibility, and risking great injury to their children's souls.

Concerning *card-playing and gambling*, my judgement is much the same. I ask Christian people to judge it by its tendencies and consequences. Of course it would be nonsense to say there is positive wickedness in an innocent game of cards for diversion, and not for money. I have known instances of old people of lethargic and infirm body, unable to work or read, to whom cards in an evening were really useful, to keep them from drowsiness, and preserve their health. But it is vain to shut our eyes from facts. If parents once begin to play cards in the living room, children are likely to play cards in their rooms; and then there follows a whole train of evil. Besides, from simple card-playing to desperate gambling there is but a chain of steps. If parents teach young people that there is no harm in the first step, they must never be surprised if they go on to the last.

I give this opinion with much diffidence. I lay no claim to infallibility. Let every one be persuaded in his own mind. But, considering all things, it is my deliberate judgement that the Christian who wishes to keep his soul right, and to 'come out from the world', will be wise to have nothing to do with playing cards. It is a habit that seems to grow on some people so much that in the end it becomes a necessity, and they cannot live without it. 'Madam,' said Romaine to an old lady, who declared she could not make it without her cards, 'Madam, if this is the case, cards are your god, and your god is a very poor one.' Surely, in doubtful matters like these, it is best to give our souls the benefit of the doubt, and to refrain.

Concerning *sport*, I admit that it is not easy to lay down a strict rule. I cannot go the lengths of some, and say that galloping across the country, or shooting grouse, partridges, or pheasants, or catching salmon or trout, are in themselves positively sinful occupations and distinct marks of an unconverted heart. There are many, I know, to whom intense outdoor exercise and complete diversion of mind are absolute necessities, for the preservation of their bodily and mental health. But in all these matters the chief question is one of degree. Much depends on the company men are thrown into, and the lengths to which they go. The great danger lies in excess. It is possible to be 'excessive' about hunting as well as about drinking. We are commanded in Scripture to be 'moderate in all things', if we would be successful in the Christian life; and those who are addicted to sport should not forget this rule.

The question, however, is one about which Christians must be careful in expressing an opinion, and moderate in their judgements. The man who can neither ride, nor shoot, nor throw a fly, is hardly qualified to speak dispassionately about such matters. It is cheap and easy to condemn others for doing things that you cannot do yourself, and are utterly unable to enjoy! One thing only is perfectly certain — all overindulgence or excess is sin. The man who is wholly absorbed in sport, and spends all his years in such a manner that he seems to think God only created him to be a 'hunting, shooting, and fishing animal', is a man who at present knows very little of scriptural Christianity. It is written, 'For where your treasure is, there your heart will be also' (Matthew 6:21).

Be moderate in the use of lawful and innocent recreations

He who desires to 'come out from among the world, and be separate' must be moderate in the use of lawful and innocent recreations. No sensible Christian will ever think of condemning all recreation. In a world of work and stress like the one that we live in, occasional relaxation is good for everyone. Body and mind alike require seasons of lighter occupation, and opportunities of letting off high spirits, especially when they are young. Exercise itself is a positive necessity for the preservation of mental and bodily health. I see no harm in field sports, rowing, running and other athletic recreations. I find no fault with those who play chess and other such games of skill. We are all fearfully and wonderfully made. No wonder the poet says,

> Strange that a harp of thousand strings
> Should keep in tune so long!

Anything which strengthens nerves, and brain, and digestion, and lungs, and muscles, and makes us more fit for Christ's work, so long as it is not in itself sinful, is a blessing, and ought to be thankfully used. Anything that will occasionally divert our thoughts from their usual grinding path, in a healthy manner, is good and not evil.

But it is the excess of these innocent things that a true Christian must watch against, if he wants to be separate from the world. He must not devote his whole heart, and soul, and mind, and strength, and time to them, as many do, if he wishes to serve Christ. There are hundreds of lawful things that are good in moderation, but bad when taken in excess. Healthy medicine taken in small quantities is good, but downright poison when swallowed down in huge doses. In nothing is this so true as in the matter of recreation. Their use is one thing, their abuse is another. The Christian who uses them must know when to stop, and how to say 'Enough!' Do they interfere with his private religion? Do they take up too much of his thoughts and attention? Have they a secularizing effect on his soul? Have they a tendency to pull him down to earth? Then let him be very careful. All this will require courage, self-denial and firmness. It is a line of conduct that will often bring on us the ridicule and contempt of those who do not know what moderation is, and who spend their lives in making trifles serious things and serious things trifles. But if we mean to come out from the world we must not mind this. We must be 'temperate' even in lawful things, whatever others may think of us. This is genuine scriptural separation.

Be careful in friendships and relationships with worldly people

Last, but not least, he who desires to 'come out from among the world, and be separate' must be careful in friendships, intimacies and close relationships with worldly people. We cannot help meeting many unconverted people as long as we live. We cannot avoid associating with them, and doing business with them, unless we 'go out of the world' (1 Corinthians 5:10). To treat them with the utmost courtesy, kindness and charity, whenever we do meet them, is a positive duty. But acquaintance is one thing, and intimate friendship is quite another. To join their circle without reason, to choose their company, to cultivate intimacy with them, is very dangerous to the soul. Human nature is so constituted that we cannot associate with other people without it having an effect on our own character. The old proverb will never fail to prove true: 'Tell me with whom a man chooses to live, and I will tell you what he is.' The Scripture says expressly, 'He who walks with wise men will be wise, but the companion of fools will be destroyed' (Proverbs 13:20). If then a Christian who desires to live consistently chooses for his friends those who either do not care for their souls, or the Bible, or God, or Christ, or holiness, or regard them as of secondary importance, it seems to me impossible for him to prosper in his Christianity. He will soon find that their ways are not his ways, nor their thoughts his thoughts, nor their tastes his tastes; and that, unless they change, he must give up close friendship with them. In short, there must be separation. Of course such separation will be painful. But if we have to choose between the loss of a friend and the injury of our souls, there ought to be no doubt in our minds. If friends will not walk in the narrow way with us, we must not walk in the broad way to please them. But let us distinctly understand that to attempt to keep up close intimacy between a converted and an unconverted person, if both are consistent with their natures, is to attempt the impossible.

The principle laid down here ought to be carefully remembered by all unmarried Christians in the choice of a husband or wife. I fear it is too often entirely forgotten. Too many seem to think of everything except religion in choosing a partner for life, or to suppose that it will come somehow as a matter of course. Yet when a praying, Bible-reading, God-fearing, Christ-loving, church-honouring Christian marries a person who takes no interest whatever in serious Christianity, what can the result be but injury to the Christian, or immense unhappiness? Health is not infectious, but disease is! As a general rule, in such cases, the good go down to the level of the bad; the bad do not come up to the level of the good. The subject is a delicate one, and I do not care to dwell upon it.

But I say confidently to every unmarried Christian man or woman — if you love your soul, if you do not want to fall away and backslide, if you do not want to destroy your own peace and comfort for life, resolve never to marry any person who is not a true and devoted Christian, whatever the resolution may cost you. It would be better for you to die than to marry an unbeliever. Hold on to this resolution, and let no one ever persuade you out of it. Depart from this resolution, and you will find it almost impossible to 'come out and be separate'. You will find you have tied a millstone around your own neck in running the race towards heaven; and, if saved in the end, it will be 'so as through fire' (1 Corinthians 3:15).

I offer these six general hints to all who wish to follow Paul's advice, and to come out from the world and be separate. In giving them, I lay no claim to infallibility; but I believe they deserve consideration and attention. I do not forget that the subject is full of difficulties, and that scores of doubtful cases are continually arising in a Christian's course, in which it is very hard to say what is the path of duty, and how to behave. Perhaps the following pieces of advice may be found useful.

1. In all doubtful cases, we should first pray for wisdom and sound judgement. If prayer is worth anything, it must be especially valuable when we desire to do right, but do not see our way.

2. In all doubtful cases, let us often judge ourselves by remembering that God has his eye on us. Should I go to

such and such a place, or do such and such a thing, if I really believed God was looking at me?

3. In all doubtful cases, let us never forget the second coming of Christ and the Day of Judgement. Would I like to be found in such and such company, or employed in such and such ways?

4. Finally, in all doubtful cases, let us find out what the conduct of the holiest and best Christians has been under similar circumstances. If we do not clearly see our own way, we need not be ashamed to follow good examples.

I throw out these suggestions for the use of all who are in difficulties about disputable points over the matter of separation from the world. I cannot help thinking that they may help to untie many knots, and solve many problems.

The secrets of real victory over the world

I shall now conclude the whole subject by trying to show the secrets of real victory over the world. To come out from the world, of course, is not an easy thing. It cannot be easy so long as human nature is what it is, and a busy devil is always near us. It requires a constant struggle and exertion; it entails incessant conflict and self-denial. It often places us in exact opposition to members of our own families, to relatives and neighbours; it sometimes obliges us to do things that cause great offence, and bring upon us ridicule and petty persecution. It is precisely this that makes many hang back and shrink from resolute Christianity. They know they are not right; they know that they are not so 'thorough' in Christ's service as they ought to be, and they feel uncomfortable and ill at ease. But the fear of man keeps them back. And so they linger on through life with aching, dissatisfied hearts — with too much religion to be happy in the world, and too much of the world to be happy in their religion. I fear this is a very common situation, if the truth were known.

Yet there are some in every age who seem to get the victory over the world. They come out decidedly from its ways, and are unmistakably separate. They are independent of its opinions, and unshaken by its opposition. They move on like planets in an orbit of their own, and seem to rise equally above the world's smiles and frowns. What are the secrets of their victory? I will set them down.

A right heart

The first secret of victory over the world is a right heart. By a right heart, I mean a heart renewed, changed and sanctified by the Holy Spirit — a heart in which Christ dwells, a heart in which old things have passed away, and all things become new. The grand mark of such a heart is the bias of its tastes and affections. The owner of such a heart no longer likes the world and the things of the world, and therefore finds it no trial or sacrifice to give them up. He no longer has any appetite for the company, the conversation, the amusements, the occupations, the books that he once loved, and to 'come out' from them seems natural to him. Great indeed is the explosive power of a new principle! Just as the new spring-buds in a hedge push off the old leaves and make them quietly fall to the ground, so does the new heart of a believer invariably affect his tastes and likes, and make him drop many things he once loved and lived in because he now likes them no more. May he who wants to 'come out from among the world and be separate' make sure first and foremost that he has got a new heart. If the heart is really right, everything else will be right in time. 'If therefore your eye is good, your whole body will be full of light' (Matthew 6:22). If the affections are not right there never will be right action.

A lively practical faith in unseen things

The second secret of victory over the world is a lively practical faith in unseen things. What does the Scripture say? 'This is the victory that has overcome the world — our faith' (1 John 5:4). To attain and keep up the habit of looking steadily at invisible things, as if they were visible — to set before our minds every day, as grand realities, our souls, God, Christ, heaven, hell, judgement, eternity; to cherish an abiding conviction that what we do not see is just as real as what we do see, and ten thousand times more important — this, this is one way to be conquerors over the world. This was the faith that made the noble army of saints, described in the eleventh chapter of Hebrews, obtain such a glorious testimony from the Holy Spirit. They all acted under a firm persuasion that they had a real God, a real Saviour, and a real home in heaven, though unseen by mortal eyes. Armed with this faith, a man regards this world as a shadow compared to the world to come, and cares little for its praise or blame, its hatred or its rewards. Let he who wants to come out from the world and be separate, but shrinks and hangs back for fear of things seen, pray and strive to have this faith. 'All things are possible to him who believes' (Mark 9:23). Like Moses, he will find it possible to forsake Egypt, seeing him that is invisible. Like Moses, he will not care what he loses and who is displeased, because he sees afar off, like one looking through a telescope, a substantial recompense of reward (Hebrews 11:26).

Attaining and cultivating the habit of boldly confessing Christ

The third and last secret of victory over the world is to attain and cultivate the habit of boldly confessing Christ on all proper occasions. In saying this I don't want to be misunderstood. I want no one to blow a trumpet before him, and thrust his Christianity on others all the time. But I do wish to encourage all who strive to come out from the world to show their colours, and to act and speak out like men who are not ashamed to serve Christ. A steady, quiet assertion of our own principles, as Christians; an habitual readiness to let the children of the world see that we are guided by other rules than they are, and do not mean to swerve from them; a calm, firm, courteous maintenance of our own standard of things in every company — all this will insensibly form a habit within us, and make it comparatively easy to be a separate man. It will be hard at first, no doubt, and cost us many a struggle; but the longer we go on, the easier it will be. Repeated acts of confessing Christ will produce habits. Habits once formed will produce a settled character. Once our characters are known, we shall be saved a lot of trouble. Men will know what to expect from us, and will count it no strange thing if they see us living the lives of separate peculiar people. It is a great thing to be able to say 'No' decidedly, but courteously, when asked to do anything which conscience says is wrong. He who shows his colours boldly from the first, and is never ashamed to let men see 'whose he is and whom he serves', will soon find that he has overcome the world and will be let alone. Bold confession is a long step towards victory.

Some words of application

It only remains for me now to conclude the whole subject with a few short words of application. The danger of the world ruining the soul, the nature of true separation from the world, the secrets of victory over the world, are all before my readers. I now ask their attention for the last time over this subject, while I try to say something directly for their personal benefit.

A question

My first word will be a *question*. Are you overcoming the world, or are you overcome by it? Do you know what it is to come out from the world and be separate, or are you still entangled by it, and conformed to it? If you have any desire to be saved, I entreat you to answer this question.

If you know nothing of 'separation' I warn you affectionately that your soul is in great danger. The world passes away; and those who cling to the world, and think only of the world, will pass away with it to everlasting ruin. Wake up and see your peril before it is too late. Awake and flee from the wrath to come. The time is short. The end of all things is at hand. The shadows are lengthening. The sun is going down. The night comes when no man can work. The great white throne will soon be set. The judgement will begin. The books will be opened. Awake, and come out from the world while it is called today.

Yet a little while, and there will be no more worldly occupations and worldly amusements — no more getting and spending money — no more eating, and drinking, and feasting, and dressing, and dancing, and theatres, and races, and cards, and gambling. What will you do when all these things have passed away for ever? How can you possibly be happy in an eternal heaven, where holiness is all in all, and worldliness has no place? Oh, consider these things, and be wise! Awake, and break the chains that the world has thrown around you! Awake, and flee from the wrath to come!

A counsel

My second word will be a *counsel*. If you want to come out from the world, but don't know what to do, take the advice that I give you this day. Begin by applying direct, as a penitent sinner, to our Lord Jesus Christ, and put your situation in his hands. Pour out your heart before him. Tell him your whole story, keeping nothing back. Tell him that you are a sinner wanting to be saved from the world, the flesh and the devil, and beg him to save you.

That blessed Saviour 'gave himself for our sins, that he might deliver us from this present evil age' (Galatians 1:4). He knows what the world is, for he lived in it for thirty-three years. He knows what the difficulties of a man are, for he was made man for our sakes, and dwelt among men. High in heaven, at the right hand of God, he is able to save to the uttermost all who come to God by him; able to keep us from the evil of the world while we are still living in it; able to give us power to become the sons of God; able to keep us from falling; able to make us more than conquerors. Once more I say, 'Go direct to Christ with the prayer of faith, and put yourself wholly and unreservedly in his hands.' Hard as it may seem to you now to come out from the world and be separate, you shall find that with Jesus nothing is impossible. You, even you, shall overcome the world.

Encouragement

My third and last word will be *encouragement*. If you have learned by experience what it is to come out from the world, I can only tell you to take comfort and persevere. You are on the right road; you have no cause to be afraid. The everlasting hills are in sight. Your salvation is nearer than when you believed. Take comfort and press on.

No doubt you have had many a battle, and made many a false step. You have sometimes felt ready to faint, and been half disposed to go back to Egypt. But your Master has never entirely left you, and he will never allow you to be tempted above what you are able to bear. Then persevere steadily in your separation from the world, and never be ashamed of standing alone. Settle it firmly in your mind that the most dedicated Christians are always the happiest, and remember that no one ever said at the end of his course that he had been too holy, and lived too near to God.

318   Practical religion

Hear, last of all, what is written in the Scriptures of truth:

'Whoever confesses me before men, him the Son of Man
    also will confess before the angels of God' (Luke 12:8).

'There is no one who has left house or brothers or sisters or
    father or mother or wife or children or lands, for my sake
    and the gospel's, who shall not receive a hundredfold
    now in this time — houses and brothers and sisters and
    mothers and children and lands, with persecutions — and
    in the age to come, eternal life' (Mark 10:29-30).

'Therefore do not cast away your confidence, which has
    great reward. For you have need of endurance, so that
    after you have done the will of God, you may receive the
    promise: "For yet a little while, And he who is coming will
    come and will not tarry"' (Hebrews 10:35-37).

Those words were written and spoken for our sakes. Let us lay
hold of them, and never forget them. Let us persevere to the
end, and never be ashamed of coming out from the world, and
being separate. We may be sure it brings its own reward.

13.
Riches and poverty

'There was a certain rich man who was clothed in purple and fine linen and fared sumptuously every day. But there was a certain beggar named Lazarus, full of sores, who was laid at his gate, desiring to be fed with the crumbs which fell from the rich man's table. Moreover the dogs came and licked his sores. So it was that the beggar died, and was carried by the angels to Abraham's bosom. The rich man also died and was buried. And being in torments in Hades, he lifted up his eyes and saw Abraham afar off, and Lazarus in his bosom'
(Luke 16:19-23).

There are probably very few readers of the Bible who are not familiar with the parable of the rich man and Lazarus. It is one of those passages of Scripture that leaves an indelible impression on the mind. Like the parable of the Prodigal Son, once read it is never forgotten.

The reason for this is clear and simple. The whole parable is a most vividly painted picture. The story, as it goes, carries our senses with it with irresistible power. Instead of readers, we become onlookers. We are witnesses of all the events described. We see. We hear. We believe we could almost touch. The rich man's table — the purple — the fine linen — the gate — the beggar lying by it — the sores — the dogs — the crumbs that fell from the rich man's table — the two deaths — the rich man's burial — the ministering angels — Abraham's side — the rich man's fearful waking up — the fire — the gulf — the hopeless remorse — all, all stand out before our eyes in bold relief, and stamp themselves upon our minds. This is the attainment of the famous Arabian standard of eloquence: 'He speaks the best who turns the ear into an eye.'

But, when all is said and done, it is one thing to admire the masterly composition of this parable, and quite another to receive the spiritual lessons it contains. The eye of the intellect can often see beauty while the heart remains asleep, and sees nothing at all. Hundreds read *Pilgrim's Progress* with deep interest, to whom the struggle for the celestial city is foolishness. Thousands are familiar with every word of the parable before us now, who never consider how it comes home to themselves. Their conscience is deaf to the cry that ought to ring in their ears as they read: 'You are the man.' Their heart never turns to God with the solemn inquiry, 'Lord, is this a picture of me? Lord, is it I?'

I invite my readers now to consider the leading truths that this parable is meant to teach. I am purposely noting only that part of it that is shown at the beginning of the chapter. May the Holy Spirit give us a teachable spirit, and an understanding heart, and so produce lasting impressions on our souls!

The conditions that God allots to different men

Let us observe, first of all, how different are the conditions that God allots to different men. The Lord Jesus begins the parable by telling us about a rich man and a beggar. He does not say a word in praise of either poverty or riches. He describes the circumstances of a wealthy man and the circumstances of a poor man; but he neither condemns the earthly position of one, nor praises that of the other.

The contrast between the two men is painfully striking. Look closely at the picture before us. Here is one who possessed an abundance of this world's good things. 'A certain rich man who was clothed in purple and fine linen and fared sumptuously every day.'

Here is another who literally has nothing. He is a friendless, diseased, have-starved destitute person. 'But there was a certain beggar named Lazarus, full of sores, who was laid at his gate,' and he begs for crumbs. Both are children of Adam. Both came from the same dust, and belonged to one family. Both are living in the same land and subject to the same government. And yet how different is their condition!

But we must take heed that we do not draw lessons from the parable that it was never meant to teach. The rich are not always bad men, and do not always go to hell. The poor are not always good men, and do not always go to heaven. We must not rush into the extreme of supposing that it is sinful to be rich. We must not run away with the idea that there is anything wicked in the difference of condition described here, and that God intended all men to be equal. There is nothing in our Lord Jesus Christ's words to warrant any such conclusion. He simply describes things as they are often seen in the world, and as we must expect to see them.

Universal equality is a very artificial expression and a favourite idea with visionary men. Many in every age have disturbed society by stirring up the poor against the rich, and by preaching the popular doctrine that all men ought to be equal. But so long as the world is under the present order of things this universal equality cannot be attained. Those who speak against the vast inequality of men's lots will doubtless never lack an audience; but so long as human nature is what it is, this inequality cannot be prevented.

So long as some are wise and some are foolish, some strong and some weak, some healthy and some diseased, some lazy and some diligent, some prudent and some careless; so long as children reap the fruit of their parent's misconduct; so long as sun, and rain, and heat, and cold, and wind, and waves, and drought, and plague, and storms, and tempests are beyond man's control — so there will always be some rich and some poor. All the political order in the world will never erase the fact that 'the poor will never cease from the land' (Deuteronomy 15:11).

Take all the property in our country by force this day, and divide it equally among the inhabitants. Give every man above the age of twenty an equal portion. Let everyone share and share alike, and begin the world over again. Do this, and see where you would be at the end of fifty years. You would just have come around to the point where you began. You would find things just as unequal as before. Some would have worked, and some would have been idle. Some would have always been careless, and some always conniving. Some would have sold, and others would have bought. Some would have wasted, and others would have saved. And the result would be that some would be rich and others poor.

Let no man listen to those vain and foolish talkers who say that all men were meant to be equal. They might as well tell you that all men ought to be of the same height, weight, strength and cleverness — or that all oak trees ought to be of the same shape and size — or that all blades of grass ought to always be the same length.

Settle it in your mind that the main cause of all the suffering you see around you is sin. Sin is the great cause of the enormous luxury of the rich, and the painful degradation of the poor — of the heartless selfishness of the highest classes, and the helpless poverty of the lowest class. Sin must first be cast out of the world. The hearts of all men must be renewed and sanctified. The devil must be bound. The Prince of Peace must come down and take his great power and reign. All this must be done before there can ever be universal happiness, or the gulf that now divides the rich and the poor can be filled up.

Beware of expecting a millennium to be brought about by any method of government, by any system of education, by any political party. Work hard to do good to all men. Pity your poorer brethren, and make every reasonable endeavour to raise them from their low estate. Seek to help to increase knowledge, to promote morality, and to improve the temporal condition of the poor. But never, never forget that you live in a fallen world, that sin is all around you, and that the devil and the demons are everywhere. And be very sure that the rich man and Lazarus are emblems of two classes, which will always be in the world until the Lord comes.

A man's temporal condition is no test of the state of his soul

Let us observe, in the next place, that a man's temporal condition is no test of the state of his soul. The rich man in the parable appears to have been the world's pattern of a prosperous man. If life as it is now is all there is, then he seems to have everything that a heart could wish for. We know that he was 'clothed in purple and fine linen and fared sumptuously every day'. We needn't doubt that he had everything else which money could buy. The wisest men had good reason for saying, 'But money answers everything.' 'The rich [have] many friends' (Ecclesiastes 10:19; Proverbs 14:20).

But who can read this story completely through without seeing that in the highest and best sense the rich man was pitiably poor? Take away the good things of his life, and he had nothing left — nothing after death — nothing beyond the grave — nothing in the world to come. With all his riches he had no 'treasure laid up in heaven'. With all his purple and fine linen he had no garment of righteousness. With all his rich and successful friends he had no Friend and Advocate at God's right hand. With all his sumptuous food he had never tasted the bread of life. With all his splendid palace he had no home in the eternal world. Without God, without Christ, without faith, without grace, without forgiveness, without holiness, he lives for himself for a few short years, and then goes down hopelessly into the pit of hell. How hollow and unreal was all his prosperity! Judge what I say: 'The rich man was very poor.'

Lazarus appears to have been one who had literally nothing in the world. It is hard to conceive a case of greater misery and destitution than his. He had neither house, nor money, nor food, nor health, nor, in all probability, even clothes. His picture is one that can never be forgotten. He 'was a certain beggar … full of sores, who was laid at [the rich man's] gate'. He longed, 'to be fed with the crumbs which fell from the rich man's table'. Moreover, 'the dogs came and licked his sores'. Indeed the wise man might well say, 'The poor man is hated even by his own neighbour, but the rich has many friends.' 'The destruction of the poor is their poverty' (Proverbs 14:20; 10:15).

But anyone who reads the parable to the end can't fail to see that in the highest sense Lazarus was not poor, but 'rich'! He was a child of God. He was an heir of glory. He possessed durable riches and righteousness. His name was in the Book of Life. His place was prepared for him in heaven. He had the best of clothing — the righteousness of a Saviour. He had the best of friends — God himself was his advocate. He had the best of food — he had food to eat the world knew nothing of. And, best of all, he had these things for ever. They supported him in life. They did not leave him in the hour of death. They went with him beyond the grave. They were with him in eternity. Surely from this point of view we may well say, not 'poor Lazarus', but 'rich Lazarus'.

We would do well to measure all men by God's standard — to measure them not by the amount of their income, but by the condition of their souls. When the Lord God looks down from heaven and sees the children of men, he takes no account of many things that are esteemed by the world. He does not look at men's money, or lands, or titles. He looks only at the state of their souls, and judges them accordingly. Oh, that you would strive to do likewise! Oh, that you would value grace above titles, or intellect, or gold! Often, far too often, the only question asked about a man is, 'How much is he worth?' It would be good for us all to remember that every man is tragically poor until he is rich in faith, and rich towards God (James 2:5).

Wonderful as it may seem to some, all the money in the world is worthless in God's balances, compared to grace! Hard as the saying may sound, I believe that a converted beggar is far more important and honourable in the sight of God than an unconverted king. The one may glitter like the butterfly in the sun for a little season, and be admired by an ignorant world; but his end is darkness and misery for ever. The other may crawl through the world like a crushed worm, and be despised by everyone who sees him; but his end is a glorious resurrection and a blessed eternity with Christ. Of him the Lord says, 'I know your works, tribulation, and poverty (but you are rich)' (Revelation 2:9).

King Ahab was ruler over the ten tribes of Israel. Obadiah was nothing more than a servant in his household. Yet who can doubt who was most precious in God's sight: the servant or the king?

Ridley and Latimer were deposed from all their dignities, cast into prison as criminals, and eventually burnt at the stake. Bonner and Gardiner, their persecutors, were raised to the highest point of ecclesiastical greatness, enjoyed large incomes, and died unmolested in their beds. Yet who can doubt which of the two parties was on the Lord's side?

Baxter, the famous clergyman, was persecuted with savage hostility, and condemned to a long imprisonment by a most unjust judgement. Jeffreys, the Chief Justice who sentenced him, was a man of shameful character without either morality or religion. Baxter was sent to jail and Jeffreys was loaded with honours. Yet who can doubt which was the good man of the two, the Lord Chief Justice Jeffreys or the author of the Christ-honouring book *Saint's Everlasting Rest?*

We may be very sure that riches and worldly greatness are no certain marks of God's favour. They are often, on the contrary, a snare and hindrance to a man's soul. They make him love the world and forget God. What does Solomon say? 'Do not overwork to be rich; because of your own understanding, cease!' (Proverbs 23:4). What does Paul say? 'But those who desire to be rich fall into temptation and a snare, and into many foolish and harmful lusts which drown men in destruction and perdition' (1 Timothy 6:9).

We can be sure that poverty and trial are not certain proofs of God's anger. They are often blessings in disguise. They are always sent in love and wisdom. They often serve to wean man from the world. They teach him to set his affections on things above. They often show the sinner his own heart. They often make the saint fruitful in good works. What does the book of Job say? 'Happy is the man whom God corrects; therefore do not despise the chastening of the Almighty' (Job 5:17). What does Paul say? 'For whom the LORD loves he chastens, and scourges every son whom he receives' (Hebrews 12:6).

One great secret of happiness in this life is to have a patient, contented spirit. Strive daily to realize the truth that this life is not the place of reward. The time of retribution and reward is yet to come. Judge nothing hastily before that time. Remember the words of the wise man: 'If you see the oppression of the poor, and the violent perversion of justice and righteousness in a province, do not marvel at the matter; for high official watches over high official, and higher officials are over them' (Ecclesiastes 5:8).

Yes! There is a Day of Judgement yet to come. That day will put everyone in their right places. At last there will be seen a distinction 'between the righteous and the wicked, between one who serves God and one who does not serve him' (Malachi 3:18). The children of Lazarus and the children of the rich man will in time be seen in their true colours, and every one will receive according to his works.

All classes alike come to the grave

Let us observe, in the third place, how all classes alike come to the grave. The rich man in the parable died, and Lazarus died too. Different and divided as they were in their lives, they both had to drink of the same cup at the end. Both went to the grave. Both went to that place where rich and poor meet together. Dust they were, and to dust they returned (Genesis 3:19).

This is the lot of all men. It will be our own, unless the Lord shall first return in glory. After all our scheming, and contriving, and planning and studying — after all our inventions, and discoveries, and scientific attainments, there remains one enemy we cannot conquer and disarm, and that is death. The chapter in Genesis which records the long lives of Methuselah, and the others who lived before the flood, winds up the simple story of each by two expressive words: 'he died'. And now, over 5000 years later, what more can be said of the greatest among ourselves? The histories of Marlborough, and Washington, and Napoleon, and Wellington, arrive at just the same humbling conclusion. The end of each, after all his greatness, is just this: 'he died'.

Death is a mighty leveller. He spares none and he waits for none. He will not wait till you are ready. Doors, and bars, and locks will not keep him out. The Englishman boasts that his home is his castle, but with all his boasting, he cannot exclude death. An Austrian nobleman would not allow death and the smallpox to be named in his presence. But, named or not named, it matters little; in God's appointed hour, death will come.

One man rolls easily along the road in the most elegant carriage that money can buy. Another toils wearily along the path on foot. Yet both are sure to meet at last under the earth, in the grave.

One man, like Absalom, has fifty servants to wait upon him and do his bidding. Another has none to lift a finger to do him a service. But both are travelling to a place where they must lie down alone.

One man is the owner of hundreds of thousands of pounds. Another has scarcely a penny to call his own. Yet neither one nor the other can carry one cent with him into the unseen world.

One man owns half a county. Another doesn't even have a small garden of herbs. And yet six feet of the vilest earth will be amply sufficient for either of them when they are dead.

One man pampers his body with every possible delicacy, and clothes it in the richest and softest apparel. Another scarcely has enough food to eat, and seldom enough clothes to put on. Yet both alike are hurrying on to a day when 'ashes to ashes, and dust to dust' shall be proclaimed over them, and fifty years later no one will be able to say, 'These are the rich man's bones, and these are the bones of the poor,' for they will both be nothing but dust.

I know that these are familiar thoughts. I do not deny it for a moment. I am writing stale old things that all men know. But I am also writing things that all men do not 'perceive'. Oh, no! If they did perceive them, then they would not speak and act as they do.

You wonder sometimes at the tone and language of ministers of the gospel. You marvel that we press upon you for an immediate decision. You think we are extreme, and extravagant,

and eccentric in our views, because we urge you to yield your
total self to Christ — to leave nothing uncertain — to make
sure that you are born again and ready for heaven. You hear,
but do not approve. You go away, and say to one another,
'The man means well, but he goes too far.'

But don't you see that the reality of death is continually for-
bidding us from using another language? We see him gradually
thinning our congregations. We miss face after face in our assemblies. We do not know whose turn may come next. We
only know that when the tree falls there it will lie, and that 'after
death comes the judgement'. We must be bold and decided
and uncompromising in our language. We would rather run the
risk of offending some, than of losing any. We would aim at the
standard established by that grand old preacher Baxter:

> I will preach as though I never would preach again
> And as a dying man to dying men.

It was said of one bold and courageous preacher: 'That man
preaches as though death was following close behind his back.
When I hear him I cannot go to sleep.'

Oh, that men would learn to live with an awareness that
one day they are going to die! Truly it is a waste of time to set
our affections on a dying world and its short-lived comforts
and pleasures, and for the sake of momentary pleasures to
lose a glorious eternity in heaven! Here we are toiling, and
labouring, and wearying ourselves about little things, and running here and there like ants upon an anthill; and yet after a
few years we will all be gone, and another generation will take
our place.

Let us live for eternity. Let us seek his Kingdom and his
righteousness that can never be taken from us. And let us never
forget John Bunyan's golden rule: 'He that would live well, let
him make the thoughts of his dying day his daily friend.'

How precious a believer's soul is in the sight of God

Let us observe, in the fourth place, how precious a believer's soul is in the sight of God. The rich man, in the parable, dies and is buried. Perhaps he had an impressive funeral — a funeral in proportion to his wealth while he was yet alive. But we hear nothing further of the moment when soul and body were divided in death. The next thing we hear of is that he is in hell.

The poor man, in the parable, dies also. We don't know what manner of burial he had. A destitute person's funeral among us is a sad affair. The funeral of Lazarus was probably no better. But this we do know, that the moment Lazarus dies he is carried by the angels into Abraham's bosom — carried to a place of rest, where all the faithful are waiting for the resurrection of the just.

To my mind, there is something very striking, very touching, and very comforting in the parable's expression. I ask you to pay particular attention to it. It throws great light on the relation of all sinners who believe in Christ, to their God and Father. It shows a little of the care bestowed on the least and lowest of Christ's disciples by the King of kings.

No man has such friends and attendants as the believer, however little he may think about it. Angels rejoice over him on the day that he is born again of the Spirit. Angels minister to him all through his life. Angels encamp around him in the wilderness of this world. Angels take charge of his soul in his hour of death, and transport it safely home. Yes! Vile as he may be in his own eyes, and lowly in his own sight, the very poorest and humblest believer in Jesus is cared for by his Father in heaven, with a care that passes understanding. The Lord has become his Shepherd, and he 'shall not want' (Psalm 23:1). Only let a man come honestly and truthfully to Christ, and be joined to him, and he shall have all the benefits of being a child of the living God.

Is he weighed down with many sins? 'Though his sins are like scarlet, they shall be as white as snow.'

Is his heart hard and prone to evil? A new heart shall be given to him, and a new spirit put in him.

Is he weak and cowardly? He who enabled Peter to confess Christ before his enemies will make him bold.

Is he ignorant? He who was patient with Thomas' slowness shall be patient with him, and guide him into all truth.

Is he alone in his position? He who stood by Paul when all men abandoned him shall also stand by his side.

Is he undergoing a particular trial? He who enabled men to be saints in Nero's household shall also enable him to persevere.

The very hairs of his head are all numbered. Nothing can harm him without God's permission. Whoever hurts him hurts the apple of God's eye, and injures a brother and member of Christ himself.

His trials are all wisely ordered. Satan can only harass him, as he did Job, when God permits him. He can suffer no temptation above what he is able to bear. All things are working together for his good.

His steps are all ordered from grace to glory. He is kept on earth till he is ripe for heaven, and not one moment longer. The harvest of the Lord must have its appointed proportion of sun and wind, of cold and heat, of rain and storm. And then when the believer's work is done, the angels of God shall come for him, as they did for Lazarus, and carry him safely home.

No, the men of the world think little about who they are despising when they mock Christ's people. They are mocking those whom angels are not ashamed to attend to. They are mocking the brothers and sisters of Christ himself. Little do they consider that these are the ones for whose sakes the days of tribulation are shortened. These are the ones by whose intercession kings reign peacefully. Little do they consider that the prayers of men like Lazarus have more weight in the affairs of nations than hosts of armed men.

Believers in Christ, who may possibly be reading these pages, how little you know of the full extent of your privileges and possessions. Like children at school, you don't know half of what your Father is doing for your welfare. Learn to live by faith more than you have done. Acquaint yourselves with the fulness of the treasure laid up for you in Christ even now. This world, no doubt, must always be a place of trial while we are in the body. But still there are comforts provided for the brothers of Lazarus, which many never enjoy.

The danger of the sin of selfishness!

Observe, in the last place, how dangerous and soul-ruining is the sin of selfishness. You have the rich man, in the parable, in a hopeless state. If there was no other picture of a lost soul in hell in the entire Bible you have it here. You meet him in the beginning, clothed in purple and fine linen. You part with him at the end, tormented in the everlasting fire.

And yet there is nothing to show that this man was a murderer, or a thief, or an adulterer, or a liar. There is no reason to say that he was an atheist, or an infidel, or a blasphemer. For all we know, he attended to all the ordinances of the Jewish religion. But we do know that he was lost for ever!

To my mind there is something very solemn in this thought. Here is a man whose outward life in all probability was correct.

In all events we know nothing against him. He dresses richly, but then he had money to spend on his apparel. He gives splendid feasts and parties, but then he was wealthy, and could well afford it. We read nothing recorded against him that might not be recorded of hundreds and thousands in the present day, who are counted respectable and a good sort of people. And yet the end of this man is that he goes to hell. Surely this deserves serious attention.

Beware of living for ourselves

I believe this is meant to teach us to beware of living only for ourselves. It is not enough that we are able to say, 'I live a moral and respectable life. I pay every one his due. I discharge all the relations of life with propriety. I attend church, I read the Bible, I pray to God.' This still leaves another question, to which the Bible requires an answer. 'To whom do you live? To yourself or to Christ? What is the great end, aim, object and ruling motive in your life?' Let men call the question extreme if they please. For myself, I can find nothing short of this in Paul's words: 'He died for all, that those who live should live no longer for themselves, but for him who died for them and rose again' (2 Corinthians 5:15). And I come to the conclusion, that if, like the rich man, we live only for ourselves, we shall destroy our souls.

The consequences of the sins of omission

I believe, further, that this passage is meant to teach us the damnable nature of the sins of omission. It does not seem that it was so much the things the rich man did, but the things he left undone, which made him miss heaven. Lazarus was at his gate, and he left him alone. But is not this exactly in keeping with the history of the judgement, in the twenty-fifth chapter of Matthew? Nothing is said there of the sins of commission of which the lost are guilty. How does the charge read? 'I was hungry and you gave me no food; I was thirsty and you gave me no drink; I was a stranger and you did not take me in, naked and you did not clothe me, sick and in prison and you did not visit me' (Matthew 25:42-43).

The charge against them is simply that they did not do certain things. On this their sentence is based. And I conclude again, that, unless we are careful, sins of omission may ruin our souls. Truly it was a solemn saying of godly Usher, on his deathbed: 'Lord, forgive me all my sins, but especially my sins of omission.'

The particular dangers of riches

I believe, further, that the passage is meant to teach us that riches bring special dangers with them. Yes! Riches, which the vast majority of men are always seeking after; riches for which they spend their lives, and of which they make an idol — riches cause their possessors immense spiritual peril! The possession of riches has a very hardening effect on the soul. They chill. They freeze. They petrify the inward man. They close the eye to the things of faith. They insensibly produce a tendency to forget God.

And doesn't this stand in perfect harmony with all the language of Scripture on the same subject? What does our Lord say? 'How hard it is for those who have riches to enter the kingdom of God!' 'It is easier for a camel to go through the eye of a needle than for a rich man to enter the kingdom of God' (Mark 10:23, 25). What does Paul say? 'For the love of money is a root of all kinds of evil, for which some have strayed from the faith in their greediness, and pierced themselves through with many sorrows' (1 Timothy 6:10).

What can be more striking than the fact that the Bible has frequently spoken of [the love of] money as a most fruitful cause of sin and evil. For money Achan brought defeat on the armies of Israel, and death on himself. For money Balaam sinned against God, and tried to curse God's people. For money Delilah betrayed Samson to the Philistines. For money Gehazi lied to Naaman and Elisha, and became a leper. For money Ananias and Sapphira became the first hypocrites in the Early Church, and lost their lives. For money Judas Iscariot sold Christ, and was ruined eternally. Surely these facts speak loudly.

Money, in truth, is one of the most *unsatisfying of possessions*. It takes away some cares, no doubt; but it brings with it quite as many cares as it takes away. There is trouble getting it. There is anxiety in keeping it. There are temptations in using it. There is guilt in abusing it. There is sorrow in losing it. There is perplexity in disposing of it. Two-thirds of all the strife, quarrels and lawsuits in the world, arise from one simple cause — money!

Money most certainly is one of the most *ensnaring and heart-changing of possessions*. It seems desirable at a distance. It often proves a poison when in our hand. No man can possibly tell the effect of money on his soul, if it suddenly falls to his lot to possess it. Many people live close to God when they are poor, but then forget God when they are rich.

I conclude that those who have money, like the rich man in the parable, ought to take double pains about their souls. They live in a most unhealthy atmosphere. They have double need to be on their guard.

The particular dangers of selfishness in the last days

I believe, not least, that the passage is meant to stir up special carefulness about selfishness in these last days. You have a special warning in 2 Timothy 3:1, 2: 'But know this, that in the last days perilous times will come: for men will be lovers of themselves, lovers of money, boasters, proud, blasphemers, disobedient to parents, unthankful, unholy.' I believe we have come to the last days, and that we ought to beware of the sins mentioned here, if we love our souls.

Perhaps we are poor judges of our own times. We are apt to exaggerate and magnify their evils, just because we see and feel them. But, after making every allowance, I doubt whether there ever was more need of warnings against selfishness than in the present day. I am sure there never was a time when all classes of people ever had so many comforts and so many temporal good things. And yet I believe there is an utter disproportion between men's expenditure on themselves and their outlay on works of charity and works of mercy. I see this in the miserable miniscule donations, which many rich men give to charity. I see it in the languished condition of many of our best religious mission organizations, and the painfully slow growth of their annual incomes. I see it in the small number of names that appear on the list of contributors to any good work. There are, I believe, thousands of rich people in this country who literally give away nothing at all. I see it in the notorious fact, that few, even of those who give, give anything proportionate to their means. I see all this, and mourn over it. I regard it as the selfishness and covetousness predicted to arise in 'the last days'.

I know that this is a painful and delicate subject. But the minister of Christ must not, on that account, avoid it. It is a subject for the times, and it needs pressing home. I desire to speak to myself, and to all who make any profession of Christianity. Of course I cannot expect worldly and utterly ungodly persons to view this subject in Bible light. To them the Bible is no rule of faith and practice. To quote texts to them would be of little use.

But I do ask all professing Christians to consider well what Scripture says against covetousness and selfishness and on behalf of liberality in giving money. Is it for nothing that the Lord Jesus spoke the parable of the rich fool, and blamed him because he was not 'rich toward God'? (Luke 12:21). Is it for nothing that in the parable of the sower he mentions the 'deceitfulness of riches' as one reason why the seed of the Word bears no fruit? (Matthew 13:22). Is it for nothing that he says, 'Make friends for yourselves by unrighteous mammon' (Luke 16:9). Is it for nothing that he says, 'When you give a dinner or a supper, do not ask your friends, your brothers, your relatives, nor rich neighbours, lest they also invite you back, and you be repaid. But when you give a feast, invite the poor, the maimed, the lame, the blind. And you will be blessed, because they cannot repay you; for you shall be repaid at the resurrection of the just' (Luke 14:12-14). Is it for nothing that he says, 'Sell what you have and give alms; provide yourselves money bags which do not grow old, a treasure in the heavens that does not fail, where no thief approaches nor moth destroys' (Luke 12:33).

Is it for nothing that he says, 'It is more blessed to give than to receive?' (Acts 20:35). Is it for nothing that he warns us against the example of the priest and Levite, who saw the wounded traveller, but passed by on the other side? Is it for nothing that he praises the Good Samaritan, who denied himself to show kindness to a stranger? (Luke 10:34). Is it for nothing that Paul classes covetousness with sins of the grossest description, and denounces it as idolatry? (Colossians 3:5). And is there not a striking and painful difference between this language and the habits and feeling of society about money? I appeal to anyone who knows the world. Let him judge what I say.

I only ask my readers to consider calmly the passages of Scripture to which I have referred. I cannot think they were meant to teach nothing at all. That the habits of the East and our own are different, I freely concede. That some of the expressions I have quoted are figurative, I freely admit. But still, after all, a principle lies at the bottom of all these expressions. Let us take heed that this principle is not neglected. I wish that many a professing Christian in this day, who perhaps dislikes what I am saying, would endeavour to write a commentary on these expressions, and try to explain to himself what they mean.

To know that giving money to the poor cannot atone for sin is good. To know that our good works cannot justify us is excellent. To know that we may give all our goods to feed the poor, and build hospitals and churches, without any real charity, is most important. But let us beware lest we go to the other extreme, and because our money cannot save us, give away no money at all.

Does anyone reading these pages have money? Then 'Take heed and beware of covetousness, for one's life does not consist in the abundance of the things he possesses' (Luke 12:15). Remember you are carrying extra weight in the race towards heaven. All men are naturally in danger of being lost for ever, but you are doubly so because of your possessions. Nothing will put out a fire so quickly as dirt being thrown upon it. Nothing I am sure has such a tendency to quench the fire of Christianity as the possession of money. It was a solemn message which Buchanan, on his deathbed, sent to one of his old pupils: 'He was going to a place where few kings and great men would come.'

No doubt it is possible for the rich to be saved as well as others. With God nothing is impossible. Abraham, Job and David were all rich and yet saved. But oh, be careful! Money is a good servant, but a bad master. Let that saying of our Lord's sink down into your heart: 'How hard it is for those who have riches to enter the kingdom of God!' (Mark 10:23). It was well said by an old godly Christian, 'The outer and upper surface above gold mines is generally very barren.' Old Latimer began one of his sermons quoting three times the Lord's words: 'Take heed and beware of covetousness,' and then saying, 'What if I should say nothing else for the next three or four hours?' There are few prayers wiser and more necessary than this petition, 'In the time of our wealth, good Lord deliver us.'

Has anyone with little or no money read these pages? Then do not envy those who are richer than you. Pray for them. Pity

them. Be charitable to their faults. Remember that high places
are unsteady places, and don't be too hasty in your condemnation of their conduct. Perhaps if you had their difficulties you
would do no better yourself. Beware of the 'love of money'. It
is a 'root of all kinds of evil' (1 Timothy 6:10). A man may
greatly love money without having any at all. Beware of the
love of self, it may be found in a poor man's home as well as
in a mansion. And beware of thinking that poverty alone
will save you. If you would sit down with Lazarus in glory,
you must not only have fellowship with him in suffering, but
also in grace.

Does any reader desire to know the remedy against that
love of self which ruined the rich man's soul, and cleaves to us
all by nature, like our skin? I tell him plainly there is only one
remedy, and I ask him to mark well what that remedy is. It is
not the fear of hell. It is not the hope of heaven. It is not any
sense of duty. Oh, no! The disease of selfishness is far too
deeply rooted to yield to such secondary motives as these.
Nothing will ever cure it but a personal and intimate knowledge of Christ's redeeming love. You must know the misery
and guilt of your own sin. You must experience the power of
Christ's atoning blood sprinkled upon your conscience, and
making you whole. You must taste the sweetness of peace
with God through the mediation of Jesus, and feel the love
of a reconciled Father poured into your heart by the Holy
Spirit.

Then, and not till then, the root of selfishness will be destroyed. Then, knowing the immensity of your debt to Christ,
you will feel that nothing is too great and too costly to give to
him. Feeling that you have been loved much when you deserved
nothing, you will heartily love in return, and cry, 'What shall I
render to the LORD for all his benefits toward me?' (Psalm
116:12). Feeling that you have freely received countless mercies,
you will consider it a privilege to do anything to please the one

to whom you owe everything. Knowing that you have been 'bought at a price', and are no longer your own, you will labour to glorify God with body and spirit, which are his (1 Corinthians 6:20).

Yes; I repeat. I know no effective remedy for the love of self, but a committed belief in the love of Christ. Other remedies may soften the pain of the disease: this alone will heal it. Other antidotes may hide its deformity: this alone will work a perfect cure.

An easy, good-natured temper may cover over selfishness in one man. A love of praise may conceal it in another. A self-righteous spirit of self-denial may keep it out of sight in a third. But nothing will ever cut out selfishness by the roots but the love of Christ revealed in the mind by the Holy Spirit, and felt in the heart by simple faith. Once you let a man see the full meaning of the words, 'Christ loved me and gave himself for me,' then he will delight to give himself to Christ, and all that he has to his service. He will live to him, not in order that he may be secure, but because he is secure already. He will work for him, not that he may have life and peace, but because life and peace are his already.

Go to the cross of Christ, all you who want to be delivered from the power of selfishness. Go and see what a price was paid there to provide a ransom for your soul. Go and see what an astounding sacrifice was made there, that an open door to eternal life might be provided for poor sinners like you. Go and see how the Son of God gave himself for you, and give yourself to him.

The disease that ruined the rich man in the parable may be cured. But oh, remember there is only one real remedy! You must not live for yourself, but you must live for Christ. See to it that this remedy is not only known, but applied — not only heard of, but used.

Conclusion

And now let me conclude all by urging on every one of my readers the great duty of self-examination.

Questions to ask yourself

A passage of Scripture like this parable surely ought to cause many to search their hearts: 'Who am I? Where am I going? What am I doing? What is likely to happen to me after death? Am I prepared to leave the world? Have I any home to look forward to in the world to come? Have I put off the old man of sin and put on the new life in Christ? Am I really one with Christ, and a pardoned soul?' Surely such questions as these may well be asked when the story of the rich man and Lazarus has been heard. Oh, that the Holy Spirit may incline many a reader's heart to ask these questions!

Seek salvation while it can be found

In the next place, I invite all readers who desire to be saved, and have come to realize that they are lost in their sins, to seek salvation while it can be found. I do entreat you to seek him — the only one by whom man can enter heaven and be saved — Jesus Christ the Lord. He has the keys of heaven. He is sealed and appointed by God the Father to be the Saviour of all who will come to him. Go to him in earnest and hearty prayer, and tell him your situation. Tell him that you have heard that he 'receives sinners', and that you come to him as one (Luke 15:2). Tell him that you desire to be saved by him in his own way, and ask him to save you. Oh, that you may take this course without delay. Remember the hopeless end of the rich man. Once a person dies his soul can change its condition no more.

Give generously

I entreat all professing Christians to encourage themselves in habits of generosity towards all causes of charity and mercy. Remember that you are God's stewards, and give money generously, freely and without grudging, whenever you have an opportunity. You cannot keep your money for ever. You must give account one day as to how it has been spent. Oh, use it with an eye on eternity while you can!

I do not ask rich men to leave their situations in life, give away all their property, and go to live in the slums. This would be refusing to fill the position of a steward for God. I ask no man to neglect his worldly calling, and to stop providing for his family. Diligence in business is a positive Christian duty. Provision for those dependent on us is proper Christian wisdom. But I ask all to look around continually as they journey on, and to remember the poor — the poor in body and the poor in soul. We are here for a few short years. How can we do most good with our money while we are here? How can we so spend it as to leave the world somewhat happier and somewhat holier when we are removed from it? Might we not restrain some of our luxuries?

Might we spend less on ourselves, and give more to Christ's cause and Christ's poor? Is there no one we can give help to? Are there no sick, no poor, no needy, whose sorrows we might lessen, and whose comforts we might increase? Such questions will never fail to elicit an answer from some quarter. I am thoroughly persuaded that the income of every religious and charitable organization might easily be increased ten times, if Christians would give in proportion to their means.

There are surely none to whom such appeals ought to come home with such power as professing believers in the Lord Jesus. The parable of the text is a striking illustration of our position by nature, and our debt to Christ. We all lay, like Lazarus, at heaven's gate, sick unto the death, helpless and starving. Blessed be God! We were not neglected, as he was. Jesus came to relieve us. Jesus gave himself for us, that we might have hope and live. For a poor Lazarus-like world he came down from heaven, and humbled himself to become a man. For a poor Lazarus-like world he went everywhere doing good, caring for men's bodies as well as souls, until he died for us on the cross.

I believe that in giving to support works of charity and mercy, we are acting according to the mind of Christ — and I ask my readers to begin the habit of giving, if they have never begun it before; and if they were already giving, then to give more.

I believe that in offering a warning against worldliness and covetousness, I have done no more than bring forward a warning especially called for by the times, and I ask God to bless the consideration of these pages to many souls.

14.
The best friend

'This is my friend' (Song of Solomon 5:16).

A friend is one of the greatest blessings on earth. Don't tell me about money: love is better than money; sympathy is better than owning property. He is a poor man who has no friends.

This world is full of sorrow because it is full of sin. It is a dark place. It is a lonely place. It is a disappointing place. A friend is like the brightest ray of the sun on a spring day. Friendship eliminates half of our troubles and doubles our joys.

A real friend is scarce and rare. There are many who will eat, and drink, and laugh with us in the sunshine of prosperity. There are few who will stand by us in the days of darkness — few who will love us when we are sick, helpless and poor — few, above all, who will care for our souls.

Do any of my readers want a real friend? I am writing this to recommend one to you this day. I know of one who 'is a friend who sticks closer than a brother' (Proverbs 18:24). I know of one who is ready to be your friend for time and for eternity, if you will receive him.

The friend I want you to know is Jesus Christ. Happy is the family in which Christ has the prominent place! Happy is the person whose chief friend is Christ!

A friend in need

Do we want a friend in need? Such a friend is the Lord Jesus Christ.

Man is the neediest creature on God's earth, because he is a sinner. There is no need so great as that of sinners: poverty, hunger, thirst, cold, sickness, are all nothing in comparison. Sinners need forgiveness, and they are utterly unable to provide it for themselves; they need deliverance from a guilty conscience and the fear of death, and they have no power of their own to obtain it. This is the need the Lord Jesus Christ came into the world to relieve. 'Christ Jesus came into the world to save sinners' (1 Timothy 1:15).

We are all by nature *poor dying creatures*. From the king on his throne to the pauper in the slums, we are all sick of a mortal disease of the soul. Whether we know it or not, whether we feel it or not, we are all dying daily. The plague of sin is in our blood. We cannot cure ourselves: we are getting worse every hour. The Lord Jesus undertook to remedy all this. He came into the world to 'bring it health and healing'; he came to deliver us from 'the second death'; he 'abolished death and brought life and immortality to light through the gospel' (Jeremiah 33:6; Revelation 2:11; 2 Timothy 1:10).

We are all by nature *imprisoned debtors*. We owed our God millions of dollars, and did not even have a penny to our name. We were wretched bankrupts, without the hope of freeing ourselves. We could never have freed ourselves from our load of liabilities, and were daily getting deeper in debt. The Lord Jesus saw all of this and undertook to help us. He undertook to 'ransom and redeem us'; he came to 'proclaim liberty to the captives, and the opening of the prison to those who are bound'; he 'has redeemed us from the curse of the law' (Hosea 13:14; Isaiah 61:1; Galatians 3:13).

We were all by nature *sinking and rejected*. We could never have reached the harbour of everlasting life. We were sinking in the midst of the waves, lethargic, helpless and powerless; tied and bound by the chain of our own sins, floundering under the burden of our own guilt, and likely to become the easy prey of the devil. The Lord Jesus saw all of this and undertook to help us. He came down from heaven as 'one who is mighty'; he came to 'seek and to save that which was lost'; and to 'deliver [us] from going down to the pit' (Psalm 89:19; Luke 19:10; Job 33:24).

Could we have been saved without the Lord Jesus Christ coming down from heaven? It would have been impossible, so far as our eyes can see. The wisest men of Egypt, and Greece and Rome never found out the way to have peace with God. Without the friendship of Christ we would all have been lost for ever in the torments and agonies of hell.

Was the Lord Jesus Christ obliged to come down to save us? Oh, no! No! Never! It was his own free love, mercy and pity that brought him down. He came unsought and unasked because he was gracious.

Let us think on these things. Search all of history from the beginning of the world — look around the whole circle of those you know and love: you never heard of such friendship among the sons of men. There never was such a real friend who was willing to help us in our desperate time of need as was Jesus Christ.

A friend capable of meeting all your needs

Do you want a friend who is absolutely capable of meeting all your needs? Such a friend is the Lord Jesus Christ.

The true extent of a man's friendship must be measured by his deeds. Don't tell me what he says, and feels and wishes;

don't tell about his words and letters: rather tell me what he does. 'A real Friend is measured by what a real Friend does.'

What the Lord Jesus Christ has done for man is the grand proof of his friendly feeling towards him. Never were there such acts of kindness and self-denial as those that he has performed on our behalf. He has not loved us in word only but in action and deed.

For our sakes he took our nature upon him, and was born of a woman. He who was very God himself, and absolutely equal with the Father, laid aside his glory, for a period of time, and took upon him flesh and blood like our own. The almighty Creator of all things became a little babe like any of us, and experienced all our bodily weaknesses and ailments, apart from sin. 'Though he was rich, yet for your sakes he became poor, that you through his poverty might become rich' (2 Corinthians 8:9).

For our sakes he lived thirty-three years in this evil world, despised and rejected by men and women, a man of sorrows, and acquainted with grief. Though he was King of kings, he had no place to lay his head: though he was Lord of lords, he was often weary, and hungry, and thirsty, and poor: '[he] made himself of no reputation, taking the form of a bondservant, and coming in the likeness of men. And being found in appearance as a man, he humbled himself...' (Philippians 2:7-8).

For our sakes he suffered the most painful of all deaths — the death of crucifixion on a cross. Though innocent, and without fault, he allowed himself to be condemned, and found guilty. He who was the Prince of Life was led as a lamb to the slaughter, and poured out his soul unto death. He 'died for us' (1 Thessalonians 5:10).

Was he obliged to do this? Oh no! He could have summoned to his aid more than twelve legions of angels, and scattered his enemies with a word from his mouth. He suffered voluntarily and of his own free will, to make atonement for our sins. He knew that nothing but the sacrifice of his body and blood could ever make peace between sinful man and a holy God. He laid down his life to pay the price of our redemption: he died that we might live; he suffered that we might reign; he bore shame that we might receive glory. 'Christ also suffered once for sins, the just for the unjust, that he might bring us to God.' '[God] made him who knew no sin to be sin for us, that we might become the righteousness of God in him' (1 Peter 3:18; 2 Corinthians 5:21).

Such friendship as this passes man's understanding. Sometimes we may have heard of friends who would die for those who love them. But who can find a man who would lay down his life for those who hate him? Yet this is what Jesus has done for us. 'God demonstrates his own love toward us, in that while we were still sinners, Christ died for us' (Romans 5:8).

Ask all the tribes of mankind, from one end of the world to the other, and you will nowhere hear of a deed like this. No one was ever so exalted and stooped down so low as Jesus the Son of God: no one ever gave so costly a proof of his friendship; no one ever paid so much and endured so much to do good to others. Never was there such a friend as Jesus Christ!

A mighty and powerful friend

Do we want a mighty and powerful friend? Such a friend is Jesus Christ.

Power to help is something that few possess in this world. Many have the desire to do good to others, but no power. They feel for the sorrows of others, and would gladly relieve them if they could: they can weep with their friends in distress, but are unable to take their grief away. But though man is weak, Christ is strong — though the best of our earthly friends is feeble, Christ is almighty: Jesus said, 'All authority has been given to me in heaven and on earth' (Matthew 28:18). No one can do so much for those whom he helps as Jesus Christ. Others can help their bodies a little: he can help both body and soul. Others can do a little for them for a time: he can be a friend both for time and eternity.

Able to pardon

He is able to pardon and save the very chief of sinners. He can deliver the most guilty conscience from all its burdens, and give it perfect peace with God. He can wash away the vilest stains of wickedness, and make a man's soul whiter than snow in the sight of God. He can clothe a poor weak child of Adam in everlasting righteousness, and give him a title to heaven that can never be overthrown. In a word, he can give any one of us peace, hope, forgiveness and reconciliation with God, if we will only trust in him. 'The blood of Jesus Christ his Son cleanses us from all sin' (1 John 1:7).

Able to convert

He is able to convert the hardest of hearts, and create in man a new spirit. He can take the most thoughtless and ungodly people, and give them another mind by the Holy Spirit, which he puts in them. He can cause old things to pass away, and everything to become new. He can make them love the things which they once hated, and hate the things they once loved. '[He can give] the right to become children of God.' 'If anyone is in Christ, he is a new creation; old things have passed away; behold, all things have become new' (John 1:12; 2 Corinthians 5:17).

Able to preserve

He is able to preserve to the end all who believe in him, and become his disciples. He can give them grace to overcome the world, the flesh and the devil, and fight a good fight to the end. He can lead them on safely in spite of every temptation, carry them home through a thousand dangers, and keep them faithful, though they stand alone and have no one to help them. 'He is also able to save to the uttermost those who come to God through him' (Hebrews 7:25).

Able to give

He is able to give those that love him the best of gifts. He can give them inward comforts in life, which money can never buy — peace in poverty, joy in sorrow, patience in suffering. He can give them bright hopes in death, which enable them to walk through the dark valley without fear. After death he can give them a crown of glory, which never fades, and a reward that no king or country on earth could ever match.

This is power indeed: this is true greatness; this is real strength. Go and look at the poor Hindu idolater, seeking peace in vain by afflicting his body; and, after fifty years of self-imposed suffering, is still unable to find it. Go and look at the blind Roman Catholic, giving money to his priest to pray for his soul, and yet dying without salvation. Go and look at rich men, spending thousands in search of happiness, and yet always discontented and unhappy. Then turn to Jesus, and think what he can do, and is daily doing for all who trust him. Think how he heals all the broken-hearted, comforts all the sick, cheers all the poor who trust in him, and supplies all their daily need. The fear of man is strong, the opposition of this evil world is mighty, the lusts of the flesh rage, the fear of death is distressing, the devil prowls around like a roaring lion looking for someone to devour; but Jesus is stronger than them all. Jesus can make us conquerors over all these foes. And now I ask you whether it is not a true statement, that there never was so mighty a friend as Jesus Christ.

A loving and affectionate friend

Do we want a loving and affectionate friend? Such a friend is Jesus Christ.

Kindness is the very essence of true friendship. Money, advice and help lose half their good will, if not given in a loving manner. What kind of love does the Lord Jesus have towards man? It is called 'the love ... which passes knowledge' (Ephesians 3:19).

Love shines forth in his *reception of sinners*. He refuses none who come to him for salvation, however unworthy they may be. Though their lives may have been most wicked, though their sins may be more in number than the stars of heaven, the Lord Jesus is ready to receive them, and give them pardon and peace. There is no end to his compassion: there are no limits to his mercy. He is not ashamed to be a friend and to help those whom the world casts off as hopeless. There are none too bad, too filthy, and too diseased with sin, to be admitted into his home. He is willing to be the friend of any sinner: he has kindness and mercy and healing medicine for all. He has long proclaimed this to be his rule: 'the one who comes to me I will by no means cast out' (John 6:37).

Love shines forth in his *dealings with sinners*, after they have believed in him and become his friends. He is very patient with them, though their conduct is often very trying and provoking. He is never tired of hearing their complaints, however often they may come to him. He sympathizes deeply in all their sorrows. He knows what pain is: he is 'acquainted with grief' (Isaiah 53:3). In all their afflictions he is afflicted. He never allows them to be tempted above what they are able to bear: he supplies them with daily grace for their daily conflict. Their poor service is acceptable to him: he is well pleased with them as a parent is with his child's efforts to speak and walk. He has caused it to be written in his book, that 'The Lord takes pleasure in his people,' and that 'the LORD takes pleasure in those who fear him' (Psalm 149:4; 147:11).

There is no love on earth that can be named alongside this! We love those in whom we see something that deserves our affection, or those who are our flesh and bone: the Lord Jesus loves sinners in whom there is nothing good. We love those from whom we get something in return for our affection: the Lord Jesus loves those who can do little or nothing for him, compared to what he does for them. We love where we can give some reason for loving: the great Friend of sinners draws his reasons out of his own everlasting compassion. His love is purely impartial, purely unselfish, purely free. Never, never was there a so truly loving friend as Jesus Christ.

A wise and prudent friend

Do we want a wise and prudent friend? Such a friend is the Lord Jesus Christ.

Man's friendship is sadly blind. He often injures those he loves by overbearing kindness: he often errs in the counsel he gives; he often leads his friends into trouble by bad advice, even when he means to help them. He sometimes keeps them back from the way of life, and entangles them in the vanities of the world, when they have almost escaped. The friendship of the Lord Jesus is not like that: it always does us good, never evil.

Never spoils

The Lord Jesus never spoils his friends by extravagant indulgence. He gives them everything that is really for their benefit; he withholds nothing from them that is really good; but he requires them to take up their cross daily and follow him. He commands them to endure hardships as good soldiers: he calls on them to fight the good fight against the world, the flesh and the devil. His people often dislike it at the time, and think it difficult; but when they reach heaven they will see it was all well done.

Makes no mistakes

The Lord Jesus makes no mistakes in managing his friends' affairs. He orders all their concerns with perfect wisdom: all things happen to them at the right time, and in the right way. He gives them as much sickness and as much health, as much poverty and as much riches, as much sorrow and as much joy, as he sees their souls require. He leads them by the right way to bring them to the city that will be their eternal home. He mixes their bitterest cups like a wise physician, and takes care that they do not have a drop too little or a drop too much. His people often misunderstand his dealings; they are silly enough to imagine that their course of life might have been better ordered: but in the resurrection day they will thank God that not their will but Christ's will was done.

Look around the world and see the harm that friends continually inflict upon each other. Note how much more ready men are to encourage one another in worldliness and levity, than to spur one another on towards love and good deeds. Think how often they meet together, not for the better, but for the worse — not to quicken one another's souls on the way to heaven, but to confirm one another in the love of this present world. Yes, there are thousands who are wounded unexpectedly in the house of their friends!

Then turn to the great Friend of sinners, and see how different his friendship is from that of man. Listen to him as he walks by the way with his disciples; notice how he comforts, reproves and exhorts with perfect wisdom. Observe how he times his visits to those he loves, as to Mary and Martha at Bethany. Hear how he converses, as he dines on the shore of the Sea of Galilee: 'Simon, son of Jonah, do you love me?' (John 21:16). His company is always sanctifying. His gifts are always for our soul's good; his kindness is always wise; his fellowship always edifies us. One day with the Son of Man is better than a thousand days in the company of earthly friends: one hour spent in private communion with him is better than a year in kings' palaces. Never, never was there such a wise friend as Jesus Christ.

A tried and proved friend

Do we want a tried and proved friend? Such a friend is Jesus Christ.

More than six thousand years have passed since the Lord Jesus began his work of being a friend to mankind. During that long period of time he has had many friends in this world. Billions of people, unhappily, have refused his offers and been miserably lost for ever; but millions upon millions have enjoyed the mighty privilege of his friendship and been saved. He has had great experience of being a friend of sinners.

He has had friends of *every rank and station* in life. Some of them were kings and rich men, like David, and Solomon, and Hezekiah, and Job; some of them were very poor in this world, like the shepherds of Bethlehem, and James, and John, and Andrew: but every one of them was Christ's friend.

He has had friends of *every age* that man can pass through. Some of them never knew him till they were advanced in years, like Manasseh, and Zacchaeus, and probably the Ethiopian Eunuch. Some of them were his friends even from their earliest childhood, like Joseph, and Samuel, and Josiah, and Timothy. But every one of them was Christ's friend.

He has had friends of *every possible temperament and disposition*. Some of them were simple plain men and women, like Isaac; some of them were mighty in word and deed, like Moses; some of them were fervent and warm-hearted, like Peter; some of them were gentle and retiring spirits, like John; some of them were active and stirring, like Martha; some of them loved to sit quietly at his feet, like Mary; some lived unknown among their own people, like the Shunamite; some have gone everywhere and turned the world upside down, like Paul. But every one of them was Christ's friend.

He has had friends of *every condition in life*. Some of them were married, and had sons and daughters, like Enoch; some of them lived and died unmarried, like Daniel and John the Baptist; some of them were often sick, like Lazarus and Epaphroditus; some of them were strong and laboured hard, like Persis, and Tryphena, and Tryphosa; some of them were masters, like Abraham and Cornelius; some of them were servants, like the saints in Nero's household; some of them had bad servants, like Elisha; some of them had bad masters, like Obadiah; some of them had bad wives and children, like David. But every one of them was Christ's friend.

He has had friends of *almost every nation, and people and language*. He has had friends in hot countries and in cold; friends among highly civilized nations, and friends among the simplest and rudest tribes. His Book of Life contains the names of Greeks and Romans, of Jews and Egyptians, of bond and of free. There are to be found on its lists reserved Englishmen and cautious Scotsmen, impulsive Irishmen and fiery Welshmen, volatile Frenchmen and dignified Spaniards, refined Italians and solid Germans, rude Africans and refined Indians (from India), cultivated Chinese and half-savage New Zealanders. But every one of them was Christ's friend.

All these have tested Christ's friendship, and proved it to be good. They all found nothing lacking when they began: they all found nothing lacking as they advanced in the friendship. No lack, no defect, no deficiency was ever found by any one of them in Jesus Christ. Each found his own soul's needs fully supplied; each found every day, that in Christ there was enough and plenty to spare. Never, never was there a friend so fully tried and proved as Jesus Christ.

An unfailing friend

Last, but not least, do we want an unfailing friend? Such a friend is the Lord Jesus Christ.

The saddest part of all the good things of earth is their instability. Riches make themselves wings and fly away; youth and beauty are but for a few years; strength of body soon decays; mind and intellect are soon exhausted. All is perishing. All is fading. All is passing away. But there is one splendid exception to this general rule, and that is the friendship of Jesus Christ.

The Lord Jesus is *a friend who never changes*. There is no fickleness about him: those whom he loves, he loves to the end. Husbands have been known to forsake their wives; parents have been known to cast off their children; human vows and promises of faithfulness have often been forgotten. Thousands have been neglected in their poverty and old age, who were honoured by all when they were rich and young. But Christ never changed his feelings towards one of his friends. He is 'the same yesterday, today, and for ever' (Hebrews 13:8).

The Lord Jesus *never goes away from his friends*. There is never a parting and goodbye between him and his people. From the time that he makes his home in the sinner's heart, he abides in it for ever. The world is full of separations and departures: death and the passage of time break up the most united family; sons move on to make their way in life; daughters are married, and leave their father's house for ever. Scattering, scattering, scattering, is the yearly history of the happiest home. How many we have tearfully watched as they drove away from our doors, whose pleasant faces we have never seen again! How many we have sorrowfully followed to the grave, and then come back to a cold, silent, lonely house! But, thanks be to God, there is one who never leaves his friends! The Lord Jesus has said, 'I will never leave you nor forsake you' (Hebrews 13:5).

The Lord Jesus *goes with his friends wherever they go*. There is no possible separation between him and those he loves. There is no place or position on earth, or under the earth, that can divide them from the great Friend of their souls. When the path of duty calls them far away from home, he is their companion; when they pass through the fire and water of fierce suffering, he is with them; when they lie down on the bed of sickness, he stands by them and makes all their trouble work for good; when they go down the valley of the shadow of death, and friends and relatives stand still and can go no further, he goes down by their side. When they wake up in the unknown world of paradise, they are still with him; when they rise with a new body at the Judgement Day, they will not be alone. He will acknowledge them as his friends, and say, 'They are mine: let them go free.' He will make good his own words: 'I am with you always, even to the end of the age' (Matthew 28:20).

Look around the world, and see how failure is written on all men's schemes. Add up the partings, and separations, and disappointments, and bereavements that you have experienced, heard about or observed. Think what a privilege it is that there is one at least who never fails, and in whom no one was ever disappointed! Never, never was there so unfailing a friend as Jesus Christ.

Some words of application

And now, permit me to conclude this chapter with a few plain words of application. I don't know who you are or what state your soul may be in; but I am sure that the words I am about to say deserve your serious attention. Oh, that these words may not find you careless of spiritual things! Oh, that you may be able to give a few thoughts to Christ!

Is Christ your friend?

I call upon you to *solemnly consider whether Christ is your friend and you are his*. There are millions, I grieve to say, who are not Christ's friends. Baptized in his name, outward members of his church, attending church services, taking the Lord's Supper, praying, reading the Bible — but they are not Christ's 'friends'.

Do they hate the sins that Jesus died for? No.
Do they love the Saviour who came into the world to save them? No.
Do they care for the souls that were so precious in his sight? No.
Do they delight in the word of reconciliation? No.
Do they try to speak with the Friend of sinners in prayer? No.
Do they seek close fellowship with him? No.

Oh, reader, is this your situation? How is it with you? Are you, or are you not, one of Christ's friends?

A poor miserable being

If you are not one of Christ's friends, *you are a poor miserable being*. I write this down deliberately. I do not say it without thought. I say that if Christ is not your friend, you are a poor miserable being.

You are in the midst of a failing, sorrowful world, and you have no real source of comfort, or refuge for a time of need. You are a dying creature, and you are not ready to die. You have sins, and they are not forgiven. You are going to be judged, and you are not prepared to meet God: you can be, but you refuse to use the one and only Mediator and Advocate. You love the world better than Christ. You refuse the great Friend of sinners, and you have no friend in heaven to plead your cause. Yes, it is sad but true! You are a poor, miserable being. It matters nothing what your income is: without Christ's friendship you are very poor.

Christ is willing to be your friend

If you really want a friend, *Christ is willing to become your friend*. He has long wanted you to join his people, and he now invites you by my hand. He is ready to receive you, all unworthy as you may feel, and to write your name down on the list of his friends. He is ready to pardon all the past, to clothe you with righteousness, to give you his Spirit, to make you his own dear child. All he asks you to do is to come to him.

He commands you to come with all your sins, only acknowledging your wickedness, and confessing that you are ashamed. Just as you are — waiting for nothing — unworthy of anything in yourself — Jesus commands you to come and be his friend.

Oh, come and be wise! Come and be safe. Come and be happy. Come and be Christ's friend.

Great privileges

If Christ is your friend, *you have great privileges*, and ought to walk worthy of them. Seek every day to have closer communion with the one who is your friend, and to know more of his grace and power. True Christianity is not merely believing a certain set of dry abstract propositions: it is to live in daily personal communication with an actual living person — Jesus the Son of God. 'For to me,' said Paul, 'to live is Christ' (Philippians 1:21).

Seek every day to glorify your Lord and Saviour in all your ways. 'A man who has friends must himself be friendly' (Proverbs 18:24), and surely no man is under such mighty obligations as the friend of Christ. Avoid everything that would grieve your Lord. Fight hard against the sins that so easily entangle, against inconsistency, against being ashamed to confess him before men. Say to your soul, whenever you are tempted to do what is wrong, 'Soul, soul, is this your kindness to your Friend?'

Think, above all, of the mercy that has been shown you, and learn to rejoice daily in your Friend! What if your body is bent over with disease? What if the poverty and trials of your life are overwhelming? What if your earthly friends all forsake you, and you are alone in this world? All this may be true: but if you are in Christ, then you have a friend, a mighty Friend, a loving Friend, a wise Friend, a Friend that never fails. Oh, think, think habitually about your Friend!

Yet in a little while and your Friend will come to take you home, and you will live with him for ever. Yet a little while and you will see him as you have been seen by him, and know him as you have been known by him. And then you will hear the glorified saints in heaven proclaim that he *who has had Christ for his friend is the rich and happy man.*

15.
Sickness

'He whom you love is sick' (John 11:3).

The chapter from which this text is taken is well known to all Bible readers. In lifelike description, in touching interest, in sublime simplicity, there is no writing in existence that can compare with that chapter. A narrative like this is, to my mind, one of the great proofs of the inspiration of Scripture. When I read the story of Lazarus, I feel 'There is something here that the unbeliever can never account for.' 'This is nothing else but the finger of God.'

The words that I chiefly dwell upon in this chapter are especially moving and instructive. They record the message that Martha and Mary sent to Jesus when their brother Lazarus was sick: 'Lord, behold, he whom you love is sick.' That message was short and simple. Yet almost every word is deeply suggestive.

Note the childlike faith of these holy women. They turned to the Lord Jesus in their hour of need, as the frightened infant turns to its mother, or the compass needle turns to the North Pole. They turned to him as their Shepherd, their almighty Friend and their Brother born for adversity. As different as they were in natural disposition, the two sisters were entirely agreed in this matter. Christ's help was their first thought in the day of trouble. Christ was the refuge to which they fled in the hour of need. Blessed are all those who do likewise!

Note the simple humility of their language about their brother
Lazarus. They call him, 'he whom you love'. They don't say,
'He who loves you, believes in you, serves you,' but 'he whom
you love'. Martha and Mary had a deep understanding of God.
They had learned that Christ's love towards us, and not our
love towards Christ, is the true basis of hope, and the true foundation of faith. Blessed, again, is everyone who has learned
these same truths! To look inward to our love towards Christ is
painfully unsatisfying: to look outward to Christ's love towards
us is peace.

Note, lastly, the touching circumstance that the message of
Martha and Mary reveals: 'Lord, he whom you love is sick.'
Lazarus was a good man, converted, believing, renewed, a
friend of Christ, and an heir of glory. And yet Lazarus was sick!
Therefore, sickness is not a sign that God is displeased. Sickness is intended to be a blessing to us, and not a curse. 'We
know that all things work together for good to those who love
God, to those who are the called according to his purpose'
(Romans 8:28). 'The world or life or death, or things present or
things to come — all are yours. And you are Christ's, and Christ
is God's' (1 Corinthians 3:22-23). I say again, blessed are those
who have learned this! Happy are those who can say, when
they are sick, 'This is my Father's doing. It must be good.'

I invite the attention of my readers to the subject of sickness. The subject is one we ought frequently to look squarely
in the face. We cannot avoid it. You don't have to be a prophet
to see sickness coming to each one of us some day. Let us turn
aside for a few moments and, as Christians, consider sickness.
Reflection upon it will not accelerate its coming, and by God's
blessing, examining it may teach us wisdom.

In considering the subject of sickness, three points appear to me to demand attention. On each I will say a few
words.

1. The universal prevalence of sickness and disease.
2. The general benefits which sickness bestows on mankind.
3. The special duties to which sickness calls us.

The universal prevalence of sickness

Firstly, the universal prevalence of sickness. I do not need to dwell very long on this point. To elaborate on the proofs of it would only be multiplying self-evident truths, which the majority of people already acknowledge.

Sickness is everywhere. In Europe, in Asia, in Africa, in America; in hot countries and in cold, in civilized nations and in savage tribes — men, women and children get sick and die.

Sickness is found in all classes. Grace does not lift a believer out of its reach. Riches will not buy exemption from it. Rank cannot prevent its assaults. Kings and their subjects, presidents and their people, masters and servants, rich men and poor, educated and uneducated, teachers and students, doctors and patients, ministers and their congregation, all alike go down before this great foe. 'The rich man's wealth is his strong city' (Proverbs 18:11). A man's house is called his castle; but there are no doors and barricades that can keep out disease and death.

Sickness comes in a variety of ways. From the top of our head to the sole of our feet we are prone to disease. Our capacity for suffering is something fearful to contemplate. Who can count up the ailments by which our bodies may be attacked? It is not so amazing to me that men die so soon, as it is that they should live so long.

Sickness is often one of the most humbling and distressing trials that can come upon men and women. It can turn the strongest into a little child, and make him feel helpless. It can unnerve the boldest, and make him tremble at the sound of a leaf being blown by the wind. The connection between body and mind is curiously close. The influence that some diseases can exercise upon the mood and spirits is very great. There are diseases of the brain, the liver and the nerves, which can bring down a Solomon in mind to a state little better than that of a baby. He who wants to know to what depths of humiliation man can fall has only to spend a little time visiting the sick.

Sickness cannot be prevented by anything man can do. The average duration of life may doubtless be somewhat lengthened. The skill of the doctor may continually discover new remedies, and accomplish remarkable cures. The enforcement of wise sanitary regulations may greatly lower the death rate in a country. But, in the end, whether in healthy or unhealthy localities, whether in mild climates or in cold, whether treated with home remedies or modern medicines' latest drug — men and women will get sick and die. 'The days of our lives are seventy years; and if by reason of strength they are eighty years, yet their boast is only labour and sorrow; for it is soon cut off, and we fly away' (Psalm 90:10). That witness is indeed true. It was true over 3,300 years ago. It is still true.

Now what can we make of the great fact of the universal prevalence of sickness? How shall we account for it? What explanation can we give for it? What answer will we give to our inquiring children when they ask, 'Father, why do people get sick and die?' These are grave questions. A few words on them will not be out of place.

Can we suppose for a moment that God created sickness and disease at the beginning? Can we imagine that he who formed our world in such perfect order was the Creator of needless suffering and pain? Can we conceive that he who made all things 'very good', made Adam's race subject to sickness and death? The idea is, to my mind, revolting. It introduces a grand imperfection into the midst of God's perfect works. I must find another solution as to the origin of sickness to satisfy my mind.

The only explanation that satisfies me is that which the Bible gives. Something has come into the world that has dethroned man from his original position, and stripped him of his original privileges. Something has come in, which, like a handful of gravel thrown into the midst of machinery, has marred the perfect order of God's creation. And what was that 'something'? I answer in one word: it is sin. 'Sin entered the world, and death through sin' (Romans 5:12). Sin is the cause of all sickness, and disease, and pain, and suffering, which prevail on the earth. They are all part of the curse that came into the world when Adam and Eve ate the forbidden fruit and fell. There would have been no sickness if there had been no fall. There would have been no disease if there had been no sin.

I pause for a moment at this point, and yet in pausing I do not depart from my subject. I pause to remind my readers that there is no ground so untenable as that which is occupied by the atheist, the deist, or the unbeliever in the Bible. Boldly, I say that it requires far more faith to be an atheist than to be a Christian. Boldly, I say that there are numerous and obvious facts in the condition of mankind, which nothing but the Bible can explain, and that one of the most striking of these facts is the universal prevalence of pain, sickness and disease. In short, one of the greatest difficulties in the teachings of atheists and deists is with the physical body of man.

Surely you have heard of atheists. An atheist is one who professes to believe that there is no God, no Creator, no first cause, and that all things came together in this world by mere chance. Now shall we listen to such a doctrine as this? Go, take an atheist to one of the excellent surgical schools of our land, and ask him to study the wonderful structure of the human body. Show him the matchless skill with which every joint, and vein, and valve, and muscle, and sinew, and nerve, and bone, and limb, has been formed. Show him the perfect adaptation of every part of the human body to the purpose that it serves. Show him the thousand devices for confronting wear and tear, and replenishing the daily loss of strength. And then ask this man who denies the existence of a God, and a great first cause, if all this wonderful system of components is the result of chance. Ask him if it came together at first by luck or accident. Ask him if he thinks about the watch he looks at each day, and the bread he eats, and of the coat he wears. Oh, no! Design is an insurmountable difficulty in the atheist's way. *There is a God.*

You have certainly heard of deists. A deist is one who professes to believe that there is a God who made the world and everything in it. But he does not believe the Bible. 'A God, but no Bible! A Creator, but no Christianity!' This is the deist's creed. Now, shall we listen to this doctrine? Go again, I say, and take a deist to a hospital, and show him some of the awful handiwork of disease. Take him to the bed where lies some tender child, scarcely knowing good from evil, with an incurable cancer. Send him to the ward where there is a loving mother of a large family in the last stage of some excruciating disease. Show him some of the agonizing pains and sufferings that flesh has inherited, and ask him to account for them. Ask this man, who believes there is a great and wise God who made the world, but cannot believe the Bible — ask him how he accounts for these traces of disorder and imperfection in his God's creation. Ask this man, who sneers at Christian theology and is too wise to believe the fall of Adam — ask him to explain the origin of the universal prevalence of pain and disease in the world. You will ask in vain! You will not get a satisfactory answer. Sickness and suffering are insurmountable obstacles in the deist's way. 'Man has sinned, and therefore man suffers.' Adam fell from his original position of joy and bliss, and therefore Adam's children get sick and die.

The universality of sickness is one of the indirect evidences that the Bible is true. The Bible explains it. The Bible answers the questions concerning it that will originate in every inquiring mind. No other systems of religion can do this. They all fail here. They are silent. They are confused. Only the Bible looks the subject directly in the face. It boldly proclaims the fact that man is a fallen creature, and with equal boldness proclaims a vast corrective system to meet his needs. I am forced to conclude that the Bible is from God. Christianity is a revelation from heaven. 'Your word is truth' (John 17:17).

Let us stand firm on the old ground, that the Bible, and the Bible only, is God's revelation of himself to man. Don't be moved by the many new assaults which modern scepticism is making on the inspired Word of God. Don't be concerned about the difficult questions that the enemies of the faith are fond of raising about Bible difficulties, and to which perhaps you often feel unable to give an answer. Anchor your soul firmly on this safe principle — that the whole book is God's truth. Tell the enemies of the Bible that, in spite of all their arguments, there is no book in the world that will bear comparison with the Bible; none that so thoroughly meets the needs of man; none that explains so much of the state of mankind. As to the difficult things in the Bible, tell them you are content to wait. You find enough obvious truth in the book to satisfy your conscience and save your soul. The difficult things will be cleared up one day. What you don't know now, you will know then.

The benefits of sickness to mankind

The second point I propose to consider is the general benefits that sickness confers on mankind. I use the word 'benefits' cautiously. I feel it is of the utmost importance to see this part of our subject clearly. I know well that sickness is one of the supposed weak points in God's government of the world, on which sceptical minds love to dwell: 'Can God be a God of love, when he allows pain? Can God be a God of mercy, when he permits disease? He could prevent pain and disease; but he doesn't. How can these things be?' This is the reasoning that often comes across the heart of man.

I reply to all such sceptics, that their doubts and questionings are most unreasonable. They might as well doubt the existence of a Creator, because the order of the universe is disturbed by earthquakes, hurricanes and storms. They might as well doubt the providence of God, because of the horrible massacres that have occurred in history. All this would be just as reasonable as to doubt the mercy of God, because of the presence of sickness in the world.

I ask all who find it hard to reconcile the prevalence of disease and pain with the love of God, to focus their eyes on the world around them, and to note what is going on. I ask them to observe the extent to which men constantly submit to present loss for the sake of future gain, present sorrow for the sake of future joy, present pain for the sake of future health. The seed is buried in the ground, and rots: but we sow in the hope of a future harvest. Children are sent to school amidst many tears: but we send them in the hope of their getting future wisdom. The father of a family undergoes some fearful surgery: but he bears it, in the hope of future health — I ask men to apply this great principle to God's government of the world. I ask them to believe that God allows pain, sickness and disease, not because he loves to torment man, but because he desires to benefit man's heart, and mind, and conscience, and soul, for all of eternity.

I repeat, once more, that I speak of the 'benefits' of sickness on purpose and cautiously. I know the suffering and pain that sickness entails. I admit to the misery and wretchedness that it often brings. But I cannot regard it as an unmixed evil. I see in it a wise permission of God. I see in it a useful provision to check the ravages of sin and the devil among men's souls. If man had never sinned I would have been at a loss to discern the benefit of sickness. But since sin is in the world, I can see that sickness is good for man. It is a blessing just as much as a curse. I admit that it is a rough schoolmaster. But it is a real friend to man's soul.

It reminds men of death

Sickness helps to remind men of death. Most people live as if they were never going to die. They follow business, or pleasure, or politics, or science, as if the earth was their eternal home. They plan and scheme for the future, like the rich fool in the parable, as if they had a long lease on life, and were not simply tenants whose length of stay is brief. A serious illness sometimes goes a long way to dispel these delusions. It awakens men from their daydreams, and reminds them that they have to die as well as to live. Now this I say emphatically is a mighty advantage of sickness.

It makes men think seriously of God

Sickness helps to make men think seriously of God, their souls, and the world to come. While they are enjoying good health most people can find no time for such thoughts. They dislike them. They ignore them. They regard them troublesome and unpleasant. Now a severe disease has sometimes a wonderful power of gathering and rallying these thoughts, and bringing them before the eyes of a man's soul. Even a wicked king like Ben-hadad, when sick, thought of Elisha (2 Kings 8:8). Even heathen sailors, when death was in sight, were afraid, and 'every man cried out to his god' (Jonah 1:5). Surely anything that makes men think is good.

It softens men's hearts

Sickness helps to soften men's hearts, and teach them wisdom. The natural (unsaved) heart is as hard as stone. It can see no good in anything that is not of this life, and no happiness except what is found in this world. A long illness sometimes goes a long way to correct these ideas. It exposes the emptiness and hollowness of what the world calls 'good' things and teaches us to hold them loosely. The businessman finds that money alone is not the answer to everything the heart desires. The woman of the world finds that expensive clothes, and the reading of novels, and the accounts of grand parties and operas, are miserable comforters in a hospital room. Surely anything that causes us to alter our value of earthly things is a real benefit.

It levels and humbles us

Sickness helps to level and humble us. We are all naturally proud and somewhat conceited. Few, even of the poorest class, are free from the infection. Few are to be found who do not look down on somebody else, and secretly flatter themselves that they are 'not like other men'. A sickbed is a mighty tamer of such thoughts. It forces on us the mighty truth that we are all poor debased creatures, that we 'dwell in houses of clay', and are 'crushed before a moth' (Job 4:19), and that kings and subjects, masters and servants, rich and poor, are all dying creatures, and will soon stand side by side in judgement, in front of God. In the sight of the coffin and the grave it is not easy to be proud. Surely anything that teaches that lesson is good.

It tests men's religion

Finally, sickness helps to test the kind of religion men have. Most people on earth have some kind of religion, yet few have a religion that will hold up under inspection. Most are content with traditions received from their fathers, and can furnish no reason for the hope that is in them. Now disease is sometimes most useful to a man in exposing the utter worthlessness of the foundation of his soul. It often shows him that he has nothing solid under his feet, and nothing firm to hold on to with his hand. It causes him to realize that, although he may have had a form of religion, he has, for all of his life, been worshipping 'an unknown God'. Many a belief looks good on the smooth waters of health, but turns out utterly unsound and useless on the rough seas of the sickbed. The winter storms often bring out the defects in a man's house, and sickness often exposes the depravity of a man's soul. Surely anything that makes us find out the real character of our faith is good.

I am not saying that sickness bestows these benefits to everyone who is overcome with illness. Sadly, I can say nothing of the kind! Every year an innumerable number are overcome with illness, and restored to health, who evidently learn no lesson from their sickbeds, and return again to the world. Myriads are yearly passing through sickness to the grave, and yet receive no more spiritual understanding from it than the animals that perish. While they live they have no feeling, and when they die, 'they have no struggles' (Psalm 73:4). These are awful things to say. But they are true. The degree of deadness to which man's heart and conscience may attain is a depth which I cannot pretend to understand.

But does sickness bestow the benefits of which I have been speaking on only a few? I will allow nothing of the kind. I believe that in very many cases sickness produces feelings and thoughts much like those I have just mentioned. I believe that in many minds sickness is God's 'day of visitation', and that feelings are continually aroused on a sickbed which might, by God's grace, result in salvation. I believe that in heathen lands sickness often paves the way for the missionary, and makes the idolater listen to the good news of the gospel. I believe that in our own country sickness is one of the greatest aids to the minister of the gospel, and that sermons and teachings that we have neglected in the day of health are often brought home in the day of disease. I believe that sickness is one of God's most important secondary instruments in the saving of men, and that though the feelings it calls forth are often temporary, it is also often a means whereby the Spirit works effectually on the heart. In short, I firmly believe that the sickness of men's bodies has often led, in God's wonderful providence, to the salvation of men's souls.

I leave this branch of my subject here. It needs no further remark. If sickness can do the things of which I have been speaking (and who will contradict it?), if sickness in a wicked world can help to make men think of God and their souls, then sickness confers benefits on mankind.

We have no right to murmur at sickness, and grieve at its presence in the world. Rather we ought to thank God for it. It is God's witness. It is the soul's counsellor. It is a stimulator to the conscience. It is a purifier to the heart. Surely I have a right to tell you that sickness is a blessing and not a curse — an aid and not an injury — a gain and not a loss — a friend and not a foe to mankind. So long as we have a world where there is sin, it is a mercy that it is a world where there is sickness.

The duties that sickness requires of us

The third and last point that I propose to consider concerns the special duties that the prevalence of sickness requires of each one of us. I would be sorry to leave the subject of sickness without saying something on this point. I hold it to be of fundamental importance not to be content with generalities in delivering God's message to the soul. I am anxious to impress on each one of my readers his own personal responsibility in this matter. I desire that no one lay down this publication unable to answer the questions, 'What practical lesson have I learned? What should I do in a world of disease and death?'

Be prepared to meet God

One paramount duty that the prevalence of sickness requires of man is to habitually live prepared to meet God. Sickness is a reminder of death. Death is the door through which we must all pass to judgement. Judgement is the time when we all must finally meet God face to face. Surely the first lesson that the inhabitant of a sick and dying world should learn should be to prepare to meet his God.

When are you prepared to meet God? Never till your sins are forgiven, and covered! Never till your heart is renewed, and your will taught to delight in the will of God! You have many sins. Only the righteousness of Christ can make you acceptable in the sight of God. Only faith, simple childlike faith, can give you an interest in Christ and his benefits. Are you prepared to meet God? Then where is your faith? Your heart is naturally unsuitable for God's company. You have no real pleasure in doing his will. The Holy Spirit must transform you into the image of Christ. Old things must pass away. All things must become new. Are you prepared to meet God? Then where is your grace? Where are the evidences of your conversion and sanctification?

I believe that this, and nothing less than this, is preparedness to meet God. Forgiveness of sin and fitness for God's presence; justification by faith and sanctification of the heart; the blood of Christ sprinkled on us, and the Spirit of Christ living in us — these are the grand essentials of the Christian faith. These are not mere words and names to furnish bones of contention for disputing theologians. These are sober, solid, substantial realities. To actually possess these things, in a world full of sickness and death, is the first duty that I impress upon your soul.

Always be ready to bear sickness patiently

Another important responsibility that sickness requires of man is to live a life that is constantly ready to bear it patiently. Sickness is no doubt trying to flesh and blood. To feel our nerves weakened, to be obliged to sit still and be cut off from all our usual pastimes, to see our plans destroyed and our purposes disappointed, to endure long hours and days, and nights of weariness and pain — all this is a severe strain on poor sinful human nature. Is it any wonder that irritability and impatience are brought out by disease! Surely in such a dying world as this we should study patience.

How will we learn to bear sickness patiently, when it is our turn to suffer? We must lay up stores of grace in the time of health. We must seek for the sanctifying influence of the Holy Spirit over our undisciplined tempers and personalities. We must make a real business of our prayers, and regularly ask for strength to endure God's will as well as to do it. Such strength is ours for the asking: 'If you ask anything in my name, I will do it' (John 14:14).

I do not think it needless to dwell on this point. I believe the passive graces of Christianity receive far less notice than they deserve. Peace, gentleness, faithfulness, patience, are all mentioned in the Word of God as fruits of the Spirit. They are passive graces that especially glorify God. They often make men think, who normally despise the active side of the Christian character. Never do these graces shine so brightly as they do in the sickroom. They enable many a sick person to preach a silent sermon, which those around him never forget. Would the doctrine you profess shine forth? Would you make your Christianity beautiful to the eyes of others? Then take hold of my suggestion this day. Store up a reserve of patience for the day of sickness that is sure to come. Then, even if your sickness does not end in death, it will be for 'the glory of God' (John 11:4).

Always be ready to help your fellow men

One more important responsibility that sickness requires of you is to always be ready to sympathize with and help your fellowmen. Sickness is never very far from us. There are only a few families who do not have some sick relative. There are few church congregations where you will not find someone ill. But wherever there is sickness, there is a call to duty. In some cases a little timely aid; in others, a kindly visit, a friendly inquiry, a mere expression of sympathy, may all do a vast amount of good. These are the sort of things that soften bitterness, and bring men together, and promote good feelings. These are ways by which you may ultimately lead men to Christ and save their souls. These are good works to which every professing Christian should be ready to perform. In a world full of sickness and disease we ought to 'Bear one another's burdens', and 'be kind to one another' (Galatians 6:2; Ephesians 4:32).

These things, I dare say, may appear to some ineffectual and trivial. They must always be doing something great, and grand, and striking, and heroic! Allow me to say that careful attention to these little acts of brotherly kindness is one of the clearest evidences of having 'the mind of Christ'. They are acts in which our blessed Master himself abounded. He always 'went about doing good' to the sick and sorrowful (Acts 10:38). They are acts to which he attaches great importance in that most solemn passage of Scripture, the description of the last judgement. He says there: 'I was sick and you visited me' (Matthew 25:36).

Have you any desire to prove the reality of your love — that blessed grace which so many talk of, and so few practise? If you have, beware of callous selfishness and neglect of the sick around you. Search them out. Assist them if they need aid. Show your sympathy with them. Try to lighten their burdens. Above all, strive to do good to their souls. It will do you good even if it does no good to them. It will keep your heart from murmuring. It may prove a blessing to your own soul. I firmly believe that God is testing and proving us by every case of sickness within our reach. By permitting suffering, he tests whether Christians have any feeling. Beware, lest you be weighed in the balance and found wanting. If you can live in a sick and dying world and not feel for others, then you still have a lot to learn.

I leave this part of my subject here. I throw out the points I have suggested, and pray to God that they may work in many minds. I repeat, that constantly being ready to meet God — constantly being ready to suffer patiently — constantly being willing to sympathize — are clear duties that sickness requires of everyone. They are duties within the reach of everyone. In naming them I ask nothing extravagant or unreasonable. I ask no man to retire into a monastery and ignore the duties of his occupation. I only want men to realize that they live in a sick and dying world, and to live accordingly. And I say boldly, that the man who lives the life of faith, and holiness, and patience, and love, is not only the most true Christian, but the most wise and reasonable man.

Some words of practical application

And now I conclude everything with four words of practical application. I want the subject of this chapter to be turned to some spiritual use. My heart's desire and prayer to God in placing it in this volume is to do good to souls.

A question

Firstly, I offer a question to all my readers, to which, as God's ambassador, I plead for their most serious attention. It is a question that naturally grows out of the subject that I have been writing about. It is a question that concerns everyone, of every rank, and class, and condition. I ask you: What will you do when you are sick?

The time must come when you, as well as others, must go down the dark valley of the shadow of death. The hour must come when you, like all your forefathers, must become sick and die. The time may be near or far off. God only knows. But whenever the time may be, I ask again: What are you going to do? Where do you plan to turn for comfort? On what do you plan to rest your soul? On what do you plan to build your hope? From where will you get your relief?

I plead with you not to ignore these questions. Allow them to work on your conscience, and do not rest until you can give them a satisfactory answer. Do not play with that precious gift, an immortal soul. Do not defer considering the matter to a more convenient time. Do not presume on a deathbed repentance. The most important business surely ought not be left to the last. One dying thief was saved that men might not despair, but only one, that none might presume. I repeat the question. I am sure that it deserves an answer. 'What will you do when you are sick?'

If you were going to live for ever in this world then I would not address you as I do. But it cannot be. There is no escaping the common lot of all mankind. Nobody can die in our place. The day must come when we must each go to the place where we will spend an eternity. I want you to be prepared when you face that day. The body that now takes up so much of your attention — the body that you now dress and feed with so much care — that body must again return to the dust. Oh, think of what an awful thing it would be in the end to have provided for everything except the one thing that was necessary — to have provided for the body, but to have neglected the soul — to die, and 'give no sign' of being saved! Once more I ask the question of your conscience: 'What will you do when you are sick?'

Counsel

In the next place, I offer counsel to all who feel they need it and are willing to take it — to all who feel they are not yet prepared to meet God. That counsel is short and simple. Seek after the Lord Jesus Christ, and be saved.

Either you have a soul or you do not. Surely, you will never deny that you have one. Then if you do, seek that soul's salvation. Of all the gambling in the world, there is none so reckless as that of the man who lives unprepared to meet God, and yet puts off repentance. Either you have sins or you have none. If you have (and who will dare to deny it?), turn away from them without delay. Either you need a Saviour or you do not. If you do, flee to the only Saviour this very day, and strongly cry to him to save your soul. Pursue Christ at once. Seek him by faith. Commit your soul into his keeping. Cry mightily to him for forgiveness and peace with God. Ask him to pour out the Holy Spirit on you, and make you a true Christian. He will hear you. No matter what you have been, he will not refuse your prayer. He has said, 'the one who comes to me I will by no means cast out' (John 6:37).

Beware, I beg you, of a vague and indefinite Christianity. Do not be content with a general hope that all is right because you belong to an old established church denomination, and that all will be well in the end, because God is merciful. Do not rest without a personal union with Christ himself. Do not rest until you have the witness of the Spirit in your heart, and are washed, sanctified, justified, one with Christ, and Christ in you. Do not rest until you can say with the apostle, 'I know whom I have believed and am persuaded that he is able to keep what I have committed to him until that day' (2 Timothy 1:12).

Vague, indefinite and indistinct religion may seem to work fine during a period of good health. It will never do in the day of sickness. A mere formal, mechanical Christianity may carry a man through the sunshine of youth and prosperity. It will break down entirely when death is in sight. Nothing will do then but real heart-union with Christ. Christ interceding for us at God's right hand; Christ known and believed as our Priest, our Physician, our Friend — Christ alone can rob death of its sting and enable us to face sickness without fear. He alone can deliver those who through the fear of death are in bondage. I say to everyone who wants advice, 'Be one with Christ.' If you are ever to have hope and comfort on the bedside of sickness, then be one with Christ. Seek Christ. Pursue Christ.

Take every care and trouble to him when you are one with him. He will keep you and carry you through everything. Pour out your heart before him, when your conscience is burdened. He is the true Confessor. He alone can forgive you and take the burden away. Turn to him first in the day of sickness, like Martha and Mary. Keep on looking to him to the very last breath of your life. Christ is worth knowing. The more you know him the better you will love him. Be one with Jesus Christ.

Lie quiet in God's hand when sick

In the third place, I exhort all true Christians who are reading this to remember how much they glorify God in the time of sickness, and to 'lie quiet in God's hand when they are sick'.

I feel it is very important to touch on this point. I know how ready the heart of a believer is to faint, and how busy Satan is in suggesting doubts and questionings when the body of a Christian is weak. I have seen something of the depression and despondency that sometimes comes upon the children of God when they are suddenly laid aside by disease, and obliged to sit still. I have noted how prone some good people are to torment themselves with morbid thoughts at such times, and to say in their hearts, 'God has forsaken me: I am cast out of his sight.'

I earnestly entreat all sick believers to remember that they may honour God as much by patient suffering as they can by active work. It often shows more grace to sit still than it does to go here and there, and perform great deeds. I entreat them to remember that Christ cares for them as much when they are sick as he does when they are well, and that the very chastisement they feel so acutely is sent in love, and not in anger. Above all, I beg them to remember the sympathy of Jesus for all his weak members. They are always tenderly cared for by him, but never so much as in their time of need. Christ has had great experience with sickness. He knows the heart of a sick man. He used to see 'all kinds of sickness and all kinds of disease among the people' (Matthew 4:23) when he was on earth. He especially felt for the sick in the days of his flesh, and he especially feels for them now. Sickness and suffering, I often think, make believers more like their Lord in experience than health would. 'He himself took our infirmities and bore our sicknesses' (Isaiah 53:4; Matthew 8:17). The Lord Jesus was a 'Man of sorrows, and acquainted with grief'. No one has such an opportunity of learning the mind of a suffering Saviour as suffering disciples.

Maintain close communion with Christ

I conclude with a word of 'exhortation' to all believers, which I heartily pray that God would impress upon their souls. I exhort you to keep up a habit of close communion with Christ, and never be afraid of 'going too far' in your religion. Remember this, if you wish to have 'great peace' in your times of sickness.

I observe with regret a tendency in some quarters to lower the standard of practical Christianity, and to denounce what are called 'extreme views' about a Christian's daily walk in life. I remark with pain that even religious people will sometimes look coldly on those who withdraw from worldly society, and will censure them as 'exclusive, narrow-minded, selfish, unkind, bitter', and the like. I warn every believer in Christ who is reading this to beware of being influenced by such censures. I entreat him, if he wants light in the valley of death, to 'keep [himself] unspotted from the world', to 'follow [the Lord] fully', and to walk very closely with God (James 1:27; Numbers 14:24).

I believe that the lack of *thoroughness* concerning many people's Christianity is one reason for their lack of peace, both in health and sickness. I believe that the religion of 'compromise', which satisfies many in the present day, is offensive to God, and sows thorns in dying pillows, which hundreds never discover until it is too late. I believe that the weakness and feebleness of such a religion never reveals itself so clearly as it does on a sickbed.

If you and I want to *have strong consolation* in our time of need, we must not be content with a barren union with Christ (Hebrews 6:18). We must seek to know something of a heartfelt, experimental 'communion' with him. Never, never let us forget that 'union' is one thing, and 'communion' another. Thousands, I fear, who know what 'union' with Christ is, know nothing of 'communion'.

The day may come when after a long fight with disease, we shall feel that medicine can do no more, and that nothing remains but to die. Friends will be standing by, unable to help us. Hearing, eyesight, even the power of praying, will be fast failing us. The world and its shadows will be melting beneath our feet. Eternity, with its realities, will be looming large before our minds. What will support us in that trying hour? What will enable us to say, 'I will fear no evil'? (Psalm 23:4). Nothing, nothing can do it but close communion with Christ. Christ living in our hearts by faith; Christ putting his right arm under our heads; Christ sitting by our side; Christ alone can give us the complete victory in the last struggle.

Let us cling to Christ more closely, love him more wholeheartedly, live to him more thoroughly, copy him more exactly, confess him more boldly, follow him more fully. Religion like this will always bring its own reward. Worldly people may laugh at it. Weak brethren may think it extreme. But it will wear well. At the evening time of our lives it will bring us light. In sickness it will bring us peace. In the world to come it will give us a crown of glory that will never fade away.

The time is short. This world is passing away. A few more sicknesses, and it will all be over. A few more funerals, and our own funeral will take place. A few more storms and gales, and we will be safe in the harbour. We travel towards a world where there is no more sickness, where parting, and pain, and crying, and mourning, are done for evermore. Every year heaven is becoming more full of God's beloved children, and the earth more empty. The friends that have gone before us are becoming more numerous than the friends left behind. 'For yet a little while, and he who is coming will come and will not tarry' (Hebrews 10:37). In his presence will be fulness of joy. Christ will wipe away all tears from his people's eyes. The last enemy that will be destroyed is death. But he *will* be destroyed. Death himself will one day die (Revelation 20:14).

In the meantime let us live the life of faith in the Son of God. Let us lean all our weight on Christ, and rejoice in the thought that he lives for evermore.

Yes, blessed be God! Christ lives, though we may die. Christ lives, though friends and families are carried to the grave. He lives who abolished death, and brought life and immortality to light by the gospel. He lives who said, 'I will ransom them from the power of the grave; I will redeem them from death. O death, I will be your plagues! O grave, I will be your destruction!' (Hosea 13:14). The one who will one day change our vile body and make it like his glorious body is alive. In sickness and in health, in life and in death, let us lean confidently on him. Surely we ought to say daily with one of old, 'Blessed be God for Jesus Christ!'

16.
The family of God

'The whole family in heaven and earth' (Ephesians 3:15).

The words that form the title of this chapter ought to always stir some feelings in our minds. There is not a man or woman on this earth who is not a member of some 'family'. The poorest as well as the richest has his relative and kin, and can tell you something of his 'family'.

We all know that family gatherings at certain times of the year, such as Christmas, are very common. Thousands of homes are crowded then, if at no other time of the year. The young man in town snatches a few days away from business, and takes a run down to visit his parents at home. The young woman gets a short holiday, and comes to visit her father and mother. Brothers and sisters meet for a few hours. Parents and children look one another in the face. There is so much to talk about! So many questions to be asked! So many interesting things to be told! It is indeed a happy home in which 'the whole family' is gathered at Christmas.

Family gatherings are natural, and right, and good. I approve of them with all my heart. It does me good to see them kept up. They are one of the very pleasant things that have survived the fall of man. Next to the grace of God, I see no principle that unites people so much in this sinful world as family sentiments. Community of blood is a most powerful tie. An American naval officer made a fine statement when his men insisted on helping the English sailors fighting the Taku forts in China: 'I cannot help it: blood is thicker than water.' I have often observed that people will stand up for their relatives, merely because they are their relatives, and refuse to hear a word against them, even when they have no sympathy with their tastes and ways. Anything that helps to keep up the family sentiment ought to be commended. It is a wise thing, when it can be done, to gather 'the whole family' together at Christmas.

Family gatherings, nevertheless, are often sorrowful things. It would be strange indeed, in such a world as this, if they were not. There are few family circles that do not show gaps and vacant places as years pass by. Changes and deaths make sad havoc as time goes on. Thoughts will rise up within us, as we grow older, about faces and voices no longer with us, which no Christmas merriment can entirely keep down. When the young members of the family have once begun to launch forth into the world, the old heads may long survive the scattering of the nest; but after a certain time, it seldom happens that you see 'the whole family' together.

There is one great family to which I want all my readers to belong. It is a family despised by many, and not even known by some. But it is a family of far more importance than any family on earth. To belong to it entitles a man to far greater privileges than to be the son of a king. It is the family of which Paul speaks to the Ephesians, when he tells them of the 'whole family in heaven and earth'. It is the family of God.

I ask for the attention of every one of my readers while I try to describe this family, and recommend it to him. I want to tell you of the amazing benefits that membership of this family conveys. I want you to be found as a member of this family, when it is finally gathered together in the end — a gathering without separation, or sorrow, or tears. Hear me while, as a minister of Christ, and friend to your soul, I speak to you for a few minutes about 'the whole family in heaven and earth'.

First of all, what is this family?
Secondly, what is its present position?
Thirdly, what are its future prospects?

I wish to unfold these three things before you, and I invite you to seriously consider them. Our family gatherings on earth must one day come to an end. Our last earthly Christmas must come. Happy indeed is the Christmas that finds us prepared to meet God!

What is this family?

What is the family that the Bible calls 'the whole family in heaven and earth'? Of whom does it consist?

The family before us consists wholly of real Christians: all who have the Holy Spirit living within them; all true believers in Christ; all the saints of every age, and church, and nation, and language. It includes the blessed company of all faithful people. It is the same as the elect of God, the household of faith, the mystical body of Christ, the bride, the living temple, the sheep that never perish, the church of the firstborn, the holy universal church. All these expressions are other names for 'the family of God'.

Membership in 'the family of God' does not depend on any earthly connection. It does not come by natural birth, but by new birth. Ministers cannot impart it to their hearers. Parents cannot give it to their children. You may be born in the most godly family in the land, and enjoy the sweetest fellowship of grace that any church can supply, and yet never belong to the family of God. To belong to it you must be born again. No one but the Holy Spirit can make you a living member of this family. It is his special function and prerogative to bring into the true church all those who will be saved. Those who are born again are born, 'not of blood, nor of the will of the flesh, nor of the will of man, but of God' (John 1:13).

Do you want to know the reason why the Bible gives this name to all true Christians? Would you like to know why they are called 'a family'? Listen and I will tell you.

They all have one Father

True Christians are called 'a family' because they all have one Father. They are all children of God by faith in Christ Jesus. They are all born of one Spirit. They are all sons and daughters of the Lord Almighty. They have received the Spirit of adoption, whereby they cry, 'Abba, Father' (Galatians 3:26; John 3:8; 2 Corinthians 6:18; Romans 8:15). They do not regard God with a cringing kind of fear, as they would to a harsh Being that is always ready to punish them. They look up to him with tender confidence, as a reconciled and loving parent — as one forgiving evil and sin, to all who believe in Jesus — and full of pity even to the least and feeblest. The words, 'Our Father in heaven,' are no mere form of prayer in the mouth of true Christians. No wonder they are called God's 'family'.

They all rejoice in one name

True Christians are called 'a family', because they all rejoice in one name. That name is the name of their great Head and Elder Brother, even Jesus Christ the Lord. Just as a common family name is the uniting link to all the members of a clan, so does the name of Jesus tie all believers together in one vast family. As members of outward visible churches they have various names and distinguishing classifications. As living members of Christ, they all, with one heart and mind, rejoice in one Saviour. Every heart among them feels drawn to Jesus as the only object of hope. Every tongue among them would tell you that 'Christ is all'. Sweet to them all is the thought of Christ's death for them on the cross. Sweet is the thought of Christ's intercession for them at the right hand of God. Sweet is the thought of Christ's coming again to unite them to himself in one glorified fellowship for ever. In fact, you might as well take away the sun out of heaven, as take away the name of Christ from believers. To the world his Name may not mean much, but to believers, it is full of comfort, hope, rest and peace. No wonder they are called 'a family'.

They have a strong family resemblance

True Christians, above all, are called 'a family' because here is so strong a family resemblance among them. They are all led by one Spirit, and are marked by the same general features of life, heart, taste and character. Just as there is a general bodily resemblance among the brothers and sisters of a family, so there is a general spiritual resemblance among all the sons and daughters of the Lord Almighty. They all hate sin and love God. They all rest their hope of salvation on Christ, and have no confidence in themselves. They all endeavour to 'come out and be separate' from the ways of the world, and to set their affections on things above. They all naturally turn to the same Bible, as the only food for their souls and the only sure guide in their pilgrimage towards heaven: they find it 'a lamp to [their] feet and a light for [their] path' (Psalm 119:105). They all go to the same throne of grace in prayer, and find it as needful to speak to God as to breathe. They all live by the same rule, the Word of God, and strive to conform their daily life to its precepts. They all have the same inward experience. They all are, in varying degrees, acquainted with repentance, faith, hope, love, humility and inward conflict. No wonder they are called 'a family'.

This family likeness among true believers is something that deserves special attention. To my own mind it is one of the strongest indirect evidences of the truth of Christianity. It is one of the greatest proofs of the reality of the work of the Holy Spirit. Some true Christians live in civilized countries, and some in the midst of heathen lands. Some are highly educated, and some are unable to read a single letter of the alphabet. Some are rich and some are poor. Some are old and some are young. And yet, despite all these differences, there is a marvellous oneness of heart and character among them. Their joys and their sorrows, their love and their hatred, their likes and their dislikes, their preferences and their aversions, their hopes and their fears, are all most curiously alike. Let others think what they please, I see in all this the finger of God. His handiwork is always one and the same. No wonder that true Christians are compared to 'a family'.

Take a converted Englishman and a converted Hindu, and let them suddenly meet for the first time. I assure you, if they can understand one another's language, they will soon find common ground between them, and feel at home. The one may have been brought up at Oxford, and enjoyed every privilege of English civilization. The other may have been trained in the midst of gross heathenism, and accustomed to habits, ways and manners as unlike the Englishman's as darkness compared to light. And yet in half an hour they feel that they are friends! The Englishman finds that he has more in common with this Hindu brother than he has with many of his old college companions. Who can account for this? How can it be explained? Nothing can account for it but the unity of the Holy Spirit's teaching. It is 'one touch' of grace (not nature) 'that makes the whole world family'. God's people are in the brightest sense 'a family'.

This is the family to which I wish to direct the attention of my readers here. This is the family to which I want you to belong. I ask you this day to consider it carefully, if you never considered it before. I have shown you the Father of the family — the God and Father of our Lord Jesus Christ. I have shown you the Head and Elder Brother of the family — the Lord Jesus himself. I have shown you the features and characteristics of the family. All its members have great marks of resemblance. Once more I say, consider it well.

Outside this family, remember, there is no salvation. No one but those who belong to it, according to the Bible, are on the road that leads to heaven. The salvation of our souls does not depend on union with one church or separation from another. Anyone who thinks it does is miserably deceived, and will find this out to their loss one day, unless they wake up. No! The life of our souls depends on something far more important. This is eternal life, to be a member of 'the whole family in heaven and earth'.

What is its present position?

I now pass on to the second thing that I promised to consider. What is the present position of the whole family in heaven and earth? The family to which I am directing the attention of my readers now is divided into two great parts. Each part has its own residence or dwelling place. Part of the family is in heaven, and part is on earth. For the present the two parts are entirely separated from one another. But they form one body in the sight of God, though resident in two places; and their union is sure to take place one day.

Remember, two places, and only two, contain the family of God. The Bible tells us of no third habitation. There is no such thing as purgatory, despite what some may falsely teach! There is no house of purifying, training, or probation for those who are not true Christians when they die. Oh, no! There are only two parts of the family — the part that is seen and the part that is unseen, the part that is in 'heaven' and the part that is on 'earth'. The members of the family that are not in heaven are on earth, and those that are not on the earth are in heaven. Two parts, and only two! Two places, and only two! Let this never be forgotten.

Some of God's family are safe *in heaven*. They are at rest in that place which the Lord Jesus expressly calls 'paradise' (Luke 23:43). They have finished their course. They have fought their battle. They have finished their appointed work. They have learned their lessons. They have carried their cross. They have passed through the waves of this troublesome world and have reached the harbour. As little as we know about them, we know that they are happy. They are no longer troubled by sin and temptation. They have said goodbye for ever to poverty and anxiety, to pain and sickness, to sorrow and tears. They are with Christ himself, who loved them and gave himself up for them, and in his company they are indeed very happy (Philippians 1:23). They have nothing to fear in looking back to the past. They have nothing to dread in looking forward to things to come. There are only three things lacking that would make their happiness complete. These are the second coming of Christ in glory, the resurrection of their own bodies, and the gathering together of all believers.

Some of God's family are still *on the earth*. They are scattered everywhere in the midst of a wicked world, a few in one place and a few in another. All are more or less occupied in the same way, according to the measure of grace given them. All are running a race, doing a work, fighting a warfare, carrying a cross, striving against sin, resisting the devil, crucifying the flesh, struggling against the world, witnessing for Christ, mourning over their own hearts, hearing, reading and praying, however feebly, for the life of their souls. Each is often disposed to think no cross is so heavy as his own, no work so difficult, no heart so hard. But each and every one is steadfast in their way — a wonder to the ignorant world around them, and often a wonder to themselves.

But, however divided God's family may be at the present time, on the earth, it is still one family. Both parts of it are still one in character, one in possessions, and one in relation to God. The part in heaven does not have as much superiority over the part on earth as at first sight may appear. The difference between the two is only one of degree.

Love the same Saviour

Both parts of the family love the same Saviour, and delight in the same perfect will of God. But the part on earth loves with much imperfection and weakness, and lives by faith, not by sight. The part in heaven loves without weakness, or doubt, or distraction. It walks by sight and not by faith, and sees what it once believed.

Saints

Both parts of the family are saints. But the saints on earth are often poor weary pilgrims, who find that the 'flesh lusts against the Spirit, and the Spirit against the flesh; and these are contrary to one another, so that you do not do the things that you wish' (Galatians 5:17). They live in the midst of an evil world, and are often sick of themselves and of the sin they see around them. The saints in heaven, on the contrary, are delivered from the world, the flesh and the devil, and enjoy glorious liberty. They are called 'the spirits of just men made perfect' (Hebrews 12:23).

God's children

Both parts of the family are equally God's children. But the children in heaven have learned all their lessons, have finished their appointed tasks, have begun an eternal holiday. The children on earth are still in school. They are daily learning wisdom, though slowly and with much trouble, and often needing to be reminded of their past lessons by chastisement and the rod. Their graduation day is yet to come.

God's soldiers

Both parts of the family are equally God's soldiers. But the soldiers on earth are still engaged in the battle. Their fight is not over. Every day they need to put on the whole armour of God. The soldiers in heaven are all triumphant. No enemy can hurt them now. No fiery dart of Satan can reach them. They have laid aside both helmet and shield. They can at last say to the sword of the Spirit, 'Rest and be still.' They can finally sit down, and not have to watch and stand on their guard.

Safe and secure

Last, but not least, both parts of the family are equally safe and secure. As wonderful as this may sound, it is true. Christ cares as much for his family members on earth as his family members in heaven. You might as well think to pluck the stars out of heaven, as to pluck one saint, however feeble, out of Christ's hand. Both parts of the family are equally secure by 'an everlasting covenant, ordered in all things and secure' (2 Samuel 23:5). The members on earth, through the weakness of their flesh and the smallness of their faith, may neither see, nor know, nor feel their own safety. But they are safe, though they may not see it. The whole family is 'kept by the power of God through faith for salvation' (1 Peter 1:5). The family members still on the road to the Father's house are as secure as the members who have already made it home. On the last day no one will be found missing. The words of the Christian poet will be proved true:

More happy, but not more secure,
The glorified saints in heaven.

Now before I leave this part of my subject, I ask every one of my readers to thoroughly understand the present situation of God's family, and to form an accurate assessment of it. Do not measure its numbers nor its privileges by what you see with your eyes. You see only a small body of believers at the present time. But you must not forget that a great number has already made it safely to heaven, and that when all are assembled at the last day, there will be 'a great multitude which no one could number' (Revelation 7:9).

You only see that part of the family that is struggling on earth. You must never forget that the greater part of the family has already made it home and is resting in heaven. You see the militant part, but not the triumphant. You see the part that is carrying the cross, but not the part that is safe in paradise. The family of God is far more rich and glorious than you suppose. Believe me, it is no small thing to belong to the 'whole family in heaven and on earth'.

What are its future prospects?

I will now pass on to the last thing that I proposed to consider. What are the future prospects of the whole family in heaven and earth?

The future prospects of a family! What a vast amount of uncertainty these words open up when we look at any family we now see in the world! How little we can tell of the things coming upon any of us! What a mercy it is that we do not know the sorrows and trials and separations that our beloved children may have to experience, after we have left the world! It is a mercy that we do not know 'what a day may bring forth', and a far greater mercy that we do not know what may happen in the next twenty years (Proverbs 27:1). Sadly, foreknowledge of the future prospects of our household would spoil many a family gathering, and fill the whole party with gloom!

Think how many a fine boy, who is now the delight of his parents, will in time follow the path of a reckless son, and never return home! Think how many a fair daughter, the joy of a mother's heart, will in a few years follow her own stubborn will, and insist on some miserably mistaken marriage! Think how disease and pain will often lay low the loveliest of a family circle, and make her life a burden and wearisome to herself, if not to others! Think of the endless disagreements and divisions that will arise out of money matters! Yes, there is many a lifelong quarrel over a small sum of money, between those who once played joyfully together in the same nursery! Think of these things. The 'future prospects' of many a family that meets together every Christmas are a solemn and serious subject. Hundreds, to say the least, are gathering together for the last time: when they part they will never meet again.

But, thank God, there is one great family whose 'prospects' are very different. It is the family of which I am speaking here, and commending your attention. The future prospects of the family of God are not uncertain. They are good, and only good; happy and only happy. Listen to me, and I will try to set them in order before you.

Brought safely home

The members of God's family will all be brought safely home one day. Here on earth they may be scattered, tried, tossed with storms of life, and bowed down with afflictions. But not one of them will perish (John 10:28). The weakest lamb will not be left to perish in the wilderness; the feeblest child will not be missing when the roll call is announced on the last day. In spite of the world, the flesh, and the devil, the whole family will get home. 'For if when we were enemies, we were reconciled to God through the death of his Son, much more, having been reconciled, we shall be saved by his life' (Romans 5:10).

Have glorious bodies

The members of God's family will one day all have glorious bodies. When the Lord Jesus Christ comes the second time, the dead saints will all be raised and the living will all be changed. They will no longer have a vile mortal body, full of weaknesses and infirmities: they will have a body like that of their risen Lord, without the slightest vulnerability to sickness and pain. They will no longer be clogged and hindered by an aching frame, when they want to serve God: they will be able to serve him night and day without any weariness, and to attend to him without any distraction. The former things will have passed away. The word will be fulfilled, 'I make all things new' (Revelation 21:5).

Gathered into one company

One day, the members of God's family will all be gathered into one company. It does not matter where they have lived or where they have died. They may have been separated from one another both by time and space. One may have lived in tents, with Abraham, Isaac, and Jacob, and another travelled by the modern transportation of our day. One may have his bones laid to rest in an Australian desert, and another may have been buried in an English churchyard. It makes no difference. All will be gathered together from north and south, and east and west, and meet in one happy assembly, never to part again. The earthly partings of God's family are only for a few days. Their meeting is for eternity. Little does it matter where we live. It is a time of scattering now, not of gathering. Little does it matter where we die. All graves are equally near to paradise. But it does matter whether we belong to God's family. If we do, we are sure to meet again in the end.

United in mind and judgement

One day the members of God's family will all be united in mind and judgement. They are so divided now about many little things. About the things necessary for salvation there is a marvellous unity among them. About many speculative points in religion, about forms of worship and church government, they often sadly disagree. But one day there will be no disagreement among them at all. Ephraim will no longer disturb Judah, nor Judah Ephraim. Partial knowledge and dim vision will be ended for ever. Divisions and separations, misunderstandings and misinterpretations, will all be buried and forgotten. Since there will only be one language, so there also will be only one opinion. At last, after thousands of years of strife and clashing, perfect unity and harmony will be found. A family will finally be shown to angels and men in which all are of one mind.

Perfected in holiness

One day the members of God's family will all be perfected in holiness. They are not now literally perfect, although they 'are complete in him' (Colossians 2:10). Though they are born again, and renewed after the image of Christ, they stumble and fall short in many things (James 3:2). No one knows it better than they do themselves. It is their grief and sorrow that they do not love God more heartily and serve him more faithfully. But one day they will be completely free of all corruption. They will rise again at Christ's Second Coming without any of the disorders and sicknesses that now cleave to them in their lives. Not a single evil temper or corrupt inclination will be found in them.

They will be presented by their Lord and Husband to the Father, without spot, or wrinkle, or any such thing — perfectly holy and without blemish — fair as the moon, and clear as the sun (Ephesians 5:27; Song of Solomon 6:10).

Grace, even now, is a beautiful thing, when it lives, and shines, and flourishes in the midst of imperfection. But how much more beautiful will grace appear when it is seen pure, unmixed, unmingled and alone! And it will be seen so when Christ comes to be glorified in his saints at the last day.

Eternally provided for

Last, but not least, one day, the members of God's family will be eternally provided for. When the affairs of this sinful world are finally wound up and settled, there will be an everlasting reward for all the sons and daughters of the Lord Almighty. Not even the weakest of them will be overlooked and forgotten. There will be something for everyone, according to their faithfulness. The smallest vessel of grace, as well as the greatest, will be filled to the brim with glory. It would be pure folly to pretend to describe the precise nature of that glory and reward. It is a thing which 'eye has not seen, nor ear heard, nor have entered into the heart of man' (1 Corinthians 2:9). It is enough for us to know that each member of God's family, when he awakes from the grave to his Master's likeness, will be 'satisfied' (Psalm 17:15). Above all, it will be enough to know that their joy, and glory, and reward will be for ever. They will never lose what they will receive in the day of the Lord. The inheritance reserved for them, when they come of age, is 'an inheritance incorruptible and undefiled and that does not fade away' (1 Peter 1:4).

These prospects of God's family are great realities. They are not vague shadowy talk of man's invention. They are real and true, and will be seen as such before long. They deserve your serious consideration. Examine them well.

Look around the families on earth you are acquainted with: the richest, the greatest, the noblest and the happiest. Who among them all can show prospects to compare with those you have just heard about? The earthly riches, in many a case, will be gone in a hundred years or so. The noble blood, in many a case, will not prevent some disgraceful deed from staining the family name. The happiness, in many a case, will be found hollow and illusive. Few, indeed, are the homes that do not have a secret sorrow, or a 'skeleton in the closet'. Whether for present possessions or future prospects, there is no family so well off as 'the whole family of God in heaven and earth'. Whether you look at what they now have, or what they will have in heaven, there is no family like the family of God.

Some words of practical application

My task is done. This chapter is drawing to a close. It only remains to close it with a few words of practical application. Give me your attention for the last time. May God bless what I am going to say for the good of your soul!

Do you really belong to the family of God?

I ask you a simple question. Take it with you to every family gathering that you join at any season of the year. Take it with you, and amidst all your happiness make time to think about it. It is a simple question, but a solemn one: Do you really belong to the family of God?

To the family of God, remember! This is the point of my question. It is no answer to say that you are a Protestant, or belong to such-and-such a denomination, or are an Evangelical. I want to hear of something more and better than that. I want you to have some soul-satisfying and soul-saving religion:

a religion that will give you peace while you live, and hope when you die. To have such peace and hope you must be something more than a Protestant, or a member of such-and-such a denomination, or an Evangelical. You must belong to 'the family of God'. I firmly believe that thousands around you do not belong to the family. But that is no reason why you should not.

If you do not yet belong to God's family, I invite you this day to join it without delay. Open your eyes to see the value of your soul, the sinfulness of sin, the holiness of God, the danger of your present condition, the absolute necessity of a mighty change. Open your eyes to see these things, and repent this very day. Open your eyes to see the great Head of God's family, even Christ Jesus, waiting to save your soul. See how he has loved you, lived for you, died for you, risen again for you, and obtained complete redemption for you. See how he offers you free, full, immediate pardon, if you will only believe in him. Open your eyes to see these things. Seek Christ at once. Come and believe in him, and commit your soul to his keeping this very day.

I know nothing of your family or past history. I do not know where you go to spend your holidays, or what company you are going to be in. But I am bold to say, that if you join the family of God you will find it the best and happiest family in the world.

Learn to be more thankful

If you really belong to the whole family in heaven and earth, count up your privileges, and learn to be more thankful. Remember what a mercy it is to have something that the world can neither give nor take away — something that makes you independent of sickness and poverty — something that is your own for evermore. The old family home will soon be empty and up for sale. The old family gatherings will soon be past and gone for ever. The loving faces we now delight to gaze on are rapidly leaving us. The cheerful voices that now welcome us will be silent in the grave. But, thank God, if we belong to Christ's family there is a better gathering yet to come. Let us often think of it, and be thankful!

The family gathering of all God's people will make up for all that their religion now costs them. A meeting where none are missing; a meeting where there are no gaps and empty places; a meeting where there are no tears; a meeting where there is no parting — such a meeting as this is worth a fight and a struggle. And such a meeting is yet to come to 'the whole family in heaven and earth'.

In the meantime let us strive to live worthy of the family to which we belong. Let us labour to do nothing that may cause our Father's house to be spoken against. Let us endeavour to make our Master's name beautiful by our disposition, conduct and conversation. Let us love as brethren, and abhor all quarrels. Let us behave as if the honour of 'the family' depended on our behaviour.

So living, by the grace of God, we will make our calling and election sure, both to ourselves and others. So living, we will have the sure hope of receiving a rich welcome into the eternal kingdom of our Lord and Saviour Jesus Christ (2 Peter 1:11). So living, we will recommend our Father's family to others, and perhaps by God's blessing induce them to say, 'We will go with you.'

17.
Our home

'Lord, you have been our dwelling place in all generations'
(Psalm 90:1).

There are two reasons why the text above should ring in our hearts with special power. It is the first verse of a deeply solemn psalm — the first bar of a wondrous piece of spiritual music. I cannot tell how others feel when they read the ninetieth psalm. It always makes me lean back in my chair and think.

For one thing, this ninetieth psalm is the only psalm composed by 'Moses the man of God'. It expresses that holy man's feelings, as he saw the whole generation whom he had led out of Egypt, dying in the wilderness. Year after year he saw the fearful judgement that Israel brought on itself by unbelief being fulfilled: 'The carcasses of you who have complained against me shall fall in this wilderness, all of you who were numbered, according to your entire number, from twenty years old and above' (Numbers 14:29).

One after another he saw, laying in the desert, the bones of the heads of the families whom he had led out of Egypt. For forty long years he saw the strong, the swift, the wise, the tender, the beautiful, who had crossed the Red Sea with him in triumph, cut down and withering like grass. For forty years he saw his companions continually changing, becoming weaker and passing away. Who can wonder that he should say, 'Lord, you have been our dwelling place.' We are all pilgrims and strangers on the earth, and we have no place to dwell. 'Lord, you are our home.'

For another thing, the ninetieth psalm forms part of the Burial Service of the Church of England. Whatever fault men may find with the prayer-book, I do not think anyone can deny the singular beauty of the Burial Service. Beautiful are the texts that it puts into the minister's mouth as he meets the coffin at the churchyard gate, and leads the mourners into the church. Beautiful is the chapter from the first Epistle to the Corinthians about the resurrection of the body. Beautiful are the sentences and prayers appointed to be read as the body is laid in its home beneath the earth. But especially beautiful, to my mind, are the psalms that are selected for reading when the mourners have just taken their places in church. I know of nothing that sounds so soothing, honouring, heart-touching, and moving to man's spirit at that trying moment, as the wondrous utterance of the old inspired law-giver: 'Lord, you have been our dwelling place.' 'Lord, you are our home.'

I want to draw from these words two thoughts that may do my readers some good. An English home is famous all over the world for its happiness and comfort. It is a little bit of heaven left upon the earth. But even an English home is not for ever. The family nest is sure to be taken down, and its residents scattered. Bear with me for a few short minutes, while I try to set before you the best, truest and happiest home.

What the world is

The first thought that I will offer you is this: I will show you what the world is. I freely admit that it is a beautiful world in many respects. Its seas and rivers, its sunrises and sunsets, its mountains and valleys, its harvests and its forests, its fruits and its flowers, its days and its nights, all, all are beautiful in their way.

The heart that never finds a day in the year when it can admire anything in nature must be cold and unfeeling! But beautiful as the world is, there are many things in it to remind us that it is not home. It is an inn, a tent, a tabernacle, a lodging, a training school. But it is not home.

It is a changing world. Everything around us is continually moving, altering and passing away. Families, properties, landlords, tenants, farmers, labourers, tradesmen — all are continually on the move. To find the same name in the same dwelling for three generations running is so uncommon that it is the exception rather than the rule. A world so full of change cannot be called home.

It is a trying and disappointing world. Whoever lives to be fifty years old has paid the cost and knows it to be true. Trials in married life and trials in single life; trials with children and trials with brothers and sisters; trials in money matters and trials in health — how many they are! Their number is legion. And not one tenth of them ever comes to light. Indeed, there are few families that do not have 'a skeleton in the closet'. A world so full of trial and disappointment cannot be called home.

It is a dying world. Death is continually around us and near us, and meets us at every turn. When Christmas comes around there are few family gatherings in which there are not some empty chairs and vacant places. There are few men and women, nearing middle age, who could not number a long list of names, deeply cut for ever in their hearts — names of beloved ones now dead and gone. Where are our fathers and mothers? Where are our ministers and teachers? Where are our brothers and sisters? Where are our husbands and wives? Where are our neighbours and friends? Where are the old grey-headed worshippers, whose reverent faces we remember so well from when we first came to church? Where are the boys and girls we played with when we went to school? How many must reply, 'Dead, dead, dead! The daisies are growing over their graves, and we are left alone.' Surely a world so full of death can never be called a home.

It is a scattering and dividing world. Families are continually breaking up and going in different directions. How rarely the members of a family ever meet together again, after the surviving parent is laid in the grave! The band of union seems snapped, and nothing welds it again. The cement seems withdrawn from the parts of the building, and the whole principle of cohesion is lost. How often some miserable squabble about trinkets, or some wretched wrangle about money, causes a breach that is never healed, and, like a crack in china, though riveted, can never be cured! Indeed, rarely do those who played in the same nursery lie down in graves in the same churchyard, or keep peace with one another till they die. A world so full of division can never be home.

These are old things. It is useless to be surprised at them. They are the bitter fruit of sin, and the sorrowful consequence of the Fall. Change, trial, death and division all entered into the world when Adam and Eve sinned. We must not murmur. We must not fret. We must not complain. We must accept the situation in which we find ourselves. We must each do our best to lighten the sorrows, and increase the comforts of our position. We must steadily resolve to make the best of everybody and everything around us. But we must never, never, never, forget that the world is not home.

Are you young? Does everything around and before you seem bright, and cheerful, and happy? Do you secretly think in your own mind that I am taking too gloomy a view of the world? Be careful. You will not say that as time goes by. Be wise. Learn to moderate your expectations. Depend on it, the less you expect from people and things here below the happier you will be.

Are you prosperous in the world? Have death, and sickness, and disappointment, and poverty, and family troubles, passed over your door up to this time, and not come in? Are you secretly saying to yourself, 'Nothing can hurt me much. I will die quietly in my bed, and see no sorrow.' Be careful. You are not yet in the harbour. A sudden storm of unexpected trouble may make you change your tune. Do not set your affection on things below. Hold them with a very loose hand, and be ready to surrender them at a moment's notice. Use your prosperity well while you have it; but do not lean all your weight on it, lest it break suddenly and pierce your hand.

Have you a happy home? Are you going to spend Christmas around a family fireplace, where sickness, and death, and poverty, and partings, and quarrellings, have never yet been seen? Be thankful for it: oh, be thankful for it! A really happy Christian home is the nearest thing to heaven on earth. But be careful. This state of things will not last for ever. It must have an end; and if you are wise, you will never forget that! 'But this I say, brethren, the time is short, so that from now on even those who have wives should be as though they had none, those who weep as though they did not weep, those who rejoice as though they did not rejoice, those who buy as though they did not possess, and those who use this world as not misusing it. For the form of this world is passing away' (1 Corinthians 7:29-31).

What Christ is to true Christians

The second thought that I will offer you is this: I will show you what Christ is, even in this life, to true Christians. Heaven, beyond a doubt, is the last home in which a true Christian will finally live. Towards that end he is travelling daily: each day he is coming nearer to that place. 'For we know that if our earthly house, this tent, is destroyed, we have a building from God, a house not made with hands, eternal in the heavens'

(2 Corinthians 5:1). Body and soul united once more, renewed, glorified, and perfected, will live for ever in the Father's great house in heaven. To that home we have not yet come. We are not yet in heaven.

But is there in the meantime no home for our souls? Is there no spiritual dwelling place to which we may continually go to in this desolate world, and, going there, find rest and peace? Thank God, there is no difficulty in finding an answer to that question. There is a home provided for all labouring and heavy-laden souls, and that home is Christ. To know Christ by faith, to live the life of faith in him, to abide in him daily by faith, to flee to him in every storm of conscience, to use him as our refuge in every day of trouble, to employ him as our Priest, Confessor, Absolver and spiritual Director, every morning and evening in our lives — this is to be at home spiritually, even before we die. To all sinners of mankind who by faith use Christ in this fashion, Christ is in the highest sense a dwelling place. They can truly say, 'We are all pilgrims and strangers on earth, and yet we have a home.'

Of all the emblems and figures under which Christ is set before man, I know few more cheering and comforting than the one set before us. Home is one of the sweetest, most tender words in the English language. Home is the place to which our most pleasant thoughts are closely tied. Everything that the best and happiest home is to its residents is what Christ is to the soul who believes in him. In the midst of a dying, changing, disappointing world, a true Christian always has something that no power on earth can take away. Morning, noon and night, he has near him a living Refuge — a living home for his soul. You may rob him of life, and liberty, and money; you may take from him health, and lands, and house, and friends; but, do what you will, you cannot rob him of his home. Like those humblest of God's creatures, which carry their shells on their backs wherever they are, so the Christian carries his home wherever he goes. No wonder that holy preacher Baxter sings,

What if in prison I must dwell,
May I not then converse with Thee?
Save me from sin, Thy wrath, and hell,
Call me Thy child, and I am free!

Room for all

No home like Christ! In him there is room for all, and room for all sorts. None are unwelcome guests and visitors, and none are refused admission. The door is always open, and never locked. The best robe, the fatted calf, the ring and the shoes are always ready for all comers. What if in time past you have been the vilest of the vile, a servant of sin, an enemy of all righteousness, a Pharisee of Pharisees, a Sadducee of Sadducees, a tax collector of tax collectors? It matters nothing: there is yet hope. All sins may be pardoned, forgiven and forgotten. There is a home and refuge where your soul may be admitted this very day. That home is Christ. 'Come to me,' he cries. 'Knock, and it will be opened to you' (Matthew 11:28; 7:7).

Mercy for all

No home like Christ! In him there is boundless and unwearied mercy for all, even after admission.

None are rejected and cast out again after probation, because they are too weak and bad to stay. Oh no! Whoever he receives, he always keeps. Where he begins, there he brings to a good end. Whoever he admits, he at once fully justifies. Whoever he justifies, he also sanctifies. Whoever he sanctifies, he also glorifies. No hopeless characters are ever sent away from his house. No men or women are ever found to be too bad to heal and renew. Nothing is to hard for him to do who made the world out of nothing. He, who is himself the home, has said it, and will guarantee it: 'the one who comes to me I will by no means cast out' (John 6:37).

Kindness, patience and gentle dealing

No home like Christ! In him there is unchanging kindness, patience and gentle dealing for all.

He is not 'a harsh man', but 'gentle and lowly in heart' (Matthew 11:29). None who apply to him are ever treated roughly, or made to feel that their company is not welcome. A feast of the best foods is always provided for them. The Holy Spirit is placed in their hearts, and dwells in them as in a temple. Leading, guiding and instruction are provided daily for them. If they sin, they are brought back into the right way; if they fall, they are raised again; if they sin wilfully, they are disciplined to make them better. For the rule of the whole house is love.

No change

No home like Christ! In him there is no change. From the youngest to the eldest he loves all who come to him, and is never tired of doing good to them. Earthly homes, I am sorry to say, are full of fickleness and uncertainty. Favour is deceitful. Courtesy and civility are often on men's lips, while inwardly they are weary of your company and wish you were gone. You seldom know how long your presence is welcome, to what extent your friends really care to see you. But it is not so with Christ. He 'is the same yesterday, today, and for ever' (Hebrews 13:8).

Will never be broken off

No home like Christ! Communion once begun with him will never be broken off.

Once joined to the Lord by faith, you are joined to him for an endless eternity. Earthly homes always come to an end sooner or later: the precious old furniture is sold and dispersed; the dear old heads of the family are gathered to their fathers;

the dear old nest is pulled to pieces. But it is not so with Christ. Faith will in time be swallowed up in sight: hope will at last be changed into certainty. We will one day see with our eyes, and no longer need to believe. We will be moved from the lower chamber to the upper, and from the outer court to the Holy of Holies. But once in Christ, we will never be out of Christ. Once let our name be placed in the Lamb's book of life, and we belong to a home that will continue for evermore.

Conclusion

Have you got a home for your soul?

And now, before I conclude, let me ask every one of my readers a simple question. Have you got a home for your soul?

Is it safe? Is it pardoned? Is it justified? Is it prepared to meet God? With all my heart I wish you a happy home. But remember my question. Amidst the greetings and salutations of home, amidst the meetings and partings, amidst the laughter and merriment, amidst the joys and sympathies and affections, think, think of my question: Have you got a home for your soul?

Our earthly homes will soon be closed for ever. Time moves on with giant strides. Old age and death will be upon us before many years have passed away. Oh, seek an abiding home for the better part of you — the part that never dies! Before it is too late, seek a home for your soul.

Seek Christ, that you may be safe. Woe to the man who is found outside the ark when the flood of God's wrath finally bursts upon a sinful world! Seek Christ, that you may be happy. No one has a real right to be cheerful, merry, light-hearted, and at ease, except those who have a home for their souls. Once more I say: Seek Christ without delay.

A friendly caution

If Christ is the home of your soul, accept a friendly caution. Beware of being ashamed of your home in any place or company.

The man who is ashamed of the home where he was born, ashamed of the parents that brought him up when he was but a baby, ashamed of the brothers and sisters that played with him — that man, as a general rule, may be considered a mean and despicable person. But what will we say of the man who is ashamed of the one who died for him on the cross? What will we say of the man who is ashamed of his religion, ashamed of his Master, ashamed of his home?

Be careful that you are not that man. Whatever others around you think, don't you ever be ashamed of being a Christian. Let them laugh, and mock, and jest, and scoff, if they will. They will not scoff in the hour of death and in the Day of Judgement. Hoist your flag; show your colours; nail them to the mast. You may certainly be ashamed of drinking, gambling, lying, swearing, idleness, pride, and failing to go to church on the Lord's Day. But of reading the Bible, praying, and belonging to Christ, you have no cause to be ashamed at all. Let those laugh who will. A good soldier is never ashamed of the colours of his nation's flag, and his uniform. Be careful that you are never ashamed of your Master. Never be ashamed of your home.

A piece of friendly advice

If Christ is the home of your soul, accept a piece of friendly advice. Let nothing tempt you to stray away from home.

The world and the devil will often try hard to make you drop your religion for a little while, and walk with them. Your own flesh will whisper that there is no danger in going a little way with them, and that it can do you no real harm. Be careful, I say: be careful when you are tempted in this fashion. Be careful of looking back, like Lot's wife. Do not forsake your home.

No doubt there are pleasures in sin, but they are not real and satisfying. There is an excitement and short-lived enjoyment in the world's ways, beyond all question, but it is joy that leaves a bitter taste in the end. Oh, no! Only wisdom's ways are ways of pleasantness, and only wisdom's paths are paths of peace. Cleave to them strictly and do not turn aside. Follow the Lamb wherever he goes. Stick close to Christ and his rule, even if people say all kinds of evil about you. The longer you live, the happier you will find his service: the more ready you will be to sing, in the highest sense, 'There is no place like home.'

A hint about your duty

If Christ is the home of your soul, accept a hint about your duty. Be sure that you take every opportunity of telling others about your happiness. Tell them *that*, wherever you are. Tell them that you have a happy home.

Tell them, if they will listen to you, that you find Christ a good Master, and Christ's service a happy service. Tell them that his yoke is easy, and his burden is light. Tell them that, whatever the devil may say, the rules of your home are not harsh, and that your Master pays far better wages than the world does! Try to do a little good wherever you are. Try to enlist more residents for your happy home. Say to your friends and relatives, if they will listen, as one did centuries ago, 'Come with us, and we will treat you well; for the LORD has promised good things to Israel' (Numbers 10:29).

18.
Heirs of God

'For as many as are led by the Spirit of God, these are sons of God' (Romans 8:14).
'For you did not receive the spirit of bondage again to fear, but you received the Spirit of adoption by whom we cry out, "Abba, Father"' (Romans 8:15).
'The Spirit himself bears witness with our spirit that we are children of God' (Romans 8:16).
'and if children, then heirs — heirs of God and joint heirs with Christ, if indeed we suffer with him, that we may also be glorified together' (Romans 8:17).

The people of whom the apostle Paul speaks in the verses before us now are the richest people on the earth. It just has to be. They are called 'heirs of God and joint heirs with Christ'.

The inheritance of these people is the only inheritance *really worth having*; all others are unsatisfying and disappointing. They bring with them many concerns. They cannot cure an aching heart, or lighten a heavy conscience; they cannot prevent family troubles; they cannot prevent sicknesses, misfortunes, separations and deaths. But there are no disappointments among the 'heirs of God'.

The inheritance I speak of is the only inheritance that *can be kept for ever*; all others must be left in the hour of death, if they have not been taken away before. Those who are extremely wealthy cannot carry anything with them beyond the grave. But it is not so with the 'heirs of God'. Their inheritance is eternal.

The inheritance I speak of is the only inheritance that *is within everybody's reach*. Most men can never obtain riches and greatness, though they work hard for them all their lives; but glory, honour and eternal life are offered freely to every man who is willing to accept them on God's terms. 'Whoever wants to,' may be an 'heir of God and joint heirs with Christ'.

If any reader wishes to have a portion of this inheritance, let him know that he must be a member of that one family on earth to which it belongs, and that is the family of all true Christians. If you desire to have glory in heaven, then you must become one of God's children on earth. I am writing this to persuade you to become a child of God today, if you are not one already. I am writing to persuade you to be absolutely certain that you are one, if at present you only have a vague hope, and nothing more. Only true Christians are the children of God! Only the children of God are heirs of God! Give me your attention, while I try to unfold these things to you, and show you the lessons contained in the above verses.

1. Let me show *the relationship of all true Christians to God*. They are 'sons of God'.
2. Let me show *the special evidences of this relationship*. True Christians are 'led by the Spirit'. They have 'the Spirit of sonship'. They have the 'testimony of the Spirit'. They 'share in the sufferings of Christ'.
3. Let me show *the privileges of this relationship*. True Christians are 'heirs of God and co-heirs with Christ'.

The relationship of all true Christians to God

First let me show the relationship of all true Christians to God. They are God's *sons*. I know of no greater and more wonderful word that could have been chosen. To be servants of God —

to be subjects, soldiers, disciples, friends — all these are excellent titles; but to be the 'sons' of God is an even more superior designation. The Scripture says, 'A slave does not abide in the house for ever, but a son abides for ever' (John 8:35).

To be a son of the rich and noble people in this world; to be the son of princes and kings of the earth — this is commonly considered a great temporary advantage and privilege. But to be a son of the King of kings, and Lord of lords; to be a son of the High and Holy One, who lives and dwells in eternity — this is something far greater. And yet this is the privilege of every true Christian.

The son of an earthly parent naturally looks to his father for affection, support, provision and education. There is a home always open to him. There is love which, generally speaking, no amount of bad behaviour can completely extinguish. All these are things that generally belong to all the sons of this world. Think then how great is the privilege of that poor sinner of mankind who can say of God, 'He is my Father.'

But how can sinful men like ourselves become sons of God? When do we enter into this glorious relationship? We are not the sons of God by nature. We were not born as 'sons of God' when we came into the world. No man has a natural right to look to God as his Father. It is a vile heresy to say that he has. Men are said to be born poets and painters — but men are never born sons of God. The Book of Ephesians tells us, '[we] were by nature children of wrath, just as the others' (Ephesians 2:3). The Book of John says, 'In this the children of God and the children of the devil are manifest: Whoever does not practise righteousness is not of God' (1 John 3:10). The doctrine of the Church of England wisely follows the doctrines of the Bible, and teaches, 'By nature we are born in sin, and children of wrath.' Yes, we are all, in our natural state, children of the devil, rather than children of God! Sin is indeed hereditary, and runs in the family of Adam. Grace is not hereditary, and holy men do not have, as a matter of course, holy sons. Then how and when does this mighty change and transformation take place? When and how do sinners become the 'sons and daughters' of the LORD Almighty? (2 Corinthians 6:18).

Men become sons of God on the day that the Holy Spirit leads them to believe in Jesus Christ for salvation, and not before. (Note: the reader will of course understand that I am not speaking of children who die in infancy, or of persons who live and die so mentally retarded that they could not begin to understand the gospel.) What does the Book of Galatians say? 'You are all sons of God through faith in Christ Jesus' (Galatians 3:26). What does the Book of 1 Corinthians say? 'But of him you are in Christ Jesus' (1 Corinthians 1:30). What does the Book of John say? 'But as many as received him, to them he gave the right [or privilege] to become children of God, to those who believe in his name' (John 1:12). Faith unites the sinner to the Son of God and makes him one of his members. Faith makes him one of those in whom the Father sees no spot, and is well pleased.

Faith marries him to the beloved Son of God, and entitles him to be counted among the sons. Faith gives him 'fellowship with the Father and with his Son Jesus Christ' (1 John 1:3). Faith grafts him into the Father's family, and opens up to him a room in the Father's house. Faith gives him life instead of death, and makes him a son, instead of being a servant. Show me a man that has this faith, and then, despite whatever church he goes to, I will say that he is a son of God.

This is one of those points we should never forget. You and I know nothing of a man's sonship *until he believes*. No doubt the sons of God are foreknown and chosen from all eternity, and predestined to adoption. But remember, it is not until they are called in due time, and believe — it is not until then that you and I can be certain they are sons. It is not until they repent and believe that the angels of God rejoice over them. The angels cannot read the book of God's election: they do not know who his 'sheltered ones' are on the earth (Psalm 83:3). They rejoice over no man until he believes. But when they see some poor sinner repenting and believing, then there is joy among them — joy that one more burning stick is snatched from the fire, and one more son and heir is born again to the Father in heaven (Amos 4:11; Luke 15:10). But once more I say, you and I know nothing certain about a man's sonship to God *until he believes in Christ.*

I warn you to beware of the delusive notion that all men and women are children of God, whether they have faith in Christ or not. It is a wild theory that many are clinging to in these days, but one that cannot be proved from the Word of God. It is a dangerous dream, with which many are trying to comfort themselves, but one from which there will be a fearful waking in the last day.

I do not pretend to deny that God, in a certain sense, is the universal Father of all mankind. He is the great first cause of all things. He is the Creator of all mankind and, in him alone, all men, whether Christians or heathens, 'live and move and have their being'. All this is unquestionably true. In this sense Paul told the Athenians that their own poet had said, 'We are his offspring' (Acts 17:28). But this 'offspring' status gives no man a title to heaven. The 'offspring' status that we have by creation is one that belongs to stones, trees, animals, or even to the demons, as much as to us (Job 1:6).

I do not deny that God loves all mankind with a love of pity and compassion. 'His tender mercies are over all his works.' He is 'not willing that any should perish but that all should come to repentance'. He has 'no pleasure in the death of one who dies'. All this I admit completely. In this sense our Lord Jesus tells us, 'God so loved the world that he gave his only begotten Son, that whoever believes in him should not perish but have everlasting life' (Psalm 145:9; 2 Peter 3:9; Ezekiel 18:32; John 3:16).

I utterly deny the doctrine that God is a reconciled and pardoning Father to anyone who has not united themselves to his Son Jesus Christ, and that anyone can be united with Jesus Christ who does not believe in him for salvation. The holiness and justice of God stand against such a doctrine. They make it impossible for sinful men to approach God, except through the Mediator. They tell us that God is 'a consuming fire' (Hebrews 12:29) against those who are without Christ. The whole New Testament is against the doctrine. It teaches that no man can claim an interest in Christ unless he will receive him as his Mediator, and believe on him as his Saviour. Where there is no faith in Christ it is a dangerous error to say that a man may take comfort in God as his Father. God is a reconciled Father to no one but those who are united with Christ.

It is unreasonable to talk of the view I am now upholding as being narrow-minded and harsh. The gospel sets an open door before every man. Its promises are wide and full. Its invitations are earnest and tender. Its requirements are simple and clear: 'Believe in the Lord Jesus, and you will be saved.' But to say that proud men, who will not bow their necks to the easy yoke of Christ, and worldly men who are determined to have their own way and their sins — to say that such men have a right to claim an interest in Christ, and a right to call themselves sons of God, is to say what never can be proved from Scripture. God offers to be their Father; but he does it on certain clear terms — they must draw near to him through Christ. Christ offers to be their Saviour; but in doing so he gives one simple requirement — they must commit their souls to him, and give him their hearts. They refuse the *terms*, and yet dare to call God their Father! They scorn the *requirement*, and yet dare to hope that Christ will save them! God is to be their Father — but on their own terms! Christ is to be their Saviour — but on their own conditions! What can be more unreasonable? What can be more proud? What can be more unholy than such a doctrine as this? Let us beware of it, for it is a common doctrine in these latter days. Let us beware of it, for it is often falsely put forward and sounds beautiful and loving in the mouth of poets, novelists, sentimentalists and tender-hearted women. Let us beware of it, unless we intend to throw aside our Bible altogether, and set ourselves up to be wiser than God. Let us stand fast on the old scriptural ground: *No sonship to God without Christ! No interest in Christ without faith!*

I pray to God there was no need to give this kind of warning. But I have every reason to think they need to be given clearly and unmistakably. There is a school of theology rising up in this day, which appears to me most eminently calculated to promote unfaithfulness, to help the devil, and to ruin souls. It comes to us like Joab to Amasa, with the highest professions of kindness, generosity and love. According to this theology, God is all mercy and love — his holiness and justice are completely ignored! Hell is never spoken of in this theology — it speaks only of heaven! Damnation is never mentioned — it is treated as an impossible thing — they say that all men and women will be saved! Faith, and the work of the Spirit, are refined away into nothing at all! 'Everyone who believes anything has faith! Everyone who thinks anything has the Spirit! Everyone is right! No one is wrong! No one is to blame for any action they may commit! It is the result of his position in life. It is because of his circumstances! He is not accountable for his opinions, any more than for the colour of his skin! He must be what he is! The Bible is an imperfect book! It is old-fashioned! It is obsolete! We may believe just as much of it as we please, and no more!' I solemnly warn men to beware of all this kind of theology. In spite of all the fashionable words used, such as 'generosity', and 'kindness', and 'openness' and 'freedom from bigotry', and so forth, I do believe it is a theology that leads people directly into hell.

Facts

Facts speak directly against the teachers of this theology. Let
them visit Mesopotamia, and see what desolation reigns where
Nineveh and Babylon once stood. Let them go to the shores of
the Dead Sea, and look down into its mysterious bitter waters.
Let them travel in Palestine, and ask what has turned that fertile country into a wilderness. Let them observe the wandering
Jews, scattered over the face of the world, without a land of
their own, and yet never absorbed among other nations. And
then let them tell us, if they dare, that God is so entirely a God
of mercy and love that he never does and never will punish sin.

The conscience of man

The conscience of man speaks directly against these teachers.
Let them go to the bedside of some dying child, and try to
comfort him with their doctrines. Let them see if their puffed-
up theories will calm his gnawing, restless anxiety about the
future, and enable him to die in peace. Let them show us, if
they can, a few well-authenticated cases of joy and happiness
in death without Bible promises — without conversion, and
without that faith in the blood of Christ, which old-fashioned
theology commands. Yes, when men are leaving this world,
conscience makes sad work of the new systems of theology
preached in these latter days. In a dying hour conscience is not
easily satisfied that there is no such place as hell.

Future state

Every reasonable conception that we can form of a future state
speaks directly against these teachers. Imagine a heaven that
would contain all of mankind! Imagine a heaven in which holy
and unholy, pure and impure, good and bad, would be all

gathered together in one confused mass! What point of union would there be in such a company? What would be the common bond of harmony and brotherhood? What unity, what harmony, what peace, what oneness of spirit could exist? Surely the mind rebels against the idea of a heaven in which there would be no distinction between the righteous and the wicked, between Pharaoh and Moses, between Abraham and the Sodomites, between Paul and Nero, between Peter and Judas Iscariot, between the man who dies in the act of murder or drunkenness, and men like Baxter, and M'Cheyne! Surely an eternity in such a miserably confused crowd would be worse than annihilation itself! Surely such a heaven would be no better than hell!

Holiness and morality

Holiness and morality speak directly against these teachers. If all men and women are God's children, regardless of the difference between them in their lives — and every one of them is going to heaven, however different they may be from one another here in the world, then what is the use of striving after holiness? What motive remains for living soberly, righteously and godly? What does it matter how men conduct themselves, if everyone goes to heaven, and nobody goes to hell? Surely the heathen poets and philosophers of Greece and Rome could tell us something better and wiser than this! Surely a doctrine that is subversive of holiness and morality, and takes away all motives to seek to be pure, carries the stamp of its origin on its face. It is of earth, and not of heaven. It is of the devil, and not of God.

The Bible

The Bible speaks against these teachers from beginning to end. Hundreds of texts might be quoted that are diametrically opposed to their theories. These texts must be totally rejected if the Bible is to square with their views. To suit their theology, these Bible truths must be thrown away! At this rate the authority of the whole Bible is soon destroyed. And what do men give us in its place? Nothing, nothing, at all! They rob us of the bread of life, and do not even give us a stone in its place.

Once more I warn everyone into whose hands this publication may fall to beware of this theology. I charge you to hold fast to the doctrine that I have been endeavouring to uphold in this chapter. Remember what I have said, and never let it go. No inheritance of glory without sonship to God! No sonship to God without an interest in Christ! No interest in Christ without your own personal faith! This is God's truth. Never forsake it.

Who now among my readers *desires to know whether he is a son of God*? Ask yourself this question, and ask it this day — and ask it in God's sight, whether you have repented and believed. Ask yourself whether you are personally acquainted with Christ, and united to him in heart. If not, you may be very sure you are no son of God. You are not yet born again. You are still in your sins. God may be your Creator, but he is not your reconciled and pardoning Father.

Yes! Though the church and the world may agree to tell you to the contrary, though clergy and laity unite in flattering you — your sonship is worth little or nothing in the sight of God. Let God be true and every man a liar. Without faith in Christ you are no son of God: you are not born again.

Who among my readers *desires to become a son of God*? Let that person see and feel his sins, and flee to Christ for salvation, and this day he will be placed among the children. Just acknowledge your iniquity, and grab hold of the hand that Jesus holds to you this day, and sonship, with all its privileges, is yours. Just confess your sins, and bring them to Christ, and

God is 'faithful and just to forgive us our sins and to cleanse us from all unrighteousness' (1 John 1:9). This very day old things will pass away, and all things become new. This very day you will be forgiven, pardoned, 'to the praise of the glory of his grace, by which he made us accepted in the Beloved' (Ephesians 1:6). This very day you will have a new name given to you in heaven. You began reading this as a child of wrath. You will lie down tonight as a child of God. Mark this, if your professed desire after sonship is sincere — if you are truly weary of your sins, and have really something more than a lazy wish to be free — there is real comfort for you. It is all true. It is all written in Scripture, just as I have written here. I dare not raise barriers between you and God. This day I say, 'Believe in the Lord Jesus Christ,' and you will become 'a son', and be saved.

Who among my readers is *truly a son of God*? Rejoice, I say, and be extremely thankful and joyful for your privileges. Rejoice, for you have good cause to be thankful. Remember the words of the beloved apostle: 'Behold what manner of love the Father has bestowed on us, that we should be called children of God!' (1 John 3:1). How wonderful that heaven should look down on earth — that the holy God should set his affections on sinful man, and admit him into his family! Even though the world does not understand you! Even though the men of this world laugh at you, and reject your name as evil! Let them laugh if they will. God is your Father. You have no need to be ashamed. The Queen can create a nobleman. The bishops can ordain clergymen. But Queen, bishops, priests and deacons — all together cannot, of their own power, make one son of God, or one of greater dignity than a son of God. The man who can call God his Father, and Christ his elder brother — that man may be poor and lowly, yet he never needs to be ashamed.

The special evidences of the true Christian's relation to God

Let me show, in the second place, the special evidences of the true Christian's relation to God.

How can a man be sure of his own sonship? How can he find out whether he has come to Christ by faith and been born again? What are the marks and signs by which the 'sons of God' may be known? This is a question that all who love eternal life ought to ask. This is a question to which the verses of Scripture I am asking you to consider, like many others, supply an answer.

Led by his Spirit

The sons of God, for one thing, are all led by his Spirit. What does the first of our texts say? 'For as many as are led by the Spirit of God, these are sons of God' (Romans 8:14).

They are all under the leading and teaching of a power that is almighty, though unseen — the power of the Holy Spirit. They no longer turn to their own way, nor walk in the light of their own eyes, nor follow their own natural heart's desire. The Spirit leads them. The Spirit guides them. There is a movement in their hearts, lives and affections, which they feel, though they may not be able to explain, and which is always more or less in the same direction.

They are led away from sin — away from self-righteousness — away from the world. This is the road by which the Spirit leads God's children. Those whom God adopts he teaches and trains. He shows them their own hearts. He makes them weary of their own ways. He makes them long for inward peace.

They are led to Christ. They are led to the Bible. They are led to prayer. They are led to holiness. This is the beaten path along which the Spirit makes them travel. Those whom God adopts he always sanctifies. He makes sin very bitter to them. He makes holiness very sweet. It is the Spirit who leads them to Sinai, and first shows them the law, so that their hearts may be broken. It is he who leads them to Calvary, and shows them the cross, so that their hearts may be healed. It is he who leads them up the slopes to the top of Pisgah, and gives them a clear view of the Promised Land, so that their hearts may be cheered. When they are taken into the wilderness, and taught to see their own emptiness, it is the leading of the Spirit. When they are carried up to Mount Tabor or Mount Hermon, and uplifted with glimpses of the glory to come, it is the leading of the Spirit. Each and every one of God's sons is the subject of these leadings. Each and every one is a 'volunteer in the day of [God's] power', and yields himself to it. And each and every one is led by a straight way to a city where they could settle (Psalm 110:3; 107:7).

Be convinced in your heart, and do not let it go. The sons of God are a people 'led by the Spirit of God', and always led more or less in the same way. Their experience will wonderfully agree when they compare notes in heaven. This is one mark of sonship.

Adopted children

Furthermore, all the sons of God have the feelings of adopted children towards their Father in heaven. What does our second text say? 'You did not receive the spirit of bondage again to fear, but you received the Spirit of adoption by whom we cry out, "Abba, Father"' (Romans 8:15).

The sons of God are delivered from that cringing fear of God that sin generates in the natural heart. They are redeemed from that feeling of guilt which made Adam 'hide from the presence of the LORD God among the trees of the garden', and Cain to go 'out from the presence of the LORD' (Genesis 3:8; 4:16).

They are no longer afraid of God's holiness, and justice, and majesty. They no longer feel that there is a great gulf and barrier between themselves and God. They no longer feel that God is angry with them, and must be angry with them, because of their sins. The sons of God are delivered from these chains and shackles of the soul.

Their feelings towards God are now those of peace and confidence. They see him as a Father reconciled in Christ Jesus. They look on him as a God whose justice and holiness is satisfied by their great Mediator and Peacemaker, the Lord Jesus. They see him as a God who is 'just and the justifier of the one who has faith in Jesus' (Romans 3:26). As a Father, they draw near to him with boldness: as a Father, they can speak to him with freedom. They have exchanged the spirit of bondage for that of liberty, and the spirit of fear for that of love. They know that God is holy, but they are not afraid; they know that they are sinners, but they are still not afraid. Though holy, they believe that God is completely reconciled; though sinners, they believe they are completely clothed with Jesus Christ. Such is the feeling of the sons of God.

I admit that some have this feeling more vividly than others. There are some who still carry about scraps and remnants of the old spirit of bondage to their dying day. Many of them still have moments when they shake with the resurrected fears of their old sinful nature. But the overwhelming majority of the sons of God would say, if cross-examined, that since they knew Christ their feelings towards God are very different from what they had ever been before. They feel as if something like the old Roman form of adoption had taken place between themselves and their Father in heaven. They feel as if he had said to each one of them, 'Will you be my son?' and their hearts had replied, 'I will.'

Let us also try to understand this, and hold on to it tightly. The sons of God are a people who feel towards God in a way that the children of the world do not. God's children no longer feel a cringing fear of God; rather, their feelings towards him are as a reconciled parent. This, then, is another mark of sonship.

The witness of the Spirit

Again, the sons of God have the witness of the Spirit in their consciences. What does our third text say? 'The Spirit himself bears witness with our spirit that we are children of God' (Romans 8:16).

The sons of God have something within their hearts that tells them there is a relationship between themselves and God. They feel something that tells them that old things have passed away and all things have become new: that guilt is gone, that peace is restored, that heaven's door is open, and hell's door is shut. They have, in short, what the children of the world do not have — a felt, positive and reasonable hope. They have what Paul calls the 'seal' and 'deposit' of the Spirit (2 Corinthians 1:22; Ephesians 1:13).

I do not for a moment deny that this witness of the Spirit varies to the extent to which the sons of God possess it. With some it is a loud, clear, ringing, distinct testimony of conscience: 'I am Christ's, and Christ is mine.' With others it is a little, feeble, stammering whisper, which the devil and the flesh often prevent from being heard. Some of the children of God race on their course towards heaven with full assurance. Others are tossed back and forth on their voyage, and will scarcely believe they have got faith. But take the least and lowest of the sons of God: ask him if he will give up the little bit of religious hope that he has attained? Ask him if he will exchange his heart, with all its doubts and conflicts, its wrestlings and fears — ask him if he will exchange that heart for the heart of the downright worldly and careless man? Ask him if he would be content to turn around and throw down the things he has got hold of, and go back to the world? Who can doubt what the answer would be? 'I cannot do that,' he would reply. 'I do not know whether I have faith, and I do not feel sure I have got grace; but I have got something within me I would not like to part with.' And what is that 'something'? I will tell you — it is the witness of the Spirit.

Let us also try to understand this, that the sons of God have the witness of the Spirit in their consciences. This is another mark of sonship.

Suffer with Christ

Let me add one more thing. All the sons of God take part in suffering with Christ. What does our fourth text say? 'If children, then heirs — heirs of God and joint heirs with Christ, if indeed we suffer with him' (Romans 8:17).

All the children of God have a cross to carry. They have trials, troubles and afflictions to go through for the gospel's sake. They have trials from the world, trials from the flesh, and trials from the devil. They have trials of hurt feelings from their relatives and friends — cruel words, harsh treatment and unmerciful judgement. They have trials in the matter of character: slander, misrepresentation, mockery, insinuation of false motives — all these often fall heavily on them. They have trials in the matter of worldly interests. They often have to choose whether they will please man and lose glory for God, or gain glory for God and offend man. They have trials from their own hearts. In general, they each have their own thorn in the flesh — their own resident devil, who is their worst foe. This is the experience of the sons of God.

Some of them suffer more, and some less. Some of them suffer in one way, and some in another. God measures out their portions like a wise physician, and cannot err. But I believe there never was one child of God who reached paradise without a cross.

Suffering is the daily provision of the Lord's family. 'For whom the LORD loves he chastens.' 'If you are without chastening, of which all have become partakers, then you are illegitimate and not sons.' 'We must through many tribulations enter the kingdom of God.' 'All who desire to live godly in Christ Jesus will suffer persecution' (Hebrews 12:6, 8; Acts 14:22; 2 Timothy 3:12). When the godly Latimer was told by his landlord that he had never had any trouble in his life, 'Then,' said Latimer, 'God cannot be here.'

Suffering is a part of the process by which the sons of God are made holy. They are chastened to wean them from the world, so they may share in God's holiness. The Captain of their salvation was made 'perfect through sufferings', and so are they (Hebrews 2:10; 12:10). There never was a great saint who had not experienced either great hardships, or great persecutions. An early church father, Melancthon, said, 'Where there are no cares there will generally be no prayers.'

Let us try to settle this in our hearts also. The sons of God all have a cross to bear. A suffering Saviour generally has suffering disciples. The Bridegroom was a man of sorrows. Therefore, the Bride must not be a woman of pleasures and unacquainted with grief. Blessed are they that mourn! Let us not murmur at the cross. This also is a sign of sonship.

I warn men never to assume that they are sons of God unless they have the scriptural marks of sonship. Beware of a sonship without evidences. Again I say, beware. When a man has no leading of the Spirit to show me, no spirit of adoption to tell of, no witness of the Spirit in his conscience, no cross in his experience — is this man a son of God? Whatever others may think I would not dare to say he is! It is to his shame that he is not one of God's children (Deuteronomy 32:5). He is no heir of glory.

Do not tell me that you have been baptized and taught the catechism of the church, and therefore must be a child of God.

I tell you that the church register is not the book of life. I tell you that to be christened a child of God, and called regenerate as an infant is one thing; but to be a child of God in fact is another thing altogether. Go and read that catechism again. It is the 'death unto sin and the new birth unto righteousness' that makes men *children of grace*. Unless you know these things by experience, you are no son of God.

Do not tell me that you are a member of Christ's church and therefore you must be a son. I answer that the sons of the church are not necessarily the sons of God. Such sonship is not the sonship of the eighth chapter of Romans. That is the sonship you must have if you are to be saved.

And now, I do not doubt that some of my readers will want to know if they may be saved without the witness of the Spirit. My answer is that if you mean by the witness of the Spirit, the full assurance of hope — then without question you may be saved. But if you want to know whether a man can be saved without any inward sense, or knowledge, or hope of salvation, I would answer that, ordinarily, he cannot. I warn you plainly to cast aside all indecision over your state before God, and make your calling sure. Clear up your position and relationship. Do not think there is anything praiseworthy in always doubting. Leave that to the Roman Catholics. 'Assurance', said a godly Puritan, 'may be attained: and what have we been doing all our lives, since we became Christians, if we have not attained it?'

I do not doubt that some true Christians who are reading this will think their evidence of sonship is too small to be good, and will think bad things about themselves. Let me try to cheer them up. Who gave you the feelings you possess? Who made you hate sin? Who made you love Christ? Who made you long and strive after holiness? Where did these feelings come from? Did they come from nature? There are no such feelings in a natural man's heart. Did they come from the devil? He would try to prevent such feelings at any cost. Cheer up, and take courage. Fear not, and do not be downcast. Press forward, and go on. There is hope for you after all. Strive. Labour. Seek. Ask. Knock. Press on. You will yet see that you are 'sons of God'.

The privileges of the true Christian's relation to God

Let me show, in the last place, the privileges of the true Christian's relation to God.

Nothing can be conceived more glorious than the prospects of the sons of God. The words of Scripture at the beginning of this chapter contain a rich mine of good and comfortable things. 'If children,' says Paul, 'then heirs — heirs of God and joint heirs with Christ, if indeed we suffer with him, that we may also be glorified together' (Romans 8:17).

True Christians, then, are 'heirs'. Something is prepared for each one of them, which is yet to be revealed.

They are 'heirs of God'. To be heirs of the rich on earth is something. How much more then is it to be son and heir of the King of kings!

They are 'co-heirs with Christ'. They will share in his majesty, and take part in his glory. They will be glorified together with him.

And this, we must remember, is for all the children of God. Abraham took care to provide for all his children, and God takes care to provide for his. None of them are disinherited. None will be cast out. None will be cut off. Each will stand in his place and have a share, in the day when the Lord brings many sons and daughters to glory.

Who can tell us of the full nature of the inheritance of the saints? Who can describe the glory that is yet to be revealed and given to the children of God? Words fail us. Language falls short. Mind cannot fully conceive, and tongue cannot express perfectly, the things that are comprised in the glory yet to come upon the sons and daughters of the Lord Almighty. Oh, it is indeed a true saying of the apostle John: 'What we will be has not yet been made known' (1 John 3:2).

The very Bible itself only lifts a little of the veil that hangs over this subject. How could it do more? We could not thoroughly understand more if more had been told us. Our mental capacity is as yet too earthly — our understanding is as yet too carnal to appreciate more if we had it. The Bible generally deals with the subject in negative terms and not in positive assertions. It describes what there will not be in the glorious inheritance that we may, therefore, have some faint idea of what there will be. It paints the *absence* of certain things, in order that we may drink in a little the blessedness of the *present* things.

It tells us that the inheritance 'can never perish, spoil or fade'. It tells us that 'the crown of glory will never fade away'. It tells us that the devil is to be 'bound', that 'there will be no night there and no longer will there be any curse', that 'death and Hades were thrown into the lake of fire', that 'every tear will be wiped from their eyes', and that the inhabitant will never say, 'I am ill.' And these are indeed glorious things. No corruption! No fading! No withering! No devil! No curse of sin! No sorrow! No tears! No sickness! No death! Surely the cup of the children of God will surely run over! (1 Peter 1:4; 5:4; Revelation 20:2; 21:25; 22:3; 20:14; 21:4; Isaiah 33:24).

But there are positive things told to us about the glory yet to come upon the heirs of God, which ought not to be kept back. There are many sweet, pleasant and unspeakable comforts in their future inheritance, which all true Christians would do well to consider. There are enjoyable refreshments for fainting pilgrims in many words and expressions of Scripture, which you and I ought to store up for the time of need.

1. Is *knowledge* pleasant to us now?

Is the little that we know of God, and Christ, and the Bible precious to our souls, and do we long for more? We will have perfect knowledge in heaven. What does the Scripture say? 'Now I know in part, but then I shall know just as I also am known' (1 Corinthians 13:12). Blessed be God, there will be no more disagreements among believers! All will finally see eye to eye. The former ignorance will have passed away. We will marvel to find how childish and blind we have been.

2. Is *holiness* pleasant to us now?

Is sin the burden and bitterness of our lives? Do we long for entire conformity to the image of God? We will have perfect holiness in heaven. What does the Scripture say? 'Christ also loved the church and gave himself for her,' not only that he might sanctify her on earth, but also 'that he might present her to himself a glorious church, not having spot or wrinkle or any such thing, but that she should be holy and without blemish' (Ephesians 5:27). Oh, the blessedness of an eternal goodbye to sin! Oh, how little even the best of us are presently doing! Oh, what unutterable evil sticks, like glue, to all of our motives, all of our thoughts, all of our words, and all of our actions! Oh, how many of us are godly in our words, but, so weak in our works! Thank God, all this will be changed.

3. Is *rest* pleasant to us now?

Do we often feel 'exhausted but still in pursuit'? (Judges 8:4). Do we long for a world in which we will not need to always be watching and doing battle? We will have perfect rest in glory. What does the Scripture say? 'There remains therefore a rest for the people of God' (Hebrews 4:9). The daily, hourly conflict with the world, the flesh and the devil will finally come to an end. The enemy will be subdued. The warfare will be over. The wicked will finally stop causing us trouble. The weary will finally be at rest. There will be a great calm.

4. Is *service* pleasant to us now?

Do we find it sweet to work for Christ, and yet groan being burdened by such a feeble body? Is our spirit often willing, but hampered and clogged by the poor weak flesh? Have our hearts burned within us when we have been allowed to give a cup of cold water for Christ's sake, and have we sighed to think what unprofitable servants we are? Let us take comfort. We will be able to serve perfectly in glory, and without weariness. What does the Scripture say? 'They serve him day and night in his temple' (Revelation 7:15).

5. Is *satisfaction* pleasant to us now?

Do we find the world empty? Do we long for the filling up of every empty place in our hearts? We will have perfect satisfaction in glory. We will no longer have to mourn over cracks in all our earthen vessels, and thorns in all our roses, and bitter residue in all our sweet cups. We will no longer lament with Jonah over withered gourds. We will no longer say with Solomon, 'All is vanity and grasping for the wind.' We will no longer cry with aged David, 'I have seen the consummation of all perfection.' What does the Scripture say? 'I shall be satisfied when I awake in your likeness' (Ecclesiastes 1:14; Psalm 119:96; Psalm 17:15).

6. Is *communion with the saints* pleasant to us now?

Do we feel that we are never so happy as when we are with the 'excellent ones'? Do we feel most at home when we are in their company? (Psalm 16:3). We will have perfect communion in heaven. What does the Scripture say? 'The Son of Man will send out his angels, and they will gather out of his kingdom all things that offend, and those who practise lawlessness.' 'He will send his angels with a great sound of a trumpet, and they will gather together his elect from the four winds' (Matthew 13:41; 24:31). Praise be to God! We will see all the saints whom we have read about in the Bible, and in whose steps we have tried to walk. We will see apostles, prophets, patriarchs, martyrs, reformers, missionaries and ministers, of whom the world was not worthy. We will see the faces of those we have known and loved in Christ while on earth, and over whose departure we shed bitter tears. We will see them more bright and glorious than they ever were before. And best of all, we will see them without hurry and anxiety, and without feeling that we only meet to part again. In the coming glory there is no death, no parting, no farewell.

7. Is *communion with Christ* pleasant to us now?

Do we find his name precious to us? Do we feel our hearts burn within us at the thought of his dying love? We will have perfect communion with him in heaven. 'We shall always be with the Lord' (1 Thessalonians 4:17). We will be with him in paradise (Luke 23:43). We will see his face in the kingdom. These eyes of ours will behold those hands and feet that were pierced with nails, and that head which was crowned with thorns. Where he is, there also will be the sons of God. When he comes, they will come with him. When he sits down in his glory, they will sit down by his side. This is indeed a blessed expectation! I am a dying man in a dying world. All before me is dark. The world to come is an unknown harbour. But Christ is there, and that is enough. Surely if there is rest and peace in following him by faith on earth, there will be far more rest and peace when we see him face to face. If we have found it good to follow the pillar of cloud and fire in the wilderness, we will find it a thousand times better to sit down in our eternal inheritance, with our Joshua, in the promised land.

If any one of my readers is not yet among the sons and heirs, I pity you with all my heart! How much you are missing! How little true comfort you are enjoying! There you are, struggling on, and toiling in the fire, and wearing yourself out for mere earthly ends — seeking rest and finding none — chasing shadows and never catching them — wondering why you are not happy, and yet refusing to see the cause — hungry, and thirsty, and empty, and yet blind to the abundance within your reach. Oh, that you were wise! Oh, that you would hear the voice of Jesus, and learn from him!

If you are one of the sons and heirs, you may rightly rejoice and be happy. You can wait with joy, like the boy Patience in *Pilgrim's Progress*: your best things are yet to come. You can easily bear crosses without murmuring: your light affliction is but for a moment. Your 'sufferings of this present time are not worthy to be compared with the glory which shall be revealed'. 'When Christ who is our life appears, then you also will appear with him in glory' (Romans 8:18; Colossians 3:4). You have no need to envy the sinner and his prosperity. You are the truly rich. It was well said by a dying believer in my own church: 'I am richer than I ever was in my life.' You may say as Mephibosheth said to David: 'Let him take it all, inasmuch as my lord the king has come back in peace to his own house' (2 Samuel 19:30). You may say as Alexander said when he gave all his riches away, and was asked what he kept for himself: 'I have hope.' You need not be discouraged by sickness: the eternal part of you is safe and provided for, despite what happens to your body. You can calmly look at death: it opens a door between you and your inheritance. You need not have excessive sorrow over the things of the world — over partings and bereavements, over losses and crosses: the day of gathering is before you. Your treasure is beyond reach of harm. Every year heaven is becoming more full of those you love, and earth more empty. Glory in your inheritance. It is all yours if you are a son of God: 'If children, then heirs.'

Conclusion

And now, in concluding this chapter, let me ask every one reading it: Whose child are you?

Whose child are you?

Are you the child of nature or the child of grace? Are you the child of the devil or the child of God? You cannot be both at once. Which are you?

Settle the question without delay, for eventually you must die as either one or the other. Settle it, for it can be settled, and it is folly to leave it in doubt. Settle it, for time is short, the world is getting old, and you are quickly drawing near to the judgement seat of Christ. Settle it, for death is near, the Lord is at hand, and who can tell what a day might bring forth? Oh, that you would never rest till the question is settled! Oh, that you may never feel satisfied till you can say, 'I have been born again: I am a son of God!'

Become one without delay

If you are not a son and heir of God, I plead with you to become one without delay.

Do you want to be rich? There are unsearchable riches in Christ. Do you want to be exalted? You will be a king. Do you want to be happy? You will have a peace that transcends understanding and that the world can never give and never take away. Oh, come out and take up the cross and follow Christ! Come out from among the thoughtless and worldly, and hear the word of the Lord: 'I will be a Father to you, and you shall be my sons and daughters, says the Lᴏʀᴅ Almighty' (2 Corinthians 6:18).

Walk worthy

If you are a son of God, I plead with you to walk worthy of your Father's house.

I solemnly charge you to honour him with your life; and above all to honour him by implicit obedience to all of his commands, and to give sincere love to all of his children. Make the effort to travel through the world like a child of God and heir to glory. Let men be able to trace a family likeness between you and your heavenly Father. Live a heavenly life. Seek things that are above. Do not seem to be building your nest below. Behave like a man who seeks a city that is not visible, whose citizenship is in heaven, and who would be content with many hardships till he gets home.

Labour to *feel like a son of God* in every circumstance in which you are placed. Never forget you are on your Father's ground so long as you are here on earth. Never forget that a Father's hand sends to you all your mercies and crosses. Cast every care on him. Be happy and cheerful in him. Indeed, why would you ever be sad if you are the King's son? Why should men ever doubt, when they look at you, whether it is a pleasant thing to be one of God's children?

Labour to *behave towards others like a son of God.* Be blameless and harmless in your day and generation. Be a 'peacemaker' (Matthew 5:9). Seek for your children sonship to God, above everything else: seek for them an inheritance in heaven, whatever else you do for them. No man leaves his children so well provided for as he who leaves them sons and heirs of God.

Persevere in your Christian calling, if you are a son of God, and press forward more and more. Be careful to lay aside every weight, and the sin that most easily entangles you. Keep your eyes fixed steadily on Jesus. Remain in him. Remember that apart from Jesus you can do nothing and with Jesus you can do everything (John 15:5; Philippians 4:13). Watch and pray every day. Be steadfast, unmovable, and always abounding in the work of the Lord. Settle it in your heart that never will a cup of cold water, given because you are a disciple of Jesus, ever lose its reward, and that every year you are coming closer to your home in heaven.

'For yet a little while, and he who is coming will come and will not tarry' (Hebrews 10:37). Then the creation itself will be liberated from its bondage to decay and brought into the glorious freedom of the children of God (Romans 8:19, 21). Then will the world acknowledge that God's children were the truly wise. Then the sons of God will finally come of age, and will no longer be waiting for their inheritance, but will actually possess it. Then they will hear with exceeding joy those comforting words, 'Come, you blessed of my Father, inherit the kingdom prepared for you from the foundation of the world' (Matthew 25:34). Surely that day will make amends for everything!

19.
The great gathering

'Concerning the coming of our Lord Jesus Christ and our gathering together to him'
(2 Thessalonians 2:1).

The text above contains an expression that deserves our most careful attention. That expression is 'our gathering together'.

'Our gathering together!' These three words ought to find a response in every part of the world. Man is by nature a social being: he does not like to be alone. Go wherever you want on earth, and you will find that people generally like meeting together, and seeing one another's faces. It is the exception, and not the rule, to find children of Adam who do not like 'being gathered together'.

For example, Christmas is noted as a time when British people 'gather together'. It is the season when family gatherings have almost become a national institution. In cities and in the country, among rich and among poor, from the palace to the home of the poor, Christmas cheer and Christmas parties are universal experiences. It is often the one time in the whole year for many to see their friends. Sons snatch a few days from the city to run down and see their parents; brothers take time away from the desk to spend a week with their sisters; friends accept long-standing invitations to pay a visit to other friends; students rush home from college, and rejoice in the warmth and comfort of their parents' house. For a little while business comes to a standstill: the spinning wheel of ceaseless labour almost seems to stop spinning for a few hours. In short, all over the nation, there is a general spirit of 'gathering together'.

It is a happy land where such a state of things exist! Long may it last in our country, and may it never end! The philosophy that sneers at Christmas gatherings is poor and shallow. The religion that frowns at them, and denounces them as wicked is cold and hard. Family affection lies at the root of a well-ordered society. It is one of the few good things that has survived the Fall, and prevents men and women from being mere devils. It is the secret oil on the wheels of our social system that keeps the whole machine going, and without which the power of the machine is useless. May the Christmas day never arrive when there are no family gatherings!

But, despite what I have just said, earthly gatherings also have something about them that is sad and sorrowful. The happiest parties sometimes contain disagreeable members. The merriest Christmas parties last only for a short time. Moreover, as the years roll on, the hand of death makes painful gaps in the family circle. Even in the midst of Christmas merriment we cannot help remembering those who have passed away. The longer we live, the more we feel that we are standing alone. The old faces will rise before the eyes of our minds, and old voices will sound in our ears, even in the midst of holiday merriment and laughter. People do not talk much about such things, but there are few who do not feel them. We need not intrude our inmost thoughts on others, especially when all around us everyone is bright and happy; but I suspect there are many reaching middle age who would admit, if they spoke honestly, that there are sorrowful things inseparably mixed up with a Christmas party. In short, there is no unmixed pleasure about any earthly gathering.

But is there no better 'gathering' yet to come? Is there no bright prospect on our horizon of an assembly that will far outshine the assemblies of Christmas and New Year — an assembly in which there will be joy without sorrow, and merriment without tears? I thank God that I can give a plain answer to these questions; and that is my simple object now. I ask my readers to give me their attention for a few minutes, and I will soon show them what I mean.

The future gathering together of Christians

There is a 'gathering together' of true Christians that is yet to come. What is it, and when will it be?

The gathering I speak of will take place at the end of the world, in the day when Christ returns to earth the second time. He went away in the clouds of heaven, and in the clouds of heaven he will return. Visibly, in the body, he will return. And the very first thing that Christ will do will be to 'gather' his people. 'He will send his angels with a great sound of a trumpet, and they will gather together his elect from the four winds, from one end of heaven to the other' (Matthew 24:31).

The manner of this 'gathering' is plainly revealed in Scripture. The dead saints will all be raised, and the living saints will all be changed. It is written, 'The sea gave up the dead who were in it, and death and Hades delivered up the dead who were in them.' 'And the dead in Christ will rise first. Then we who are alive and remain shall be caught up together with them in the clouds to meet the Lord in the air.' 'We shall not all sleep, but we shall all be changed — in a moment, in the twinkling of an eye, at the last trumpet. For the trumpet will sound, and the dead will be raised incorruptible, and we shall be changed' (Revelation 20:13; 1 Thessalonians 4:16-17; 1 Corinthians 15:51-52). And then when every member of Christ is found, and not one is left behind, when soul and body, those old companions, are once more reunited, then will it be the great 'gathering'.

The object of this 'gathering together' is as clearly revealed in Scripture as its manner. It is partly for the final reward of Christ's people: that their complete justification from all guilt may be declared to all creation; that they may receive the 'crown of glory that will never fade away', and the 'kingdom prepared for them since the creation of the world'; that they may be admitted publicly into the joy of their Lord! It is partly for the safety of Christ's people, that, like Noah in the ark and Lot in Zoar, they may be hid and covered before the storm of God's judgement comes down on the wicked; that when the last plagues are falling on the enemies of the Lord, they may be untouched, as Rahab's family in the fall of Jericho, and unscathed as the three children in the midst of the fire. The saints have no reason to fear in the day of gathering, however fearful the signs that may accompany it. Before the final crash of all things begins, they will be hidden in the secret place of the Most High. The great gathering is for their safety and their reward. 'Do not be afraid,' will the gathering angels say, 'for I know that you seek Jesus who was crucified.' 'Come, my people,' will their Master say, 'enter your chambers, and shut your doors behind you; hide yourself, as it were, for a little moment, until the indignation is past' (Matthew 28:5; Isaiah 26:20).

A great gathering

This gathering will be a *great* one. All children of God who have ever lived, from Adam, the first saint, down to the last born in the day that our Lord comes — everyone of every age, and nation, and church, and people, and tongue — everyone will be gathered together. No one will be overlooked or forgotten. The weakest and feeblest will not be left behind. Now, when 'scattered', true Christians seem like a little flock; then, when 'gathered', they will be found to be a multitude that no man can number.

A wonderful gathering

This gathering will be a *wonderful* one. The saints from distant lands, who never saw each other in the flesh, and could not understand each other's speech if they met, will all be brought together in one harmonious fellowship. Those who live in Australia will find they are as near to heaven and will arrive there as quickly as those living in Britain. The believers who died five thousand years ago and whose bones are mere dust will find their bodies raised and renewed as quickly as those who are alive when the trumpet sounds. Above all, miracles of grace will be revealed. We will see some in heaven whom we never expected would have been saved at all. The confusion of tongues will finally be reversed, and done away. The assembled multitude will cry with one heart and in one language, 'Oh, what God has done!' (Numbers 23:23).

A humbling gathering

This gathering will be a *humbling* one. There will be an end to bigotry and narrow-mindedness for ever. The Christians of one denomination will find themselves side by side with those of another denomination; if they would not tolerate them on earth, they will be obliged to tolerate them in heaven. Those Christians, who will neither pray together nor worship together now, will discover to their shame that they must praise together for all eternity. The very people who will not allow us to sit with them at the Lord's Table now will be obliged to acknowledge us before our Master's face, and to let us sit down by their side. Never will the world see such a complete overthrow of sectarianism, party spirit, unbrotherliness, religious jealousy and religious pride. Finally, we will all be completely 'clothed with humility' (1 Peter 5:5).

This 'being gathered to him' is the mighty and wonderful gathering which ought to be foremost in men's thoughts. It deserves consideration; it demands attention. Gatherings of other kinds are incessantly occupying our minds: political gatherings, scientific gatherings, gatherings for pleasure, gatherings for gain. But the hour comes, and will soon be here, when gatherings of this kind will be completely forgotten. Only one thought will swallow up men's minds; that thought will be, 'Will I be gathered with Christ's people into a place of safety and honour, or be left behind to everlasting agony?' *Let us be careful that we are not left behind.*

Why should we desire it?

Why is this gathering together of true Christians something to be desired? Let us try to get an answer to that question.

Paul evidently thought that the gathering at the last day was an object of great joy that Christians ought to keep before their eyes. He classes it with the second coming of our Lord, which, he says elsewhere, believers love and long for. He exalts it in the distant horizon as one of those 'good things that are coming', which should animate the faith of every pilgrim to walk the narrow path. He seems to say that not only will each servant of God have rest, and a kingdom, and a crown; but he will also find himself truly blessed by 'being gathered to him'. Now, where is the peculiar blessedness of this gathering? Why is it something that we ought to look forward to with joy, and expect with pleasure? Let us see.

Something totally unlike their present state

For one thing, when all true Christians are 'gathered to him' they will be in a state totally unlike their present condition. To

be scattered, and not gathered, seems the rule of man's existence now. Of all the millions who are born into the world each
year, how few continue together till they die! Children who live
their first days under the same roof, and play in the same living
room, are sure to be separated as they grow up, and will draw
their last breath in a far distant place from one another. The
same law applies to the people of God. They are spread abroad
like salt, one in one place and one in another, and never allowed to continue long by each other's side. Without a doubt it
is for the good of the world that it is this way. A town would be
a very dark place at night if all the lights were crowded together
into one room. But, good as it is for the world, it is a big trial to
believers. There are many days when they feel desolate and
alone; many times they long for a little more communion with
their brethren, and a little more fellowship with those who love
the Lord! Well, they may look forward with hope and comfort,
for the hour is coming when they will have no lack of companions. Let them lift up their heads and rejoice, for they soon will
be 'gathered to him'.

An assembly of one mind

For another thing, when all true Christians are 'gathered to him'
they will be an assembly entirely of one mind. There are no
such assemblies now, for hypocrisy and false profession creep
in everywhere. Wherever there is wheat there are sure to be
weeds. Wherever there are good fish there are sure to be bad
ones too. Wherever there are wise virgins there are sure to be
foolish ones too. There is no such thing as a perfect church
now. There is a Judas Iscariot at every communion table, and a
Demas who will desert the church because of his love for the
world; and wherever the 'sons of God' come together Satan is
sure to appear among them (Job 1:6). But all this will come to
an end one day. Our Lord will finally present to the Father a

perfect church, 'not having spot or wrinkle or any such thing' (Ephesians 5:27). How glorious such a church will be! To meet with half-a-dozen believers together now is a rare event in a Christian's year, and one that cheers him like a sunny day in winter: it makes him feel his heart burn within him, as the disciples felt on the way to Emmaus. But how much more joyful it will be to meet a 'multitude that no man can number'! To find too, that everyone we meet is finally of one opinion and one judgement, and sees eye to eye; to discover that all our unfortunate controversies are buried for ever, and that one group of Christians no longer quarrels with other Christian groups; to join a company of Christians in which there is neither squabbling, nor discord, and where every man has complete holiness, and all of his former sins, that so easily entangled him on earth, have dropped off like the leaves of a tree in autumn — all this will indeed be happiness! No wonder that Paul invites us to look forward.

None will be absent

For another thing, when all true Christians are 'gathered to him' it will be a gathering in which none will be absent. The weakest lamb will not be left behind in the wilderness: the youngest babe that ever drew breath will not be overlooked or forgotten. We will once more see our beloved friends and relatives who fell asleep in Christ, and left us in sorrow and tears, and they will be better, brighter, more beautiful, and more pleasant than we ever found them on earth. We will hold communion with all the saints of God who have fought the good fight before us, from the beginning of the world to the end. Patriarchs and prophets, Apostles and Fathers, martyrs and missionaries, Reformers and Puritans, all the host of God's elect will be there. If reading their words and works has been pleasant, how much better it will be to see them! If hearing them, and being stirred by their example has been useful, how much more delightful it will be to talk with them, and ask them questions! To sit down with Abraham, Isaac and Jacob, and hear how they kept the faith without a Bible; to converse with Moses, Samuel, David, Isaiah and Daniel, and to hear how they could believe in a Christ that was yet to come; to converse with Peter, Paul, Lazarus, Mary and Martha, and to listen to their wondrous tale of what their Master did for them — all this will indeed be sweet! No wonder that Paul invites us to look forward.

Without a parting

In the last place, when all true Christians are 'gathered to him' it will be a gathering without a parting.

There are no such meetings now. We seem to live in a time of endless hurry, and can hardly sit down and catch our breath before we are off again. 'Goodbye' treads on the heels of 'How are you?' The cares of this world, the necessary duties of life, the demands of our families, the work of our various callings in life — all these things appear to eat up our days, and to make it impossible to have long quiet times of communion with God's people. But, blessed be God, it will not always be this way. The hour is coming and will soon be here, when 'goodbye' and 'farewell' will be words that are laid aside and buried for ever, when we will meet in a world where the former things have passed away, where there will be no more sin and no more sorrow — no more poverty and no more money — no more labour of body or labour of brains — no more need of anxiety for families — no more sickness, no more pain, no more old age, no more death, and no more change. When we meet in that endless state of being calm, and restful, and unhurried, who can tell what a blessed change it will be? No wonder that Paul invites us to look up and to look forward.

Some applications for ourselves

I lay these things before all who are reading this, and ask them to give it their serious attention. If I know anything of a Christian's experience, I am sure they contain food for reflection. This, at least, I say confidently: the man who sees nothing much in the second coming of Christ and the public 'gathering' of Christ's people — nothing happy, nothing joyful, nothing pleasant, nothing desirable — such a man has every reason to doubt whether he himself is a true Christian.

Where will you be?

I ask you a simple question. Do not turn away from it and refuse to look it in the face. Will you be gathered by the angels into God's home when the Lord returns, or will you be left behind?

One thing, at any rate, is very certain. There will only be two groups of mankind at the last great day: those who are on the right hand of Christ, and those who are on the left; those who are counted righteous, and those who are wicked; those who are safe in the ark, and those who are outside; those who are gathered like wheat into God's barn, and those who are left behind like weeds to be burned. Now, what group will you belong to?

Perhaps you do not know yet. You cannot say. You are not sure. You hope for the best. You trust it will be all right in the end: but you won't undertake to give an opinion. Well, I only hope you will never rest until you do know. The Bible will tell you plainly who are those who will be 'gathered to him'. Your own heart, if you are honest with yourself, will tell you whether you are one of the number. Do not rest, do not rest, until you know!

How can men stand the partings and separations of this life if they have no hope of anything better; how can they bear to say 'goodbye' to sons and daughters, and launch them on the troublesome waves of this world, if they have no expectation of a safe 'gathering' in Christ at the last day; how they can part with beloved members of their families, and let them journey to the other side of the globe, not knowing if they will ever meet happily in this life or the life to come — how this can be, completely baffles my understanding. I can only suppose that most people never think, never consider, never look forward. Once a man begins to think, then he will never be satisfied until he has found Christ and is safe.

Test the condition of your soul

If you want to know your own chance of being gathered into God's home, then I offer you a simple way of testing the condition of your soul. Ask yourself what kind of gatherings you like best here on earth? Ask yourself whether you really love being gathered together with God's people?

How could the man who takes no pleasure in meeting with true Christians on earth enjoy meeting true Christians in heaven? How can the heart that is completely focused on parties, sporting events, entertainment, and worldly assemblies, and who thinks that earthly worship is wearisome — how can such a heart be in tune for the company of saints, and only the saints? It is impossible. It cannot be.

Never, never let it be forgotten, that our tastes on earth are a sure evidence of the state of our hearts; and the state of our hearts here is a sure indication of our eternal destiny. Heaven is a prepared place for a prepared people. He who hopes to be gathered with the saints in heaven while he only loves the gathering of sinners on earth is deceiving himself. If he lives and

dies in that state of mind he will find in the end that it would
have been better for him if he had never been born.

Look forward

If you are a true Christian, I exhort you to be frequently looking
forward. Your good things are yet to come. Your redemption is
drawing near. The night is almost over. The day is at hand. For
in just a very little while, he who is coming will come and will
not delay. When he comes, he will bring the saints from heaven
with him and change the ones that are still alive on the earth.
Look forward! There is a 'gathering together' yet to come.

The morning after a shipwreck is a sorrowful time. The joy
of half-drowned survivors, who have safely reached the land,
is often sadly marred by the memory of shipmates who have
sunk to rise no more. There will be no such sorrow when believers gather together around the throne of the Lamb. Not one
of the ship's company will be found absent. Some got 'on boards
and some on parts of the ship. And ... all escaped safely to
land' (Acts 27:44). The great waters and raging waves will swallow none of God's elect. When the sun rises everyone will be
seen safe and 'gathered together'.

Even the day after a great victory is a sorrowful time. The
triumphant feelings of the conquerors are often mingled with
bitter regrets for those who fell in action and died on the battle-
field. The list of 'killed, wounded and missing' breaks many a
heart, fills many a home with mourning, and brings many a
grey head sorrowing to the grave. The great Duke of Wellington often said, 'There was but one thing worse than a victory,
and that was a defeat.' But, thanks be to God, there will be no
such sorrow in heaven! The soldiers of the great Captain of our
salvation will all answer when their names are called in the end.
The roll call will be as complete after the battle as it was before.
Not one believer will be 'missing' in the great 'gathering together'.

Does Christmas, for instance, bring with it sorrowful feelings and painful associations? Do tears come to your eyes when you note the empty places around the dinner table? Do grave thoughts come sweeping over your mind, even in the midst of your children's festivity, when you remember the dear old faces and much loved voices of some that sleep in the grave? Well, look up and look forward! The time is short. The world is growing old. The coming of the Lord is drawing near. There is yet to be a meeting without parting, and a gathering without separation. Those believers whom you laid in the grave with many tears are in good keeping: you will yet see them again with joy. Look up! I say once more. Lay hold by faith 'the coming of our Lord Jesus Christ and our gathering together to him'. Believe it, think of it, rest on it. It is all true.

Do you feel lonely and deserted as every December comes around? Do you find few people left to pray with, few to praise with, few to open your heart to, few to exchange experience with? Do you increasingly learn that every year heaven is becoming more full and earth more empty? Well, it is an old story. You are only drinking a cup that myriads have drunk before. Look up and look forward. The lonely time will soon be past and over: you will have plenty of company in the future. '[You] shall be satisfied when [you] awake, in [his] likeness' (Psalm 17:15). Yet a little while and you will see a congregation that will never break up, and a day of rest that will never end. 'The coming of our Lord Jesus Christ and our gathering together to him' will make amends for everything.

20.
The great separation

'His winnowing fan is in his hand, and he will thoroughly clean out his threshing floor, and gather his wheat into the barn; but he will burn up the chaff with unquenchable fire'
(Matthew 3:12).

The verse of Scripture that is now before our eyes contains words that were spoken by John the Baptist. They are a prophecy about our Lord Jesus Christ, one that has not yet been fulfilled. They are a prophecy that we will see fulfilled one day, and God alone knows how soon.

I invite every reader to consider seriously the great truths that this verse contains. I invite you to give me your attention, while I unfold them and set them before you in order. This text may possibly prove to be a timely word to your soul. Who knows, maybe this text will help to make this the happiest day of your life.

The two great classes

Let me show you, in the first place, the two great classes into which mankind may be divided.

There are only two classes of people in the world in the sight of God, and both are mentioned in our text. There are those who are called the wheat, and there are those who are called the chaff.

Viewed with the eye of man, the earth contains many different sorts of inhabitants. Viewed with the eye of God it only
contains two. Man's eye looks at the outward appearance —
this is all he thinks of. The eye of God looks at the heart — this
is the only part of which he takes any account. And tested by
the state of their hearts, there are only two classes into which
people can be divided — either they are wheat, or they are
chaff.

Who are the wheat?

Who are the wheat in the world? This is a point that demands
special consideration.

The wheat refers to all men and women who are believers in
the Lord Jesus Christ; all who are led by the Holy Spirit; all who
have felt themselves sinners, and fled for refuge to the salvation offered in the gospel; all who love the Lord Jesus and live
to the Lord Jesus, and serve the Lord Jesus; all who have taken
Christ for their only confidence and the Bible for their only guide,
and regard sin as their deadliest enemy, looking to heaven as
their only home. All such people, of every church, name, nation,
people and language; of every rank, occupation and condition
— all such people are God's 'wheat'.

Show me people like this anywhere, and I know what they
are. I do not know whether they and I may agree in every detail, but I see in them the handiwork of the King of kings, and I
ask no more. I do not know where they came from and where
they found their religion; but I know where they are going and
that is enough for me. They are the children of my Father in
heaven. They are part of his 'wheat'.

All such people, though sinful and vile, and unworthy in
their own eyes, are the precious part of mankind. They are the
sons and daughters of God the Father. They are the delight of
God the Son. They are a dwelling place of God the Holy Spirit.

The Father sees no iniquity in them — they are the members of his dear Son's mystical body: he sees them in him, and is well pleased. The Lord Jesus sees in them the fruit of his own suffering and work upon the cross, and is well satisfied. The Holy Spirit regards them as spiritual temples, which he himself has created, and rejoices over them. In a word, they are the 'wheat' of the earth.

Who are the chaff?

Who are the chaff in the world? This again is a point that demands special attention.

The chaff refers to all men and women who have no saving faith in Christ, and no sanctification of the Spirit. Some of them are atheists, and some are 'Christians' in name only. Some are sneering Sadducees, and some self-righteous Pharisees. Some of them make a point of keeping up a kind of Sunday religion, and others are utterly careless of everything except their own pleasure and the world. But every one of them has the two great marks already mentioned — no faith and no sanctification; every one of them is 'chaff'. Those who attend church and can think of nothing but outward ceremonies — the unconverted admirer of sermons — all are standing in one class before God; every one of them is 'chaff'.

They bring no glory to God the Father, because, 'He who does not honour the Son does not honour the Father who sent him' (John 5:23). They neglect the mighty salvation that countless millions of angels admire. They disobey the Word that was graciously written for their understanding. They do not listen to the voice of the one who condescended to leave heaven and die for their sins. They do not serve nor love the one who gave them 'life and breath and everything else'. And therefore God takes no pleasure in them. He pities them, but he considers them no better than 'chaff'.

Yes! You may have rare intellectual gifts and great mental attainments: you may sway kingdoms by your counsel, move millions by your pen, or keep crowds in breathless attention by your tongue; but if you have never submitted yourself to the rule of Christ, and never honoured his gospel by receiving it in your heart, then you are nothing in his sight. The most insignificant insect that crawls in the dirt is a nobler being than you are; it fills its place in creation and glorifies its Maker with all its power, and you do not. You do not honour God with heart, and will, and intellect, and with the members of your body, which are all his. You overturn his order and arrangement, and live as if your time on earth was more important than eternity, and the body better than the soul. You dare to neglect God's greatest gift — his own incarnate Son. You are cold about the subject that fills heaven with hallelujahs. And as long as this is the case, then you belong to the worthless part of mankind. You are the 'chaff' of the earth.

Let this thought be engraved deeply in the mind of every one of my readers, whatever else he forgets. Remember there are only two kinds of people in the world. There are wheat, and there are chaff.

There are many nations in Europe. Each differs from the rest. Each has its own language, its own laws, and its own unique customs. But God's eye divides Europe into two great parties — the wheat and the chaff.

There are many classes in England. There are peers and commoners — farmers and shopkeepers — masters and servants — rich and poor. But God's eye only sees two classes — the wheat and the chaff.

There are many and various minds in every congregation that gathers for religious worship. There are some who attend merely out of habit, and some who really desire to meet Christ; some who come there to please others, and some who come to please God; some whose hearts are open and very alert to the message, and some who have closed their hearts and consider the whole service a drudgery. But the eye of the Lord Jesus only sees two divisions in the congregation — the wheat and the chaff.

There were millions of visitors to the Great Exhibition of 1851. From Europe, Asia, Africa and America — from north and south, and east and west — crowds came together to see what skill and industry could do. People from all over the world, who had never seen each other before, met face to face under one roof. But the eye of the Lord only saw two groups crowding that large palace of glass — the wheat and the chaff.

I know full well that the world dislikes this way of dividing professing Christians. The world tries hard to convince us that there are three classes of people and not two. The first class of people are the very good and the very strict; however, this does not suit the world: they cannot and will not be saints. Yet, the third class, which has no religion at all, does not suit the world either: it would not be respectable. 'Thank God,' they will say, 'we are not as bad as they are.' Then there is the second class — a safe middle class, the world thinks — and in this middle class is where the majority of men persuade themselves they belong. In this class a person only needs enough religion to be saved, and yet not go to extremes; to be minimally good, and yet not be exceptional; to have a quiet, easy-going, moderate kind of Christianity, and go comfortably to heaven when they die — this is the world's favourite class.

I denounce this notion of a middle class as an immense and soul-ruining delusion. I warn you strongly not to be carried away by it. It is as vain an invention as the Roman Catholic's purgatory. It is a refuge of lies — a castle in the air — a Russian ice-palace — a vast unreality — an empty dream. Nowhere is there such a middle class of Christians spoken of in the Bible.

There were two classes in the day of Noah's flood: those who were inside the ark, and those who were outside; two in the parable of the gospel-net: those who are called the good fish, and those who are called the bad; two in the parable of the ten virgins: those who are described as wise, and those who are described as foolish; two in the account of the Judgement Day: the sheep and the goats; two sides of the throne: the right hand and the left; two abodes when the last sentence has been passed: heaven and hell.

And just as there are only two classes in the visible church on earth — those who are in their natural state of unbelief and sin, and those who are in the state of grace; those who are on the narrow road, and those who are travelling on the broad road; those who have faith, and those who do not have faith; those who have been converted, and those who have not been converted; those who are with Christ, and those who are against him; those who gather with him, and those who scatter; those who are 'wheat', and those who are 'chaff' — into these two classes the whole professing church of Christ may be divided. There is no other class apart from these two.

You must examine yourselves! Are you among the wheat, or among the chaff? Neutrality is impossible. Either you are in one class, or in the other. Which is it of the two?

Perhaps you attend church. You go to the Lord's Table. You like good people. You can distinguish between good preaching and bad. You think Roman Catholicism is a false religion, and heartily oppose it. You think Protestantism is true and warmly support it. You attend Christian meetings. You sometimes read Christian books. It is good: it is all very good. It is more than can be said of many. But still this is not a straightforward answer to my question — are you wheat or are you chaff?

Have you been born again? Are you a new creature? Have you put off the old man and put on the new? Have you ever felt convicted of your sins and repented of them? Are you looking only to Christ for the forgiveness of your sins and eternal life? Do you love Christ? Do you serve Christ? Do you hate your sins and fight against them? Do you long for perfect holiness and strive after it? Have you come out from the world? Do you delight in the Bible? Do you wrestle in prayer? Do you love Christ's people? Do you try to do good to the world? Are you vile in your own eyes and willing to take the lowest place? Do you live like a Christian at work, and on weekdays, and also in the privacy of your own home? Oh, think, think, think on these things, and then perhaps you will be better able to tell the state of your soul.

I implore you not to turn away from my question, however unpleasant it may be. Answer it, though it may prick your conscience and convict your heart. Answer it, though it may prove you in the wrong and expose your fearful danger. Do not rest, do not rest, until you know how it is between you and God. It is a thousand times better to find out that you are living an evil life of sin, and repent immediately, than live on in uncertainty and be eternally lost.

The separation of the two classes

Let me show you, in the second place, the time when the two great classes of mankind will be separated.

Our text tells us of a coming separation. It says that Christ will one day do to his professing church what the farmer does to his corn. He will sift it. He 'will clean out his threshing floor'. And then the wheat and the chaff will be divided.

There is no separation yet. Good and bad are now all mingled together in the visible church of Christ. Believers and unbelievers — converted and unconverted — holy and unholy — all are to be found now among those who call themselves Christians. They sit side by side in our churches. They kneel side by side in prayer. They listen side by side to our sermons. They sit side by side at the Lord's Table and receive the same bread and wine from our hands.

But it will not always be so. Christ will come the second time with his winnowing fork in his hand. He will purge his church, even as he purified the temple. And then the wheat and the chaff will be separated, and each will go to its own place.

No separation now

Before Christ comes *separation is impossible.* It is not in man's power to make the separation. There is no minister on earth who can read the hearts of every person in his congregation. He may speak decidedly about some, but not everyone. Who has oil in their lamps, and who has not; who has grace as well as profession, and who has profession only and no grace; who are the children of God, and who are the children of the devil — all these are questions that in many cases we cannot accurately answer. The winnowing fork was not put into our hands.

There are some Christians whose grace is sometimes so weak and feeble that they look like unbelievers. Unbelievers sometimes are so convincing and well dressed that they look like Christians. I believe that many of us would have said that Judas was as good as any of the Apostles; and yet he proved to be a traitor. I believe that we would have said that Peter was a reprobate when he denied his Lord; and yet he repented immediately. We are fallible men. 'For we know in part and we prophesy in part' (1 Corinthians 13:9). We scarcely understand our own hearts. Is it any great wonder that we cannot read the hearts of others?

But it will not always be this way. There is one coming who never makes a mistake in judgement and is perfect in knowledge. Jesus will purge his floor. Jesus will sift the chaff from the wheat. I wait for this. Till then I will lean to the side of love in my judgements. I would rather tolerate a lot of chaff in the church than to cast out one grain of wheat. He will soon come with 'his winnowing fork in his hand', and then everyone's identity will be known.

No perfect church now

Before Christ comes *it is useless to expect to see a perfect church.* There cannot be a perfect church. In this life the wheat and the chaff will always be found together. I pity those who leave one church and join another because of a few faults and questionable members. I pity them because they are fostering ideas that can never be realized. I pity them because they are seeking something that cannot be found. I see 'chaff' everywhere. I see imperfections and weaknesses in every congregation on earth. I believe there are only a few communion tables of the Lord, if any, where all the communicants are converted. I often see loud-talking Christians exalted as saints. I often see holy and contrite believers looked upon as having no grace at all. I believe that those who demand a perfect church will go fluttering about, like Noah's dove, all their days, and never find rest.

Do any of my readers desire a perfect church? You must wait for the second coming of Christ. Then, and not until then, you will see 'a glorious church, not having spot or wrinkle or any such thing' (Ephesians 5:27). Then, and not until then, the threshing floor will be purged.

No conversion of the world

Before Christ returns *it is vain to look for the conversion of the world.* How can the whole world be converted, if the Bible says that Christ will find wheat and chaff growing side by side in the day of his Second Coming? I believe some Christians expect missions to fill the earth with the knowledge of Christ, and that in time sin will disappear and a state of perfect holiness will gradually be manifest. I cannot agree with them. I think they are mistaking God's purposes, and sowing for themselves bitter disappointment. I expect nothing of the kind. I see nothing in the Bible or in the world around me to make me expect it. I have never heard of a single congregation in all of England or Scotland, which was entirely converted to God — so why am I to look for a different result from the preaching of the gospel in other countries of the world? I only expect to see a few raised up as witnesses to Christ in other nations, some in one place and some in another. Then I expect the Lord Jesus will come in glory with his winnowing fork in his hand. And when he has purged his floor, and not until then, his kingdom will begin.

No separation and no perfection until Christ comes! This is my creed. I am not moved when the unbeliever asks me, 'How can Christianity be true if the whole world is not converted?' I answer, 'It was never promised that the whole world would be saved before the return of Christ.' The Bible tells me that believers will always be few in number, that evil and divisions and heresies will always abound, and that when my Lord returns to earth he will find plenty of chaff.

No perfection until Christ comes! I am not disturbed when men say, 'You must make all the people good Christians at home before you send missionaries to the heathen abroad.' I answer, 'If I am to wait for that, I may wait for ever.' When we have done all that we can at home, the church will still be a mixed body — it will contain some wheat and a lot of chaff.

But Christ will come again. Sooner or later there will be a separation of the visible church into two companies — that will be a fearful separation. The wheat will make up one company. The chaff will make up another. The one company will be all godly. The other company will be all ungodly. Each will be by themselves, and a great gulf will exist between them that no one can cross. Blessed indeed will the righteous be in that day! They will shine like stars, no longer obscured with clouds. They will be beautiful as the lily, no longer choked with thorns (Song of Solomon 2:2). The wretched will be most ungodly! How corrupt will corruption be when left without one grain of salt to season it! How dark will darkness be when left without one spark of light! No, it is not enough to respect and admire the

Lord's people! You must belong to them, or you will one day be separated from them for ever. There will be no chaff in heaven. There are many, many families where one will be taken and the other left (Luke 17:34).

Who among my readers sincerely loves the Lord Jesus Christ? If I know anything of the heart of a Christian, you experience your greatest trials when you are in the company of worldly people, and you experience your greatest joys when in the company of the saints. Yes! There are many days when your spirit feels broken and crushed by the 'worldliness' of all those around you — days when you could cry out with David, 'Woe is me, that I dwell in Meshech, that I dwell among the tents of Kedar!' (Psalm 120:5). And yet there are hours when your soul is so refreshed and revived by meeting some of God's dear children that it seems like heaven on earth. Am I not speaking to your heart? Are these things not true? Then you should long for the time when Christ will return. You should pray daily that the Lord would expedite his coming kingdom, and say to him, 'Come, Lord Jesus!' (Revelation 22:20). Then, and only then, will there be a pure unmixed communion. Then, and only then, will the saints all be together and will not go out from one another's presence again. Wait a little while. Wait a little while. Scorn and contempt will soon be over. Laughter and ridicule will soon be ended. Slander and misrepresentation will soon cease. Your Saviour will come and plead your case. And then, as Moses said to Korah, 'the LORD will show who is his' (Numbers 16:5).

This is certain — when the elect are all converted, then Christ will come to judgement. As he that rows a boat stays till all the passengers are taken into his boat, and then he rows away; so Christ stays till all the elect are gathered in, and then he will hasten away to judgement.

Thomas Watson, 1660

Is there anyone among my readers who knows that his heart is not right in the sight of God? You should fear and tremble at the thought of Christ's appearing. Fear, indeed, for anyone who lives and dies with nothing better than a pretext of religion! You will have your true colours exposed in the day that Christ comes and separates the chaff from the wheat. You may deceive ministers, friends and neighbours — but you cannot deceive Christ. The paint and varnish of a heartless Christianity will never stand the fire of that day. The Lord is a God of knowledge, and he will examine and judge every action. You will find that the eye that saw Achan's and Gehazi's sins has also read your secrets and searched out the hidden things of your heart. You will hear that awful word, 'Friend, how did you come in here without a wedding garment?' and you too will be speechless (Matthew 22:12). Oh, tremble at the thought of the day of sifting and separation! Surely hypocrisy is a losing proposition. Surely acting the part of a Christian without its reality will fail. Surely you will suffer like Ananias and Sapphira who pretended to give something to God and yet kept back their heart. It all fails in the end. Your joy will last for only a moment. Your hopes will be no better than a dream. Oh, tremble, tremble: tremble and repent!

The inheritance for Christ's people

Let me show, in the third place, the inheritance that Christ's people will receive when he comes to purge his threshing floor.

Our text tells us, with words of comfort, that Christ will 'gather his wheat into the barn'. When the Lord Jesus comes the second time, he will gather his believing people into a place of safety. He will send his angels and gather them from the four winds. The sea will give up the dead that are in it, and the graves the dead that are in them, and those who are alive will be changed. Not one poor sinner of mankind, who has ever believed in Jesus Christ by faith, will be missing from that company. Not one single grain of wheat will be missing and left outside, when judgements fall upon a wicked world. There will be a barn for the wheat of the earth and all the wheat will be brought into it.

It is a sweet and comfortable thought, that 'the Lord takes pleasure in his people' and 'knows those who trust in him' (Psalm 149:4; Nahum 1:7). But I fear that little is known, and only dimly seen, of exactly how much the Lord cares for them. Beyond question, believers have a great many trials. The flesh is weak. The world is full of snares. The cross is heavy. The way is narrow. The companions are few. But still they have great consolations, if only their eyes were open to see them. Like Hagar, they have a well of water near them, even in the wilderness, though often they do not see it. Like Mary, they have Jesus standing by their side, though often they are not aware of it because of their very tears (Genesis 21:19; John 20:14).

Bear with me while I try to tell you something about Christ's care for poor sinners who believe in him. We live in a day of weak and feeble preaching. The danger of the natural state of man is feebly exposed. The privileges of the state of grace are feebly set forth. Faltering souls are not encouraged. Disciples are not established and confirmed. The man without Christ is not properly alerted. The man in Christ is not properly built up. The one sleeps on and seldom has his conscience pricked. The other creeps and crawls all his days and never thoroughly understands the riches of his inheritance. Truly this is a painful disease, and one that I would gladly help to cure. Truly it is a sad thing that the people of God never go up to mount Pisgah and, therefore, never know the length and breadth of their possessions. To be brethren of Christ and sons of God by adoption; to have full and perfect forgiveness and the renewing of the Holy Spirit; to have a place in the book of life and a name on the breastplate of the Great High Priest in heaven — all these are truly glorious things. But still they are not everything that the believer will receive.

Loves his people

The Lord takes pleasure in his believing people. Though stained and spotted in their own eyes, they are beautiful and honourable in his. They are all lovely. He sees 'no spot' in them (Song of Solomon 4:7). Their weaknesses and shortcomings do not break off the union between him and them. He chose them, knowing everything in their hearts. He took them for his own, with a perfect understanding of all their debts, liabilities and weaknesses, and he will never break his covenant and cast them off. When they fall, he will raise them up again. When they wander, he will bring them back. Their prayers are pleasant to him. As a father loves the first stammering efforts of his child to speak, so the Lord loves the poor feeble petitions of his people. He endorses them with his own mighty intercession and gives them power on high. Their acts of service are pleasant to him. As a father delights in the first daisy that his child picks and brings him, so the Lord is pleased with the weak attempts of his people to serve him. Not a single cup of cold water will ever lose its reward. Not a word spoken in love will ever be forgotten. The Holy Spirit inspired the writer of Hebrews to tell of Noah's faith, but not of his drunkenness — of Rahab's faith, but not of her lie. It is a blessed thing to be God's wheat!

In life

The Lord cares for his believing people in their lives. Their dwelling place is well known. The street called 'Straight' where Judas lived, and Paul lodged — the house by the seaside where Peter prayed, were all familiar to their Lord. No one has such attendants as they have: angels rejoice when they are born again; angels minister to them; and angels encamp around them. No one has such food — their bread is given them and their water is sure, and they have meat to eat that the world knows nothing about. No one has such company as they have: the Holy Spirit lives within them; the Father and the Son come to them and make their home with them (John 14:23). Their steps are all ordered from grace to glory: those who persecute them persecute Christ himself, and those who hurt them hurt the apple of the Lord's eye. A wise Physician measures out all their trials and temptations: not a grain of bitterness is ever mingled in their cup that is not good for the health of their souls. Their temptations, like Job's, are all under God's control. Satan cannot touch a hair of their head without their Lord's permission, nor even tempt them above that which they will be able to bear. 'As a father pities his children, so the LORD pities those who fear him.' 'He does not afflict willingly, nor grieve the children of men' (Psalm 103:13; Lamentations 3:33). He leads them down the right path. He withholds nothing that would be for their good. Come what may, any pain they receive will always be necessary. When they are placed in the furnace, it is so that they may be purified. When they are chastened, it is so that they may become more holy. When they are pruned, it is to make them more fruitful. When they are transplanted from place to place, it is that they may bloom more brightly. All things are continually working together for their good. Like the bee, they extract sweetness even out of the bitterest flowers.

In death

The Lord cares for his believing people in their deaths. Their times are all in the Lord's hand. The hairs of their heads are all numbered and not one can ever fall to the ground without their Father's permission. They are kept on earth until they are ripe and ready for glory and not one moment longer. When they have had enough sun and rain, enough wind and storm, enough cold and heat — when the fruit is ripe — then, and not until then, they are harvested. They are all immortal until their work is done. There is not a disease that can take their lives until the Lord gives the word. A thousand may fall at their right hand, but there is not a plague that can touch them till the Lord sees fit. There is not a physician who can keep them alive when the Lord gives the word to bring them home. When they come to their deathbed, the everlasting arms are wrapped around them. When they die, they die like Moses, 'according to the word of the LORD', and at the right time, and in the right way (Deuteronomy 34:5). And when they breathe their last, they fall asleep in Christ and are immediately carried, like Lazarus, to Abraham's bosom. Yes! It is a blessed thing to be Christ's wheat! When the sun of other men is setting, the sun of the believer is rising. When other men are laying aside their honours, he is putting his on. Death locks the door on the unbeliever and shuts him out from hope; but death opens the door to the believer and lets him into paradise.

When he appears

The Lord will care for his believing people in the dreadful day of his appearing. The flaming fire will not come near them. The voice of the Archangel and the trumpet of God will not proclaim any terrors to their ears. Sleeping or waking, alive or dead, decomposing in the coffin, or going about their daily duties — believers will be secure and immovable. They will lift up their heads with joy when they see redemption drawing near. They will be changed and will put on their beautiful heavenly robes in the twinkling of an eye. They will be caught up 'to meet the Lord in the air' (1 Thessalonians 4:17). Jesus will do nothing to a sin-laden world till all his people are safe. There was an ark for Noah when the flood began. There was the town of Zoar for Lot to flee to when the fire fell on Sodom. There was a place of refuge for early Christians when Jerusalem was besieged. There was a Zurich for English Reformers when Mary, a supporter of Roman Catholicism, came to the throne. And there will be a safe and secure barn for all the wheat of the earth on the last day. Yes! It is a blessed thing to be Christ's wheat!

I often wonder at the miserable faithlessness of those of us who are believers. Next to the hardness of the unconverted heart, I call it one of the greatest wonders in the world. I am amazed that with such mighty reasons for confidence we can still be so full of doubts. I marvel, above all things, how any can deny the doctrine that Christ's people persevere to the end, and can imagine that he who loved them so much that he died for them upon the cross will ever abandon them. I do not think it possible. I do not believe the Lord Jesus will ever lose one of his flock. He will not let Satan pluck away from him so much as one sick lamb. He will not allow one bone of his mystical body to be broken. He will not allow one jewel to fall from his crown. He and his bride have been joined into an everlasting covenant and they will never, never be put asunder. The trophies won by earthly conquerors have often been wrested from them and carried off; but this will never be said of the trophies of the one who triumphed for us on the cross. 'My sheep...' he says, 'shall never perish' (John 10:28). I take my stand on that text. I do not know how it can be evaded. If words have any meaning then for sure, the perseverance of Christ's people is there.

I do not believe that when David had rescued the lamb from the paws of the lion, that he left it weak and wounded to perish in the wilderness. I cannot believe that when the Lord Jesus has delivered a soul from the snare of the devil that he will ever leave that soul to take his chances and wrestle on in his own feebleness, against sin, the devil and the world.

I am absolutely positive that if you were present at a shipwreck and saw some helpless child tossed on the waves, that you would plunge into the sea and save him at the risk of your own life. I am absolutely positive that you would not be content with merely bringing that child safely to shore. You would not lay him down when you had reached the land, and say, 'I will do no more. He is weak — he is unconscious — he is cold: it does not matter. I have done enough — I have delivered him from the waters: he is not drowned.' You would not do it. You would not say such things. You would not treat that child in such a manner. You would lift him in your arms; you would carry him to the nearest house; you would use every means to restore his health and vigour: you would never leave him until his recovery was certain.

Now, do you suppose the Lord Jesus Christ is less merciful and less compassionate? Do you think he would suffer on the cross and die and yet leave it uncertain whether believers in him would be saved? Do you think he would wrestle with death and hell and go down to the grave for our sakes, and yet allow our eternal life to hang on such a thread as our poor miserable endeavours?

Oh, no! He does not do it that way! He is a perfect and complete Saviour. Those whom he loves, he loves to the end. Those whom he washes in his blood, he never leaves nor forsakes. He puts his fear into their hearts so that they will not depart from him. Where he begins a work, there he also finishes. All whom he plants in his garden on earth, he transplants sooner or later into paradise. All whom he revives by his Spirit, he will also bring with him when he enters his kingdom. There is a barn for every grain of wheat. All will appear before God in Zion.

Man may fall from false grace. I never doubted this. I see proof of it continually. Men never fall from true grace. They never did, and they never will. If they commit sin, like Peter, they will repent and rise up again. If they stray from the right path, like David, they will be brought back. It is not their own strength or power that keeps them from apostasy. They are kept secure because of the power and love, and promises of the Trinity. The election of God the Father will not be fruitless;

the intercession of God the Son will not be ineffectual; the love of God the Holy Spirit will not labour in vain. The Lord 'will guard the feet of his saints' (1 Samuel 2:9). They will all be more than conquerors through him who loved them. They all will conquer, and none will die eternally.

> Blessed forever and ever is that mother's child whose faith has made him the child of God. The earth may shake, the pillars of the world may tremble under us, the countenance of the heaven may be horrified, the sun may lose its light, the moon its beauty, the stars their glory: but concerning the man that trusts in God — what is there in the world that will change his heart, overthrow his faith, alter his affection towards God, or the affection of God to him?

> *Richard Hooker, 1585*

If you have not yet taken up the cross and become Christ's disciple, then you have little idea of the privileges you are missing. Peace with God now and glory in the future; the ever-lasting arms to guide and protect you on your way to heaven and the shelter of safety in the end — all these are freely offered to you without money and without cost. You may say that Christians have trials — you forget that they also have comforts. You may say they have unique sorrows — you forget they also have unique joys. You only see half of the Christian life. You do not see everything. You see the warfare but not the daily sustenance and the rewards. You see the struggles and conflicts of the outward part of Christianity but you do not see the hidden treasures that lie deep within. Like Elisha's servant you see the enemies of God's children but you do not, like Elisha, see the chariots and horses of fire that protect them. Oh, do not judge by outward appearances! Be sure that the smallest drop of the 'water of life' is better than all the rivers of the world. Remember the place of shelter and the crown. Be wise as you live on this earth.

If you feel that you are a weak disciple, then do not think that weakness shuts you out from any of the privileges I have been speaking about. Weak faith is true faith, and weak grace is true grace and both are a gift from the one who never gives in vain. Do not fear and do not be discouraged. Do not doubt, nor despair. 'A bruised reed he will not break, and smoking flax he will not quench' (Isaiah 42:3). The infants in a family are as much loved and thought of as the elder brothers and sisters. The tender seedlings in a garden are as diligently looked after as the old trees. The lambs in the flock are as carefully tended by the good shepherd as the old sheep. Oh, rest assured, it is just the same in Christ's family, in Christ's garden, in Christ's flock! All are loved. All are tenderly thought of. All are cared for. And in the end all will be found in his barn.

What remains for all who are not Christ's people

Let me show in the last place, the portion that remains for all who are not Christ's people.

The text at the beginning of this chapter describes this in words that should make our ears tingle: Christ will 'burn up the chaff with unquenchable fire'. When the Lord Jesus Christ comes to clear his floor he will punish all who are not his disciples with a fearful punishment. All who are found to be unrepentant and unbelieving; all who have suppressed the truth by their wickedness; all who have clung to sin, loved the world, and set their affections on things below; all who are without Christ — all of them will come to an awful end. Christ will 'burn up the chaff'.

Their punishment will be *most severe*. There is no pain like that of burning. If you doubt this, then put your finger in the flame of a candle for a moment. Fire is the most destructive and devouring of all elements. Look into the mouth of a blast furnace and think what it would be like to be in there. Of all elements, fire is the most opposed to life. Creatures can live in air, and earth, and water; but nothing can live in fire. Yet fire is the doom to which the Christless and the unbelieving will come. Christ will 'burn up the chaff with fire'.

Their punishment will be *eternal*. Millions of ages will pass away and the fire into which the chaff is thrown will still burn on. That fire will never burn low and become dim. The fuel of that fire will never be consumed. It is 'unquenchable fire'.

These are sad and painful things to speak of! I have no pleasure in dwelling on them. I would rather say, with the apostle Paul, as I write, 'I have great sorrow and continual grief in my heart' (Romans 9:2). But they are things written for our learning and it is good to consider them. They are a part of that Scripture which is 'profitable', and they ought to be heard. Painful as the subject of hell is, it is one about which I dare not, cannot, and must not be silent. Who would desire to speak of the fires of hell if God had not spoken of it? When God has spoken so plainly about it, then who can safely keep from speaking of it?

I dare not shut my eyes to the fact that a deep-rooted indifference lurks in men's minds on the subject of hell. I see it oozing out in the utter apathy of some: they eat, and drink, and sleep, as if there was no wrath to come. I see it creeping forth in the coldness of others about their neighbours' souls: they show little anxiety to snatch the burning sticks from the fire. I denounce such indifference with all my might; believing that there are 'terrors of the Lord', as well as the 'giving of rewards', I call on all who profess to believe the Bible to be on their guard.

I know that some *do not believe that hell exists*. They think it impossible there can be such a place. They call it inconsistent with the mercy of God. They say it is too awful an idea to be really true. The devil, of course, rejoices in the views of such people. They help his kingdom greatly. They are preaching his own favourite doctrine: 'You will not surely die' (Genesis 3:4).

Furthermore, I know that some *do not believe that hell is eternal.* They tell us it is incredible that a compassionate God will punish men for ever; he will surely open the prison doors some day. This also is a great assistance to the devil's cause. 'Take it easy,' he whispers to sinners: 'if you do make a mistake, never mind, it is not for ever.' A wicked woman was overheard in the streets of London, saying to an evil companion, 'Come along: do not be afraid. In fact, some preachers say there is no hell.'

I also know that some *do believe there is a hell, but do not believe that anybody is going there.* They believe that every-one, along with they themselves, are declared and made 'good' as soon as they die, because all were sincere, all meant well, and all, they hope, made it to heaven. Oh, what a common delusion this is! I can clearly understand the feeling of the little girl who asked her mother where all the wicked people were buried, 'because all the gravestones in the cemetery say that these were good people'.

And I know very well that some *believe there is a hell but never like it to be spoken of.* In their opinion, it is a subject that should always be avoided. They see no profit in bringing it up and are rather shocked when it is mentioned. This also is an immense aid to the devil. 'Quiet, quiet!' says Satan, 'Say nothing about hell.' The hunter does not want to make any noise when he sets his traps. The wolf would like the shepherd to stay asleep while he prowls around the fold. The devil rejoices when Chris-tians are silent about hell.

All these notions are the opinions of man. But what does it matter to you and me what man thinks about religion? Man will not judge us at the last day. Man's thoughts and traditions are not to be our guide in this life. There is only one point to be settled: 'What does the Word of God say?'

Hell is real and true

Do you believe the Bible? Then depend upon it, hell is real and true.

It is as true as heaven; as true as justification by faith; as true as the fact that Christ died on the cross; as true as the Dead Sea. If you doubt hell, then there is no fact or doctrine in the Bible that you cannot also doubt. Disbelieve hell and you unscrew and unsettle everything in Scripture. You may as well throw your Bible away, for there are only a few steps from 'no hell' to 'no God'.

Hell will have inhabitants

Do you believe the Bible? Then depend upon it, hell will have inhabitants.

The wicked will certainly be sent to hell, and all the people who forget God. 'These will go away into everlasting punishment' (Matthew 25:46). The same blessed Saviour who now sits on a throne of grace will one day sit on a throne of judgement, and men will see that there is such a thing as 'the wrath of the Lamb' (Revelation 6:16). The same lips that now say, 'Come: come to me!' will one day say, 'Depart from me, you who are cursed!' How awful the thought of being condemned by Christ himself, judged by the Saviour, and sentenced to misery by the Lamb!

Hell will be an intense and unutterable misery

Do you believe the Bible? Then depend upon it, hell will be an intense and unutterable misery.

It is vain to talk of all the expressions of hell as only being figures of speech. The pit, the prison, the maggot, the fire, the thirst, the blackness, the darkness, the weeping, the gnashing of teeth, the second death — all these may be figures of speech if you please. But beyond all doubt, figures of speech, in the Bible, mean something, and here they mean something which man's mind can never fully understand. The anguish of mind and conscience are far worse than those of the body. The whole extent of hell — the present suffering, the bitter recollection of the past, the hopeless prospect of the future — will never be thoroughly known except by those who go there.

Hell is eternal

Do you believe the Bible? Then depend upon it, hell is eternal.

It must be eternal or words have no meaning at all. For ever and ever — everlasting — unquenchable — eternal — all these are expressions used about hell that cannot be explained away. It must be eternal or the very foundations of heaven are destroyed. If hell has an end, heaven has an end too. They both stand or fall together. It must be eternal or else every doctrine of the gospel is undermined. If a man without faith in Christ or without the sanctification of the Spirit can escape hell, then sin is no longer an infinite evil and there was no great need for Christ to make an atonement. And where in the Bible is there warrant for saying that hell can ever change a heart or make it fit for heaven? It must be eternal or hell would cease to be hell altogether. Give a man hope, and he will bear anything. Grant a hope of deliverance, however distant, and hell is but a drop of water. Oh, these are solemn things! It has been well said, that, 'For ever is the most solemn saying in the Bible.' For a day in hell will have no tomorrow. It will be a place where men will seek death and not find it, and will desire to die, but death will flee from them! 'Who among us shall dwell with the devouring fire? Who among us shall dwell with everlasting burnings?' (Revelation 9:6; Isaiah 33:14).

Hell is a subject that ought not to be kept back

Do you believe the Bible? Then depend upon it, hell is a subject that ought not to be kept back.

It is obvious to note the many texts about hell in the Scriptures. It is interesting to observe that no one said so much about hell as did our Lord Jesus Christ, that gracious and merciful Saviour, and the apostle John, whose heart seems full of love. Truly, it is doubtful whether we ministers speak of it as much as we ought. I cannot forget the words of a dying person to his minister, 'Sir, you often told me of Christ and salvation, but why didn't you often remind me of hell and danger?'

Let others hold their peace about hell if they will — I dare not do so. I see it plainly in Scripture and I must speak of it. I fear that thousands are on that broad road that leads to it, and I would willingly arouse them to a sense of the peril before them. What would you say of the man who saw his neighbour's house on fire and never raised his voice and cried out, 'Fire!'? What would be said about us as ministers, who call ourselves watchmen of souls, but see the fires of hell raging in the distance, and never give the alarm? Call it bad taste, if you like, to speak of hell. Call it love to speak about pleasant things, and speak smoothly, and soothe men with a constant lullaby of peace. May I always be delivered from such notions of taste and love! My notion of love is to warn men plainly of danger. My notion of taste in the ministerial office is to declare the whole counsel of God. If I never spoke of hell, I would be holding something back that was profitable, and would look on myself as an accomplice of the devil.

I implore, with all tender affection, everyone reading this to beware of false views of the subject that I have been dwelling on. Beware of new and strange doctrines about hell and eternal punishment. Beware of manufacturing a God of your own

— a God who is all mercy, but not just — a God who is all love, but not holy — a God who has a heaven for everybody, but a hell for none — a God who can allow good and bad to exist side by side on earth, and will make no distinction between good and bad in eternity. Such a God is an idol of your own creation as real as Jupiter or Moloch — as true an idol as any snake or crocodile in an Egyptian temple—as true an idol as ever was moulded out of brass or clay. The hands of your own notions and emotions have made him. He is not the God of the Bible; and aside from the God of the Bible there is no God at all. Your heaven would be no heaven at all. A heaven containing all sorts of indiscriminate characters would surely be a place of miserable discord. Oh, what a miserable eternity such a heaven would be — there would be little difference between it and hell! There is a hell! There is a fire for the chaff! Be careful that you do not find it out too late — to your own loss.

Beware of thinking yourself wiser than that which is written in God's Word. Beware of forming fanciful theories of your own, and then trying to make the Bible agree with them. Beware of taking selections from the Bible to suit your taste — refusing, like a spoiled child, whatever you think might taste bitter — grabbing, like a spoiled child, whatever you think might be sweet. What is all of this but the same as taking Jehoiakim's penknife and cutting out portions of Scripture and throwing them into the fire? (Jeremiah 36:23). What does it amount to but telling God that you, a poor short-lived worm, know better than he what is good for you. It will not do: it will not do. You must take the Bible as it is. You must read it all and believe it all. You must read it with the spirit of a little child. Do not dare to say, 'I believe this verse, because I like it. I reject that one, because I don't like it. I accept this verse, for I can understand it. I refuse that one, for I cannot reconcile it with my views.' May this never be! 'But indeed, O man, who are you to reply against God?' (Romans 9:20). By what right do you talk in this way?

Surely it would be better to say over every chapter in the Word, 'Speak, LORD, for your servant is listening.' If men would do this, then they would never deny hell, the chaff and the fire.

Conclusion

And now, let me say four things in conclusion, and then I will be done. I have shown the two great classes of mankind, the wheat and the chaff. I have shown the separation that will one day take place. I have shown the safety of the Lord's people. I have shown the fearful fate of the unbelievers — those without Christ. In the sight of God, I urge these things on the conscience of every reader.

These things are real and true

First of all, be convinced in your own mind that the things of which I have been speaking are real and true.

I do believe that many never see the great truths of religion in this light. I firmly believe that many never listen to the things they hear from ministers as realities. They regard it all as nothing but 'names and words', and nothing more; a huge shadow — a formal acting part — an immense sham. The latest novel, the most recent news from France, India, Australia, Turkey, or New York — all these are things they comprehend: they feel interested and excited about them. But as to the Bible, and heaven, and the kingdom of Christ, and the Judgement Day — these are subjects that do not affect their hearts: they do not really believe them. If an archaeologist had dug up anything at the excavation of Nineveh that would damage the truth and authority of the Old Testament Scriptures, it would not have interfered with their peace for one moment.

If this is your frame of mind, then I ask you to cast it off for ever. Awaken to a thorough conviction that the things I have brought before you here are real and true. The wheat, the chaff, the separation, the barn, the fire — all these are great realities — as real as the sun in heaven, as real as the paper that your eyes see. For me, I believe in heaven, and I believe in hell. I believe in a coming judgement. I believe in a day of sifting. I am not ashamed to say so. I believe them all, and therefore write as I do. Oh, take a friend's advice — live as if these things were true.

They concern you personally

In the second place, be convinced in your own mind that the things I write about concern you personally. They are your business, your affair, and your concern.

Many, I believe, never look on religion as a matter that concerns them. They are careful to attend to its outward form in a decent and proper fashion. They listen to sermons. They read religious books. They have their children christened. But all the while they never ask themselves, 'What does all of this really mean to me?' They sit in our churches like spectators in a theatre or a court of law. They read our writings as if they were reading a report of an interesting trial, or of some event far away. But they never say to themselves, 'I am the man.'

If you have this kind of feeling, then you can depend on it, that will never do. All of this thinking must come to an end if you are ever to be saved. I write to whoever is reading this — you are that person. I do not write especially to the rich. I do not write especially to the poor. I write to everybody who will read, whatever his rank may be. It is because of your very soul that I am pleading, not another's. You are the one spoken of in the verse at the beginning of this chapter. You are this very day either among the 'wheat' or among the 'chaff'. Your destiny will one day either be the barn or the fire. Oh, if only men were wise, and would take these things to heart! Oh, that they would not trifle, dally, linger, or live on as false Christians, meaning well, but never acting boldly and finally, realizing in the end that it is too late!

The Lord Jesus Christ is willing to receive you

In the third place, be convinced in your mind that if you are willing to be one of the wheat of the earth, then the Lord Jesus Christ is willing to receive you.

Does anyone suppose that Jesus is not willing to see his barn filled? Do you think he does not desire to bring many to glory? Oh, if you can think such a thought then you know very little of the depth of his mercy and compassion! He wept over unbelieving Jerusalem. He mourns over the unrepentant and the indifferent in the present day. He sends you invitations by my words this very hour. He invites you to hear and live, to forsake the way of the foolish and go down the path of understanding. The sovereign Lord declares, 'I have no pleasure in the death of one who dies. Therefore turn and live!' (Ezekiel 18:32).

Oh, if you never came to Christ for life before, come to him this very day! Come to him with the repentant sinners' prayer for mercy and grace. Come to him without delay. Come to him while the subject of this chapter is still fresh in your mind. Come to him before another sun rises on the earth, and let the morning find you a new creature.

If you are determined to have the world and the things of the world, its pleasures and its rewards, its follies and its sins; if you must have your own way, and cannot give up anything for Christ and your soul; if this is your situation, there is but one end for you. I honestly warn you — I tell you plainly: you will sooner or later be thrown into the eternal fire.

But if any man is willing to be saved, the Lord Jesus Christ stands ready to save him. 'Come to me,' he says, 'all you who labour and are heavy laden, and I will give you rest.' Oh, come, guilty and sinful soul, and I will give you free pardon. Come, lost and ruined soul, and I will give you eternal life (Matthew 11:28).

Let that passage be a timely word to your soul. Wake up and call on the Lord. Let the angels of God rejoice over one more saved soul. Let the courts of heaven hear the good news that one more lost sheep is found.

Christ will never allow your soul to perish

Last of all, be convinced in your mind that if you have committed your soul to Christ, then Christ will never allow your soul to perish.

The everlasting arms are around you. Lean back in them and know your safety. The same hand that was nailed to the cross is holding you. The same wisdom that created the heavens and the earth is engaged to maintain your cause. The same power that redeemed the twelve tribes from the house of bondage is on your side. The same love that sustained and carried Israel from Egypt to Canaan is pledged to keep you. Yes! Those whom Christ keeps are well kept! Our faith may rest calmly on such a bed as Christ's omnipotence. Take comfort, doubting believer. Why are you downcast? The love of Jesus is not shallow water: no man has ever yet seen its bottom. The compassion of Jesus is a fire that never yet burned low: the cold, grey ashes of that fire have never yet been seen. Take comfort. In your own heart you may find little cause for rejoicing, but you may always rejoice in the Lord.

You say your faith is small. But where is it said that none will be saved except those whose faith is great? And after all, 'Who gave you this faith?' The very fact that you have any faith at all is a sign of God's grace.

You say you have too many sins. But where is the sin or the heap of sins that the blood of Jesus cannot wash away? After all, 'Who told you that you had any sins?' That feeling never came from you. Greatly blessed is the person who really knows and feels that he is a sinner.

I say once more, take comfort, if you have truly come to Christ. Take comfort, and know your privileges. Cast every care on Jesus. Tell your every want to Jesus. Roll every burden onto Jesus: sins — unbelief — doubts — fears — anxieties — lay them all on Christ. He loves to see you do so. He loves to be employed as your High Priest. He loves to be trusted. He loves to see his people ceasing from the vain effort to carry their burdens for themselves.

I commend these things to the notice of every one into whose hands this book may fall. Be among Christ's 'wheat' now, and then in the great day of separation, as sure as the Bible is true, you will be in Christ's 'barn' for ever.

21.

Eternity!

'For the things which are seen are temporary, but the things which are not seen are eternal'
(2 Corinthians 4:18).

A subject stands out on the face of this text that is one of the most solemn and heart-searching in the Bible. That subject is eternity.

The subject is one that the wisest man can only take in a little at a time. We have no eyes to see it fully, and no mind to grasp it; and yet we must not refuse to consider it. There is a depth of stars in the heavens above us, which the most powerful telescope cannot pierce; yet it is well worth it to look into them and learn something, even if we cannot learn everything. There are heights and depths about the subject of eternity that mortal man can never comprehend; but God has spoken of it, and we have no right to turn away from it completely.

The subject is one that we must never approach without the Bible in our hands. The moment we depart from 'God's written Word' in considering eternity and the future state of man, we are likely to fall into error. In examining points like these we must have nothing to do with preconceived notions as to what God's character is like, and what we think God ought to be, or ought to do with man after death. We only have to find out what is written. What does the Scripture say? What does the Lord say? It is foolish to tell us that we ought to have 'noble thoughts about God', independent of, and over and above, Scripture. The noblest thoughts about God, which we have a right to hold, are the thoughts that he has been pleased to reveal to us in his 'written Word'.

I ask for the attention of everyone into whose hands this publication may fall, while I offer a few thoughts about eternity. As a mortal man, I deeply feel my own insufficiency to handle this subject. But I pray that God the Holy Spirit, whose strength is made perfect in weakness, may bless the words I speak, and make them seeds of eternal life in many minds.

Everything is temporal

The first thought that I bring to your attention is that we live in a world where all things are temporary and passing away. Surely, a man who cannot realize this must be blind. Everything around us is decaying, dying and coming to an end. There is a sense, no doubt, in which 'matter' is eternal. Once created, it will never entirely cease to exist. But in a popular practical sense, everything about us is dying except our souls. No wonder the poet says:

Change and decay all around me I see:
O You who does not change, abide with me!

We are all going, going, going, whether eminent or unimportant, gentle or cruel, rich or poor, old or young. We are all going and will soon be gone.

Beauty is only temporary. Sarah was once the fairest of women, and the admiration of the Court of Egypt; yet a day came when even Abraham, her husband, said, 'Give me property for a burial place among you, that I may bury my dead out of my sight' (Genesis 23:4). Strength of the body is only temporary. David was once a mighty man of valour, the slayer of the lion and the bear, and the champion of Israel against Goliath; yet a day came when even David had to be nursed and ministered to in his old age like a child. Wisdom and power of the brain are only temporary. Solomon was once a marvel of knowledge, and all the kings of the earth came to hear his wisdom, yet even Solomon in his latter days played the fool, and allowed his wives to 'turn away [their] hearts after their gods' (1 Kings 11:2).

Humbling and painful as these truths may sound, it is good for all of us to realize them and take them to heart. The houses we live in, the homes we love, the riches we accumulate, the professions we follow, the plans we formulate, the relations we enter into — they are only for a time. 'The things which are seen are temporary.' 'The form of this world is passing away' (2 Corinthians 4:18; 1 Corinthians 7:31).

The thought is one that ought to awaken everyone who is living only for this world. If his conscience is not completely seared, it should stir in him a great searching of his heart. Oh, be careful what you are doing! Awake to see things in their true light before it is too late. The things you live for now are all temporary and passing away. The pleasures, the amusements, the recreations, the profits, the earthly callings, which now absorb all your heart and drink up your entire mind, will soon be over. They are poor fleeting things that cannot last. Oh, do not love them too much; do not hold on to them too tightly; do not make them your idols! You cannot keep them, and you must leave them. Seek first the kingdom of God, and then everything else will be given to you. 'Set your minds on things above, not on things on the earth.' Oh, you who love the world, get wisdom! Never, never forget that it is written, 'The world is passing away and the lust of it; but he who does the will of God abides for ever' (Colossians 3:2; 1 John 2:17).

The same thought ought to cheer and comfort every true Christian. Your trials, crosses and conflicts are all temporary.

They will soon come to an end; and even now they are working for you 'a far more exceeding and eternal weight of glory' (2 Corinthians 4:17). Receive them patiently; bear them quietly; look upward, forward, onward, and far beyond them. Fight your daily fight under a steadfast conviction that it is only for a little while, and rest is not far off. Carry your daily cross always remembering that 'what is seen is temporary'. The cross will soon be exchanged for a crown, and you will sit down with Abraham, Isaac and Jacob in the kingdom of God.

Everything is eternal

The second thought that I bring to your attention is that we are all moving towards a world where everything is eternal. That great unseen state of existence, which lies beyond the grave, is for ever. Whether it is happy or miserable, whether it is a condition of joy or sorrow, we know that in one respect it will be utterly unlike anything in this world — it will be for ever. There will be no change and decay, no end, no goodbye, no mornings and evening, no alteration, and no annihilation. Whatever there is beyond the tomb, when the last trumpet has sounded, and the dead are raised, we know it will be endless, everlasting and eternal. 'What is unseen is eternal.'

We cannot fully realize this condition. The contrast between now and then, between this world and the next, is so very great that our feeble minds cannot grasp it all. How we live our lives in this world brings consequences in the next that are so tremendous that they almost take away our breath, and we shrink back from looking at them. But when the Bible speaks plainly we have no right to turn away from a subject, and with the Bible in our hands we will do well to look at the 'unseen things that are eternal'.

Let us settle it then in our minds, for one thing, that the *future happiness* of those who are saved is eternal. However little we may understand it, it is something that will have no end: it will never cease, never grow old, never decay, and never die. 'In your presence is fulness of joy; at your right hand are pleasures for evermore' (Psalm 16:11). Once they arrive in paradise, the saints of God will never ever leave that wonderful place. Their inheritance 'is incorruptible and undefiled and ... does not fade away'. They will 'receive the crown of glory that does not fade away' (1 Peter 1:4; 5:4). Their warfare is finished; their fight is over; their work is done. 'Never again will they hunger; never again will they thirst.' They are travelling on towards an 'eternal glory that far outweighs' all their struggles; towards a home that will never be broken up, a meeting without a parting, a family gathering without a separation, a day without night. Faith will be swallowed up in sight, and hope in certainty. They will see as they have been seen, and know as they have been known, and 'always be with the Lord'. I am not surprised that the apostle Paul adds, 'Therefore comfort one another with these words' (1 Thessalonians 4:17-18).

For another thing, let us be convinced in our minds, that the *future misery* of the unbelievers who are lost is eternal. I am aware that this is an awful truth, and flesh and blood naturally shrink from the contemplation of it. But I am one of those who believe it is clearly revealed in Scripture, and I dare not keep it back in the pulpit. To my eyes eternal future happiness and eternal future misery appear to stand side by side. I fail to see how you can distinguish the duration of one from the duration of the other. If the joy of the believer is for ever, then the sorrow of the unbeliever is also for ever. If heaven is eternal, likewise so is hell. It may be my ignorance, but I do not know how the conclusion can be avoided.

I cannot reconcile the concept of a 'non-eternal' punishment with the *language of the Bible*. Its advocates talk loudly about

love and kindness, and say that it does not harmonize with the
merciful and compassionate character of God. But what does
the Scripture say? Who ever spoke such loving and merciful
words as our Lord Jesus Christ? Yet his are the lips which three
times over describe the consequence of refusing to repent of
sin, as 'their worm does not die, and the fire is not quenched'.
He is the person who speaks in one sentence of the wicked
going away to 'everlasting punishment', and the righteous to
'eternal life' (Mark 9:43-48; Matthew 25:46).

> If God had intended to have told us that the punishment
> of wicked man shall have no end, the languages wherein
> the Scriptures are written do hardly afford fuller and more
> certain words than those that are used in this case,
> whereby to express a duration without end; and likewise,
> which is almost a peremptory decision of the thing, the
> duration of the punishment of wicked men is in the very
> same sentence expressed by the very same word which
> is used for the duration of happiness of the righteous.[1]

Who does not remember the apostle Paul's words about love?
Yet he is the very Apostle who says the wicked 'shall be punished with everlasting destruction' (2 Thessalonians 1:9). Who
does not know the spirit of love that runs through all John's
Gospel and Epistles? Yet the beloved Apostle is the very writer
in the New Testament who, in the book of Revelation, dwells
most strongly on the reality and eternity of future agony. What
will we say to all these things? Will we be wiser than that which
is written? Will we admit the dangerous principle that words in
Scripture do not mean what they appear to mean? Is it not far
better to put our hands over our mouths and say, 'Whatever
God has written must be true.' 'Even so, Lord God Almighty,
true and righteous are your judgements' (Revelation 16:7).

I cannot reconcile the 'non-eternal' punishment with the *language of our church's own prayer book*. The very first petition

in our matchless litany contains this sentence: 'From everlasting damnation, good Lord, deliver us.' The Catechism teaches every child who learns it that whenever we repeat the Lord's Prayer we desire our heavenly Father to 'keep us from our spiritual enemy and from everlasting death'. Even in the Burial Service we pray at the graveside, 'Deliver us not into the bitter pains of eternal death.' Once more I ask, 'What will we say to these things?' Shall our congregations be taught that even when people live and die in sin we may hope for their happiness after death? Surely the common sense of many of our worshippers would reply that if this is the case then the words of the prayer book mean nothing at all.

I lay no claim to any unusual knowledge of Scripture. I daily feel that I am no more infallible than the Bishop of Rome. But I must speak according to the light that God has given to me; and I do not think I would be doing my duty if I did not raise a warning voice on this subject, and try to put Christians on their guard. About six thousand years ago sin entered into the world by the devil's daring lie: 'You will not surely die' (Genesis 3:4). At the end of six thousand years the great enemy of mankind is still using his old weapon, and trying to persuade men that they may live and die in sin, and yet at some distant time in the future they will finally be saved. Let us not be ignorant of his schemes. Let us walk steadily in the old paths. Let us hold on tight to the old truth, and believe that just as the happiness of the saved is eternal, so also is the misery of the lost.

There is nothing that Satan desires more than that we should believe that he does not exist, and that there is no such a place as hell, and no such things as eternal torments. He whispers all this into our ears, and he rejoices when he hears a layman, and much more when he hears a clergyman, deny these things, for then he hopes to make them and others his victims.[2]

For truth

Let us be faithful because of the truths revealed in Christianity. What was the use of God's Son becoming incarnate, agonizing in Gethsemane, and dying on the cross to make atonement, if men can ultimately be saved without believing on him? Where is the slightest proof that saving faith in Christ's blood can ever be achieved after death? Where is the need of the Holy Spirit, if sinners can enter heaven without conversion and renewal of heart? Where can we find the smallest evidence that after a person dies in an unregenerate state, he can still be born again later, and have a new heart? If a man without faith in Christ or sanctification of the Spirit can escape eternal punishment, then sin is no longer an infinite evil and there was no need for Christ to make atonement.

For holiness and morality

Let us be faithful because of holiness and morality. I can imagine nothing so pleasant to our flesh and blood as the deceptive theory that we may live in sin, and yet escape eternal damnation; and that although we are 'enslaved by all kinds of passions and pleasures' while we are here, we will somehow all eventually get to heaven! Just tell the young man who 'squandered his wealth in wild living' that heaven is available even for those who live and die in sin, and he is never likely to turn from it. Why should he repent and take up the cross, if he can eventually get to heaven without repenting?

For the hopes of God's saints

Finally, let us be faithful because of the common hopes of all God's saints. Let us distinctly understand that every blow struck at eternal punishment is an equally heavy blow at the eternity of heaven's bliss. It is impossible to separate the two things. No ingenious theological definition can divide them. They stand or fall together. The same language is used, the same figures of speech are employed, when the Bible speaks about either condition. Every attack on the duration of hell is also an attack on the duration of heaven. It is true that if we take away the fear of hell from sinners, then we also have taken away our own hope.

I turn from this part of my subject with a deep sense of its painfulness. I strongly agree with Robert M'Cheyne that 'It is a hard subject to handle lovingly.' But I turn from it with an equally deep conviction that if we believe the Bible, then we must never give up anything that it contains. Dear Jesus, deliver us from hard, austere and unmerciful theology! If men are not saved it is because they 'are not willing to come to [Christ]' (John 5:40). But we must not be wise above that which is written. No morbid love of liberality, so called, must induce us to reject anything that God has revealed about eternity. Men sometimes talk exclusively about God's mercy and love and compassion, as if he had no other attributes, and leave out his holiness and his purity, his justice and his unchangeableness, and his hatred of sin. Let us beware of falling into this delusion. It is a growing evil in these last days. Low and inadequate views of the absolute vileness and filthiness of sin, and of the indescribable purity of the eternal God, are fertile sources of error about man's future state. Let us think about the mighty being whom we are subject to, as he himself declared his character to Moses saying, 'And the LORD passed before him and proclaimed, "The LORD, the LORD God, merciful and gracious, longsuffering, and abounding in goodness and truth, keeping mercy for thousands, forgiving iniquity and transgression and sin."' But let us not forget the solemn clause that concludes the sentence: 'by no means clearing the guilty' (Exodus 34:6-7). Unrepented sin is an eternal

evil, and can never cease to be sin; and the one we are subject
to is an eternal God.

The words of Psalm 145 are strikingly beautiful: 'The LORD is
gracious and full of compassion, slow to anger and great in
mercy. The LORD is good to all, and his tender mercies are over
all his works...The LORD upholds all who fall, and raises up all
who are bowed down ... The LORD is righteous in all his ways,
gracious in all his works. The LORD is near to all who call on
him, to all who call upon him in truth ... The LORD preserves all
who love him.' Nothing can exceed the mercifulness of this
language! But what a striking fact it is that the passage goes on
to add the following solemn conclusion: 'But all the wicked he
will destroy' (Psalm 145:8-20).

Our eternal state depends upon our present state

The third thought that I bring to your attention is that our future
state in the unseen world of eternity depends entirely on what
we are in the present.

The life that we live on the earth is short and soon gone. 'We
finish our years like a sigh.' 'What is your life? It is even a vapour that appears for a little time and then vanishes away' (Psalm
90:9; James 4:14). The life that is before us when we leave this
world is an endless eternity, a bottomless sea, and an ocean
without a shore. 'With the Lord one day is as a thousand years,
and a thousand years as one day' (2 Peter 3:8). In that world
there will be no more time. But short as our life is here, and
endless as it will be in eternity, the life we now live will have a
tremendous impact on eternity. Our lot after death depends,
humanly speaking, on what we are while we are alive. It is
written, God 'will render to each one according to his deeds:
eternal life to those who by patient continuance in doing good
seek for glory, honour, and immortality; but to those who are

self-seeking and do not obey the truth, but obey unrighteousness — indignation and wrath' (Romans 2:6-8).

We must never forget that every one of us, while we live, are in a state of probation. We are constantly sowing seeds that will spring up and bear fruit, every day and every hour of our lives. There are eternal consequences resulting from all our thoughts and words and actions, which we pay too little attention to. 'For every idle word men may speak, they will give account of it in the day of judgement' (Matthew 12:36). Our thoughts are all numbered; our actions are weighed. No wonder that Paul says, 'For he who sows to his flesh will of the flesh reap corruption, but he who sows to the Spirit will of the Spirit reap everlasting life' (Galatians 6:8). In a word, what we sow in life we will reap after death, and reap throughout all eternity.

There is no greater delusion than the common idea that it is possible to live wickedly, and yet rise again gloriously — to be without Christ in this world, and yet to be a saint in the next. When that great preacher George Whitefield revived the doctrine of conversion, in the eighteenth century, it is reported that one of his listeners came to him after a sermon and said, 'It is all quite true, sir. I hope I will be converted and born again one day, but not till after I am dead.' I fear there are many like him. I fear the false doctrine of the Roman Catholic purgatory has many secret friends even within the confines of the true church today! However carelessly men may go on while they live, they secretly cling to the hope that they will be found among the saints when they die. They seem to embrace the idea that there is some cleansing, purifying effect produced by death, and that, whatever they may be in this life, they will be found 'suitable for the inheritance of the saints' in the life to come. But it is all a delusion.

The Scripture never represents the state of future misery as a state of cleansing and purification, or anything

analogous to a state of trial, where men may conform
and qualify themselves for some better state of existence:
but always as a state of retribution, punishment, and righteous vengeance, in which God's justice (a perfection of
which some men seem to render no account) vindicates
the power of his majesty, his government, and his love,
by punishing those who have despised them.[3]

Life is the time to serve the Lord,
The time to insure the great reward.

The Bible clearly teaches that what we are when we die, whether
converted or unconverted, whether believers or unbelievers,
whether godly or ungodly, so we will be when we rise again at
the sound of the last trumpet. There is no repentance in the
grave: there is no conversion after the last breath is drawn.
Now is the time to believe in Christ, and to lay hold of eternal
life. Now is the time to turn from darkness to light, and to make
our calling and election sure. The night comes when no man
can work. As the tree falls, there it will lie. If we leave this world
refusing to repent and believe, we will rise in the same condition on resurrection morning, and find it would have been 'better
for us if we had never been born'.

This life is the time of our preparation for our future state.
Our souls will continue forever what we make them in
this world. Such a taste and disposition of mind as a man
carries with him out of this life, he will retain in the next.
It is absolutely true that heaven perfects those holy and
virtuous dispositions, which are begun here; but the other
world alters no man as to his main state. He that is filthy
will be filthy still; and he that is unrighteous will be
unrighteous still.[4]

I strongly advise my readers to remember this, and to make good use of their time. Regard it as the stuff of which life is made, and never waste it or throw it away. Your hours and days and weeks and months and years all have something to say to your eternal condition beyond the grave. What you sow in this life on earth you are sure to reap in a life to come. As that holy preacher Richard Baxter says, it is 'now or never'. Whatever we do in religion must be done now.

Remember this in your use of all the means of grace, from the least to the greatest. Never be careless about them. They are given as helps towards an eternal world, and not one of them ought to be thoughtlessly treated or lightly and irreverently handled. Your daily prayers and Bible-reading, your weekly behaviour on the Lord's Day, your manner of going through public worship — every one of these things is important. Use them all as one who remembers eternity.

Keep it foremost in your mind, whenever you are tempted to do evil. When sinners entice you, and say, 'It is only a little sin.' When Satan whispers in your heart, 'Never mind: what is the great harm in it? Everybody does it' — then look beyond time to a world unseen, and place in the face of the temptation the thought of eternity. There is a great saying by the martyred Reformer, Bishop Hooper, when someone urged him to recant before he was burned, saying, 'Life is sweet and death is bitter.' 'True,' said the good Bishop, 'quite true! But eternal life is more sweet, and eternal death is more bitter.'

The Lord Jesus is our help for eternity

The last thought that I bring to the attention of my readers is that the Lord Jesus Christ is the great Friend to whom we must all look to for help, both for now and eternity.

The reason why the eternal Son of God came into the world can never be declared too fully, or proclaimed too loudly. He came to give us hope and peace while we live among the 'temporary things which are seen', and glory and blessedness when we go to the 'eternal things, which are unseen'. He came to bring 'life and immortality to light', and to 'release those who through fear of death were all their lifetime subject to bondage' (2 Timothy 1:10; Hebrews 2:15). He saw our lost and bankrupt condition, and had compassion on us. And now, blessed be his name, a mortal man may pass through 'temporary things' with comfort, and look forward to 'eternal things' without fear.

Our Lord Jesus Christ has purchased these mighty privileges for us at the cost of his own precious blood. He became our Substitute, and bore our sins in his own body on the cross, and then rose again for our justification. 'Christ also suffered once for sins, the just for the unjust, that he might bring us to God.' 'He made him who knew no sin to be sin for us,' that we poor sinful creatures might have pardon and justification while we live, and glory and blessedness when we die (1 Peter 2:24; 3:18; 2 Corinthians 5:21).

And all that our Lord Jesus Christ has purchased for us he offers freely to everyone who will turn from his sins, come to him, and believe. 'I am the light of the world,' he says. 'He who follows me shall not walk in darkness, but have the light of life.' 'Come to me, all you who labour and are heavy laden, and I will give you rest.' 'If anyone thirsts, let him come to me and drink.' 'The one who comes to me I will by no means cast out.' And the terms are as simple as the offer is free: 'Believe on the Lord Jesus Christ, and you will be saved.' 'Whoever believes in him should not perish but have everlasting life' (John 8:12; Matthew 11:28; John 7:37; 6:37; Acts 16:31; John 3:16).

He who has Christ has life. He can look around at the 'temporary things', and see change and decay everywhere and yet have no fear. He has got treasure in heaven, 'where moth and rust do not destroy, and where thieves do not break in and steal'. He can look forward to the 'eternal things', and feel calm and composed. His Saviour has risen, and gone to prepare a place for him. When he leaves this world he will have a crown of glory, and be for ever with his Lord. He can look down even into the grave, as the wisest Greeks and Romans could never do, and say, 'O Death, where is your sting? O Hades, where is your victory?' (1 Corinthians 15:55).

Let us all settle it firmly in our minds that the only way to pass through 'what is seen' with comfort, and look forward to 'what is unseen' without fear, is to have Christ for our Saviour and Friend, to lay hold of Christ by faith, to become one with Christ and Christ in us, and while we live in the flesh to live the life of faith in the Son of God (Galatians 2:20).

How vast is the difference between the state of the one who has faith in Christ, and the one who has none! Blessed indeed is that man or woman, who can say, with truth, 'I trust in Jesus: I believe.' When the Roman Catholic Cardinal Beaufort lay on his deathbed, our mighty poet describes King Henry as saying, 'He dies, but gives no sign [of comfort].' When John Knox, the Scottish Reformer, was drawing to his end, and unable to speak, a faithful servant asked him to give some proof that the gospel he had preached in life gave him comfort in death, by raising his hand. He heard; and raised his hand towards heaven three times, and then departed. I say again, blessed is he who believes! He alone is rich, independent, and beyond harm's reach. If you and I have no comfort among temporary things, and no hope for eternal things, then it is completely our own fault. It is because we 'are not willing to come to [Christ] that [we] may have life' (John 5:40).

Some food for thought

I leave the subject of eternity here, and pray that God may bless it to many souls. In conclusion, I offer to everyone who reads this volume some food for thought, and material for self-examination.

How are you using your time?

Life is short and very uncertain. You never know what a day may bring forth. Business and pleasure, making money, and spending money, eating and drinking, marrying and giving in marriage — all, all will soon be over and done with for ever. And you, what are you doing for your immortal soul? Are you wasting time, or using it wisely? Are you preparing to meet God?

Where will you be in eternity?

It is coming, coming, coming very fast upon us. You are going, going, going very fast into it. But where will you be — on the right hand or on the left, in the Day of Judgement? Are you among the lost or among the saved? Oh, do not rest; do not rest until your soul is secured! Be prepared: leave nothing uncertain. It is a dreadful thing to die unprepared, and fall into the hands of the living God.

Do you want to be safe now and in eternity?

Then seek Christ, and believe in him. Come to him just as you are. Seek him while he may be found, call on him while he is near. There is still a throne of grace. It is not too late. Christ waits to be gracious: he invites you to come to him. Before the door is shut and the judgement begins, repent, believe and be saved.

Do you want to be happy?

Cling to Christ and live the life of faith in him. Remain in him and live close to him. Follow him with heart and soul and mind and strength, and seek to know him better every day. By doing so, you will have great peace while you pass through the 'temporary things', and in the midst of a dying world you 'shall never die' (John 11:26). By doing so you will be able to look forward to 'eternal things' with unfailing confidence, and to feel and 'know that if the earthly house, this tent, is destroyed, we have a building from God, a house not made with hands, eternal in the heavens' (2 Corinthians 5:1).

Postscript

Since preaching the above sermon I have read Canon Farrar's volume *Eternal Hope*. I cannot agree with most of what that book contains. Anything that comes from the pen of such a renowned writer of course deserves respectful consideration. But I must honestly confess, after reading *Eternal Hope*, that I see no reason to take back anything I have said in my chapter on 'Eternity'. I have laid down Farrar's volume with regret and dissatisfaction, unconvinced and unshaken in my opinions.

I can find nothing new in Canon Farrar's statements. He hardly says anything that has not been said before, and refuted before. To everyone who wishes to fully examine the subject of the reality and eternity of future punishment, I venture to recommend some works that are far less known than they ought to be, and that appear to me far sounder, and more scriptural, than *Eternal Hope*. These are Horbery's *Enquiry into the Scripture Doctrine of the Duration of Future Punishment*, Girdlestone's *Dies Irae*, Rev. C. F. Childe's *Unsafe Anchor*, and Rev. Flavel Cook's *Righteous Judgment*; 'Bishop Pearson on the Creed', under the heading 'Resurrection', and Hodge's *Systematic Theology*, volume 3, page 868.

The plain truth is, that there are vast difficulties bound up with the subject of the future state of the wicked, which Canon Farrar seems to me to leave untouched. The amazing mercifulness of God, and the awfulness of supposing that many around us will be lost eternally, he has handled fully and with characteristic rhetoric. No doubt the compassions of God are unspeakable. He does not 'want anyone to perish'. He 'wants all men to be saved'. His love in sending Christ into the world to die for sinners is an inexhaustible subject. But this is only one side of God's character, as we have it revealed in Scripture. His character and attributes need to be looked at completely. The infinite holiness and justice of an eternal God; his hatred of evil, manifested in Noah's flood, and at Sodom, and in the destruction of the seven nations of Canaan; the unspeakable vileness and guilt of sin in God's sight; the wide gulf between natural man and his perfect Maker; the enormous spiritual change which every child of Adam must go through, if he is to dwell for ever in God's presence; and the utter absence of any implication in the Bible that this change can take place after death — every one of these are points that seem to me partly put aside, or left alone, in Canon Farrar's volume. My mind demands satisfaction on these points before I can accept the views advocated in *Eternal Hope*, and I fail to find that satisfaction in the book.

Origen, a Church Father who lived in the third century after Christ, first formally advocated the position that Canon Farrar has taken up. He boldly broached the opinion that future punishment would be only temporary; but almost all his contemporaries rejected his opinion. Bishop Wordsworth says, 'The Fathers of the Church in Origen's time and in the following centuries, among whom were many to whom the original language of the New Testament was their mother tongue, and who could not be misled by translations, minutely examined the opinion and statements of Origen and agreed for the most part in rejecting and condemning them. Irenaeus, Cyril of Jerusalem, Chrysostom, Basil, Cyril of Alexandria, and others of the Eastern Church, and Tertullian, Cyprian, Lactantius, Augustine, Gregory the Great, Bede, and many more of the Western Church, were unanimous in teaching that the joys of the righteous and the punishments of the wicked will not be temporary, but everlasting.

'Nor was this all. The Fifth General Council, held at Constantinople under the Emperor Justinian, in A. D. 553, examined the tenets of Origen, and passed a synodical decree condemning them. And for a thousand years after that time there was a unanimous acceptance in Christendom with the condemnation.'[5]

Let me add to this statement the fact that the eternity of future punishment has been held by almost all the greatest theologians from the time of the Reformation down to the present day. It is a point on which Lutherans, Calvinists, Arminians, Episcopalians, Presbyterians and Independents have always, with a few exceptions, been of one mind. Search the writings of the most eminent and learned Reformers, search the works of the Puritans, search the few literary remains of the men who revived English Christianity in the eighteenth century, and, as a rule, you will always get one harmonious answer. Within the last few years, no doubt, the 'non-eternity of future punishment' has found several zealous advocates. But up to a comparatively modern date, I unhesitatingly assert that the supporters of Canon Farrar's views have always been an extremely small minority among orthodox Christians. That fact is, at any rate, worth remembering.

As to the *difficulties* surrounding the old or common views of future punishment, I admit their existence, and I do not pretend to explain them. But I always expect to find many mysteries in Christianity, and I do not stumble over them. I see other difficulties in the world, which I cannot solve, and I am content to wait for their solution. What a mighty theologian has called, 'The mystery of God, the great mystery in his allowing wickedness and confusion to prevail'; the origin of evil; the permission of cruelty, oppression, poverty and disease; the allowance of

sickness and death of infants before they know good from evil;
the eternal doom of the heathen who never heard the gospel;
the times of ignorance which God had purposely overlooked;
the condition of China, India and Central Africa, for the last
2000 years — all these things are to my mind great knots which
I am unable to untie, and depths that I am unable to fathom.
But I wait for light, and I have no doubt everything will be
made plain. I rest in the thought that I am a poor ignorant
mortal, and that God is a being of infinite wisdom, and is doing
everything right. 'Will not the Judge of all the earth do right?'
(Genesis 18:25). It is a wise statement by Butler: 'Every thing
that appears to be unjust and cruel in the providence of God
will be understood and clarified, if we would keep in mind that
every merciful allowance will be made, and no more will be
required of anyone, than what might have been expected of
him from the circumstances in which he was placed, and not
what might have been expected from him had he been placed
in other circumstances.'[6] It is a great saying of Elihu, in the Book
of Job, 'As for the Almighty, we cannot find him; he is excellent
in power, in judgement and abundant justice; he does not op-
press' (Job 37:23).

It may be perfectly true that many Roman Catholic theologians, and even some Protestants, have made extravagant and
offensive statements about the bodily sufferings of the lost in
another world. It may be true that those who believe in eternal
punishment have occasionally misunderstood or mistranslated
texts, and have pressed figurative language too far. But it is
hardly fair to make Christianity responsible for the mistakes of
its advocates. It is an old saying that 'Christian errors are unbeliever's arguments.' Thomas Aquinas, Dante, Milton, Thomas
Boston and Jonathan Edwards were not inspired and infallible,
and I decline to be answerable for all they may have written
about the physical torments of the lost. But after every allowance,
admission and deduction, there remains, in my humble opinion,

a mass of scriptural evidence in support of the doctrine of eternal punishment, which can never be explained away, and which no revision or new translation of the English Bible will ever overthrow. It is undeniable that there are degrees of misery as well as degrees of glory in the future state, and that the eternal sufferings of some who are lost will be far worse than that of others. But that the punishment of the wicked will ever have an end, or that length of time alone will change a heart, or that the Holy Spirit continues to work for the salvation of the dead, or that there is any purging, purifying process beyond the grave, by which the wicked, in the fires of hell, will eventually be saved and transferred to heaven, these are positions that I maintain are utterly impossible to prove by Scripture. Rather, there are texts of Scripture that teach an utterly different doctrine. 'It is surprising,' says Horbery, 'that if hell is such a state of purification, it should always be represented in Scripture as a place of punishment.'[7] 'Nothing' says Girdlestone, 'but clear statements of Scripture could justify us in believing, or preaching to ungodly men, the doctrine of repentance after death; and not one clear statement on this subject is to be found.'[8] Once we begin to invent doctrines, which we cannot prove by the Bible, or refuse the evidence of texts in Scripture because they lead us to conclusions we do not like, then we may as well throw away our Bibles.

The favourite argument of some, that no religious doctrine that is rejected by the 'common opinion' and popular feeling of mankind can be true; that any texts which contradict this common popular feeling must be wrongly interpreted; and that, therefore, eternal punishment cannot be true, because the inward feeling of the multitude revolts against it — this argument appears to me most dangerous and unsound. It is dangerous, because it strikes a direct blow at the authority of Scripture as the only rule of faith. What good is the Bible, if the 'common opinion' of mortal man carries more weight than the declarations of God's Word? It is unsound, because it ignores the great fundamental principle of Christianity — that man is a fallen creature, with a corrupt heart and understanding, and that in spiritual things his judgement is worthless. There is a veil over our hearts: 'But the natural man does not receive the things of the Spirit of God, for they are foolishness to him' (1 Corinthians 2:14). To say, in the face of such a text, that any doctrine that the majority of men dislike, such as eternal punishment, must therefore be untrue, is simply absurd! The 'common opinion' is more likely to be wrong than right!

After all, there is great doubt as to what the 'common feeling' or opinion of the majority of mankind is when it comes to the duration of future punishment. Of course we have no means of ascertaining it: and it would signify little either way. In such a matter the only point is: What does the Scripture say? But I have a strong suspicion, if the world could be polled, that we would find that the majority of mankind believed in eternal punishment! There is little dispute about the opinion of the Greeks and Romans on eternal punishment. If anything is clearly taught in the stories of their mythology it is the endless nature of the sufferings of the wicked. Butler says, 'Gentile writers, both moralist and poetic, speak of the future punishment of the wicked, both as to duration and degree, in a like manner of expression and description as the Scripture does.'[9] The strange and weird legends of Tantalus, Sisyphus, Ixion, Prometheus and the Danaides, all have one common feature about them — in each case the punishment is eternal! This is a fact worth noting. Therefore, the opponents of eternal punishment should not talk too confidently about the 'common opinion of mankind'.

As to the doctrine of the annihilation of the wicked, to which many adhere, it appears to me so utterly irreconcilable with the words of our Lord Jesus Christ, who said, 'those who have done evil [rise] to the resurrection of condemnation', and 'the worm does not die, and the fire is not quenched', and also

Paul's words about 'the resurrection of the dead' (John 5:29; Mark 9:43-48; Acts 24:15). Until those words can be removed from the pages of inspired Scripture it seems to me a mere waste of time to argue about it.

The favourite argument of the advocates of this doctrine, that 'death, dying, perishing, destruction', and the like, are phrases that can only mean 'cessation of existence', is so ridiculously weak that it is scarcely worth noting. Every Bible reader knows that God said to Adam, concerning the forbidden fruit, 'For in the day that you eat of it you shall surely die' (Genesis 2:17). But every Christian knows that Adam did not 'cease to exist' when he broke the commandment. He died spiritually, but he did not cease to exist! Peter also says of the flood: 'by which the world that then existed perished, being flooded with water' (2 Peter 3:6). Yet, though temporarily drowned, it certainly did not cease to be; and when the water was dried up Noah lived on the earth again.

It only remains for me now to add one last word, by way of information. Those who care to investigate the meaning of the words 'eternal' and 'everlasting', as used in Scripture, will find the subject fully and exhaustively considered in Girdlestone's *Old Testament Synonyms*, chapter 30, page 495; and in the same writer's *Dies Irae*, chapters 10 and 11, page 128.

Notes

1. Archbishop Tillotson on *Hell's Torments*. See *Horbery*, volume 11, p. 42.
2. Wordsworth's *Sermons on Future Rewards and Punishments*, p. 36.
3. *Horbery*, volume II, p. 183.

4. Tillotson's *Sermon on Philippians 3:20*; see *Horbery*, volume II, p. 133.
5. Bishop Wordsworth's *Sermons*, p. 34.
6. *Analogy*, part 2, chap. 6, p. 425, Wilson's edition.
7. Vol. 2, p. 223.
8. *Dies Irae*, p. 269.
9. *Analogy*, part 1, chap. 2, p. 218.